THE CANADIAN
GENERAL
ELECTION
OF 1957

CANADIAN GOVERNMENT SERIES

General Editors

R. MacG. DAWSON, 1946–58

J. A. CORRY, 1958–61

C. B. MACPHERSON, 1961–

The Canadian General Election of 1957

John Meisel

UNIVERSITY OF
TORONTO PRESS

© UNIVERSITY OF TORONTO PRESS, 1962
Printed in Canada

Reprinted in 2018
ISBN 978-1-4875-7872-5 (paper)

TO MY PARENTS

PREFACE

THIS VOLUME DESCRIBES THE 1957 CANADIAN ELECTION. It is, therefore, an exercise in contemporary history. But it is also a study in political science. As such, it is highly selective in what it records and analyses. No attempt is made to chronicle all the major political events that occurred during the period preceding or following the election. Consequently the existence of the present book in no sense frees Canadian historians from their duty to provide general accounts of the King-St. Laurent era, of which the events discussed below are merely its final hour.

It is proposed that future Canadian elections be given similar attention. Eventually a series of election studies may emerge, enabling the scholar, the politician, and the general reader to obtain a thorough insight into one of the central processes of our political life. Some aspects of Canadian elections, which have received detailed consideration in the ensuing pages, will be accorded only scant attention in forthcoming studies, for they vary little from election to election. Other features, neglected here, will be singled out for future examination. The usefulness of any one electoral study increases with the publication of each subsequent volume. The present analysis of similarities and differences among candidates in the 1957 election may, for instance, appear unrewarding. But when compared with corresponding information for an election twenty years hence, it may prove highly revealing about the changing nature of our parties.

The cumulative usefulness of election surveys has been demonstrated by the studies of British elections sponsored by Nuffield College in Oxford.[1] This book owes much to the pioneering work done in the field of election studies by the authors of these accounts of British general elections.

[1] R. B. McCallum and Alison Readman, *The British General Election of 1945* (London, 1947); H. G. Nicholas, *The British General Election of 1950* (London, 1951); D. E. Butler, *The British General Election of 1951* (London, 1952); *idem*, *The British General Election of 1955* (London, 1955); D. E. Butler and R. Rose, *The British General Election of 1959* (London, 1959).

Originally, it had been intended to treat the 1957 and 1958 Canadian elections as one political event, and to analyse both in one volume. It became apparent, however, that a work of this scope would be inordinately long, and that a single study of both elections would be inappropriate in any case. For, as was indicated above, the 1957 election marked the end of one epoch in Canadian politics. This book deals with the electoral aspects of the fall of the King-St. Laurent party. Among the chief interests of the 1958 contest, on the other hand, was the fact that it was the first occasion on which the new Conservative party, fashioned by Mr. Diefenbaker, appealed to the Canadian voters. In this sense, the 1958 election, though separated only by a few months from its predecessor, opened a new era in Canadian politics and should be examined in that context. The present volume, therefore, deals only with the 1957 election. It is hoped that an analysis of the 1958 contest will be forthcoming in the not too distant future. The relationship between the two elections will then be considered.

In the pages that follow, the reader may frequently wish for additional information on various aspects of the 1957 election. His wish has certainly been anticipated by the author. The absence of virtually any other Canadian election studies and of greater research resources has prevented the inclusion of some case studies of constituency contests, of detailed accounts of campaigning by provincial party organizations, and of more information about electioneering in the Maritimes and the West. The last-named omission was caused by the impossibility, pending the creation of an adequate national library, of consulting a completely representative cross-section of Canadian newspapers. The greatest lacuna in the raw material out of which this volume was fashioned, however, resulted from the dearth of attitude studies of the electorate based on adequate sample surveys.

Another omission which may prove vexing to some readers, must be ascribed to the author's conception of the 1957 federal election. That contest is here seen as, first and foremost, a struggle between the Liberals and Conservatives. The "third" parties were relatively unimportant. Neither the C.C.F. nor the Social Credit party had anything like national support. In an election in which there was a strong swing away from the government party, they succeeded in winning no more than about a third of the votes cast in their respective strongholds, Saskatchewan and Alberta. The proportion of the vote obtained by the C.C.F. in Canada was actually smaller than in the previous election, and that of the Social Credit party only slightly higher. Special studies of the role of "third" parties in Canadian politics and elections would be highly desirable, but a volume dealing with all phases of a national election can give only a cursory treatment to this intriguing question. As a consequence, the activities of the major parties are emphasized in this book and the minor parties are discussed only in so far as they contributed something unique to the election (as, for example, in terms of their programmes) or in so far as their participation affected the standing of their older rivals.

This book could not have been written without the co-operation and generosity of hundreds of people connected with the 1957 election. To all of them, I owe a very real debt of gratitude which I am happy to acknowledge. My only regret is that the number of my creditors is so great that they cannot all be mentioned. This being the case, I have decided to avoid making invidious comparisons between my numerous informants and to thank them collectively. For the same reasons I shall bestow a collective anonymity on the many generous historians, sociologists, and political scientists who commented on all or parts of this manuscript before its final revision.

It gives me much pleasure to make three notable exceptions to this wholesale expression of gratitude. My friends and colleagues, J. E. Hodgetts of the Political and Economic Science Department at Queen's and E. C. Beer of the Douglas Library, have gone over the manuscript in the most painstaking manner and have done much to improve the quality of this book. Professor Norman Ward also recommended many useful revisions. The reader will have guessed, however, that not all of their suggestions were adopted, and that the final responsibility for the substance and the form of this book is, of course, mine.

An earlier draft of this study was prepared as a doctoral thesis for the London School of Economics and Political Science under the sympathetic supervision of Mr. Reginald Bassett. My thanks are due to him and also to the following bodies which have provided the financial assistance required for the completion and publication of the book: the Canada Council, the Social Science Research Council of Canada, the Arts Research Committee of Queen's University, and the Publications Fund of the University of Toronto Press.

J. M.

Kingston, February, 1962

CONTENTS

APPENDICES

LIST OF TABLES

LIST OF CHARTS

Part I

THE PRE-ELECTION PERIOD

BEFORE
THE ELECTION

1

General Conditions Prevailing in Canada

THERE IS MUCH TRUTH in the cliché often resorted to by vanquished politicians when the election outcome is announced and they are called upon to comment on their defeat. The next campaign, they suggest, has just begun. Electoral contests certainly are shaped by and feed on the events that have taken place since the previous battle. If war is merely the continuation of diplomacy by other means, then elections are the continuation of the normal party battle by other means.

A little under four years elapsed between the elections of 1953 and 1957. In this period the Korean and Indo-Chinese wars were wound up, international tension was apparently eased with the Geneva Conference of 1954, West Germany was admitted into N.A.T.O., and the Hungarians rose against their government. Canada was involved in one way or another with all these developments, but it is doubtful whether any of them had a marked effect on the 1957 election, except perhaps to the extent that they helped to enhance the reputation of Mr. Lester Pearson, Minister of External Affairs. However, the Suez crisis, which also occurred in this period, had considerable repercussions on domestic politics, and these are discussed below.

At home the St. Lawrence seaway was begun, a railway line was completed between southern Quebec and ore-rich Labrador, bridges were constructed linking Cape Breton Island to the Nova Scotia mainland and Halifax to Dartmouth. In western Canada a number of important oil pipelines were built and in Ontario an atomic power-plant was started.

Production continued to increase and the standard of living of most Canadians improved despite inflationary pressures. The population of Canada grew by about 1,700,000, of whom about 600,000 were immigrants. Unemployment, which had reached serious proportions in 1954, declined again and just before the election stood at 3.3 per cent of the labour force. Some areas, notably those supporting numerous textile plants, suffered serious and continuous unemployment. The number of man-hours lost through strikes was lower in this period than it had been for some time and dropped noticeably in the year before the election.

Generally speaking, economic conditions gave cause for satisfaction. This was no doubt in Prime Minister St. Laurent's mind when he decided on the date of polling day; it was also one of the reasons why almost everyone was certain that the government would be returned. Only two obvious weak spots could be detected in the economy. Western farmers found it extremely difficult to dispose of their wheat and the amount of this important staple stored on the farms and in granaries was at an all-time high. Secondly, prices had risen by about four per cent in the year preceding the election. Credit restrictions caused hardship in certain industries and made it difficult for municipalities to borrow money. In some quarters anxiety was expressed over the level of American investment in Canada, and this concern was one of the factors contributing to the mild but widespread anti-Americanism prevailing in Canada during this period.

A number of violent disputes erupted between the government and the opposition in the period between the elections. The controversies which were most frequently referred to during the campaign concerned dominion-provincial relations, foreign policy (particularly the Suez crisis), the treatment of the House of Commons by the cabinet, and the pre-election budget.

Political Disputes

Federal-provincial relations had to be defined, during the period under review, in connection with hospital insurance, the construction of the Trans-Canada highway, and that aspect of assistance to the unemployed not handled exclusively by the federal government. A number of talks were held between representatives of the two levels of government, and after the usual bickering and the customary complaints by provincial leaders about federal stinginess the required agreements were signed. In April, 1957, the federal government piloted through Parliament an Act under which grants-in-aid were made available to the provinces to assist in operating publicly administered insurance plans for general hospital care. The federal government also increased its contribution to the cost of completing the Trans-Canada highway and entered into agreements with six provinces in an effort to assist them in taking care of the unusually high numbers of unemployed.

The 1952 tax rental agreements between most of the provincial governments and the Dominion expired in March, 1957, and new arrangements had therefore to be made. The matter was first raised in 1954 and was under discussion practically until polling day in 1957. Under the old agreements all provinces except Ontario and Quebec leased their personal and corporation taxes, special corporation taxes, and succession duties to the federal government in exchange for a rental fee. Ontario also agreed to lease these tax fields, with the exception of succession duties. Under these general agreements the poorer provinces received equalization payments which in effect assured some regional redistribution of income.

In 1955 and 1956 three dominion-provincial conferences were held to find a new way of allocating tax income. The meetings were often stormy and failed to produce a satisfactory solution. The poorer provinces thought that they should receive greater amounts from the federal treasury than the government was willing to grant, and the wealthy provinces thought that their taxpayers were being asked to subsidize unduly the economically less favoured regions of the country.

A new formula was finally devised by the federal government which was incorporated in the Federal-Provincial Tax-Sharing Arrangements Act passed in 1956. It changed many of the earlier features and for 1957-58 increased the revenue of the eight provinces which continued to rent all three tax fields by twenty per cent over the 1956-57 scale of payment. Ontario continued to levy its own succession duties and re-entered the corporation tax field. Quebec remained as aloof from the new arrangements as it had from the earlier ones. The terms of the 1956 Act were accepted rather reluctantly by most provinces and, as will be seen below, the whole matter became one of the issues in the election campaign.

Foreign policy does not often create serious divisions among Canadians. The Suez crisis in the autumn of 1956 aroused deep-felt emotions, however, and led to profound differences of opinion. The government, it will be recalled, was critical of what it considered to have been Israeli aggression. Canada took vigorous action at United Nations headquarters in an attempt to stop hostilities and to send the United Nations Emergency Force to the Middle East. During the crisis various members of the government made it clear that they thought the Anglo-French intervention regrettable. The Canadian delegation at the United Nations Assembly on one occasion opposed Britain's efforts to have the question removed from the Assembly's agenda.

Conservative spokesmen supported the British action in the Middle East and accused the Canadian government of "knifing Britain and France . . . in the back. . . ."[1] The government was also accused of having followed "a course of gratuitous condemnation of the action of the United Kingdom and France which was designed to prevent a major war in the Suez area," of having "meekly followed the unrealistic policies of the United States," and thereby having encouraged "a truculent and defiant attitude on the part of the Egyptian dictator," and of having placed Canada in "the humiliating position of accepting dictation from President Nasser."[2] Commenting on an unpremeditated attack by Mr. St. Laurent on the imperialist attitudes of "the supermen of Europe,"[3] Mr. Diefenbaker said he was "scandalized . . . that the Prime Minister saw fit to condemn Britain and France to the bag in which the U.S.S.R. was placed . . . ." And perhaps slightly exaggerating the care with which world communism follows the debates in the Canadian House of Commons he added: "I say this not in anger; I say it in the deepest feeling of sorrow, that Canada should have permitted the use of words which cannot hurt those against whom they are directed but will raise the hopes of communists everywhere in the world and bring solace to the Khrushchevs and Bulganins."[4]

On April 4, 1957, Mr. E. H. Norman, the Canadian Ambassador to Egypt, committed suicide in Cairo. He had been accused of Communist associations by a United States Senate subcommittee, and although the Canadian government had vigorously asserted its complete confidence in his loyalty, the attacks by the Senate subcommittee, coming at a time when he was obviously overworked, were generally believed to have been responsible for his suicide. "His death," in the words of one editorial writer, "was attributed solely to persecution by the committee and the word 'murder' was uttered by the intemperate. The

[1]For an exchange between Mr. Howard Green who used this phrase and Mr. Pearson on its precise meaning see *Canada, House of Commons Debates,* hereafter cited as *Debates* (March 15, 1957), p. 2360.

[2]The quotations are from the Conservative motion of non-confidence in the government during the special session of Parliament called because of the serious developments in Hungary and the Middle East in 1956. *Debates* (Nov. 26, 1956), p. 18.

[3]See Chapter III, p. 57.

[4]*Debates* (Nov. 29, 1956), pp. 142–3.

upsurge of national feeling revealed not only the strength of Canadian aversion to McCarthyism but also the strength of latent anti-American sentiment."[5]

Not all the criticism was directed at the Americans, however. The Canadian government, and specifically Mr. Pearson, were accused of not having given the House of Commons all the information in their possession about the late Mr. Norman and of having permitted the Royal Canadian Mounted Police to transmit unchecked and unsubstantiated gossip to the F.B.I., from whose files it had ultimately passed into the hands of the Congressional subcommittee.

It is unlikely that Mr. Pearson had consciously attempted to mislead the House. Nevertheless, the opposition probably suspected all ministers of trying to conceal vital information, for members had been given several illustrations of the government's want of candour in dealing with the twenty-second Parliament. For example, the Minister of Agriculture had tried to delete from Hansard a paragraph of a speech he had given in the House.[6] There were other instances in which it was revealed that ministers had misinformed or misled the Chamber.[7] But these were relatively minor incidents compared with two great debates which focused public attention on Parliament and on the Liberal party's attitude towards it. The first, in the summer of 1955, concerned the government's desire to amend the Defence Production Act of 1951. Passed in the first instance during the Korean war, the Act revived most of the sweeping powers originally given the government in 1939, enabling it to mobilize the material resources of the country for an all-out military effort. The 1951 version of the Act contained a five-year time-limit which would have expired in 1956. For reasons that have never been adequately explained, the government chose 1955—a year marked by the seeming relaxation of international tension—not only to renew the Act, but to place it on the statute book for an indefinite period.

Under the provisions of the Act the Minister of Defence Production and the Governor-in-Council were given extremely wide regulatory and requisitioning powers, some of them without providing for appeals to the courts against their exercise. The opposition fought bitterly

[5]*Canadian Forum*, May, 1957, p. 26.

[6]Clark Davey, "Gardiner Apologizes for Oleo Issue After Rebuke on Hansard Deletion," Toronto *Globe and Mail*, Feb. 14, 1956. See also John A. Stevenson, "Senile Decay in the Cabinet," Toronto *Saturday Night*, March 3, 1956.

[7]See, for example, the contradictory statements of ministers in the House during January, 1956, about the shipment of Canadian aircraft to Egypt. Some of these are collected in the Conservative party's *Progress Report*, vol. I, no. 5 (Feb., 1956), p. 7.

against the indefinite extension of the Act. The debate took nine Parliamentary days and forced the government to offer three different concessions. None of these was acceptable to the opposition and in the end the government capitulated.

The Minister of Defence Production, Mr. Howe, bore the brunt of the opposition attack. The Prime Minister defended the bill in general terms when he moved the second reading, but no other cabinet minister participated in the debate. It was generally thought, in consequence, that the cabinet was not in complete agreement with the proposed legislation. It was also reported that for undisclosed reasons the bill was never referred to the cabinet committee which normally examines all bills before they reach the House. In any event, the opposition was able to exploit the impatience of Mr. Howe with Parliamentary wrangling and to be gratified by his apparent distaste for constitutional and procedural argument. It tried to show the Canadian public a picture of an arrogant and autocratic government—a task facilitated by some statements by, and the general attitude of, Mr. Howe. But whatever the tactical advantage derived from the debate, "in persuading the government to retreat the Progressive Conservatives won their greatest victory in twenty years of opposition. They sustained the attack with great vigor and effectiveness, although it would be wrong to say that all the speeches were always relevant and free from weakening exaggeration."[8]

The second Parliamentary debate of unusual interest preceding the 1957 election took place in 1956 over the Northern Ontario Pipeline Crown Corporation bill. Its purpose was to establish a Crown company which would build part of a pipeline, in conjunction with the province of Ontario, for leasing (with option to purchase) to a largely American-owned private company which was to be given a government loan so that it could build another stretch of the pipeline. The legislative battle over the bill was considerably more bitter even than that which had raged over the Defence Production Act amendment and was, in fact, as tumultuous and rowdy as any witnessed in the Canadian Parliament in recent times. "As a result of the use of closure at every stage, the virtual circumvention of the committee stage, and the strained interpretation of the rules by the Chair, the bill was passed by the Government's declared deadline of June 7; and it was passed in exactly the form in which the Government had brought it down."[9]

[8]J. A. Corry, "Arms and the Man: Defence Powers in Parliament," *Queen's Quarterly*, vol. LXII, no. 3 (Autumn, 1955), p. 323.

[9]H. G. Thorburn, "Parliament and Policy-Making: The Case of the Trans-Canada Gas Pipeline," *Canadian Journal of Economics and Political Science*, vol. XXIII, no. 4 (Nov., 1957), p. 525.

In applying closure, the government claimed that the opposition had made it abundantly plain that it would obstruct the passage of the measure and that if a start was to be made on the construction of the pipeline, the bill had to become law quickly. The Speaker became deeply embroiled in the government's efforts to facilitate rapid passage of the bill through the House. On Friday, June 1 ("Black Friday" to the opposition), he took an action which reversed one of his earlier rulings and amounted to wiping out three hours' debate of the previous day. He had been visited by the government House Leader and it was generally believed that he had changed his mind under government pressure. He made some other extremely doubtful decisions, appeared throughout in a partisan light, announced that he would resign, and then failed to do so on the urging of the Prime Minister.[10]

Opposition fire was directed at the speed with which the bill was being rushed through the House and at the merciless application of closure, a device only rarely resorted to in the Canadian Parliament. The Speaker's conduct also provoked intense hostility. On points of substance the government was criticized for granting special privileges to a particular company which, in consequence, stood to make huge profits and which, to boot, was largely American-owned. Later it became known that three of the promoters of Trans-Canada Pipe Lines had been granted exceedingly advantageous options to buy shares of the company. In connection with this aspect of the project Mr. Howe had misled the House.[11] But as the debate progressed, the pipeline itself became less and less important and the government's treatment of Parliament became the major issue.

[10]The matter is obviously too complex to be explored here. The reader interested in the detailed examination of the case by scholars of differing views is advised to see the article cited above as well as the following: J. R. Mallory, "Parliament and Pipeline—Bill No. 298 to Establish the Northern Ontario Pipe Line Corporation—'Rights of Parliament'—Closure—Impartiality of the Chair—Parliamentary Procedure and the Conduct of Legislative Business," in the Case and Comment section of the *Canadian Bar Review*, vol. XXXIV, no 6 (June–July, 1956, pp. 714–30; and correspondence between Eugene Forsey and Professor Mallory in *ibid.*, vol. XXXIV, no. 6 (August–Sept., 1956), pp. 880–5; Eugene Forsey, "Constitutional Aspects of the Canadian Pipe Line Debate," *Public Law* (Spring, 1957), pp. 9–27. The official Liberal view is to be found in Hon. Walter Harris, "Parliament and the Pipeline," *Canadian Liberal*, vol. VIII, no. 4 (Fall, 1956), pp. 293–7; and particularly Hon. James Sinclair, "The Facts on the Trans-Canada Pipeline Question," *ibid.*, pp. 299–326, which is the verbatim transcript of a radio interview of some length. For the official Conservative view see "The Pipeline—The Conservative Stand," *Progress Report*, vol. I no. 7 (June, 1956), pp. 3–4, 13; and "The Speaker—Casualty of Government Conduct," *ibid.*, vol. I no. 8 (Aug., 1956), pp. 5–6.

[11]*Debates* (Feb. 25, 1956), pp. 1600–45.

As was the case in the debate on the Defence Production Act, Mr. Howe was the chief target and the most active proponent of the pipeline bill. In this instance there had also been considerable controversy among members of the cabinet about the desirability of the measure. It was known that Mr. Howe had been unable to persuade his cabinet colleagues to accept an earlier solution he had proffered of the pipeline problem. The struggle, therefore, became one in which prestige played an important part. Emboldened by its 1955 success, the opposition was pressing the government as hard as it could. Much of what it said was obviously received with discomfiture by many Liberal supporters. The government, for its part, found it difficult to give way so soon after its capitulation over the Defence Production Act, particularly since its plans were the result of protracted and delicate negotiations with the Trans-Canada Pipe Lines Company. Furthermore, Mr. Howe—unquestionably one of the ablest members of the cabinet—could not again be abandoned in the face of biting opposition onslaughts. In the end, as stated above, the government, utilizing its large majority, secured passage of the bill, but the opposition had won a moral and propaganda victory.

This was so despite the fact that, as one editorial writer suggested, when it was all over:

All parties must take some blame for the breakdown of last month. Opposition as well as Liberal M.P.'s resorted to the booing and braying, the childish tantrums and cheap posturing that brought Parliament during the pipeline debate to its lowest pitch in history. All parties made use of any sharp practices they could devise within the rules, and the Opposition made no attempt to conceal the fact that its motive was obstruction.[12]

The magazine's Ottawa correspondent probably drew the right conclusions about the partisan consequences of the episode:

If the Liberal government is beaten at the next election—a prospect less unlikely now than it has been for twenty-one years—this session of parliament will appear in retrospect as a *Gritterdaemmerung*, or Twilight of the Grits. Political historians may well conclude that the Liberals fell, not because of any one policy, and certainly not a pipeline policy of which the average voter knew little and cared less, but because they failed to observe the proper limits of power.[13]

An event which took place three months before polling day established a suitable demarcation point between the pre-election period and the

[12]"Only a New Commons Can Repair the Damage to Parliament," *Maclean's*, July 7, 1956.
[13]Blair Fraser, "How the Grits' Power Play Backfired," *ibid.*

campaign itself. The budget introduced just before an election often constitutes the opening salvo: the government hopes that it will score a hit, but in so doing also reveals the basic position it will have to defend in the forthcoming battle. In presenting his budget, Mr. Walter Harris, the Minister of Finance, painted a rosy picture of the country's progress. The gross physical output was seven per cent higher than during the previous year, even when allowance was made for the four per cent increase in the price level. The budgetary surplus was about $282,000,000 and it was possible to reduce the national debt by almost twice this amount. Despite this favourable picture the Minister regretted that he could not recommend to the House any major reductions in the general level of taxation. Noting that there were signs that the extreme inflationary pressures were moderating, Mr. Harris nevertheless warned against letting down "our guards of fiscal and monetary policy at this juncture. Too hasty action would imperil the success we have achieved so far, and an inflationary rise in prices could take away from our people far more in rising costs than they would benefit from even larger reductions in tax rates."[14]

Under these circumstances it was obvious that the government could not, or more correctly would not, present the public with tax relief. However, some modest largesse was forthcoming. The Minister of Agriculture announced, two weeks before the bringing down of the budget, increases in the subsidy on freight charges for feed grains. Similar increases were provided in the budget for greater assistance to goods being sent from the Maritime provinces to the rest of the country. The government also stated that it would be prepared to assist the Maritimes in constructing certain types of power generating equipment. Some increases in direct payments to individuals were also granted. Disabled veterans and widows and orphans of veterans received larger payments, the family allowances were increased silghtly as were also old age pensions and old age assistance to the blind and disabled. The Minister estimated that these changes in payments would affect about four and a half million Canadians. There were to be no changes in the rate of income tax paid but an important tax concession was made to individuals privately buying annuities as part of a retirement programme. The self-employed were given the opportunity of postponing the paying of income tax on pension contributions made to certain pension funds.

The new Income Tax Act also simplified the method of deducting certain medical payments and charitable donations from taxable income and eased the tax burden of those caring for the infirm or for other

[14]*Debates* (March 14, 1957), p. 2221.

dependents. The sales tax was removed from a number of food items of which coffee, tea, cocoa, and meat extracts were probably the most important. A previously imposed special tax on soft drinks was also abolished.

If these measures seemed meagre inducements for supporting the Liberal party, to those contemplating the imminent election, the government showed foresight in catering to voters who would cast their first ballots in the 1960's and 1970's: the sales tax was also removed from candy, chocolate, confectionery and chewing gum. It was this last item which induced a number of opposition speakers to apostrophize the budget as the "bubble-gum budget." But despite this touch of levity, the budget was a document which would have serious consequences on the election. For, as will be noted below, the budget and government fiscal policies in general became important issues in the election.

So far we have been considering only those features of the inter-election period which, while politically important, were not *per se* partisan in nature, although partisan use may have been made of them. Developments centring on the parties themselves during this period must now be examined.

By-elections

Of the seventeen by-elections occurring between 1953 and 1957, ten were held in 1954 and the remainder in 1955.[15] The Liberals lost three seats they had won in 1953: Selkirk, in Manitoba, to the C.C.F., Restigouche-Madawaska, in New Brunswick, and Toronto Spadina to the Conservatives. When changes in the popular vote are considered, regardless of whether any seats were won or lost, the decline in Liberal support appears to have been more widespread. In eleven constituencies the government received a smaller portion of the votes cast in the by-election than in the previous general election, whereas the Conservatives' proportion dropped only in four.

On the whole, the by-election results did not indicate that the Liberal party was losing support in any one region more than in another, or at any period of time more than at another. The government had obviously lost some ground, but it was difficult to tell whether its reverses should be ascribed to the anti-government swing characteristic of by-elections or whether a more lasting anti-Liberal sentiment was sweeping the country. The latter interpretation seemed unlikely in view of the occa-

[15]For a table summarizing the results, see Appendix A.

sional gains by the government candidates and the fact that the Liberals retained ten of the thirteen seats they had won in 1953.

Provincial Elections[16]

A less directly applicable but not entirely irrelevant barometer indicating whether the political climate in the country favoured the Liberals or the other parties was to be found in provincial elections. It is, of course, not uncommon for Canadians to support one party federally and to oppose it at the provincial level. But to win power in a province confers many advantages on a party's organization and clearly adds to its prestige. During the period between the 1953 and the 1957 elections, provincial governments went to the people in all provinces except Manitoba.

Ever since a coalition government was defeated in British Columbia in 1952 the Liberals and Conservatives had been losing ground there to the C.C.F. and Social Credit parties. In the 1956 election the Social Credit government of Premier Bennett increased its popular vote by seven per cent over the 1952 results. The Social Credit party obtained about forty-five per cent of the first ballots cast, the C.C.F. twenty-nine, and the Liberals only twenty-one. The Conservative total came to less than four per cent. On the west coast, therefore, the Social Credit party was scoring impressive gains and the major parties were enduring humiliation at the hands of the voters.

In the 1955 Alberta election, on the other hand, the Social Credit government lost about seven per cent of the vote and the Liberals gained in popularity. The Conservatives obtained a mere 21,000 votes out of a total of about 307,000. The C.C.F.'s strength declined in this province where, despite its losses, the Social Credit government was still firmly entrenched.

Saskatchewan held a provincial election in 1956. The C.C.F. government won an easy majority of seats but lost about nine per cent of the popular vote. The Liberals' strength also declined by eight percentage points. As in British Columbia the Social Credit party benefited from the losses of the other parties and the number of Conservative votes was insignificant.

Premier Frost of Ontario repeated his 1951 success by leading the Conservative party to an overwhelming victory in the 1955 provincial election. The Liberal vote increased by only two percentage points. In

[16]Most of the information in this section is based on relevant volumes of P. Normandin, *Canadian Parliamentary Guide*.

Quebec, the Liberals failed to improve their position vis-à-vis the Union Nationale government of M. Duplessis. The Conservatives showed no strength since the Union Nationale really was the provincial successor of the Conservative party in Quebec.

Newfoundland and Prince Edward Island, the two provinces with the smallest populations, gave the Liberals their greatest successes enabling them to improve their already good position. In the two other Maritime provinces, however, the reverse happened. New Brunswick in 1956 returned the Conservative government with an increased majority both of seats and of votes. The Nova Scotia Liberal government went down to defeat in 1956, at the hands of the Conservatives, having been in office since 1933.

Provincial elections, therefore, like the by-elections, seemed to indicate a slight falling-off in Liberal support. While the proportion of the popular vote obtained by the Liberals increased in Newfoundland, Prince Edward Island, Alberta and slightly in Ontario, it declined in the other provinces.

Changing Personnel of the Liberal Party

One of the charges levelled against the Liberals was that they had become too old and tired in office and that the cabinet could do with the addition of younger men of talent. Four of the nineteen ministers holding cabinet posts at the time of the dissolution, including Mr. St. Laurent, were in their seventies and four others in their sixties. Two had first assumed office in the early days of Mackenzie King's 1935 ministry. But the remainder was comparatively young. The ages of six ministers were between fifty and sixty; five were in their forties. The average age of the cabinet was a little over fifty-eight years. This figure was reduced to fifty-seven and a half by cabinet changes announced in the course of the campaign.

It had been an interesting feature of Liberal cabinets in the King-St. Laurent era that many of their members were not recruited from among the occupants of the party's front benches in the House of Commons. Mr. St. Laurent himself was brought into the cabinet during the war from a highly successful law practice. Two ministers—Mr. Pearson and Mr. John W. Pickersgill—entered the cabinet from the civil service and Mr. Milton Gregg left a university presidency to become Minister of Fisheries in 1947. Provincial Liberal leaders provided three cabinet members in the persons of Mr. Gardiner, Mr. Garson, and Mr. Marler.

In the period between the 1953 and 1957 elections, seven ministers left the cabinet. Mr. Côté died, Senator Wishart Robertson was appointed Speaker of the Senate, Mr. Abbott filled a vacancy on the Supreme Court of Canada, and Mr. Chevrier assumed the presidency of the St. Lawrence Seaway Authority. The others, Mr. Pinard, Mr. Prudham, and Mr. Claxton, retired from political life to engage in various private pursuits. Some of the cabinet vacancies were filled by the appointment of M. Jean Lesage, Senator Ross Macdonald, and Mr. Marler.

The St. Laurent cabinet was sometimes criticized for not including a representative of Toronto and a really senior and nationally respected French-speaking Canadian who would become the chief spokesman in the cabinet for Quebec when the Prime Minister retired. In part no doubt to meet these criticisms two cabinet changes were announced on April 26, 1957. Mr. Paul Hellyer, a young Toronto M.P., was made Associate Minister of National Defence, and Mr. Chevrier returned to the cabinet as Minister without Portfolio. These appointments were so obviously prompted by the impending election that they were criticized even by some friends of the government. The Winnipeg *Free Press*, for example, stated editorially that the appointment of Mr. Chevrier, who came from eastern Ontario, was an admission that the party had failed to find a rising Quebec leader. It added that the appointment of Mr. Hellyer was an obvious attempt to give Toronto a representative in the cabinet, and that it would fool nobody.[17]

The long neglect of Toronto was criticized particularly vehemently by some people who thought that in Mr. David Croll, the M.P. for the Toronto Spadina constituency, the Ontario capital had a member well qualified for a cabinet post. Mr. Croll's Jewish origin was thought to have been an impediment to his achieving cabinet rank. It is impossible to say whether these imputations of prejudice were based on fact. At any rate, in 1955 he was appointed to the Senate and it was Mr. Hellyer who became the minister from Toronto.

Mr. Croll was one of three prominent Liberals who, during the period under review, accepted senatorships. The other two, Mr. Jean-François Pouliot and the Honourable C. G. Power, were, like Mr. Croll, men of independent mind whose adherence to their party's line could never be taken for granted. Their elevation removed from the Liberal benches in the Lower House some of its most colourful and independent members. Other Senate appointments rewarded less well-known Liberals for services they had rendered their party. One exception to this statement

[17]Winnipeg *Free Press*, April 27, 1957.

must be noted: in bestowing a senatorship on Mr. J. T. Hackett, Mr. St. Laurent took the highly unusual step of honouring someone who had never supported the Liberal party and who had, in fact, been a lifelong Conservative.

As the election approached, general conditions in the country and the state of the Liberal party gave the impression to most observers that the government's chances of being returned were almost as good as in 1953, although everyone expected that it would have a reduced majority in the House of Commons. In one significant respect, however, the first half of 1957 stood in sharp contrast to the period preceding the 1953 election. The press had, on the whole, become more critical of the government than it had been at any time since the end of the Second World War. This was true particularly of newspapers which normally supported the government. Some of the actions of certain ministers were deemed arbitrary and arrogant. More important, the government's original attitude to the amendment of the Defence Production Act and, above all, to the pipeline case met with bitter and virtually universal criticism. Many writers, and not least among them well-known Liberals, thought that the government had become complacent and that the Liberal party could do with some spirited and vigorous opposition. Its majority in the House was thought by many to be too large. In any case, most of the newspapers and magazines deplored the splintering of the opposition into several small parties and regretted the weakened position of the Conservatives—the major opposition party.

This anxiety about the political condition of the country was epitomized in a thoughtful article by one of Canada's leading journalists and authors. Under the heading "The Political Vacuum" the pro-Liberal Bruce Hutchison asserted that

When . . . the Government is in a mood of sleek complacency and distended ego, the public strangely uninterested in its most vital business, and political thought largely suspended, why then an effective opposition is needed today as perhaps it was never needed before.

When a party calling itself Conservative can think of nothing better than to outbid the Government's election promises; when it demands economy in one breath and increased spending in the next; when it proposes an immediate tax cut regardless of inflationary results; when it advocates a system of parity prices which has produced chaos in American agriculture and is backfiring on us; when it cannot make up its mind on the basic issue posed by our trade deficit and capital imports; when in short, the Conservative party no longer gives us a conservative alternative after twenty-one years of Liberalism which no Liberal can define, why then our political system desperately requires an opposition prepared to stand for something more than the improbable chance of quick victory.[18]

[18]Bruce Hutchison, "The Political Vacuum," *Financial Post*, Nov. 3. 1956.

Writing on the occasion of the retirement for reasons of ill-health of the Conservative leader and at a time when the Social Credit party was beginning to look like a possible alternative to the Conservatives as the right-wing opposition party, Mr. Hutchison pointed to the very great importance of the forthcoming Conservative convention which would choose Mr. Drew's successor. "Sometime, somehow, someone is going to fill the vacuum on the Right, as enlarged by the untimely stroke of Mr. Drew's departure. Can his successors begin to fill it or will they merely strike postures and utter empty echoes in the vacuum?"

THE "DIEFENBAKER REVOLUTION"

2

Importance of the Convention

MANY LEADING CONSERVATIVES, particularly those responsible for the direction of the 1957 election campaign, think of their party's national convention in 1956 as launching the "Diefenbaker revolution." This revolution is held to have radically transformed the Conservative party and to have been the first step towards its march to power. Whatever the validity of this view, the resignation of Mr. Drew in October, 1956, and its aftermath were certainly the most important developments affecting the major parties between the election of 1953 and 1957.

There were several reasons for this. In the first place, the Conservative party had had an almost bewildering succession of leaders in its recent history. In the thirty years before 1957, there had been six changes in leadership. It was highly desirable from the Conservative point of view, to find a chief likely to stay in office long enough to revitalize the party and, if possible, lead it to victory. Secondly, the party's record in recent elections had cast doubts on its chances of survival. How much longer would the party faithful continue to support it in view of its seeming inability to elect more than fifty members? This question was of particular urgency when the Social Credit movement seemed to be gaining momentum in Canada. The Liberals, although still appearing well entrenched in Ottawa, had been in office for twenty-one years. Their defeat at the polls was to be expected within the foreseeable future. It was therefore important to select a leader who could block further successes of Social Credit and profit from the possibly imminent decline of the Liberals. Failure to achieve this might spell the demise of the national party.

A third reason for the critical importance of the 1956 convention was related to the internal life of the party, within which there had developed a number of serious divisions. Among Conservative Members of Parliament there were differences over questions of social policy. One faction was bitterly critical of what it thought to be the other's old-fashioned approach to Conservative policy. The critics were, on the whole, back-benchers and they were usually defeated. It is said that they often found it difficult even to obtain a hearing.[1]

Quarrels had also developed between the national party and its leaders on the one hand and some of the provincial associations on the other. An open attack on Mr. Drew by Deane Finlayson,[2] leader of the British Columbia Progressive Conservatives was merely a more serious and more public instance of several profound disagreements between the national organization and some of the provincial parties. These disagreements reflected, in part, a pronounced anti-Drew sentiment which had plagued the retiring leader virtually from the day he assumed office. The cause of the trouble did not reside merely in a clash of personalities, however. There was a widespread feeling that the national leadership favoured the central provinces at the expense of the others. More specifically, the leadership was accused of being under the influence of Toronto and Montreal financiers who were allegedly insensitive to the needs of Canadians with interests different from their own.

Dissension developed within the national association itself. In 1954, for example, the tradition was shattered that the president of the Progressive Conservative Association of Canada, though elected by the annual meeting of the executive officers, was in fact the nominee of, or at least acceptable to, the national leader. Mr. George Hees, a young M.P. who had done some effective organizational work for the party, decided to run for the top post in the national association. That he sought the post despite his failure to obtain the blessing of the leader constituted an unmistakable challenge to those who had been in control of the party's machinery. A journalist friendly to the party subsequently referred to Mr. Hees' capturing the presidency as "a successful rebellion of sorts against the party's 'Old Guard'."[3] Mr. Hees' candidacy may

[1]Meetings of the party caucus are, of course, secret. My information is derived from a number of Conservative Members of Parliament who were willing to discuss these matters on the understanding that nothing of what they told me should be attributed to them.

[2]In July, 1954, the B. C. Conservatives passed a vote of non-confidence in Mr. Drew's leadership. This was followed by a drawn-out struggle between the B.C. provincial organization and the federal party. Ultimately there were actually two P.C. organizations in British Columbia. See Toronto, *Globe and Mail*, July to Sept., 1954, April and May 1955, *passim*.

[3]Arthur Blakely, "Ottawa Day by Day," Montreal, *Gazette*, Sept. 25, 1956.

have been motivated by no more than personal ambition; his success attests to the existence of some support for a challenge to the established leadership.

It is difficult, particularly for an outsider, to assess the extent of dissension within the party and to judge its importance. Opposition to the leaders is to be expected in a party long out of office and seemingly no nearer to winning power. Indeed, the frequent changes in Conservative leaders suggest that the party had been in a chronic state of unrest for decades.[4] Mr. Drew's aloofness, his Toronto background and loyalty to old friends in financial circles combined to prevent him from bequeathing a united party to his successor. As the convention approached most Conservatives hoped that the new leader would reconcile the divisive forces and that he would fashion a party devoting itself with single-minded purpose to gaining office.

The difficulty lay in finding a man who could do this. Many Conservatives thought that an "old guard" had gained control of the party. There was considerable opposition to it, but there was no agreement on what, precisely, it stood for, nor even on who, exactly, belonged to it. The term "old guard" could be defined only with reference to who was designated by it and according to who used it. This confusion notwithstanding, there was probably wide agreement that the genuinely conservative Conservatives, the wealthy party supporters from Toronto and English-speaking Montreal and those close to the leadership, constituted the "old guard."

Conservatives who see in the Diefenbaker Revolution the foundations of the 1957 electoral victory claim that the revolution consisted of the defeat of the "old guard" as defined at the close of the previous paragraph. The change in *leaders* is said, this time, to have constituted a change in *leadership*. The defeat of the "old guard" by the Diefenbaker forces is alleged to have re-established unity and to have freed the party from influences which, in the past, had prevented it from making an effective appeal to the voters. It may be asked how the defeat of an important and heretofore influential faction of the party can contribute to party unity. The consideration of this and the question of how the Diefenbaker victory affected the election is left for later discussion. The problem at hand concerns the convention. To what extent did it show that the party was, as some suggest, passing through a revolution? How far was it possible for the "old guard" (which was, of course, in a

---

[4]For details of the difficulties experienced by Mr. Drew's predecessors see J. R. Williams, *The Conservative Party of Canada, 1920–1949* (Durham, N.C., 1956), chap. II.

position to control most of the arrangements) to use the convention itself as a weapon against the challengers? What light, in short, does the convention throw on the thesis that the Conservative party had undergone a Diefenbaker Revolution?

Organization

When he received Mr. Drew's letter of resignation, Mr. Léon Balcer, the president of the Progressive Conservative Association of Canada, immediately called a meeting of that group's executive officers responsible for arranging the national convention.[5] The forty members who met on October 2, 1956, decided to hold a convention in Ottawa during the week beginning on December 10.[6] General arrangements were to be much the same as during the convention which, in 1948, chose Mr. Drew.[7]

A careful scrutiny of the way in which the machinery of the convention was set up reveals no evidence of the established leadership trying to take unfair advantage of their entrenched position. It is true that the convention Executive Committee was composed entirely of members of the "old guard." The personnel of the national office did much of the fact-finding and preliminary drafting on the basis of which the association executive officers and the convention Executive Committee made their decisions. W. L. Rowe (a supporter of the "old guard")[8] was, as national director, in a position to influence many of the arrangements governing the convention. Most of the chairmanships and secretaryships of the committees went to members or supporters of the "old guard," but they did not seem to take advantage of their respective strategic positions to give the convention and its work any particular orientation.

There was only one place where it was possible to do some substantial "rigging" of the convention: whoever controlled a provincial association had a strong voice in choosing the provincial delegates-at-large and also

[5]The Association is empowered by its constitution to convene conventions (article IX) and at each annual meeting the Association officers are authorized to act for the Association between annual meetings.

[6]This decision, one correspondent maintained, was a defeat for those backing the leadership aspirations of Mr. Diefenbaker. They apparently thought that the chances for election of a Westerner would be greater in a prairie city than in the East. See Montreal *Gazette*, Oct. 3, 1956.

[7]Progressive Conservative Party of Canada, *"Structure of Convention"* (mimeo).

[8]See, for example, Gerald Waring, "PC's New National Director Gives Strength to Old Guard," Kingston *Whig Standard*, Oct. 23, 1954.

delegates from constituencies where the party organization had decayed. Mr. Léon Balcer, for example, the most prominent among the small number of Quebec Conservatives, was extremely influential in selecting the Quebec delegation. Very much a member of the "old guard," Mr. Balcer was known to be strongly opposed to Mr. Diefenbaker. In the course of the convention he went so far, despite being its chairman, as to attack him publicly. There is every reason to believe that he made sure that there would be only a minimum of Diefenbaker supporters in the Quebec delegation. Mr. Balcer had this power not by virtue of being the president of the national association, but because of his position within the Quebec party. Influential members of some western provincial associations (who supported Mr. Diefenbaker) were probably also able to assure that persons of their choice were included in their provincial delegations.

Resolutions

The Resolutions and Policy Committee was the most active body of the convention. It and its six subcommittees met almost continuously from Sunday evening, December 9, to the moment when its report was presented on Thursday morning, December 13.[9] Material from two sources was distributed to the committee members before they arrived at the convention: Conservative organizations and even individuals had prepared various resolutions which they hoped would be adopted by the party.[10] Secondly, the Research Department of the party, which advised the committee generally, laid before the committee material on a variety of topics[11] and also presented a compilation of policy statements the party had made in Parliament, at past conventions and at its annual meetings.[12] The Research Department also recommended to the com-

[9]Report of the Resolutions and Policy Committee, in "Proceedings of the National Convention," p. 83. This is the stenographic record of the convention.

[10]Progressive Conservative Party of Canada: "Suggested Resolutions Submitted by Progressive Conservative Organizations for Consideration by the Resolutions and Policy Committee of the National Convention, 1956 (mimeo). Referred to henceforth as "Suggested Resolutions."

[11]Donald Eldon, "Toward a Well Informed Parliament: the uses of research," *Queen's Quarterly*, vol. 53, no. 4 (Winter 1957), p. 522. Dr. Eldon very kindly discussed some of the material in this chapter with the author and made some valuable suggestions.

[12]Progressive Conservative Party of Canada, *Progressive Conservative Party Resolutions since 1948* (including Resolutions of the National Convention of 1942 and 1948), Research Department Report no. 59 (mimeo). Henceforth referred to as *Report no. 59*. Progressive Conservative Party of Canada, *A collection*

mittee a number of technical experts to advise it. Before the convention opened the department consulted with a number of organizations (such as trade unions) who were thought to have a special interest in some of the subjects covered by the resolutions. Drafts of resolutions were submitted to the committee by the party's Research Department.

The report of the Resolutions and Policy Committee received a good deal of attention at the convention and was the subject of some lively discussion. The proposed resolutions were under consideration for the best part of the morning and afternoon sessions of the penultimate day, and again on the morning of the last day. Mr. Sedgwick, the committee chairman, who piloted most of them through the convention, was anxious to have them considered in the time allotted for the purpose. He seemed, therefore, at times to be impatient and to press hard for the quick consideration of the various planks. Despite this pressure several items were discussed at length and many critics were able to make their views known. By no means all of the criticisms or suggestions received the approval of the convention, of course.

In addition to a number of insignificant verbal or other slight changes, eight substantive alterations were made by the convention as a whole. Of these, three were inspired by members of the resolutions committee and can be considered as extensions of the work of the committee onto the floor of the convention. The most important of these expressed the party's approval of family allowances. Of the five changes suggested by rank and file members, three added new resolutions to those already drafted. One, dealing with low-interest loans to buyers of old houses, was moved by the Mayor of Ottawa, Charlotte Whitton. The other two concerned the control of floods and support for the fisheries. Finally, two changes were made in the section of the report dealing with natural resources.[13]

The reception given the report of the Resolutions and Policy Committee by the convention does not support the view that the "old guard" tried to force its views on the convention. Nor, however, does it indicate that an organized attempt was made by any well-defined group to chal-

---

of Past Resolutions of the Progressive Conservative Party Prepared for the Deliberation of the Resolutions and Policy Committee of the 1956 National Convention, Research Department Report no. 60 (mimeo). This contains essentially the same material as *Report no. 59*, but presents the resolutions under headings corresponding to those of the six subcommittees.

[13]The resolution on family allowances is on page 15 of the Report of the Committee on Resolutions and Policy as adopted by the Convention. (*What the Progressive Conservative Party Stands For*, 2nd version) The other changes mentioned here can be found on pp. 13, 17, 18 and 16. A summary of the resolutions is placed in Appendix B, below, pp. 281–4.

lenge the views of the established leadership. Such differences of opinion and arguments as did develop surely must be expected in any party, particularly in one long out of office. Under such circumstances there are always "progressives" and "conservatives," "ins" and "outs," those who humour the court and irascible characters who are excluded from it. The English-speaking chairman of the resolutions committee may have been a member of the "old guard," but then his French counterpart was backing Mr. Diefenbaker, the leader of the attack against it.[14] That a bitter struggle for power was being waged at the convention is certain. There is little evidence, however, that the resolutions committee was used as a battlefield or that the resolutions themselves were used as weapons. This being the case, the question arises as to whether the resolutions produced by the convention represented an "old guard" view or whether they foreshadowed a revolution.

The 1956 resolutions differ in several important respects from those adopted at the previous convention. While the newer version was generally less specific than that of 1948, it was more concrete in certain areas which received particular emphasis. Differences in the fields stressed no doubt reflected in part changing conditions prevailing in the country. But it is significant that labour and natural resources were given much greater emphasis in 1956 and that the recommendations made in relation to these areas were less vague than in 1948. An important difference was noticeable in the party's agricultural policy: the unqualified support given the Wheat Board in 1956 had been withheld at the earlier convention.[15] At that time, also, there was no suggestion that low-interest loans be made available for buyers of old homes. Some earlier "ultra-conservative" resolutions were dropped in 1956, notably the heavy and repeated emphasis on "free enterprise" and the call for outlawing "communist activity."[16] There is some ground, therefore, for the argument that the party had changed its perspective on some national problems and that it did try, in 1956, to live up to the first part of its double-barrelled name.

But there is some evidence on the other side as well. Whereas in 1956 the plank dealing with the old age pensioners seemed to envisage a means test, in 1948 such a test had been repudiated.[17] Furthermore, at the earlier convention family allowances were endorsed;[18] in 1956 this

[14]Mr. Duranleau was reported as being a member of the Comité des Bleus. See below, and also Montreal *Gazette*, Nov. 30, 1956.
[15]*Report no. 59*, p. 212. For the 1948 resolutions dealing with Natural resources see *ibid.*, pp. viii, xvi–xvii; on labour see *ibid.* pp. xiii–xiv.
[16]*Ibid*, pp. vi, vii.
[17]*Ibid.*, p. xxii.
[18]*Ibid.*, p. xxii.

was done only as an after-thought.[19] In foreign affairs, support for the United Nations was given without qualifications by the convention which chose Mr. Drew as leader; in 1956 one plank seemed to place N.A.T.O. and the Commonwealth ahead of the world organization. This suggests a narrowing of the party's international horizons. On the other hand, the more recent convention did call for the establishment of a permanent United Nations police force, thereby perhaps compensating for the slight retreat from internationalism.

In weighing the "progressive" and "conservative" tendencies in the party, as revealed in a comparison of the 1956 and the 1948 resolutions, one is led to the conclusion that the 1956 resolutions were, on balance, more progressive. But there were obviously still powerful elements in the party who, while they did not have to be "dragged, screaming, into the twentieth century," were nevertheless opposed to some of the policies which have become commonplace in the modern welfare state. One is left with the impression (it cannot be called more than that) that the Research Department, the idealists, the reformers in the party, had a much greater voice in the drafting of the resolutions than their influence in the party warranted. These groups no doubt found the process of planning and of formulating resolutions rather congenial, whereas those with a more vested interest in the party—its heavy financial supporters for example—may have been sceptical of the importance of resolutions. In any case, the latter elements of the party, who can be expected to be more conservative, were probably absorbed in the fight that was being waged for the leadership. If this view is correct, then the formula- tion of the resolutions was but a skirmish before the main battle—the contest for the highest post in the party.

The Leader

During the weeks following Mr. Drew's resignation there mushroomed a wild crop of rumours about who might succeed him.[20] There were only three serious contenders: John G. Diefenbaker, Donald G. Fleming,

---

[19]"Proceedings of the National Convention."

[20]In addition to those who actually sought the leadership, the following were mentioned in the press at one time or another as possible leaders: Premier W. A. C. Bennett of British Columbia (a former Conservative, by then a Social Crediter); Henry Borden, a lawyer and magnate; James S. Duncan, top executive of Massey-Harris; John Hamilton, Toronto M.P.; George Hees; Premier Hugh J. Flemming of New Brunswick; Premier Leslie Frost of Ontario; George Nowlan; Paul Sauvé, Quebec Minister of Youth and Social Welfare; S. E. Smith, president of the University of Toronto; Dufferin Roblin, leader of the Manitoba Conservative party; and Garfield Weston, financier.

and E. Davie Fulton. Léon Balcer also announced his intention to seek the nomination, but his candidature lasted only a little more than a week.[21]

Of the three serious candidates, the forty-year-old Mr. Fulton was much the youngest. A west-coast lawyer, he came from a family which had rendered distinguished political service at both the provincial and national levels. He had been a Rhodes scholar, had a good military record in the Second World War, and was considered an able parliamentarian. His urbanity, witty turn of phrase, and somewhat academic manner made him particularly acceptable to university Conservative clubs and probably to the more intellectually inclined Conservatives generally. His Catholicism was deemed a handicap in the race for the leadership of a party which had traditionally derived its greatest strength in the Protestant parts of Canada. In Quebec, where his religion would have constituted a decided asset, he had lost some ground for having raised the question of conscripting forces for the Korean war.[22] In outlook, Mr. Fulton was considered a moderate Conservative, certainly no rebel, but neither too closely associated with the "old guard." In addition to pointing to his obviously considerable talents, his supporters emphasized his youth. Almost no one expected the Conservatives to win the forthcoming election. A leader was needed, Mr. Fulton's backers argued, who could rebuild the party and then lead it to victory in five or ten years' time. Mr. Fulton was to be this leader.

Mr. Donald Fleming was born in 1905. A lawyer by profession, he had entered Parliament in 1945, after an active career in Toronto municipal politics. He had been a candidate for the leadership in 1948, receiving less than ten per cent of the vote. Like the other aspirants for the leadership he was a front-bencher in the House where he had acquired a reputation for pugnacity. Having made himself bilingual, he had assiduously cultivated the province of Quebec. He was an active member of the United Church of Canada. More than the other candidates for the leadership Mr. Fleming was considered to be a member of the "old guard." Acceptability to Quebec was counted his greatest asset; that he represented and lived in a Toronto constituency his greatest handicap. A party long accused of being dominated by Ontario and particularly Toronto would hesitate before choosing another Torontonian to succeed Mr. Drew.

Neither his domicile nor his religion were thought to stand in the way

[21]Montreal *Gazette*, Nov. 22, 1956, and Dec. 1, 1956.
[22]Blair Fraser, "Why the Conservatives Are Swinging to Diefenbaker," *Maclean's*, Nov. 24, 1956, p. 77.

of Mr. Diefenbaker's "availability," to borrow a word from the vocabulary of American presidential nominating politics. He came from Saskatchewan where he had become a successful vote-getter and he was a Baptist. He was sixty-two years of age. A highly regarded orator, he was by far the best known of the candidates both inside and outside the party. He had unsuccessfully contested the leadership in 1942 and in 1948. By consistently and publicly defending civil rights and minority groups, Mr. Diefenbaker had acquired a Canada-wide reputation as a liberal. Despite these assets, his was probably the most controversial candidacy of the three, for the prairie lawyer not only rejoiced in almost fanatical support, but also had to contend with bitter hostility. It was said of Mr. Diefenbaker that he had shown himself a lone wolf who found it difficult to co-operate with his Parliamentary colleagues, that he was totally unacceptable to Quebec and distrusted by the Toronto and Montreal financial circles on which the party would depend for funds; he was accused of being unstable, not robust enough physically to carry the load imposed by the leadership, too old, hard to work with; in short the sort of leader who, at this critical juncture in the party's history, would more likely wreck it than lead it into office.

The full meaning of the words "Diefenbaker Revolution" emerges when it is realized that some of the doubts about Mr. Diefenbaker's qualities of leadership were entertained, singly or in combination, by virtually every one of the then leading members of the party. With two or three exceptions, every member of the Conservative front bench in the House of Commons was opposed to Mr. Diefenbaker. Mr. Drew was known not to favour him as his successor. Before the balloting began the president of the Progressive Conservative Association of Canada openly attacked him.[23] It was announced that the acting leader of the party supported Mr. Fleming.[24] A "Stop Diefenbaker" movement developed and was associated with an attempt to "draft" the president of the University of Toronto as leader.[25]

Earlier in this chapter it was seen that none of the activities associated with the drawing up of the party resolutions could properly be likened to a revolution. But to win the leadership against such opposition was something else again. Here, indeed, there was a genuine battle. And leading the challenge to the entrenched party chiefs were those who had long been on the outside where, they felt, their voices had too often been ignored. Victory would enable them to reshape the Conservative party

[23]Montreal *Gazette*, Dec. 14, 1956. See above p. 22.
[24]*Ibid.*, Dec. 11, 1956.
[25]*Ibid.*, Nov. 10, 1956, also Oct. 3, 1956.

according to their own design. This looked more like a revolution. For "some of Diefenbaker's backers, and the most vociferous," as one Ottawa correspondent observed two weeks before the convention opened, "are not merely *for* Diefenbaker. They're also *against* his opponents, the established leadership inside and outside the House of Commons. If John Diefenbaker does become national leader, these backers will expect drastic changes in the Conservative hierarchy. They'll expect the men who have been important figures for the past ten or fifteen years to become unimportant figures. . . ."[26]

From the very beginning Mr. Diefenbaker probably had considerably more support than the other candidates among the constituency and provincial organizations. The aspirants for the leadership spent the time between the resignation of Mr. Drew and the balloting in travelling widely and everywhere lining up such support as they could find or create. But whereas Mr. Fulton and Mr. Fleming waged a traditional type of pre-convention campaign, Mr. Diefenbaker had the benefit of the services of a highly competent specialist in public relations. In addition, the two Conservative front benchers who supported him, did so with immense vigour and skill. This triumvirate, made up of Mr. Allister Grosart, vice-president of McKim Advertising Ltd., Mr. Gordon Churchill, M.P. (Winnipeg South Centre), and Mr. George Hees, M.P. (Toronto Broadview), constituted an impressive High Command for the leadership campaign and it was in effect they who later became the chief strategists of the 1957 election campaign. While the other candidates for the leadership had many supporters and some competent advice, they could not match the skill and ubiquity of the team fielded for Mr. Diefenbaker. Mr. Grosart brought to the Diefenbaker campaign not only an extremely imaginative approach to the art of public relations, but also an intimate knowledge of Canadian politics and particularly of the Conservative party. He had been closely connected with the running of a number of Conservative campaigns in provincial (Ontario) general elections and in federal and provincial by-elections. Not being a politician, he had achieved a certain detachment which proved invaluable in both the Diefenbaker leadership campaign and in subsequent elections.

Mr. George Hees was something of an oddity in the Conservative party. His home and his constituency were in Toronto—the bastion of the "old guard." He was also wealthy, so that according to the folklore of Canadian politics he should have been a crusty old Tory and certainly a defender of the established order in the party. Yet it was he who had challenged the "old guard" by seeking and winning the presidency of

[26]Blair Fraser, "Why the Conservatives Are Swinging to Diefenbaker," p. 30.

the Progressive Conservative Association in 1954. During his term of office he spent an enormous amount of time travelling back and forth across the country talking to Conservative supporters and functionaries in every province and probably in every constituency. After Mr. Drew's resignation he made another trip to the West, allegedly to see how much support he himself might get in a bid for the leadership.[27] He must have encountered strong pro-Diefenbaker sentiment. At any rate, on October 5, 1956, it was announced that Mr. Hees was supporting Mr. Diefenbaker. He contributed to the Diefenbaker campaign not only his youthful aggressive enthusiasm, but also an unmatched knowledge of and contact with Conservative affairs and personalities throughout the country.

In the 1954 election for the presidency of the national association a candidate, backed by established leaders, appeared in the last minute to oppose Mr. Hees. That candidate was Mr. Gordon Churchill, a one-time Manitoba teacher and lawyer, with a distinguished military record, who had been one of the party's military spokesmen in the House of Commons. He had been regarded in the party as a highly respectable supporter of the "old guard." It was, therefore, a terrible blow for Mr. Diefenbaker's opponents and an invaluable boost to his supporters, when Mr. Churchill emerged as the spokesman for a "Draft Diefenbaker" committee of Conservative Members of Parliament. Mr. Churchill gave the Diefenbaker movement a degree of respectability among those friendly to the "old guard" which it would not have had without him. In addition he had been a keen student of Canadian politics. As a consequence he had produced two studies which played an important part in the strategy of the leadership campaign and even more so in the election which followed it.[28]

Mr. Churchill, Mr. Grosart, and Mr. Hees succeeded in making the most of Mr. Diefenbaker's already great popularity and of his undoubted ability to attract the support of delegates. Mr. Grosart was generally responsible for the public relations aspects of the campaign; Mr. Hees used his excellent nation-wide connections to prepare the ground for Mr. Diefenbaker's visits and to increase support for him. In Ottawa, meanwhile, Mr. Churchill worked on the Parliamentary group and represented the Diefenbaker interests in discussions dealing with the planning of the convention.

[27]Montreal *Gazette*, from the resignation of Mr. Drew to Oct. 5, 1956.

[28]"Forming the Government" and "Conservative Strategy for the Next Election," unpublished memoranda, dated respectively Jan., 1954, and Jan., 1956. See below pp. 166–8.

This is not the place to describe the various manoeuvres executed to ensure Mr. Diefenbaker's victory. One example must suffice as an illustration of the techniques employed by the Diefenbaker forces to win not only the leadership but also the subsequent election. The argument which probably carried considerable weight with a large number of Conservatives was that he was quite unacceptable to Quebec. It had long been an axiom of Canadian politics that no party could get itself elected in Ottawa without a reasonable degree of support from that province. If Mr. Diefenbaker was so disliked among French Canadians, how could the party, under his leadership, hope to return to power? Some of Mr. Diefenbaker's entourage questioned the hypothesis that the road to Ottawa must lead, in part, at least, through Quebec. But it was too late for the party to be converted to this heresy. There was equally not enough time to make Mr. Diefenbaker acceptable to the Quebec delegation. So the only recourse left was to create the impression that Mr. Diefenbaker was, in fact, the chosen candidate of certain factions in Quebec.

To this end at least two stratagems were attempted. In the first place the services of one of the three Conservative French-Canadian M.P.'s were enlisted in the Diefenbaker cause. Mr. Wilfrid Dufresne had become involved in some legal difficulties from which he managed to extricate himself, according to newspaper reports,[29] only with the help of a prominent member of the Diefenbaker High Command. At any rate, Mr. Dufresne made a number of speeches both in and outside Quebec[30] in which he indicated that he and many of his colleagues would vote for Mr. Diefenbaker. Every effort was made by Mr. Diefenbaker's supporters to have these speeches reported as widely as possible, in English-speaking Canada.

A similar scheme involved the setting up of Le Comité des Bleus,[31] which went on record as fully backing Mr. Diefenbaker, and met him when he visited Montreal before the convention. There were fewer than twenty members of the committee, but they contained a number of distinguished Quebec names. Three of four sons of former Conservative cabinet ministers were included, as well as the batonier of the Montreal bar and the president of the Canadian Club of Montreal. It is most unlikely that this committee, or the speeches made by some of its members,

[29]Le Devoir, Montreal, June 3, 1957.
[30]Montreal Gazette, Oct. 9 and Nov. 30, 1956.
[31]After the epithet "Bleu" ascribed to the Conservative party and its supporters in the days of Cartier.

had the slightest effect on the Quebec delegation at the convention. The purpose of these activities was to get news items indicating French-Canadian support for Mr. Diefenbaker into English-language newspapers where they might be seen by convention delegates *outside* Quebec. Two of the speeches by French Canadians supporting Mr. Diefenbaker, for example, were made to the Osgoode Hall Progressive Conservative Club in Toronto. Osgoode Hall is a law school, and the meetings could not have been attended by more than a handful of people. Yet both speeches were given impressive coverage in some newspapers and were reported by the national news agency.[32]

Neither Mr. Fleming nor Mr. Fulton went to anything like the same lengths in creating a climate of opinion favouring his election. Indeed the Diefenbaker victory was something of a revolution not only because it shifted the balance of power within the party, but also because it introduced, and showed the effectiveness of, a substantially new approach to campaigning.

One move in the Diefenbaker campaign was considered by most observers to have been a major error; it threatened almost to break up the party. Mr. Diefenbaker's name was placed in nomination by New Brunswick's Premier Hugh J. Flemming; the seconder was Major-General G. R. Pearkes of British Columbia. For a candidate who was generally suspected in Quebec this was a sure way of becoming *persona non grata* in that province. As was to be expected there was an immediate uproar, which included Mr. Balcer's attack on Mr. Diefenbaker. Later, when Mr. Diefenbaker rose to deliver his acceptance speech, a substantial number of the Quebec delegation walked out of the convention. There are several explanations of why this seemingly calculated insult was directed at Quebec, none of which is entirely satisfactory.

In thanking his mover and seconder, Mr. Diefenbaker said that "they were chosen in recognition of the fact that this party extends from the Atlantic to the Pacific."[33] He went on to remind his audience that in 1927 (the year in which the party had last chosen a future prime minister), the leader had been nominated by a New Brunswicker and a Westerner. Mr. Diefenbaker's explanation sounds no more convincing now than it did at the time it was uttered. No man in his right mind

[32]Canadian Press dispatch from Toronto, November 29, 1956. The Toronto *Telegram*'s report on Dufresne's speech was placed on the front page and entitled "Quebec Swinging to Diefenbaker."

[33]"Text of Speech Delivered by John G. Diefenbaker, Q.C., M.P., at the National Convention of the Progressive Conservative Party, December 13, 1956" (mimeo).

would risk further alienating an already hostile province for the sake of being able to make a symbolic gesture. And no one has ever doubted that Mr. Diefenbaker was very much in his right mind at the time of the convention.

It has been suggested by an otherwise well-informed lieutenant[34] that the decision to have Mr. Diefenbaker nominated by two English-speaking Canadians was made to forestall the possible victory of Mr. Fulton. The argument, which is too elaborate both to be reproduced fully here and to be quite creditable, is based on the doubtful assumption that Mr. Fulton might have received the second largest number of votes on a first, inconclusive ballot. In that event, it is argued, Mr. Diefenbaker might have lost some support on the following ballots and Mr. Fulton might ultimately have won the leadership. To forestall this possibility, it was necessary to create sympathy for Mr. Diefenbaker among large numbers of delegates. This could be done by provoking the Quebec delegates into attacking him in a manner seemingly lacking in sportsmanship. Such an attack was to be expected from *some* members of the Quebec delegation as a result of neither nominator being from Quebec. Not having Mr. Diefenbaker nominated or seconded by a French-speaking Canadian was, in this view, a calculated risk taken to create a situation in which Mr. Diefenbaker would appear to have been treated unfairly. It was a second line of defence established to guard against the possibility that Mr. Diefenbaker might not win on the first ballot and that Mr. Fulton might threaten to overtake him.

A different hypothetical explanation, probably of equally questionable validity, has at least the merit of being simple. According to it, Mr. Churchill's alleged anti-French prejudices are solely to be blamed.

Another contention is that had someone from Quebec been chosen, it would have been almost impossible not to seek the other nominator in Ontario. This would have looked as if Mr. Diefenbaker had abandoned his championship of the poorer provinces against the wealthier ones, and the party would once again have appeared to the nation as the tool of the Ontario and Quebec financial interests. This is the most plausible of the explanations offered, but even it is not entirely satisfactory.

Whatever the reason, the choice of two non-French-Canadian nominators made it almost certain that Mr. Diefenbaker would receive very few of the Quebec votes. Whether he would have received very many more, even had he not so offended Quebec, is a moot point. In any event, when the ballots were counted, Mr. Diefenbaker received 774 (60 per cent),

[34]In an interview with the author.

Mr. Fleming 393 (31 per cent), and Mr. Fulton 117 (9 per cent) of the 1284 ballots cast.[35]

Mr. Diefenbaker defeated the "old guard" but, so all observers said, he had driven Quebec farther away from the Conservative party. And without Quebec, how could the party succeed in the impending election? In his acceptance speech, the new leader made a gallant effort to placate those whom he had offended. He appealed strongly for unity and frequently referred to the great Conservative combination of Macdonald and Cartier. Speaking in French, he assured his audience that he would respect the Act of Confederation and that he would uphold the rights of language and religion, and of minorities as guaranteed by the constitution. But he soon turned away from his French compatriots and even perhaps from those attending the convention. In a characteristic passage he invited all of Canada to join him in a national crusade: "Will you, ladies and gentlemen, whether you belong to this party or not—the unseen audience that is present here in spirit—I ask you, my fellow citizens, to join with us in a national crusade, united in a dedication to our traditions, forward looking, looking forward to our tomorrows."[36]

Much of what follows in this study will concern the way in which Canadians responded to this challenge. When that response is described and analysed, some assessment will be possible of how it was affected by the Diefenbaker Revolution.

[35]"Proceedings of the National Convention."
[36]"Acceptance Speech by Mr. Diefenbaker" (mimeo).

Part II

THE CAMPAIGN

Origins of Party Programmes[1]

FOR MORE THAN TWENTY YEARS one party had been in, the other out of, power: this circumstance necessarily made for profound differences in the way in which each shaped its programme before and during the campaign. The Liberals did little more than point to their record. The central theme of their campaign was that the party had done well in the past and, if returned, would continue doing equally well in the future. The Liberal programme, such as it was, was that of the government. Not fashioned to suit the exigencies of the 1957 election, it had, in the main, evolved gradually as the consequence of the continuous interaction of the cabinet and the leading experts in the civil service.

The cabinet contains representatives of the various provinces and major regions of the country, yet departmental responsibilities make it difficult for the leading ministers to be fully sensitive to the varied shifts of opinion within the party. It is perhaps possible to make too much of the distinction between the cabinet and the party in the cabinet system: the cabinet is composed of the party leaders. But there seems to have been a tendency for the Liberal party, so long in power, to leave much of the formulating of policy to the leaders who could utilize the skill and knowledge of the civil service. Much of what had, in the years immediately before the election, been called Liberal policies or the Liberal

[1]Some of the material in this section has already been published under the title, "The Formulation of Liberal and Conservative Programmes in the 1957 Canadian General Election," *Canadian Journal of Economics and Political Science*, vol. XXVI, no. 4 (Nov., 1960), pp. 565–74.

programme was actually the product of the intimate co-operation of leading civil servants and their ministers.[2] The result of this collaboration was that the party, as such, tended to neglect the task of re-examining its programme and of devising new approaches to the problems facing the country.[3]

It is true that the normal activities of the National Liberal Federation of Canada continued throughout the post-war period. The chief organs of the Federation were the National Executive Committee of thirty members which, technically, at least, was the party's "principal executive and administrative arm"[4] and the Advisory Council of 236 members. The latter was the top policy-making committee of the Liberal party in so far as the formal allotment of functions was concerned.[5] It met once between the 1953 and 1957 elections—in March, 1955—and adopted a number of resolutions containing the party's views on current Canadian problems.

Beginning with expressions of loyalty to Her Majesty Queen Elizabeth and of confidence in Mr. St. Laurent, the resolutions commended the government for successes it had achieved in a wide variety of fields. In other areas the resolutions not only expressed satisfaction with past performance but also contained some recommendations for the future. They suggested that a contributory health insurance scheme be implemented as soon as possible by the government in conjunction with the provinces, that methods be considered for the provision of financial assistance to university students, and that a commission be established to examine broadcasting and the advisability of separating the operating functions of the C.B.C. from its regulatory ones. Other suggestions dealt with judges' salaries, unemployment, the extension of the franchise to Canadian Indians, the encouragement of research, equal pay for women,

[2]For an interesting discussion of this relation see J. E. Hodgetts, "The Liberal and the Bureaucrat," *Queen's Quarterly*, vol. LXII, no. 2 (Summer, 1955), pp. 176–83. See also *idem*, "The Civil Servant and Policy Formulation," *Canadian Journal of Economics and Political Science*, vol. XXIII, no. 4 (Nov., 1957), pp. 470–3.

[3]Some Liberals occasionally expressed concern over this development. See, e.g., the speech by C. G. Power to the 1948 leadership convention in National Liberal Federation, *Report of the Proceedings of the National Convention* (Ottawa, 1948), pp. 202–7. He elaborated these views subsequently in some private memoranda, notably in one dealing with Liberal failures in a number of by-elections and in another where he proposed a Liberal policy for the 1953 election. It seems that, on the whole, his views were ignored.

[4]"The Advisory Council of the National Liberal Federation of Canada," *Canadian Liberal*, vol. VII, no. 1 (Summer, 1955), p. 1.

[5]*Ibid.* Even the most casual student of Canadian politics will be struck by the enormous gulf separating fact from this fiction concerning the locus of decision-making in the pre-1957 Liberal party.

additional exemptions from income tax, and mortgages.[6] The government had complied with only a very small number of these recommendations before the election. In any case, none of the resolutions could be considered as having added anything new to Liberal thinking in Canada. Similar requests had been made before, both inside and outside the party.

A fuller statement of Liberal policy had been approved in 1948 by the national convention which elected Mr. St. Laurent as leader.[7] While this was in a sense the most representative expression of Liberal views, approved as it was by a national convention attended by over 1,300 delegates, it was only of minor importance in the 1957 election. Since it was almost nine years old and had served through two elections, it was not referred to very often in the course of the campaign. It should be noted, however, that the preamble to the 1948 resolutions, constituting a statement of principles, was reprinted for wide use in the 1957 election as a small leaflet entitled *Liberalism . . . a Fighting Faith.*

The Conservatives, on the other hand, had barely completed the drafting of their party resolutions when the election campaign started.[8] It was to be expected, therefore, that they would make extensive use of their newly drawn-up programme. Nothing of the sort in fact occurred. The resolutions, taken as a whole, were never used. A mimeographed version of them, as passed by the Resolutions and Policy Committee, was circulated to members of the convention and to the press. After the convention agreed upon the final version, a certain number of copies was mimeographed. No attempt was made to give the resolutions a permanent form and they were not used, as such, in the campaign. The reasons for this startling treatment of the convention's handiwork concern primarily election strategy and will be discussed at the appropriate place in chapter VIII.[9]

Although the complete version was ignored, many of the resolutions were in fact used during the election campaign. The Conservative agricultural programme, for example, was, in many respects similar to the

[6]"Resolutions Adopted by the 15th Meeting of the Advisory Council of the National Liberal Federation of Canada, March 28th, 29th and 30th, 1955," *ibid.*, pp. 21–6.

[7]National Liberal Federation of Canada, *Report of the Proceedings of the National Liberal Convention* (Ottawa, 1948), pp. 87–238 *passim.* A consolidated version of the resolutions is to be found in the Federation's *The Liberal Party* (Ottawa, 1957), pp. 9–10, 63–76, and in the *Canadian Liberal*, vol. V, no. 3 (Fall, 1952), pp. 169–205, where they are compared with legislation introduced by the Liberal government subsequent to the holding of the convention.

[8]See chap. II, pp. 22–5.

[9]See below, pp. 170–1.

agricultural resolutions adopted by the convention. The pamphlet on *Labour*, in the party's "Talking Points" series, likewise contained an almost verbatim repetition of the labour resolutions passed by the convention.

It is tempting to see in the Conservatives' failure to campaign on the basis of the 1956 resolutions further confirmation of the generally held view that Canadian parties are devoid of any ideology. It is usually argued that, like their United States counterparts, the major Canadian parties are alliances of economic and regional groups based on expediency rather than on any genuinely shared philosophical outlook or even on a well-defined programme. There is obviously much truth in this observation. A close look at the Conservative party during the period preceding the 1957 election suggests, however, that the case may sometimes be overstated.

Before the 1957 election a surprisingly large number of Conservatives tried to define the party's philosophy and put the definition in the form of a programme or a manifesto. Whatever else it may tell about the Conservative party, the failure to utilize the convention resolutions does not prove that the party was uninterested in formulating an ideology. Some of the impetus for the seemingly widespread search for a distinct Conservative philosophy undoubtedly came from tactical needs; to profit from anti-Liberal sentiment it was necessary to distinguish as sharply as possible between the two old-line parties. This need was particularly pressing in view of the repeated allegations by both the C.C.F. and the Social Credit parties that there really was no difference between the parties led by Mr. St. Laurent and Mr. Diefenbaker, except that one was in office and the other not.

Quite apart from the exigencies of the campaign, however, a number of attempts were made of redefining the party's philosophy. In the spring of 1955, for example, Mr. Gordon Churchill drafted a statement of Conservative principles as the result of discussions he had held with a number of parliamentary colleagues all of whom felt the need for a new look at their party.[10] The first part is an attempt to formulate a general Conservative philosophy. It owes much to the Christian ethic and to Edmund Burke. The second part tries to apply the general propositions of the first to specific attitudes of the party on current problems.

Later that year Mr. Donald Fleming gave an address entitled *Distinc-*

[10]Gordon Churchill, "The Conservative Position: A Statement of Philosophy and Principles," unpublished memoir dated May, 1955. Among those participating in the discussions leading towards this memoir were Mr. R. A. Bell, Mr. J. M. Macdonnell, and Mr. Davie Fulton. The last-named also produced his own version of Conservative principles.

tive Conservatism which was widely distributed.[11] Somewhat less contemplative in outlook than Mr. Churchill's, this statement of Conservatism attempted to show the historical differences between the two major parties and then listed a number of differences in policy.

Members of the Resolutions and Policy Committee of the leadership convention also exhibited a keen interest in stating the party's philosophy in clear and unmistakable terms. It was hoped that a short statement of principles could be included in a preamble to the resolutions. Mr. Alvin Hamilton, the Saskatchewan leader, submitted a long document entitled "A Declaration of Principles." It was never adopted or used, although Mr. Hamilton incorporated it into a revision he undertook of the convention resolutions.[12] This draft differed from those of Mr. Churchill and Mr. Fleming largely in emphasis. It placed greater stress on governmental responsibilities for social welfare (although, like the other documents, it reiterated the need for preventing the state from becoming too powerful) and for national development.

Although it did not adopt Mr. Alvin Hamilton's version, the convention Resolutions Committee did incorporate into its report a statement of principles, to constitute the preamble to the resolutions. It was even vaguer than these manifestoes usually are. For this reason, and also because it placed too much emphasis on free enterprise (thus, it was thought, again identifying the party with big business) this formulation of the party's general position was found unsatisfactory by the convention. Mr. William Hamilton, in collaboration with some others, redrafted it; his amendment was adopted by the convention and his formulation became part of the resolutions.[13]

It is difficult to tell how effective these attempts were in determining the party's attitudes to the election issues. In the final analysis, the leader of a party plays by far the largest part in presenting its views to the nation. He is assisted by the candidates who, as a rule, take their cues from him and their lines from material provided by the national or provincial headquarters. While the various attempts at defining the party's general position that have been mentioned so far may have influenced the way in which Mr. Diefenbaker approached the election, it is doubtful

[11]Published in Ottawa as a pamphlet, and also issued in French.

[12]"Declaration of Principles by the Progressive Conservative National Convention, Ottawa, December 12th to 14th, 1956," unpublished.

[13]This amendment was later incorporated into the new constitution as the major part of the section defining the party's objects. Press release by the Progressive Conservative party, "Summary of Changes in the Constitution of the Progressive Conservative Association of Canada Approved by the Meeting of the Executive Officers and Executive Members Qualified to Vote under the Present Constitution, November 30, 1959," p. 1.

whether they played a decisive role. There is no doubt, however, about the influence, and about the congeniality to the new leader, of still another attempt at defining Conservative principles and deducing from them the broad lines of the party's policy. Its author was not even a member of the party and produced his programme largely out of exasperation with, and fear of, the Liberal Government.[14] He had, in fact, been at one time on the staff of a Liberal cabinet minister.

Dr. Merril W. Menzies had written a doctoral dissertation for the London School of Economics in which he developed some interesting ideas about the relation, historically, of the great Canadian parties to economic growth.[15] In the autumn of 1956 he applied some of his findings to the current political and economic situation in Canada. As a consequence, he wrote a forty-page analysis of the situation which, through a relative who was an active Conservative, came to the attention of Mr. Diefenbaker just before he assumed the leadership of the party. Mr. Diefenbaker was impressed. Dr. Menzies became a member of Mr. Diefenbaker's staff and throughout the campaign assisted him in the preparation of speeches.

An adequate summary of Dr. Menzies' argument cannot be attempted here. For the purpose at hand, however, it is important to note that, on the basis of a long historical and economic analysis, Dr. Menzies concluded that if Canada were to maintain her own national identity it was essential for the government actively to foster economic development. In the nineteenth century this idea had prompted Sir John A. Macdonald's National Policy which had assured Canada of a balanced economic growth. The Conservatives should return to the ideas and general policies of their greatest Prime Minister. The Liberals, Dr. Menzies thought, had led the country brilliantly after the Second World War. By abandoning laissez-faire and committing the government to widespread and large-scale intervention in the country's economy they had led Canada through a difficult period of adjustment and of necessary economic expansion. But now they had given up this imaginative post-war approach. The time had come, so they appeared to reason, for govern-

[14]There were other non-Conservatives who felt impelled to aid in strengthening the Conservative party out of fear of what was happening to Canadian politics under Liberal rule. Professor H. G. Thorburn, for example, a political scientist then at the University of Saskatchewan, submitted a memorandum to Mr. Fulton and some of his colleagues in which he suggested what the Conservatives might do to strengthen their party. This memorandum, which was presented in Ottawa in June, 1955, was entitled "The Political Situation." It has not been published.

[15]*The Canadian Wheat Board and the International Wheat Trade: National and International Factors Influencing the Development of Canadian Wheat Policy* (London, 1956).

ment to cease vigorously promoting economic expansion and for private enterprise to act largely alone in bringing about economic growth.[16] Mesmerized by "the cult of the Gross National Product," blinded by reasonably encouraging national statistics, the Liberal Government had failed to notice that certain regions in the country were not doing nearly as well as some others. Their preoccupation with national statistics led the Liberals to the view that all that a government needs to do is to maintain welfare policies and short-run economic stability. This, Dr. Menzies argued, was inadequate:

It seems to me, then, that in regard to national policy the Liberal government is in a state of drift. It has no clear-cut objective except to keep the economy competitive and on an even keel. This is an essential objective and most of its policies designed to achieve these ends are right and sound. But the Canadian people want more than this. They ask for vision in their statesmen, a sense of national purpose and national destiny. They are offered prosperity and welfare state. There is nothing wrong in this but it is not enough. "Man does not live by bread alone." "Without a vision the people (and the nation) perish."[17]

After urging the Conservative party to abandon what he thought to have been its traditional distrust of positive government action, Dr. Menzies outlined a new national policy; it featured a proposal for a national energy grid, a comprehensive policy on natural resources,[18] and the establishment of various incentives for development. In pressing for this programme Dr. Menzies warned against some of the policies usually advocated by economic nationalists—an excessive use of the tariff, for example, or the insistence to an unreasonable degree that Canadian raw materials be processed at home.[19]

[16]The thought underlying the Liberal government's position was epitomized, so Dr. Menzies believed, in a paper by an economist at Laval University. See Maurice Lamontagne, "The Role of Government," in G. P. Gilmour, ed., *Canada's Tomorrow* (Toronto, 1954), pp. 117–52. Mr. Lamontagne became economic adviser to the federal cabinet some time after the publication of his paper.

[17]The memorandum, being in the form of a letter, has no title. This quotation is from pp. 21–2 of the typescript.

[18]Dr. Menzies, in formulating some of his ideas on a policy for the development of energy and other resources, referred to M. W. Mackenzie's paper "Canada's Natural Resources" in Gilmour, ed., *Canada's Tomorrow*, pp. 35–63. He is also indebted to G. V. Ferguson, "Likely Trends in Canadian-American Political Relations," *Canadian Journal of Economics and Political Science*, vol. XXII, no. 4 (Nov., 1956), pp. 437–48.

[19]In issuing his warnings, as well as in other parts of his analysis, Dr. Menzies cited the views contained in a presidential address to the Canadian Political Science Association: see J. Douglas Gibson, "The Changing Influence of the United States on the Canadian Economy," *Canadian Journal of Economics and Political Science*, vol. XXII, no. 4 (Nov., 1956), pp. 421–36.

The stand the Conservative party took on the major issues of the election cannot be divorced from the attitudes that had evolved within the party in the past. Nor, as was suggested above, is it wise to write off completely the effectiveness of the convention resolutions, even though they were never published. But the most important factor in the formulation of the party's position on contemporary problems was the attitude of the new leader. His constant adviser on speeches dealing with policy was Dr. Menzies, who, in turn, was in continuous contact with party headquarters, particularly with Dr. Donald Eldon, the head of the Research Department. It was thus the leader, and those whom he chose to consult, who, in the final analysis, determined the Conservative party's "line" in the election.

The economic argument elaborated by Dr. Menzies was perfectly compatible with Mr. Diefenbaker's ideas on the role of government and on the nature of Canada's problems at the time of his accession to the leadership. These ideas met the demands not only of western and Maritime provincial leaders, but also those of the strategists at national headquarters, concerned with creating an image of the party acceptable to large numbers of voters. There was, therefore, from the Conservative point of view, a happy convergence of the ideas entertained by the new leader, by a number of provincial leaders, by an intellectual element in the party, and by the managers of the campaign, whose responsibility was in the field of public relations.

The Issues

It has been argued that the main issue of the 1957 election was whether or not the Liberal party had been in power too long and, assuming this to have been the case, whether or not the Conservatives should replace it.[20] These were, of course, questions of fundamental importance, but to account for the 1957 fall of the Liberals from power in terms of the "time for a change" hypothesis takes us only part way towards an understanding of what really happened. What specific acts of commission or omission led to the Liberal defeat? What enabled the Conservatives to gain power? An attempt to answer these questions is made in the concluding part of this study. In the remainder of this chapter the most important issues are isolated and discussed in terms of the attitudes adopted towards them by the major parties.

[20]See for example, H. D. Johns, "Why Canadians Voted Conservative," *Saturday Night*, vol. LXXII, no. 17, (Aug. 17, 1957), pp. 7, 38–9.

FISCAL POLICY[21]

While it was probably rash of one Conservative member[22] to call it the most important issue in the election, it is certain that taxation was of great interest to the public. The differences between the parties in relation to it were considerable and, on the surface at least, of a kind easily comprehensible to every taxpayer. Mr. Diefenbaker set out the Conservative viewpoint in the address which constituted the formal opening of his party's campaign. He claimed that Canadians were being overtaxed "to the extent of approximately $120.00 for every four-member family." Asserting that it was time "to take the unrepentant Tax Masters at Ottawa off the backs of the Canadian people," he undertook, if elected, immediately to call a session of Parliament to reduce taxation. He was particularly critical of the government for not reducing taxes when a surplus had been accumulated in the previous fiscal year.[23]

Mr. St. Laurent also dealt with the tax problem in his first major campaign speech. He argued that the country's great prosperity could not have occurred had the government not pursued a wise tax policy. Like other Liberal speakers during the campaign he stressed that since 1953 the tax rate had been reduced and that at the same time the national debt had also been brought down by 165,000,000 dollars. This had helped to maintain Canada's reputation for sound financial policies, which in turn created a climate conducive to investment and consequently to economic development. Mr. St. Laurent attacked the opposition parties for making extravagant promises of government expenditures. The cost of these promises would inevitably drive up the tax rate. And even if no new expenditures were undertaken, what services would the opposition reduce so as to achieve the promised tax reduction?[24] To

[21]This account of the positions the parties took on the various issues is based almost exclusively on (a) leaders' speeches, (b) publications of the parties, (c) statements by some ministers who presented Liberal policies in relation to their own ministries. When information is derived from copies of speeches preserved by the parties, this is indicated by the word "mimeo" in the footnote, usually followed by a page reference. Dates refer to 1957. It should be noted that in the case of Mr. St. Laurent's speeches all the manuscripts consulted carried the caution that they contained notes for speeches. On the rare occasions when Mr. St. Laurent departed from the prepared text, however, this was noted by the newspapers. Here such departures are indicated only when they seem relevant to our argument.

[22]Dr. W. G. Blair, speaking in support of A. Clair Casselman in Kemptville, Ont., Ottawa *Journal*, June 1.

[23]Speech at Massey Hall, Toronto, April 25 (mimeo). The Conservative view is also set out in a pamphlet, *Taxation and Inflation*, in the party's "Talking Points" series.

[24]Speech in Winnipeg, April 29 (mimeo). He also dealt with the tax problem in London, Ont., on May 16 (mimeo).

this the opposition replied by saying that it would effect economies through being less wasteful than the government and that the cost of its own promises would be more than covered by the unnecessary surplus.[25]

Credit restrictions were closely related to tax policy. Large numbers of voters had undoubtedly been irritated by them and it was therefore to be expected that they would be a lively issue in the election. Mr. Diefenbaker did, in fact, mention in more than a dozen of his major election speeches "those unwise and unsound credit restrictions, which were so precipitously imposed in an attempt to cover up the failure of the Government to foresee and forestall the threat of inflation."[26] He argued that the government would have been better advised to cut its inessential spending, thereby bolstering development and productivity so that goods would be in sufficient supply for the amount of money available.[27] Mr. Diefenbaker also suggested that the same end could be achieved by reducing taxes. But whatever the alternatives, he thought that the policy of the Bank of Canada (for which he obviously held the Liberals responsible) and of the government itself discriminated against the Maritime provinces and the West and also favoured the large entrepreneurs at the expense of the small farmer, fisherman, or businessman.

The Liberal response to the Conservatives' sustained attack was a curious one: it was practicallly nonexistent. True, Mr. Harris, the Minister of Finance, had explained the government's stand in the House during the budget debate: money was "tight" because of Canada's great rate of expansion. It was necessary to offset inflationary pressures by trying to reduce the rate of spending so long as the economy could not produce the goods and services demanded. But the policy of resisting inflationary pressures when they appeared was "designed not to reduce economic growth but to increase it by stretching out the period in which conditions favourable to growth will

[25]To Mr. St. Laurent's later estimates that the Conservative promises would cost as much as $1,500,000,000, Mr. Diefenbaker replied that he thought they could be implemented for $300,000,000. He estimated the real government surplus to have been $500,000,000, Winnipeg *Free Press*, May 27.

[26]A collection of Mr. Diefenbaker's election promises assembled by the Liberal party devotes ten of its 159 pages to the Conservative leader's speeches on this subject. See National Liberal Federation, "John G. Diefenbaker's Promises to the People of Canada during the 1957 Election" (Ottawa, 1957, mimeo), pp. 89–97 (henceforth referred to as "Mr. Diefenbaker's Promises"). This quotation is cited on pp. 92–3.

[27]Speech in Hull, Que., May 3. Montreal *Star*, May 8, cited in "Mr. Diefenbaker's Promises," p. 92.

continue. . . .[28] This, in brief, was the line the government took during the budget debate. The argument was reproduced in the Liberal party's Speaker's Handbook.[29] But no major attempt was made during the campaign to explain the government's policy to the voters. Mr. St. Laurent made only passing reference to the necessity for credit restrictions. Mr. Harris, like most of the leading ministers, devoted a television speech to issues related to his Department. He discussed the problem of dividing the tax field equitably between the three levels of government, he referred to tax reductions since the previous election and to social security, but he made no reference to the tight money policy. This, then, was an issue used extensively by the Conservatives but practically ignored by the government.

AGRICULTURE

That agricultural questions would play an important role in the election was well known long before the campaign started.[30] As polling day approached it became evident that farm discontent would affect the outcome in a considerable number of constituencies. In the prairie provinces, particularly, its extent and violence must have aroused deep Liberal anxieties. Several former executives of the Manitoba Farmers Union were waging intensive campaigns as opposition candidates; even such powerful Liberals as Mr. C. D. Howe were practically refused a hearing at meetings held in largely wheat-growing constituencies.[31] It was, therefore, not surprising that both parties expended considerable energy in airing their views on Canada's agricultural problems.[32]

As they did, perforce, in relation to virtually all campaign issues, the Liberals pointed with satisfaction to their record in agriculture. Mr. St.

[28]Hon. W. E. Harris, *Debates* (March 14, 1957), p. 2216.

[29]National Liberal Federation, *Liberal Action For a Greater Canada* (Ottawa, 1957; henceforth referred to as *Liberal Action*), pp. 335–7.

[30]See, for example, Blair Fraser, "Wheat, Gas and Tory Hopes," *Maclean's*, Feb. 18, 1956, pp. 8, 57.

[31]See, for example, Michael Best, "Farmers' Revolt as a Vote Factor in Manitoba," Toronto *Globe and Mail*, June 4, or his report in the Winnipeg *Free Press*, May 14. On Mr. Howe's disastrous meeting in Morris, Man., see below, chap. IX, and a report by Ted Byfield in the Winnipeg *Free Press*, May 20.

[32]The Liberals devoted fifty pages of *Liberal Action* to agriculture, as well as two of the nine leaflets the National Federation prepared for appeals to various groups in the country. Mr. St. Laurent and other cabinet ministers devoted a number of major speeches to it and the subject was discussed on the radio and television. Mr. Diefenbaker also spent considerable time in all provinces discussing this issue. He called a special press conference in his campaign train at which a full statement of his party's agricultural policy was distributed to the correspondents. One of the ten pamphlets in the "Talking Points" series deals with agriculture.

Laurent more than once mentioned that seventeen measures had been passed by the recent Parliament to assist the farmer.[33] Conditions in agriculture, no less than in other sectors of the economy were, it was argued, generally extremely good. It was admitted that there was some hardship among wheat farmers who could not dispose of their grain, but this condition was considered to be temporary. Equally short-lived, according to government spokesmen, would be the so-called "cost-price" squeeze resulting from increasing production costs and falling farm prices. This phenomenon was thought of as a temporary by-product of Canada's rapid economic growth. The expansion would, in the long run, benefit the farmer by creating a large and steady domestic market for his produce. In sum, then, the Liberals tried to show that the farmer had shared in Canada's prosperity and that he really had little to complain about.

Of the many promises made to farmers by Conservative spokesmen, four constituted a sufficiently drastic departure from Liberal policy to merit notice. If elected, the Conservatives undertook (1) to establish and maintain a flexible price support programme to ensure "adequate parity for agricultural producers, based on a fair price-cost relationship,[34] (2) to pay cash advances on farm-stored western wheat, and (3) to safeguard Canadian producers from "unwarranted importations of agricultural products."[35] The Conservatives also promised (4) that if it became advisable to export wheat or any other farm product below the domestic price the loss would not be borne by the producer alone.

Each one of these suggestions was vigorously attacked by the Liberals. Parity prices were opposed on the grounds that they had not really been a success in the United States and that the government was not going to tell farmers what to grow and then to guarantee a set price for their produce.[36] Cash advances on farm-stored wheat would not, it was argued, result in a net advantage to the producer. The problem was a temporary one in any event and the government's 1956 Interim Financing Act offered some relief to small farmers.[37] The clearly protectionist implications of the Conservatives' agricultural programme were also rejected. The government had, however, itself placed a tariff on potatoes

[33]Notably in Winnipeg (April 29) and Edmonton (April 30th). Among the many speeches in which he discussed agriculture, those in Guelph, Ont. (May 14), Truro, N.S. (May 21), and Roberval, Que. (May 29), contained particularly useful summaries of the Liberal position. Most of his western addresses, of course, also gave prominence to farm problems.

[34]Press release, May 7, p. 5.   [35]Ibid., p. 6.

[36]Liberal Action, pp. 132–5. See also Mr. St. Laurent's speech in Regina, May 7, Winnipeg Free Press, May 8.

[37]Liberal Action, p. 154.

imported from the United States and Mr. Howe announced in the middle of the campaign that imports of cheddar cheese would henceforth be banned.[38]

The Conservatives took a more strongly protectionist stand than the Liberals who argued that their protests against United States interference with Canadian exports would carry little weight if Canada imposed too many restrictions on American commodities seeking access to the Canadian market. On similar grounds the Liberals criticized Conservative hints that they would compensate the Canadian wheat grower for lower revenues received from exports to distressed areas at below domestic prices. Such subsidies would, the Liberals feared, weaken Canadian protests in Washington against United States surplus disposal programmes. The government also expressed fear of doing anything which would affect the world wheat price adversely and reassured the farmer that soon he would be able to dispose of his surpluses for "real money."[39]

Occasionally, Liberal speakers did express the view that stronger measures might become necessary in the future to aid the wheat farmer. Mr. Howe, for example, hinted during a speech in Saskatchewan that new steps might have to be taken to meet the grain surplus if another bumper crop were harvested.[40] At no time, however, did the Liberals go as far as Mr. Diefenbaker in suggesting that one way of coping with the problem would be to establish an "international food bank under NATO in which surpluses . . . could be stored to meet any possible future emergency."[41]

One interesting feature of the campaign concerns the emphasis the Liberals gave to the Senate's Special Committee to study land use, created early in 1957. Mr. St. Laurent made surprisingly frequent reference to it, perhaps because he was personally interested in the project. It is also possible that this minor measure was played up because it suggested, to those who wished to view it in this way, that the government was both forward-looking, despite its long years in office, and interested in making the best use of Parliament, despite what was said about it as a result of the pipeline debate.

[38]Mr. St. Laurent referred to the move against potato imports while campaigning in the Maritimes, whereas Mr. Howe, naturally, talked about the cheese ban during speeches in dairy areas of Ontario. See Mr. St. Laurent's speech in Truro, May 21, and the Winnipeg *Free Press*, May 28.

[39]Mr. St. Laurent, speaking in Regina, May 7, Winnipeg *Free Press*, May 8.

[40]Melville, Sask., Winnipeg *Free Press*, May 18. See also Mr. St. Laurent's speech in St. Catharines, *ibid.*, June 5.

[41]Calgary. See Winnipeg *Free Press*, May 20.

TRADE

Conservative policy on trade followed the party resolutions much more closely than it did the ideas contained in the Menzies memorandum. The Conservatives were bitterly critical of the government for having "permitted . . . trade with the United Kingdom and other European countries to decline while Canada's dependence on trade with the United States has increased alarmingly and out of all proportion."[42] A Commonwealth trade and economic conference was promised to redress the balance. The party also undertook to pursue a policy "which will encourage more processing of Canada's raw materials in Canada, and will foster a greater financial participation (in development of industry) by Canadians."[43] Apart from suggesting a number of changes in tax policy, the Conservatives were not explicit about how they would carry out these undertakings.

Indeed, Mr. St. Laurent countered the opposition charges in this regard by asking Mr. Diefenbaker whether he would impose controls preventing businessmen from selling raw materials abroad, whether he would erect tariff barriers to protect uneconomic industries and whether he would hoard mineral, timber and agricultural products.[44] The extent of American investments did not cause the government undue concern. The Prime Minister pointed out that foreign investment had not kept pace with other aspects of Canadian economic expansion. In any case, he argued, this investment aided Canadian development and enabled Canada to make purchases in the United States which she would otherwise have to do without. The fact that Canadian exports in 1956 had increased by 12 per cent was ascribed in large part to capital investment made in the past, much of it having been American in origin.[45]

DEVELOPMENT

Economic nationalism constituted an important element in the Conservative appeal to the voters on the matter of trade and United States investment. A somewhat more broadly conceived nationalism underlay much of what was said on the related subject of national development. Here too the main parties followed the usual pattern. The Liberals pointed to what had been achieved and how much Canada had grown since they had assumed office and even since the last election; the Con-

[42]*Trade*, one of the pamphlets in the "Talking Points" series, p. 3.
[43]Mr. Diefenbaker in a speech at Massey Hall, Toronto, April 25 (mimeo), p. 5. For a fuller statement of Conservative policy see the speech by Mr. Hees in Calgary, reported in Winnipeg *Free Press*, May 10.
[44]Montreal, June 3 (mimeo), pp. 6–7.
[45]*Ibid.*, p. 6. Also Calgary, May 1 (mimeo), pp. 11–12.

servatives found fault with much that had been done and with an even larger number of things which had been left undone. Specifically, they undertook to establish a national energy board, to launch a "New Frontier" policy to develop the resources of Canada's northland, to collaborate with the provinces on joint investment programmes for the development of hydro-electric and other self-liquidating projects, and generally to promote growth and a climate favouring private investment. This, the Liberals argued, was precisely what they had been doing since the end of the Second World War. The candidates' handbook listed twenty-six large development projects undertaken by private enterprise and government since 1948.[46]

The parties disagreed on a number of specific developmental projects. Up to the time of the election, for example, the government had found it impossible to offer assistance to the proposed construction of the South Saskatchewan Dam—a scheme to which the Conservatives were committed. In the Maritimes the Liberals had consented to help in the development of more power, but the offer was made only a short time before the election. The Conservative premiers in Nova Scotia and New Brunswick were able to help Mr. Diefenbaker create the impression that he, and not the Liberal party, was more likely to assist Maritime development. Government willingness to help in the development of power on the Columbia river in British Columbia was expressed in somewhat equivocal form and was obviously the subject of difference of opinion among cabinet ministers.[47]

Most sensational of the issues touching on national development, was, of course, that concerning the Trans-Canada pipeline. It is worthwhile adding to what is said about it elsewhere in this volume,[48] that the Conservatives were critical of the Liberals' attitude to the pipeline on at least two scores. They would have preferred an all-Canadian company and they objected to the great profits made by private investors with the help of the Canadian government. "Who risked the money?" asked

[46]*Liberal Action*, pp. 171–3. Some sixty pages are devoted to production and future growth. Mr. St. Laurent often touched on the question of Canada's development. See, for example, his Edmonton speech, April 30, where he pointed to the fact that it was the Liberals who established the Department of Northern Affairs and National Resources shortly after the previous election. Television broadcasts by Mr. Howe, Mr. Marler, and Mr. Winters also dealt with national development. On the Conservative side, one pamphlet in the "Talking Points" series was devoted to it and Mr. Diefenbaker made numerous references to the subject. See, for example, his speech in northern Manitoba, reported in the Winnipeg *Free Press*, May 17.

[47]For revealing articles on this much-discussed subject see the Winnipeg *Free Press*, April 1, May 4, and May 14. See also below, p. 187.

[48]See above and below, pp. 8–10 and 59–61.

Mr. Diefenbaker. "You and I," came the reply. "Who made the profits? . . . Those pampered pets."[49]

Conservative criticism of the government's approach to Maritime and British Columbia power development and to the Trans-Canada pipeline was largely directed at its past performance. The only major difference between the parties, in relation to specific future projects, concerned the South Saskatchewan Dam. One might conclude from this that national development was not an important issue in the election. This would be erroneous. For while there seemed relatively little that separated the parties in substance, there was a vast difference in how they presented their respective views. The difference was largely in tone. Where the Liberals spoke with the soft voice of the self-confident bureaucrat, the Conservatives exhorted with the feverish zest of the visionary. Did this difference in the manner of presentation reflect a difference in enthusiasm and in the breadth of horizons that bound the vision of each party? There is some evidence that many Canadians thought the difference to have been more than merely verbal.

SOCIAL WELFARE

There were no fundamental divisions, among the major parties, on questions of social security. The idea of the welfare state had received general recognition long before 1957. During the campaign, consequently, the Conservatives promised to maintain and even expand social security measures. Specifically, they undertook to extend the government hospital insurance plan to include tubercular and mental patients, and to incorporate hospital depreciation charges in the formula used to compute the government's contribution to the cost of hospital care. Veterans were promised justice and fair treatment.[50] Nothing, here, revealed drastic divergencies of view between the government and the Conservative party.

And yet, one field of social legislation played an important part in the election. Considerable discontent had arisen over the size of the old age pension. When established in 1952, it amounted to forty dollars per month for every citizen in Canada aged seventy years or more who had been resident in the country for at least twenty years. As noted above, the government raised the amount in its last budget to forty-six dollars. The opposition considered this increase inadequate and accused the government of being mean and niggardly to the senior citizens. The growing number of so-called New Canadians were irritated by the

---

[49]Speech in Prince Edward Island. See Winnipeg *Free Press*, April 30.
[50]*Social Security*, in the "Talking Points" series, p. 3.

twenty-year waiting period. Many of them had been contributing to the fund since its inception but were not eligible for benefits paid from it.

Liberal ministers pointed to the numerous social security measures introduced by their party, arguing that to have gone beyond the present level would have been unjustifiable in relation to national productivity. Consequently they termed opposition promises irresponsible and in some instances even dishonest.[51] Liberal speakers also reminded their listeners that the Conservative party had been vigorously opposed to family allowances when these were first introduced.[52] At the same time they recalled the fact that the plank on family allowances was included in the 1956 Conservative convention resolutions only after an appeal had been made for the purpose from the floor.[53]

But it was the opposition which took the offensive in the campaign on social security and the old age pension became the main battleground. In every province anti-government candidates repeatedly promised a substantial increase in the pension. Addressing foreign language newspapermen, Mr. Diefenbaker supported a "very pronounced reduction" in the twenty-year qualifying period.[54] The government's decision not to begin paying the increase until July was also criticized. Mr. Harris had said that the reason for the delay was that the government did not wish to add to existing inflationary pressures. This argument was ridiculed by Mr. Diefenbaker who pointed out that the increase in the pension amounted to twenty cents a day per pensioner.

All the opposition parties promised to increase the pension. The C.C.F. and Social Credit parties even specified the amounts to which they proposed to raise it.[55] This the Conservatives refused to do. But in their efforts to portray the government as having become arrogant and

[51]Three of the Liberals' special leaflets were concerned with social security. *Liberal Action* devoted over thirty pages (pp. 265–308) to the subject. A number of broadcasts also set out the government's view. Notable among these were two television addresses by Mr. Martin and Mr. Lapointe, April 7 and 31, and a radio talk by Mr. Sinclair, June 6.

[52]In the text of the speech prepared for delivery in Halifax, Mr. St. Laurent asked his audience whether they thought family allowances would have been started by the Conservatives "when the Tory leader at the time fought so hard against this measure?" (mimeo, p. 3) The Canadian Press dispatch reporting the speech, dated May 22, quotes him as adding the following: "Do you think that any Canadian party can win through an election with a programme designed to repeal the Family Allowance Act?"

[53]See broadcasts by Mr. Lionel Chevrier, June 6 (mimeo), p. 4, and by Mr. Hugues Lapointe, May 16 (mimeo), pp. 5–6. See also *Liberal Action*, pp. 283–4 and *Canadian Liberal*, vol. XIX, nos. 1 & 2 (first quarter, 1957), pp. 19–20.

[54]Press Conference at Canadian Ethnic Press Club, Toronto, Ont., Winnipeg *Free Press*, April 27.

[55]See below, pp. 207, 223.

insensitive to human needs, they never tired of using the old age pension as a telling example. On his last television broadcast but one, Mr. Diefenbaker spoke of the "fantastically inadequate increase" and practically on the eve of the election, during his final television appeal, he characterized the raise as "insufficient, inequitable, niggardly."[56] Used in this way by all the opposition parties, the pension became of decided importance in the campaign.

It was an issue to which probably very large numbers of voters responded with considerable emotion.[57] A skilful appeal to this emotion by the Conservatives achieved a twofold purpose; it branded the Liberals as a party no longer sympathetic to the underdog, to the group Mr. Diefenbaker once characterized as "the humble men and women across this country who desire someone to speak for them in Parliament."[58] Secondly, it enabled the Conservatives to divest themselves of the lingering stigma of being a party of privilege. Mr. Diefenbaker was probably the first Conservative leader in this century to succeed in making credible Conservative promises of social reform. The old age pension was an important prop in his electoral performance.

DOMINION-PROVINCIAL RELATIONS

Dominion-provincial relations, particularly their fiscal aspects, were also among the important issues of the election. A substantial proportion of voters must have known that the level of municipal taxes was related to this question, and almost everyone in the country felt the pressure of rising local taxes. In addition, it affected the attitude to the election of the premiers of at least three provinces—Ontario, Nova Scotia and New Brunswick. They would almost certainly not have taken as active an interest in the election as they did, had they not expected to secure for their provinces more favourable terms from a Conservative than from a Liberal federal government.

The Conservative case rested on the assertion that the government had become excessively centralist. This, it was argued, had led to "a deliberate federal policy of invasion of the major taxation fields in order to shut out the provinces and municipalities from their main source of income and to force them to beg for hand-outs from Ottawa."[59] In the province of Quebec the same argument took the form of attacks on the

---

[56]May 29 (mimeo), p. 6, and June 5 (mimeo), p. 5.

[57]Johns, "Why Canadians Voted Conservative," pp. 7, 38. But see also below, pp. 273–4.

[58]Television broadcast, April 30 (mimeo), p. 6.

[59]*Federal-Provincial-Municipal Relations*, in the "Talking Points" series, p. 4.

government for allegedly having violated provincial rights.[60] For their part, the Conservatives promised to call a dominion-provincial conference, as soon as elected, "to bring about a settlement [of dominion-provincial differences] not in the spirit of arrogant domination, as displayed by the present government, but in the spirit of unity and amity, with mutual tolerance and respect."[61] No precise Conservative proposals were ever announced. The party left no doubt in anyone's mind, however, that it would approach the problem differently from the Liberals. While no "significant changes" were envisaged[62] the implication clearly was that the provinces would obtain more favourable terms from a Conservative than from a Liberal government. In the face of Liberal counter-attacks, Mr. Diefenbaker assured the country that no province would get less than at the time of the election and that the same equalization rate would apply to them all.[63]

Replying to criticisms of their policies vis-à-vis the provinces, government spokesmen claimed that each time a new tax-sharing agreement had been negotiated in the past, the provinces had obtained a larger share. The government thought that, although its plan was not necessarily perfect, the main objective had been attained: "to enable all the Provinces to provide a Canadian standard of Provincial services without punitive taxation."[64] On the issue of dominion-provincial relations, however, the Liberals were not satisfied to remain on the defensive. Mr. St. Laurent, particularly, made some spirited attacks on the Conservatives in this regard.

The Prime Minister criticized the alliance between Mr. Frost and Mr. Diefenbaker. Mr. Frost had indicated that the main reason for his support of the federal Conservatives was his disappointment with the way Ontario had been treated by the federal government. Ontario, he argued repeatedly, was entitled to a larger share of the tax-dollar. Mr. St. Laurent wanted to know at whose expense a Diefenbaker government would provide Ontario with larger revenues. Would Mr. Diefenbaker raise taxes or would he reduce the payments made to the other provinces? The federal government had the duty of redistributing some of the nation's taxable wealth. It was, therefore, unlikely that anyone

[60]See dispatch by Fred Manor in Winnipeg *Free Press*, May 31, and report in *La Presse*, June 1, quoted in "Mr. Diefenbaker's Promises," p. 69.

[61]Mr. Diefenbaker in Toronto, April 25 (mimeo), p. 4.

[62]Interview with Mr. Diefenbaker, Winnipeg, Man., Winnipeg *Free Press*, May 14.

[63]Speeches in Carman, Man., April 15, on television, April 30, and in Saskatoon, May 27.

[64]Mr. Walter Harris in a television broadcast, May 15 (mimeo), pp. 1–2.

would reduce the share of the poorer provinces so as to make increased payments to the more prosperous ones. Rejecting the Conservative suggestion that the increase could come from the government surplus "spent several times already" Mr. St. Laurent concluded that the Conservatives planned to increase federal taxes.[65]

Often, in the campaign, the Liberals had taken a defensive, and therefore a somewhat negative position. On dominion-provincial relations, as was shown above, they assumed a more aggressive posture. They not only challenged Mr. Diefenbaker to state, unequivocally, how he proposed to help the provinces financially without increasing federal taxes, but they also used the issue for a more general purpose. Pointing to the Frost-Diefenbaker alliance, they tried to show that the Conservative party was still very much an Ontario party, pressing the interests of the central provinces at the expense of the peripheral ones. In contrast, the Liberal party was frequently referred to as a truly national party—one which had always taken a national viewpoint and could be counted upon to continue doing so in the future.

FOREIGN POLICY

Another field in which the government thought that it had a distinct edge over the opposition was that of foreign relations. Mr. Pearson's undoubted success as Secretary of State for External Affairs was cited as an excellent example of how difficult it would be to replace the Liberal cabinet by one composed of opposition leaders.[66] The Conservatives resented Liberal attempts to give the impression that Mr. Pearson and his colleagues would serve the cause of peace better than would any other party. Mr. Diefenbaker ridiculed the Liberal slogan—"Peace, Prosperity and Social Security." It suggested, he said in Minnedosa, Manitoba, that the Liberals held themselves up "as supermen of foreign affairs . . . campaigning as though they were the only Canadian politi-

[65]Mr. St. Laurent's views were expressed at some length in speeches at Belleville, May 17, in Moncton, May 21, and Halifax, May 22. The federal-provincial tax rental agreements were explained by Mr. Garson in a speech made in Toronto in December, 1956. It is reprinted in the *Canadian Liberal*, vol. XIX, no. 3 (second quarter, 1957), pp. 50–6. Only eleven pages (pp. 350–60) in *Liberal Action* are devoted to this issue. The intensity of the Conservative interest in it is revealed in the fact that extracts from Mr. Diefenbaker's speeches on the subject took up fifteen pages (pp. 56–71) in "Mr. Diefenbaker's Promises." The extracts are taken from speeches made in about twenty localities.

[66]Mr. Marler, for example, said in a radio broadcast on May 30, "You will wonder as I do who in the Conservative party would take the place of the Honourable Lester Pearson, whose knowledge and experience of world affairs has been put to such good use in recent years" (mimeo, p. 4).

cians working for peace."[67] On another occasion the Conservative leader made it clear that he refused even to concede the Liberal claim that the government had done a good job of looking after Canada's foreign relations. In a television broadcast he said that Canadians were "asking Pearson to explain his bumbling of External Affairs."[68] But aside from these general skirmishes there were only two issues of any consequence related to foreign policy. The first of these concerned the Norman case,[69] the second the government's attitude to the Suez crisis.

It was only with reluctance that any of the leading politicians referred to the suicide of Canada's ambassador to Egypt. Such attacks as were made were directed at the government for failing to prevent United States congressional committees from subjecting Canadians to the sort of treatment which had led to the Norman tragedy. The government was also accused of acting irresponsibly in transmitting unchecked gossip collected by the Royal Canadian Mounted Police to the United States Federal Bureau of Investigation. Most vehement, however, were the attacks based on the assertion that the government had been less than candid in discussing the facts of the Norman incident.

Some bitter things were said against the government on account of its Suez policy. The Conservative party had consistently been critical of Canada's opposition to the Anglo-French intervention in the Middle East crisis. While this criticism took many forms during the campaign, it was most frequently directed at an almost chance remark of the Prime Minister. This statement of Mr. St. Laurent's was presumably thought by Conservatives to epitomize the attitude of the Liberals to which they objected. In the course of an exchange on the Suez crisis in the House of Commons Mr. St. Laurent referred to the days just before the creation of the United Nations Organization. He mentioned that the great powers —the Soviet Union, the United States and the United Kingdom—had favoured the adoption of the veto as part of the procedure of the Security Council. A member asked why the smaller countries should have been allowed to deal with the vital interests of the great states. In reply to this question Mr. St. Laurent said: "Because the members of the smaller nations are human beings just as are their people; because the era when the supermen of Europe could govern the whole world has and is coming pretty close to an end."[70] The Conservatives never let him forget that he applied the same derogatory epithets to both the Soviet Union and Britain. In his first major campaign address, for example, Mr. Diefenbaker said: "In the tradition of this Party, we did

[67]Winnipeg *Free Press*, May 17.　　[68]May 29 (mimeo), p. 2.
[69]See above, pp. 6–7.　　[70]*Debates*, Nov. 26, 1956, p. 20.

and do resent the British people being castigated and derisively condemned as those 'supermen' whose days are about over."[71]

The Suez crisis was often invoked in arguments which had no obvious connection with foreign policy or with the Middle East. Mr. Diefenbaker for example, said in Portage la Prairie, Manitoba, that "the government had wasted no time in protesting to Britain over the Anglo-French invasion of Egypt. Why, then, hadn't it been just as punctual in protesting U.S. policies which could reduce wheat to an almost valueless commodity . . ."[72] An even more tenuous link between Suez and the Canadian election was established by Miss Charlotte Whitton, a prominent Conservative and former mayor of Ottawa. Referring to the acute housing shortage in Elliot Lake, one of the communities in the hotly contested seat of Canada's Minister of External Affairs, she said in a manner typical of her campaign style: "It's too bad Nasser couldn't help Mike Pearson to cross Elliot Lake when Mr. Pearson did so much to help him along the Suez Canal."[73]

Comments on the Suez crisis prompted many Conservatives to say or imply that their party was more friendly to the Commonwealth than the Liberal party. The contextual relation of these remarks to Suez suggests that for some Conservatives "Commonwealth ties" really referred to Canada's relation to Britain and not, say, to an Asian country.[74] The contrast between the Liberals and the Conservatives in this regard is revealing. Far from admitting that it had done anything to weaken Commonwealth ties, the government insisted that it had strengthened them: "It was because Canada values the Commonwealth, because the world needed the Commonwealth, and because we wanted no nation to leave this association, that Canada was so concerned last November at the time of the Middle East crisis.[75]

With regard to foreign policy the issues that were actually discussed seemed to be raised not so much for their own sake but to create a certain general impression on the electorate. The Liberals were trying to suggest that they were more experienced and, particularly through the services of Mr. Pearson, more likely to carry out an effective foreign policy than any other party. In their somewhat casual references to the Norman case, the Conservatives appeared to be aiming at arousing the

[71]Toronto, April 25 (mimeo), p. 13.   [72]Winnipeg *Free Press*, May 15.
[73]Canadian Press dispatch from Toronto, dated June 6.
[74]See, for example, the broadcast by Mr. Gordon Churchill, Feb. 15, on the "Nation's Business" series of the Trans-Canada network of the C.B.C. (mimeo, p. 5). Another typical example is contained in a speech by Mr. Howard Green in Vancouver, May 31, reported in a C.P. dispatch.
[75]Mr. St. Laurent in London, Ont., May 16 (mimeo), p. 9.

latent anti-Americanism which permeated Canadian opinion at the time. The allusions to Suez were no doubt aimed primarily at the strongly pro-British sentiment prevalent in many parts of Canada.

PARLIAMENT

Of the many charges levelled against the government by the Conservatives, one was singled out for particular emphasis. A pamphlet was prepared to discuss it. The national office provided a full-page newspaper advertisement for candidates wishing to purchase space in local publications for the purpose of pointing to it. Mr. Diefenbaker and other party leaders referred to it as the main issue of the election. The issue in question was the alleged abuse by the government of Parliament.[76] Conservative speakers were indefatigable in accusing the government of having treated Parliament with contempt. The 1955 proposals of the government to amend the Defence Production Act[77] were referred to, statements were cited, illustrating Mr. St. Laurent's and particularly Mr. Howe's alleged impatience with, and contempt for, Parliamentary debate, incidents were recalled, revealing the government's failure fully and accurately to inform the House on important issues; the government was chastised for not making effective use of Parliamentary committees; in short, the executive's treatment of the legislature came under heavy and sustained fire.[78]

The growing tendency of the government to treat Parliament cavalierly culminated, according to the opposition, in the pipeline debate. Imposition by the government of closure and the conduct of the Speaker outraged the Conservative and C.C.F. members. To no incident or issue did Mr. Diefenbaker refer more frequently as he travelled from constituency to constituency in his bid for power. The following extract from one of his speeches is typical of the tone he adopted when discussing the case:

The events of the last few years have proved what happens when a party is too long in power. Those events had their culmination in the month of June last, on Black Friday, when the rights of Parliament were trampled on as

[76]The pamphlet and the advertisement were both entitled "Black Friday." Mr. Diefenbaker said in Saskatoon, that the preservation of Parliamentary rights transcended in importance all other issues of the election (Winnipeg *Free Press*, May 28). Mr. Fleming expressed a similar thought in a broadcast on June 6 (mimeo, p. 1).

[77]See above, pp. 7–8.

[78]The Conservative case was expounded not only in the House of Commons, but also in *Progress Report*, the party's magazine. See vol. I, 1955–56, *passim*. A summary, for election purposes, can be found in *Parliament and the People*, in the "Talking Points" series.

never before, when the rights of minorities were disregarded. That day, they tore up the rules, they changed the rules between sessions of Parliament, they tore up the Constitution, they trampled on the rights of men, the rights of free men that have been the rights of British and French tradition for hundreds of years. They did so when they applied closure before one solitary word was spoken before the House of Commons, when they denied criticism, when they prevented any discussion, when they finally succeeded in passing the legislation which they desired to have passed, they did something beyond anything that could have been expected in a free Parliament . . . [79]

To correct these alleged abuses, and to prevent their ever being repeated, the Conservative party promised to introduce the following innovations: abolition of closure; appointment of a "permanent" Speaker, as in the United Kingdom; and the revitalization of Parliamentary committees. A dominion-provincial conference was promised, to deal with the Senate. Out of this meeting, it was hoped, would emerge plans for a more effective upper chamber. The establishment of an independent commission was also promised, to carry out the decennial redistribution of seats demanded by the British North America Act.[80]

At the beginning of the campaign the Liberals made light of the Parliamentary issue. During his opening speech in Winnipeg, for example, Mr. St. Laurent referred flippantly to the matter when he said that it had been possible to begin building the natural gas pipeline eastward from Alberta only "after a debate nearly as long as the pipeline itself and quite as full of another kind of natural gas."[81] Later, more serious attempts were made to deal with opposition charges: Mr. St. Laurent devoted an important part of his final English television talk to it.[82] Neither the Prime Minister nor any other leading Liberal pleaded guilty to opposition charges. On the contrary, the government took the offensive and claimed that it was the opposition which had abused the House. Ministerial spokesmen claimed that ample time had been provided for the discussion of the pipeline: sixteen days were held to have been adequate; the fact that much of this time had been taken up by procedural wrangles was not considered to have been the government's fault. In any case, since the opposition had given notice of its filibuster in a broadcast by Mr. Diefenbaker on March 9, 1956, the government had been compelled to take steps ensuring that the will of the majority of the House prevailed. It was unthinkable that a minority should impose

[79]Television broadcast, June 5 (mimeo), pp. 2–3.
[80]The promises dealing with closure and the Senate were made by Mr. Diefenbaker in his Toronto speech, April 25 (mimeo, pp. 10–11). The other changes were outlined at Carman, Man. See the Winnipeg *Free Press*, May 16.
[81]April 29 (mimeo, p. 10).
[82]June 5 (mimeo, pp. 4–6).

its will on the majority of elected representatives. "It is our view," said Mr. St. Laurent in Owen Sound, Ontario, "that it was the Opposition which persistently tried to abuse the rules and thereby to prevent the majority in Parliament from putting through legislation which, it was felt, was in the public interest, and was wanted by the public." Blaming the government's opponents with obstruction, Mr. St. Laurent suggested that what they obviously needed was "more practice where they are so that they can do their job, in Opposition, as it should be done."[83] It was apparent from a radio address that Mr. Pickersgill shared some of the Conservative apprehensions about the future of Parliament, admittedly on grounds substantially different from those invoked by Mr. Diefenbaker. "It is very important for the future of Parliament," argued Mr. Pickersgill, "that the arrogant Tory attempt to establish minority rule should be recognized for what it was and repudiated by all fair-minded people."[84]

"TIME FOR A CHANGE?"

In addition to the issues just summarized, the parties also argued on general grounds. The Liberals pointed to their accomplishments since the previous election and since the ascent of Mr. St. Laurent to the leadership of the party. They wished to be given credit for what they had achieved and were highly sceptical of the proposition that another government would have done better. Canadians were just about as well off as could be expected. General conditions in the country were excellent and the future looked bright. The Conservatives, on the other hand, argued that improvements could be made in almost every phase of governmental activity: virtually everyone would be better off under a Conservative administration.

The government, the Conservatives insisted, had been in power too long. It had become arrogant, inflexible, and incapable of looking at problems from a new point of view. In addition, much concern was expressed over the size of the Liberal majority in the House: that it was so large was thought to weaken the effectiveness of Parliament. One of the issues in the election was, therefore, the question of whether the opposition should be strengthened.

But for those who believed that such strengthening of the opposition was desirable, the question still remained as to which of the parties was

[83]Owen Sound, May 15 (mimeo, pp. 3–4). Other important statements on this subject were made by the Prime Minister at Brantford (May 14), Ottawa (May 27), and at Montreal (June 3). Mr. Pickersgill devoted a good part of his radio broadcast on May 27 to an attack on the opposition's behaviour in Parliament.
[84]May 27 (mimeo, p. 7).

to benefit from it. Mr. Diefenbaker argued frequently and with vigour that only the Conservatives could adequately check the Liberals and that so long as the opposition to the government was divided it would be largely ineffective. Curiously enough, the Liberals were almost as busy as the Conservatives in pleading the cause of the two old parties and in attacking C.C.F.'ers and the Social Crediters. They were probably hoping to wrest some of the seats from the so-called splinter parties in the West to offset expected Liberal losses in the Maritime provinces.

In meeting the general attack of the Conservatives, the Liberals claimed that if the Canadian people continued to vote them into office, there was nothing undemocratic in their being in power for a long time. At any rate, the personnel of the party was changing, and, it was maintained, the party was as young and vigorous as ever. So long as conditions in the country were satisfactory, there was not much sense in saying that it was time for a change. "A change to what?" some Liberals asked. They saw no alternative in the Conservative party which, they argued, was making irresponsible promises in its attempt to gain power. And anyway, they asked further, *what* was the Conservative party? It seemed to have disappeared and to have become a Diefenbaker party. Had the Tories become ashamed of themselves? Was it not dangerous to support a party pursuing a Canadian variant on the cult of personality, particularly when that party was in the habit of changing its leaders with great frequency?[85]

Caught in the cross-fire of such arguments, the voter had to make up his mind about which to believe; was it time for a change, and if so, a change to what? In casting their ballots, were most voters influenced by the large, general questions or by thousands of shifting complexes of minor, more immediate issues thought to affect their immediate daily lives? In this chapter the attitudes of the parties on these issues were described. It is now possible to look at how the parties tried to present their programmes and at the electoral techniques they used.

[85]A general comparison of the ways in which the leaders dealt with the issues is made below in chap. VII and in Appendix C.

NATIONAL HEADQUARTERS

4

The National Liberal Federation

IN A FEDERAL STATE LIKE CANADA, political developments in the provinces obviously affect what happens at the national level, and *vice versa*. The national party organization is to some extent a co-ordinating body, facilitating the co-operation of a number of provincial parties. Provincial organizations, therefore, play a vital role not only in provincial but also in federal politics. They are busy enough between elections; as voting day approaches, their frenzied activity offers eloquent testimony to their deep involvement in the federal contest.

During the 1957 election campaign, much of the activity of the Liberal national office was carried out in consultation with the provincial parties. The leaflets and other campaign literature prepared under the general supervision of the Ottawa headquarters were circulated to the provincial capitals for comment and suggestion long before the writs were issued for the June 10 ballot. As the campaign began in earnest, the provincial associations, sometimes in conjunction with certain members of the cabinet, made sure that all constituency organizations selected candidates. Sometimes—in many Quebec constituencies, for example—the provincial organization nominated or confirmed the nomination of candidates. Party literature prepared by the national office was often distributed to the constituencies through the provincial organizations. In several provinces the provincial campaign committee decided on the number of the various items of publicity material which should be ordered from the National Federation. Provincial committees sometimes issued their own literature to supplement that emanating from Ottawa.

The wealthier ones engaged advertising agencies to assist them in their activities. Occasionally, a provincial group showed unusual enterprise and complemented the party's national campaign with an effort of its own, particularly suited to local conditions. The British Columbia party, for example, held a "candidates' workshop" in which campaign strategy was mapped out. It was attended, among others, by the president of the British Columbia Liberal Association and by the province's two cabinet ministers.[1]

Provincial campaign committees were also responsible for numerous arrangements pertaining to speaking tours by the national leader and other cabinet ministers. Many provincial Liberal politicians vigorously supported the federal party. This aid was particularly effective in places like Newfoundland, where a Liberal government was in power provincially and where the federal candidates benefited from the popularity of Mr. Smallwood. There were, on the other hand, instances where the provincial party clearly wished to dissociate itself from the federal wing. The federal Liberal committee in Manitoba, for instance, was dismayed by the behaviour of Liberal Premier Campbell and his cabinet during the visit to Winnipeg of Mr. St. Laurent. The provincial government ignored the Prime Minister, presumably because it thought that it had more to gain from staying aloof than from associating itself with the federal government.[2]

Notwithstanding the great importance of the party organizations within the provinces, the main actors in a federal election are the national leaders and their chief lieutenants—members of the cabinet or of the shadow cabinet. The ministers are, it is true, spokesmen in the cabinet for the provincial interests, but they are not delegates of the provinces in a federal assembly. Those ministers who become the spokesmen for

---

[1]Winnipeg *Free Press*, April 23.

[2]Winnipeg *Free Press*, April 30. See also Michael Best, "Why Manitoba Premier Boycotted Mr. St. Laurent," Toronto *Globe and Mail*, May 7, and his "Vote Fever in Manitoba," *ibid.*, June 1. Comparing the degree of co-operation between the federal and provincial branches of the various parties in Manitoba, Mr. Best said that "the coolest relations are between the two Liberal camps. The federal Liberal campaign is being handled by D. G. McKenzie, retired chairman of the Board of Grain Commissioners, from an office a respectable distance away from provincial Liberal headquarters. The federal office is staffed by persons having slight, if any, connection with the provincial Liberal organization. As the federal office fights for the June 10 election, the provincial office concentrates almost exclusively on oiling up the provincial machine." For Mr. Campbell's explanation of his conduct towards the Prime Minister, given almost a month after the snub occurred, see the Winnipeg *Free Press*, May 23. In addition to the much publicized Liberal disunity in Manitoba, there were persistent rumours of dissension between the federal Liberals and the Alberta Liberal organizations.

their provinces in the cabinet[3] are responsible *to the cabinet* for the state of the party's organization in their province; in no sense are they responsible to the provincial organization for the activities of the cabinet. It is, consequently, the task of the ministers to see that the decisions about the national campaign—the strategy and the tactics as determined by the national leadership—are carried out in the provinces and regions for which they bear particular responsibility. The decisions about how the campaign is to be run are, of course, ultimately the responsibility of the prime minister in his capacity of party leader. In 1957 it was Mr. St. Laurent, and his advisers from among the cabinet and the leadership of the National Liberal Federation, who were the architects of the Liberal campaign. And the national instrument at their disposal was the headquarters of the National Liberal Federation.

The Liberal national office had for many years been under the direction of Mr. H. E. Kidd, the general secretary of the Federation. He was assisted by M. Paul Lafond, the associate general secretary, who also had special responsibilities in relation to the French-speaking elements in the party. There were two additional administrative officers—the executive secretaries of the National Federation of Liberal Women of Canada, and of the Young Liberal Federation and the Canadian University Liberal Federation.[4] During "peace time" the staff numbered from fourteen to sixteen. As the election approached this number rose to between fifty and sixty. Secretaries, typists, and workers responsible for printing and mailing material to the constituencies accounted for most of the increase. In addition, Cockfield Brown and Company, the advertising agency of the party, put about forty people to work on the election. These included radio and television specialists, space buyers, artists, writers, and lay-out designers.[5]

The staff at headquarters constituted the party bureaucracy, and as such it served the executive officers of the National Liberal Federation. In practice this meant that Mr. Duncan K. MacTavish, the Federation's

[3]At the time of the 1957 election Mr. Pickersgill was responsible for Newfoundland, Mr. Winters for Nova Scotia, Mr. Gregg for New Brunswick, Mr. Pinard, Mr. Lapointe, Mr. Lesage and Mr. Marler for Quebec, Mr. Harris and Mr. Martin for Ontario, Mr. Garson for Manitoba, Mr. Gardiner for Saskatchewan, Mr. Prudham for Alberta, and Mr. Sinclair and Mr. Campney for British Columbia.

[4]The latter was appointed only towards the end of May, 1957.

[5]"Liberal Organization in the 1957 Campaign," a memorandum by Mr. H. E. Kidd, prepared in response to a number of questions submitted by the author. Much of the information on the organization of the Liberal national office is based on evidence derived from interviews with Mr. Kidd and Mr. Lafond and from files at the office, made available by them.

president, was responsible for the national office. It was he who provided a link between the leader of the party, his chief lieutenants in the cabinet, and the party bureaucracy. The institutional form in which these relationships found expression was a liaison committee, sometimes referred to as the cabinet liaison committee. It was composed of from eight to ten cabinet ministers appointed by the Prime Minister (party leader), and of the president and senior officers of the Federation. In the course of frequent luncheon meetings it discussed tactics in the House of Commons, political conditions in the country, and preparations for the election. The tactics to be employed during the election also received attention, but the committee lacked formal powers to implement its views. "The liaison committee . . . could make no decisions *as a committee,* and was purely a consultative committee."[6] Since it was composed of almost half the cabinet acting on behalf of the leader, the president of the Federation and its chief administrative officers, it is obvious that this committee was, in effect, of the greatest importance. Its members, as individuals, must have had a decisive influence in the cabinet and in the management of the national office. When the House was dissolved and the election campaign started in earnest, the cabinet members of the committee were, of course, dispersed throughout the country. It was then that the president of the Federation and its secretary assumed sole authority over the party's national headquarters and through it over much of the campaign.

In the long run, the most important political decisions—those of substance as well as of strategy and tactics—were made by the leader and his advisers. Mr. Pickersgill was probably his leader's most influential lieutenant in matters relating to the election. The Prime Minister, then, and his cabinet, acting in their party capacities, constituted the party's high command. Added to their voices were those of the leading members of the provincial parties and occasionally those of other friends of the government. Some journalists, the editor of the Winnipeg *Free Press*, for example, were considered to have the confidence of, and some influence over, several members of the government.

According to its own officers, the primary function of Liberal headquarters was to act as a news exchange; to provide candidates with information about the opposition, about Liberal arguments, to supply material for all communication media and, to a limited degree, also literature.[7] To exchange news is a task vastly different from that of a jobber or wholesaler who receives his wares from one source, repacks them and, parcelled out to different consignees, sends them on their way

[6]*Ibid.*, p. 6. Italics added.   [7]*Ibid.*, p. 7.

again. News and information passing through a middleman invariably are processed—weighed, selected, edited, recast. These processes affect not only the form of the news, but also the substance. By acting as a news exchange, therefore, the national office emphasized some items and played down others. Its work inevitably affected not only how the Liberal case was packaged, but also what it contained. Much that the candidates and the public learned about Liberal policies was influenced by the activities at headquarters.

A concise, clear manual for the use of riding associations was produced jointly by the headquarters staff and the advertising agency.[8] This booklet outlined a model campaign organization, set out its main tasks, and listed the duties of the chief workers: the campaign manager, enumerators, poll captains, inside scrutineers, and the field force. Some information about electoral law was also provided after consultation with the Chief Electoral Officer.

Attempts were made by headquarters to create a general climate of opinion favourable to the Liberals. The party celebrating the seventy-fifth birthday of Mr. St. Laurent illustrates this type of work. To mark the anniversary, a dinner was held in Quebec City on February 2, 1957, at which occasion a number of prominent speakers gave eloquent testimony to the Prime Minister's greatness and to his contribution to Canada. Mr. St. Laurent had always been a popular figure and it was not surprising to find his family and friends desiring to wish him the best at a celebration marking his birthday. But Mr. St. Laurent was more than a respected and well-liked man: he was one of the Liberal party's greatest assets. How better could this popularity be put to work than by holding a well-publicized, "non-political" celebration pointing to the accomplishments of Mr. St. Laurent and of his government?

There were several indications that the birthday party was more than a spontaneous, personal tribute to a well-liked public figure. Press reports stated, for example, that it had been the subject of conversations between Mr. Guy Beaudry of the Liberal party's advertising agency and Mr. Pierre Asselin, the Prime Minister's private secretary.[9] The numbers attending offered another indication of the true nature of the event. A crowd estimated at from two to three thousand people met Mr. and Mrs. St. Laurent at the station and additional thousands were said to line the streets leading to the Prime Minister's home in the Grande Allée. Four-

[8]*Organizing for General Elections*, revised according to the Canada Elections Act (1955).

[9]*Le Devoir*, Jan 12, 1957. The same paper, reporting the dinner on February 4, referred to the obviously electoral aspect of the celebrations.

teen hundred guests attended the dinner. That the publicity value of all this was not lost on the party is shown in the subsequent treatment of the celebrations: a booklet commemorating the event was prepared in both French and English and the plates were used again in the party's magazine.[10] The national office therefore made full use of this opportunity to bring the Prime Minister's and the party's accomplishments to the public's attention. That this was done in no way detracts, of course, from the genuineness of the good wishes which many Liberals and other Canadians bore the Prime Minister. The matter is mentioned here for the sole purpose of illustrating the public relations efforts of the national office. In this case news was not only transmitted; it was also made.

That the party headquarters did more than merely circulate information was further indicated by a document produced at the national office almost seven months before the election. In a shrewd analysis, its author attempted to assess the electoral chances of the main parties. After weighing the strengths and weaknesses of the Liberal party in the public's eye, the author concluded that the 1957 campaign might prove exceedingly tough. He recommended certain types of party effort (largely in the field of publicity, it is true) for the purpose of averting the unlikely but possible defeat at the impending election.[11]

Chief among the publications issued by the national office was the Speaker's Handbook, entitled *Liberal Action for a Greater Canada*.[12] This 384-page book provided Liberal candidates with summaries of governmental policies and accomplishments, refutations of a number of opposition charges, and press comments favourable to the Liberal administration. In format the volume closely resembled the party's quarterly publication, *The Canadian Liberal*. A good deal of the material in the Speaker's Handbook was, in fact, reprinted from the magazine, the same plates obviously having done double duty. Liberal arguments as here presented were usually based on speeches which had been made by Liberal ministers in the House or elsewhere. Much of the material in the Handbook was produced by writers in the advertising agency simply summarizing or reducing in size official pronouncements.

Like almost all items of party literature, the guide was also published in French. Entitled *Le Parti Liberal au pouvoir*, it was slimmer than its English mate. It contained essentially the same material as the larger volume, except that some items were excluded and that occasionally additional information, of particular interest to Quebec, was added.

[10]*Canadian Liberal*, vol. XIX, no. 3 (Second Quarter, 1957), pp. 17–47.

[11]Unsigned memorandum, dated Nov. 16, 1957, in one of the scrapbooks at the Liberal National Office.

[12]For frequent references to it see above, chap. III *passim*.

A pamphlet taking a more general approach to the party than the Speaker's Handbook was published early in 1957.[13] Almost a third of it contained an appraisal of Liberal contributions to Canadian history, under the heading "Liberalism and the Evolution of Political Freedom in Canada." The appendix included the resolutions adopted by the party at its 1948 national convention.

Less substantial items were produced and distributed in large numbers under the supervision of the national office. A small vest pocket-sized pamphlet contained the Prime Minister's television broadcast given on February 4. It summarized the government's action under two headings, national development and social security, mentioned the legislative programme foreshadowed in the previous Speech from the Throne, and concluded by expressing considerable optimism about the future. Of similar general appeal was the leaflet called *Liberalism . . . a Fighting Faith.* It referred to no one specific campaign issue but contained the statement of principles adopted as a preamble to the resolutions adopted by the party in 1948.[14] These two items were prepared before the campaign was really under way. It was desirable to have some literature available for nominating meetings, many of which took place long before Parliament was dissolved or even before the Speech from the Throne revealed what final measures the government intended to introduce just before the election.

Nine additional leaflets were made available by the national office to the constituency organizations. Each could be folded in three, the front indicating its subject and the back being left blank. The candidates could use the empty page for their own picture or message, or for the voters' addresses, in case they wanted to distribute them by mail. One of these special leaflets was designed to appeal to labour, another to fishermen, a third and fourth to western and eastern farmers respectively. Women and veterans were also singled out for particular attention. A leaflet was devoted to each of these groups. Of more general appeal were the sheets dealing with national development, social security, and with peace.[15] Each was illustrated, although the drawings were incidental

[13]*The Liberal Party of Canada: Liberal policies are creating a better life for all Canadians,* pp. 72.

[14]See above, chap. III, p. 39.

[15]The headings on the title pages of the leaflets were as follows: (1) *Canada's Labour Movement is Making RECORD PROGRESS*; (2) *Atlantic fishermen are making STEADY GAINS UNDER LIBERAL POLICY*; (3) *With higher than average exports, and a growing home market, WESTERN FARMERS, as well as farmers in other parts of Canada, can look to the future with confidence*; (4) *Our growing and thriving Home Market points to an upward trend for CANA-DIAN FARMERS . . . with less dependence on an export market*; (5) *CANA-*

to the written text. Some contained over a thousand words, others less. None had much under five hundred words. The likeness of a somewhat severe looking Mr. St. Laurent adorned each leaflet, as did also the Liberal party's device: a young family walking towards the slogan "Unity, Security, Freedom." Almost all the leaflets contained a quotation from a speech by the Prime Minister.

Services other than the provision of leaflets were tendered the constituencies by headquarters. Among these was the circulation of speeches made by party leaders; the issuing of daily campaign memoranda, consisting largely of clippings and news of the campaign; schedules of publications and other items released by the national office; information about available election favours such as match booklets; proofs of advertisements which, with small alterations or additions, could be used by local candidates; radio and television schedules, and even draft radio speeches on key topics.

A challenge was presented to the parties by television, for the 1957 election was the first in which it was extensively used in Canada. How was it to be approached? As far as the Liberal party was concerned, the first step was to engage a person thoroughly familiar with the new medium. During the middle of March he converted a garage attached to headquarters into a studio and set up a closed-circuit television unit. Headquarters had thus acquired its own radio and television workshop. The premises were used to give "illustrated" talks on the new medium to which Liberal Members of Parliament were invited. The broadcasting technique of several candidates who subsequently bought their own time on a local station was probably first developed in the makeshift studio. The party's expert also distributed information about the use of television. Among the items included were technical explanations of the new wonder, maps and tables showing "audience density," and colour charts enabling the reader to achieve sartorial perfection even in the then black and white image of the TV screen.

But the studio was not merely a training-ground. It produced, under the guidance of the party's expert, some sixty filmed programmes, a smaller number of live presentations, and some tapes of radio talks. Arrangements were made for the booking of television time and liaison maintained with the Canadian Broadcasting Corporation about the scheduling of speakers on the "free-time" programmes which the C.B.C.

DIAN WOMEN have confidence in St. LAURENT; (6) _Veterans benefits again increased_; (7) _Liberal action policies create MORE JOBS AND MORE OPPORTUNITIES . . . the record proves it!_ (8) _Increased Social Security Benefits_; (9) _Canada works for PEACE._

traditionally provides for "*bona fide* parties which are national in extent and which reflect a substantial body of opinion throughout the country."[16] The custom had grown up, in the less hectic radio era, for the parties and the C.B.C. to agree on how a limited amount of free time was to be used and divided among the chief contestants during an election. In 1957, the parties were forced to come to some agreement about television. The president and secretary of the National Federation represented the Liberal party in joint talks with the other parties and the C.B.C. The parties could not agree on the proportion of time to be allotted to each and the Canadian Broadcasting Corporation was forced to decide the issue. The Liberals were given thirty-three per cent of the time allotted the parties, the Conservatives thirty per cent and the C.C.F. and Social Credit parties twenty and seventeen per cent respectively.[17] Under this arrangement the Liberal party received fifteen quarter-hour free radio periods on the English national network and eight quarter-hour English television programmes, and comparable time on the French network. The national office was responsible for the production of these broadcasts. Additional programmes were also prepared, but were abandoned as a result of changes in campaign plans. Constituency organizations were able to use the films produced at headquarters on local stations, provided they had sufficient funds to pay the high fees demanded of them.[18]

In addition to broadcasting, the head office also dealt with national advertising in newspapers and periodicals, with posters of the leader, and with billboards. This activity, like so many others, was carried out in close conjunction with the advertising agency. Newspaper advertisements were created for national distribution and also for use, with minor additions, by local candidates. Certain groups were appealed to by placing specially designed advertisements in publications such as farm journals, labour reviews and periodicals devoted to veterans. One large advertisement, entitled "The Right Man for the Right Job" was placed in every daily and weekly newspaper in Canada. The *Star Weekly* and the *Weekend Magazine* were given a double-page advertisement pointing to the Liberal party's previous eight-year record. Considerable space was bought in French newspapers and magazines. It was used to present the same material as was used in English publicity as well as additional

[16]Canadian Broadcasting Corporation, " Political and Controversial Broadcasting: Policies and Rulings, as revised to May 27, 1953" (*mimeo*), 1957, p. 3.
[17]*Ibid. Idem.*, Minutes of Meeting with Representatives from the Four Federal Political Parties with the Canadian Broadcasting Corporation, April 15, 1957. Conservative party, "Notes on Meeting with C.B.C. Radio and T.V., March 27."
[18]See below, chap. v.

matter designed for consumption in Quebec. Specially designed publicity material was also placed in foreign language publications. But the national office was not content to seek publicity for which it had to purchase space or time. A service to weekly newspapers was provided making available news stories favourable to the Liberal party.

A large and a small poster were created showing Mr. St. Laurent in serious mood. The words "Vote Liberal" were placed in large letters at the top; at the bottom the inscription, equally prominent, read: "Louis St. Laurent, Canada's Great Leader." Billboards, as well as posters, exhorted the voters to re-elect the government. But headquarters did more than merely distribute pictures of the Prime Minister; it was instrumental in enabling many Canadians to see him in person, for it had a hand in organizing his campaign tour.[19] Much of this work was actually done by Mr. St. Laurent's own staff, but the enormous job of co-ordination was partly discharged by the national office. A speakers' bureau was also organized, to facilitate the campaign tours of cabinet ministers.

A special committee was established by the National Liberal Federation for the purpose of presenting the party's case to the service voters. It unwittingly produced one of the last-minute excitements of the campaign when it distributed a letter signed by Mr. St. Laurent to members of the armed forces, urging them to support Liberal candidates. Mr. Diefenbaker objected most violently to this letter, alleging that it took unfair advantage of the fact that the Liberal leader was also Prime Minister.[20]

The Conservative National Office

The Conservative party, being out of office, inevitably took not only a different line of argument in the election from that of its chief rival, but also organized its campaign machinery quite differently. These differences were enhanced by the fact that the Liberal organization and key Liberal personnel had been in existence for a long period of time and had fought several elections, whereas the Conservative national office and organization had undergone a series of changes and upheavals.

One of the many (and as yet unexplored) differences between the Liberal and Conservative parties in Canada concerns the leader's control over party headquarters. Possibly because no issue had ever arisen to

[19]See below, chap. VII.
[20]See below, chap. IX, p. 189.

strain and test the arrangement, the Liberal party offices are, formally at least, under the exclusive direction of the executive officers of the National Liberal Federation. The Federation's secretary is the senior full-time official in charge of headquarters and, as pointed out above, the Federation's president is the man who, in the final analysis, is accountable to the Federation for head office activities. The party leader, who is the honorary president of the Federation, has no direct responsibilities. The major decisions of the national office are of course made with his knowledge, and presumably consent.

In the Conservative party the situation is entirely different. "The national director is appointed by the leader and is responsible only to the leader."[21] In case of conflict between the leader and the executive of the National Association, "the director's first loyalty is only to the leader."[22] Recent supporting evidence is to be found in the appointment of Mr. W. Rowe as national director by Mr. Drew in 1954.[23] On this occasion the new national director was clearly the choice of the leader and not of the president of the Progressive Conservative Association of Canada. It was evident that Mr. Rowe held himself accountable to Mr. Drew and not to Mr. Hees.[24] It was not surprising, therefore, that he offered to resign as national director when Mr. Drew was replaced as leader by Mr. Diefenbaker. His resignation was accepted. On the eve of the election, therefore, Conservative headquarters was without a director.

There was considerable speculation as to which one of Mr. Diefenbaker's chief pre-convention parliamentary supporters—Mr. Hees or Mr. Churchill—would be entrusted with the all-important job of taking over control of the national office.[25] For some time these two and Mr. Allister Grosart constituted an informal committee which assisted Mr. Diefenbaker in gaining effective command over the party apparatus and in preparing for the impending election. To control headquarters by a committee, most of whose members had to be absent from Ottawa repeatedly and for considerable periods of time, was obviously a make-shift and unsatisfactory arrangement. In the end Mr. Allister Grosart assumed the post of campaign manager and national director. He took over the national office in the middle of March—only a month before

[21]John R. Williams, *Conservative Party of Canada*, p. 127.
[22]*Ibid.*
[23]Gerald Waring, "PC's New National Director Gives Strength to Old Guard," Kingston *Whig Standard*, Oct. 23, 1954.
[24]See also chap. II above, pp. 19–20.
[25]See, for example, Pierre Laporte's column in *Le Devoir*, Jan. 9, or the Toronto *Globe and Mail*, Feb. 9.

dissolution. It is to be noted that Mr. Balcer, the president of the Progressive Conservative Association of Canada, had no say whatsoever in the choice of the national director.

Before the electoral tasks of the national office are described, it will be well to consider briefly the activities of the provincial Conservative organizations and the relation between them and the Ottawa headquarters. The main job of the provincial Conservative parties during the election was, of course, similar to that of the comparable Liberal organizations. What was said of the Liberals generally applies to the Conservatives and need not be repeated here.[26] But relations between the national Liberal Federation and the various provincial Liberal parties were influenced to a large extent by the fact that there was a Liberal government in power in Ottawa at a time when there were few Liberal governments in the provinces. In the case of the Conservatives, the federal party had been out of office for a very long period of time but there were three Conservative provincial governments. It was to be expected that the degree of centralization prevailing within the Conservative organization would be considerably less than within the Liberal party. In fact, the reverse had been true for a long time. The powers of the national leader, the control imposed by the national office on the party organizations in the provinces and in the constituencies, and the virtual disappearance of local organizations in some provinces had conspired to make of the Conservative party a political machine largely dominated from the centre.

Increasing unrest in the provincial organizations during Mr. Drew's tenure as leader,[27] the coming into office of a growing number of Conservative provincial governments, and the advent to leadership of Mr. Diefenbaker and his entourage all constituted new factors which, just before the 1957 election, contributed towards a change. During the campaign, therefore, there was less domination of party activities from the centre than had been the case in any recent election. This fact notwithstanding, the organization of the Conservatives showed a greater degree of centralization than did that of the Liberals. In Ontario, for example, the party still maintained a federal office with a full-time paid staff. The national office also maintained a paid organizer for Quebec and during the election one of the most brilliant public relations experts —D. C. Camp—served in the Maritime provinces.

Occasionally, Conservative provincial or regional groups set out to supplement their routine activities and those of the national organiza-

[26]See above, pp. 63–4.
[27]See above, chap. II, p. 19.

tions. Thirty-seven Maritime candidates met in May, for example, to work out Maritime campaign planks within the framework of the national programme.[28] The Nova Scotia Conservatives were particularly energetic in raising funds in addition to those collected by the national organization.[29] A different method of co-operation between the central and provincial organizations was exemplified at a luncheon held in Toronto in March of the election year. On this occasion, Mr. Diefenbaker and Conservative Members of the Ontario legislature met to discuss the forthcoming election. Mr. Dana H. Porter, the Ontario Provincial Treasurer, assured the new national leader that all Conservative members of the provincial Legislature would support to the utmost the Conservative candidates in the forthcoming federal election.[30] In Ontario, New Brunswick, and Nova Scotia the Conservative provincial premiers and governments vigorously aided their national party.

The provincial organizations of the Conservatives played an important part in the election. But, like the Liberals, the Conservatives made their greatest impact on the election by their activities undertaken on a national scale. This was particularly so in the light of the unmistakeable appeal to the voters of the new national leader.

At the time of the election Conservative headquarters included a campaign staff of about eight, assisted by the usual clerical and mail workers.[31] The main public relations firm used by the Conservatives was that of McKim Advertising Ltd., Toronto, which had successfully looked after the account of the Conservative party in Ontario.

In view of the great authority enjoyed by the Conservative leader it was not surprising that Mr. Diefenbaker took a dominant role in designing his party's campaign plans. But to determine the strategy of an election and to decide on the best means for its implementation was not

[28]C. P. dispatch, dated May 12, from Moncton. See also "Atlantic PC's Set Program for Election," Toronto *Globe and Mail*, May 13.

[29]Interview with a Nova Scotia Member of Parliament, Ottawa, September, 1958.

[30]C.P. dispatch, dated March 13, from Toronto.

[31]In addition to the campaign manager and a general executive, the staff at national headquarters consisted of two people responsible for advertising, three general public relations people dealing with the speakers' bureau, distribution of pamphlets, pictures, and other material, and a person responsible for the activities of the Young Progressive Conservatives who also concerned himself with the service vote and supplied the campaign train with daily bulletins about the campaign. The Research Department under Dr. Eldon was not situated at headquarters. This, as well as most of the other information on headquarters activities, was made available to me by Mr. Grosart. I am greatly indebted to him for his willingness, and that of his staff, to answer every question I raised and for generously giving me free access to the files at the national office.

the job of one man. Who, then, had the new leader's confidence and who the most influence over him? Mr. Diefenbaker succeeded Mr. Drew in the face of opposition from most of the leading members of the party. It is, therefore, unlikely that he placed much confidence in the chief members of the former shadow cabinet. On the contrary, he probably suspected the judgment of those who failed to recognize his own pre-eminent claims to the highest post in the party. Those who had been his most loyal and effective supporters for the leadership were inevitably also the key men in planning the 1957 election strategy. The triumvirate of Mr. Churchill, Mr. Grosart, and Mr. Hees, mentioned in an earlier chapter,[32] constituted Mr. Diefenbaker's high command. Mr. Grosart naturally assumed special responsibilities for planning and running the campaign.

One of the most pressing tasks was to create a unified electoral machine as quickly as possible. Such discord as existed in the party towards the end of the Drew era was exacerbated by the struggle for the leadership which had preceded Mr. Diefenbaker's assumption of office. The job of re-uniting the party was begun while the convention was still in session. And on the eve of the election, the men who had recently gained control took a step deliberately designed to achieve the highest degree of unified electoral effort—they set up a national campaign committee. This move contributed not only to harmony within the party, but had the added effect of complementing the new approach to electioneering and the imaginative zeal of the new national leaders with some of the experience and knowledge of the seasoned campaigners in the provincial organizations. Two committees were actually created. A small planning group met on April 1, 1957, to prepare the two-day sessions of the full national committee. The first committee was composed of about fifteen Conservative Members of Parliament and of the national direc'or. The larger group which met in Ottawa on April 7 and had joint meetings with the Conservative Parliamentary caucus on April 8, consisted of about fifty members. The entire planning committee was included. To this nucleus were added the leaders and representatives of the provincial organizations, the national presidents of the Progressive Conservative Association, the Women's Organization, and of the Young Progressive Conservatives, and the campaign staff. The agenda for both meetings was prepared by the campaign manager, who also presided.[33]

The planning committee had a two-fold purpose. It was to enable the

[32]See above, chap. II, *passim.*
[33]Agenda of the Planning Committee Meeting, April 1, and Agenda of the National Campaign Committee, April 7 and 8 (mimeo).

provincial organizations to establish effective liaison with headquarters and with individual Members of Parliament. Secondly, the committee was expected to discuss and make decisions about the broad outlines and some details of campaign policy. An incidental purpose, but one of which the organizers were fully aware, was to give the provincial representatives a sense of participation in the planning of the national campaign and to indicate to them that the new leadership was taking into account the views of all sections within the party.

In the course of its one-day session the committee considered a short manifesto containing the party's general philosophy. A draft was presented by Mr. Fleming, but it was not adopted by the committee. The general line to be taken during the campaign was approved, however, and also the way in which it was to be presented. A number of important organizational decisions were also made. The most important of these dealt with the principle of decentralization which was to govern many of the campaign activities. The duties of headquarters, the leader's itinerary, the Speakers' Bureau, material to be sent to all candidates, advertising and finance, all received the attention of the committee. Its decisions were discussed on the following day with the Conservative Members of Parliament. Thereupon the committee dispersed—most of its members no doubt playing key roles in many provincial and constituency organizations.

National headquarters had thus launched the campaign in a unique way which was followed by the more usual and routine election activities. Every Conservative candidate, as soon as he was adopted by his constituency organization or approved by the provincial party, was sent a candidate's kit. A cornucopia of campaign aids, its contents fell into three broad categories. In the first place, there was information about electoral law as published by the Chief Electoral Officer.[34] Secondly, some indication was given of the position the Conservative party had taken towards the major political questions in the period preceding the election.[35] Thirdly—and most important—various direct electioneering aids were included. A constituency map, a poll-by-poll report on the 1953 election results, and an indication of the population changes which

[34]The following items were included: *General Election Instructions for Returning Officers, with a discussion of the Rights and Obligations of Candidates and an office consolidation of the Canada Elections Act; Instructions for Rural Enumerators; Instructions for Urban Enumerators* and the *Urban Enumerators' Manual; The Canadian Forces Voting Regulations.*

[35]Mr. Fleming's *Distinctive Conservatism,* a summary of the House of Commons discussions of the Canada Council and of national development, and the most recent issue of *Progress Report,* the party's monthly magazine, made up this portion of the kit.

had occurred in Canadian electoral districts between 1951 and 1956 gave the candidate some general information about his riding.[36] The names of individuals in the constituency on the headquarters mailing list were also provided. A small pamphlet, roughly comparable to the Liberals' *Organizing for General Elections*, outlined the scrutineer's duties at various stages of the election.[37] *Campaigning to Win* was a larger pamphlet originally prepared by Mr. Hees and slightly revised for use in the 1957 election. It contained a detailed outline and time-table of how a campaign should be organized in a constituency.

In addition to the material in the kit, the newly nominated candidates were also sent a set of *House of Commons Debates* for the 1957 session, the C.B.C. regulations governing political television and radio broadcasting, and key speeches by Mr. Diefenbaker and other leading Conservatives. A comprehensive summary of press reports critical of the government during recent sessions of Parliament was also supplied.[38]

The campaign kits were mailed to most candidates as soon as they were selected. Later, additional material was distributed by the national office. Mr. Hees' *Campaigning to Win* was supplemented with a twelve-page booklet entitled *Advertising and Publicity; Hints for Candidates*. Some of the pamphlets in the "Talking Points" series were referred to in a previous chapter. Each set reached the candidates in a pocket-sized cover resembling a truncated envelope. The same general plan was followed in almost all of the pamphlets.[39] At the beginning was placed a point-by-point summary of the Conservative party's policy or proposals on the subject of the pamphlet. The opening section was invariably followed by a description of prevailing unsatisfactory conditions, nearly always attributed to the government. The concluding section usually contained one or more quotations from speeches by Mr. Diefenbaker or other leaders either reinforcing the attack on the government or suggesting what remedies would be introduced if the Conservatives were elected.

Headquarters at Ottawa also tried to help the local candidates find

[36]The first two items were published by the Chief Electoral Officer, the last reproduced the latest reports of the Dominion Bureau of Statistics, based on the 1956 census.

[37]*Scrutineers' Manual: A guide for scrutineers and workers at federal elections* (revised).

[38]Conservative Party National Headquarters, *Press Comment on Third Session 22nd Parliament January 10 to August 14* (Ottawa, 1956).

[39]The ten pamphlets were entitled *Agriculture, External Affairs* (since only three pages were devoted to this subject, another three pages in the booklet dealt with Housing), *Federal-Provincial-Municipal Relations, Labour, National Development, Parliament and the People, Social Security, Taxation and Inflation, Trade,* and *We Have an Appointment with Destiny*.

a sufficient number of campaign workers. A folder was produced to which was attached a business reply card addressed to the candidate. On the card the sender could indicate which of six jobs he would like to undertake in the Conservative campaign in his constituency. The folder contained a description of the work that needed doing and exhorted the reader to join the campaign. Space left blank enabled the candidate to put his photograph, name and address in the appropriate place on the folder. About seven hundred thousand of these leaflets were used in sixty-eight constituencies.[40]

Another form of assistance consisted of supplying the candidates with clippings, reprints from newspapers, and summaries of speeches and election promises. Memoranda were dispatched to the constituencies reminding the campaign managers of various impending deadlines or giving them hints arising from experience obtained in the course of the campaign. Some, such as the "Candidate's Diary of Events," were quite routine. Others were of considerable interest; they gave some indication of how headquarters was reacting to the progress of the electoral battle. One memorandum, for example, issued early in May, gave detailed instructions on how to make the most out of a local meeting attended by Mr. and Mrs. Diefenbaker. At about the same time, the chairman of the Speakers' Bureau informed Conservative speakers that Mr. Diefenbaker did not wish the so-called Third Parties in the West to be designated as "splinter groups" or "splinter parties."[41] Mr. Diefenbaker's request may have been prompted in part by the fact that in some Western provinces the Conservatives were more of a splinter party than the C.C.F. or Social Credit parties.

Candidates were also informed by the national office of conditions affecting billboard advertising, about discussions between the party and representatives of weekly newspapers, and of the available advertising aids. Mats were provided enabling the candidates to make up effective local newspaper advertisements displaying not only their own name and picture, but also emphasizing the national leader and the election slogan: "It's Time for a Diefenbaker Government!" A special memorandum was issued summarizing the Canadian Forces Voting regulations. Reprints were distributed of an article in the New York *Herald Tribune* giving general hints on how politicians should deport themselves before television cameras.

[40]One previously successful Conservative candidate in a Metropolitan constituency was alleged to have found six hundred campaign workers by means of this type of folder. Memorandum from party headquarters to Progressive Conservative candidates, dated April 15.

[41]Memorandum from R. D. Coates dated May 9.

In addition to the "Talking Points" series, which was intended primarily for candidates and speakers, headquarters produced a number of leaflets and pamphlets for general distribution. The most popular of these items (about a million and a quarter were ordered by candidates in over one hundred constituencies) was typical of the general approach adopted by the Conservatives in the campaign. It consisted of a reprint of a double-page advertisement which had appeared in the Canadian edition of the *Reader's Digest*. The front and back pages were left blank for use by the candidates. As he unfolded it, the reader was confronted on the left-hand page by a photograph of Mr. Diefenbaker. On the right-hand side there were five quotations about Mr. Diefenbaker selected from about three hundred similar editorial comments in Canadian newspapers. The gist of the text was that Mr. Diefenbaker would make an admirable Prime Minister. Underneath, there appeared the reminder ". . . It's time for a Diefenbaker government!" The slogan was printed in large letters, the type used for the name of the leader being twice as large as the next largest type employed in this layout. Below the election slogan, in considerably smaller type, was placed the name of the party. Mr. Diefenbaker was also the subject of another folder.

A large pamphlet was produced, designed in part to take the place of a party manifesto and of the unpublished resolutions adopted by the 1956 convention. Entitled *A New National Policy*, it was a series of quotations from speeches by Mr. Diefenbaker. The extracts from the new leader's addresses attempted to present the highlights of Progressive Conservative Policy. Of much more limited appeal was a special pamphlet called *Progressive Conservative Agricultural Policy* which summarized, in point form, the party's promises to farmers. It did not carry a picture of the leader, but on the front page there was his personal signature. *Black Friday* was probably the most striking of the Conservative publicity releases. In addition to presenting the Conservative view of the pipeline issue, it contained cartoons and newspaper comments criticizing the government's treatment of Parliament during the pipeline debate.

Most of the activities of the Conservative national office described so far were designed specifically to assist the candidates in the constituencies. The national campaign was at least equally important. Its greatest asset was the leader. His campaign tours had to be planned and their success assured. Leadership had to be provided where the provincial organizations were weak and the efforts of the various provincial organizations co-ordinated. In addition, the Speakers' Bureau made it possible for some of the candidates to benefit from meetings attended by the less exalted but nevertheless important leaders of the party. Mr. Fleming, Mr. Fulton, and Mr. Hees were particularly active in speaking throughout the country in support of Conservative candidates. Pictures and posters displaying the national leader had to be made available to campaign managers wishing to use them.

Two extremely effective newspaper layouts were prepared. One of these repeated the text and the picture of the *Reader's Digest* leaflet. It was redesigned for use as a full-page advertisement, the insertion of which in every daily newspaper was paid for by the national party. Arrangements were made with a number of advertising agencies in different provinces so that local candidates could place their names in an appropriate spot at the bottom of this "It's time for a Diefenbaker government!" appeal. The material from *Black Friday* provided the basis for the other advertisement prepared at headquarters. The cost of placing it in the press had to be defrayed by the candidates themselves or by the provincial organizations. It could, therefore, be used only in constituencies where Conservative funds permitted it.

Responsibility for using the free television and radio time provided by the C.B.C. rested with the national organization. Although no full-time broadcasting expert was placed on the headquarters staff, considerable care was taken to make the most of radio and particularly of television. Proof of the importance attached to television was to be found in the fact that Mr. Diefenbaker's appearances were prepared and produced with meticulous care by Mr. Grosart. Five fifty-second television spot announcements were made by Mr. Diefenbaker, in addition to the free-time national broadcasts, in which he urged voters to support the local Conservative candidate. Those wishing to use any of these films had to pay for the station time out of their local campaign funds. For candidates able to go on the air themselves, the national office provided printed information about the effective use of television.

The general public relations of the Conservative party were also, of course, the concern of headquarters. During Mr. Drew's tenure as leader, a Research Department had been established which enabled the party to speak with considerable authority on policy questions. Long before the election, an officer had been appointed whose duty it was to supply the non-English and non-French press with news favourable to the party, and who was generally responsible for maintaining good relations with the organizations representing the most important ethnic minorities. These activities were, of course, intensified during the campaign.

Of more general appeal were the services rendered by the national office in supplying the press with Conservative news. The newly established leaders were particularly sensitive to the effectiveness of non-paid advertising and they did their utmost to maintain close relations with news-dispensing organizations. Candidates were encouraged to supply their local newspapers and radio stations with usable summaries of their activities. A number of national publications—some of general appeal, others catering to special interest groups—were provided with material presenting the Conservative case in a favourable light.

In this chapter an attempt has been made to sketch the activities of the national leadership and of the national office during an election campaign. The objective of all these activities was, of course, to influence favourably the voter in the constituencies. The efficacy of such efforts by the national bodies depends to some extent on the way in which the campaigns are conducted by the local committees and workers. In the following chapter this aspect of the election will be considered.

General Organization

THERE IS AGREEMENT among the major Canadian parties that the basic function of the constituency organization is to select a suitable candidate and to get him elected. This, it is thought, cannot be done primarily by *persuading* eligible voters to support one's own party, but rather by making sure that everyone who is already friendly towards it casts his or her ballot. The chief job of the riding organization, therefore, is to find out who intends to support its candidate and then to make sure that everyone with such intentions carries them out on election day. The task of persuading people to vote for a particular party or person is left to the national leader and to the candidate himself who, it is often repeated, "must sell himself to the voter." The local activities are, of course, designed to facilitate the task of the national party and of the candidate to persuade, cajole, and attract new voters, but the main effort is directed towards "bringing out the friendly vote."

Three distinct phases of campaigning are discernible in a Canadian federal election. The first consists of the enumeration period, when the parties must provide personnel used in the preparation of the Voters List. Secondly, a canvass is undertaken, based on the new lists, to ascertain who can be relied upon to support one's own party, who is certain to be opposed, and who might be persuaded to swing round to a more enlightened view, provided he is approached in an appropriate manner. The third phase consists of election day itself, when the maximum number of supporters must be induced to cast their votes. In addition to the basic operations corresponding to the three campaign phases, it is of course necessary to advertise, arrange meetings, and do the myriad things which have become a part of the election ritual.

Since both older parties hold similar views on the functions of the local organization in an election, there are only minor differences between the ways in which they organize for the contest. The main variation in electioneering techniques in Canada is to be found less between the parties (certainly as far as the Liberals and Conservatives are concerned) than among various constituencies. It is obvious that, no matter the party, campaigning for the 6,400 votes scattered in the 493,000 square miles of the riding of Mackenzie River is vastly different from trying to win the support of the 47,000 eligible voters packed into the few blocks of the Verdun constituency in Montreal. To seek votes in a rural setting requires an entirely different effort from that needed in an urban settlement; an organization suited to a French-speaking, Catholic constituency of Quebec is likely to prove ineffective in a Protestant, English-speaking seat in Ontario. In this chapter, therefore, general electioneering techniques will be emphasized, rather than differences between parties. The latter will be mentioned only when they seem relevant to the outcome of the 1957 election.

Both parties try to maintain a lively constituency organization during the periods intervening between elections. They are by no means always successful, but even where there is a vigorous local organization with an energetic executive the latter is ill-suited to the job of running an election. As the voting date approaches, therefore, an organization is built up designed specifically for the direction of the impending campaign. This organization cannot be established, however, until the candidate is nominated. The reason for this is simple: the key man in any election machine is the campaign manager who is always the personal appointee of the candidate. This is a reasonable arrangement, for the campaign is not likely to succeed in the absence of the highest degree of understanding between the two chief people planning it—the candidate and the campaign manager. Ideally, the campaign organization which results from the successful co-operation between these two persons should look something like this:[1]

[1]The model which is here described is derived from a number of sources. In the first place, it is based on the prescriptions contained in the pertinent publications of the parties: the Liberals' *Organizing for General Elections* and the Conservatives' *Campaigning to Win, Scrutineers' Manual*, and *Advertising and Publicity*. Secondly, information provided by a number of politicians with extensive experience in campaigning proved helpful. In this respect, while I cannot acknowledge the assistance of all those who were willing to discuss their experiences with me, it would be remiss not to acknowledge the assistance of two seasoned campaigners. Mr. William McL. Hamilton, former Postmaster General, gave generously

At the top, and responsible for everything done in the course of the campaign, is the candidate. He is required by law to appoint an official agent whose principal function is to act as his campaign treasurer.[2] Virtually all expenses incurred during the campaign must be authorized by the official agent who is obliged, by law, to issue a detailed statement of receipts and expenditures made by him or on his behalf in relation to the conduct of the campaign. But while the official agent is a person of considerable importance, particularly in relation to financial and legal questions, he is usually not involved directly in the day-to-day business of electioneering. Frequently, he is a somewhat shadowy figure, close to the candidate and the wealthy supporters of the party, but nevertheless aloof from the fighting force which is concerned directly with producing favourable votes.

Since the candidate's most effective way of gaining votes is, by all accounts, his meeting and talking to the maximum number of people, he must be freed from practically all administrative and "back-room" chores. The campaign manager assumes the post of the chief executive officer. Working in close harmony with the candidate, he directs operations and is the central figure to whom the party workers and the various branches of the organization are responsible.

In most instances, the candidate and his manager are assisted by a committee that fulfils the functions of a central campaign organization committee or of a strategy board. Usually, this group is composed of the chief executive officers of the permanent local party organizations. These include the presidents and secretaries of the general or men's associations, and of the women's and youth associations wherever they exist. In rural constituencies, representatives from organizations in the main population centres may be included. In addition to the constituency's permanent executives who know local conditions and have contact with the most promising reservoir of manpower, the heads of the various campaign sub-organizations are represented. Some of the latter may, of course, be on the committee both by virtue of being executives

---

of his time, knowledge, and insight. The late Mr. Lorne McDonell, one of the most experienced campaign managers in Ontario, although he did not share Mr. Hamilton's political views, did share with him that rare characteristic—a practising politician's interest in an academic study of politics. I am particularly grateful for the generosity and frankness of both Mr. Hamilton and of the late Mr. McDonell. Large numbers of students of political science at Queen's University, have helped by writing essays and term papers describing elections in their home constituencies. To them too I owe a debt. Lastly some elements in this chapter are derived from observation of election campaigns and from newspaper reports.

[2]The Chief Electoral Officer, *General Election Instructions for Returning Officers* (Book A 36), (Ottawa, 1956), p. 133, para. 353.

and of being responsible for a particular phase of the campaign. The official agent is always a member. In addition, the person responsible for the publicity must be included and, in constituencies where considerable radio and television work is done, his chief lieutenant as well. The person heading the group which is responsible for canvassing the eligible voters is also almost always a member of the committee. Others, responsible for special activities, may be added. In one constituency, for example, an organization was set up to conduct a colossal canvass inviting thousands of citizens to a meeting at which Mr. Diefenbaker spoke. The Conservative organization in Notre Dame de Grace, Montreal—a complex, metropolitan constituency—included in the executive committee the chairman of sub-groups responsible for the following: poll organization, women's committee, office and committee room, meetings and special events, intelligence, advertising and publicity, transport and distribution.[3]

Generally, all constituency organizations establish an hierarchical system at the base of which is to be found the poll organization. At this level, a well-staffed machine consists of a poll captain, assisted by two or three helpers, one of whom at least must have the use of a car. Anywhere from six to ten polling subdivision organizations will be under the direction of a group captain. In large constituencies a number of these will report to an area chairman who is directly responsible to the campaign manager.

During the 1957 election there were 44,055 polling stations in Canada.[4] More than half of these were urban stations and it is likely that both the Conservative and Liberal parties tried to establish an adequate poll organization in a vast majority of these. One of their first tasks was to nominate an enumerator to assist in the preparation of the Voters List. Officially, the two enumerators required by statute in each urban subdivision are, of course, appointed by the Deputy Returning Officer. But one of the enumerators is always the nominee of the candidate who won the previous election, and the other of the runner-up. The two enumerators must conduct a house-to-house canvass. Being familiar with the terrain on which the battle is to be fought, they usually become poll captains or at least members of his team. The fact that they are paid for enumerating means that the party has been instrumental in giving them some financial assistance; it may therefore feel free subsequently to make demands on their time.

[3]The organization of this elaborate and highly efficient electoral machine is shown in Chart I, p. 88.

[4]*Report of the Chief Electoral Officer, Twenty-third General Election, 1957* (Ottawa, 1958) Table 2, p. ix.

The poll organization attempts to contact every eligible voter in the subdivision in an effort to find out who is its party's friend or who might be persuaded to become one. On election day personal and telephone calls, baby sitters and, above all, car rides are used in an all-out bid for a large turn-out of supporters of the poll organization's own candidate. The poll organization is reinforced by additional workers. Some serve as inside scrutineers, each acting as the candidate's agent in a polling station. Here he makes sure that no unfair and illegal practices are resorted to by the other parties. In most cases, however, the really important work he does has nothing to do with keeping an eye on the opposition. As a sworn candidate's agent he obtains day-long admission to the polling station assigned to him. This enables him to check, on lists of party sympathizers prepared by the poll organization during its canvass, the names of those who have already voted and those who have yet to cast their ballots. Reports on the turnout of the party faithful are transmitted at regular intervals to the poll captain. It is on the basis of this information that the outside scrutineers contact laggards in hopes that they can be persuaded to go and vote. When the poll closes, the inside scrutineer represents his candidate during the counting of the ballots.

The largest number of workers is to be found in that part of the campaign organization which attempts to identify the friendly electors and to make sure that they vote. Other branches of the election machine are also important and are integrated in the organization. But while they are also under the direction of the campaign manager, they are outside the hierarchical line extending downward from him through the district, group and poll captains, to the canvassers and scrutineers. Some of the groups occupying a somewhat lateral position in the organization chart, off to one side of the main hierarchy, are the organizations staffing the campaign headquarters and possible subsidiary offices, the individuals concerned with advertising and public relations, those responsible for arranging meetings and the various other activities which the campaign committee, the candidate or the campaign manager might wish to embark upon for the sake of attracting votes.

To illustrate the general description given so far, two organization charts are presented below. The first shows the elaborate structure evolved by a successful Conservative candidate in a polyglot, metropolitan constituency. It cannot be considered typical, since few constituency parties were able to create an organization even remotely resembling it in completeness. The candidate who built up this organization not only drew up the chart reproduced here; he also wrote a full job analysis for his workers, describing in considerable detail the work to be done by each of the organizations depicted in it. It should be noted that the

CHART I

Organization of the Conservative Party for the 1957 General Election:
Notre Dame de Grace Constituency, Montreal.

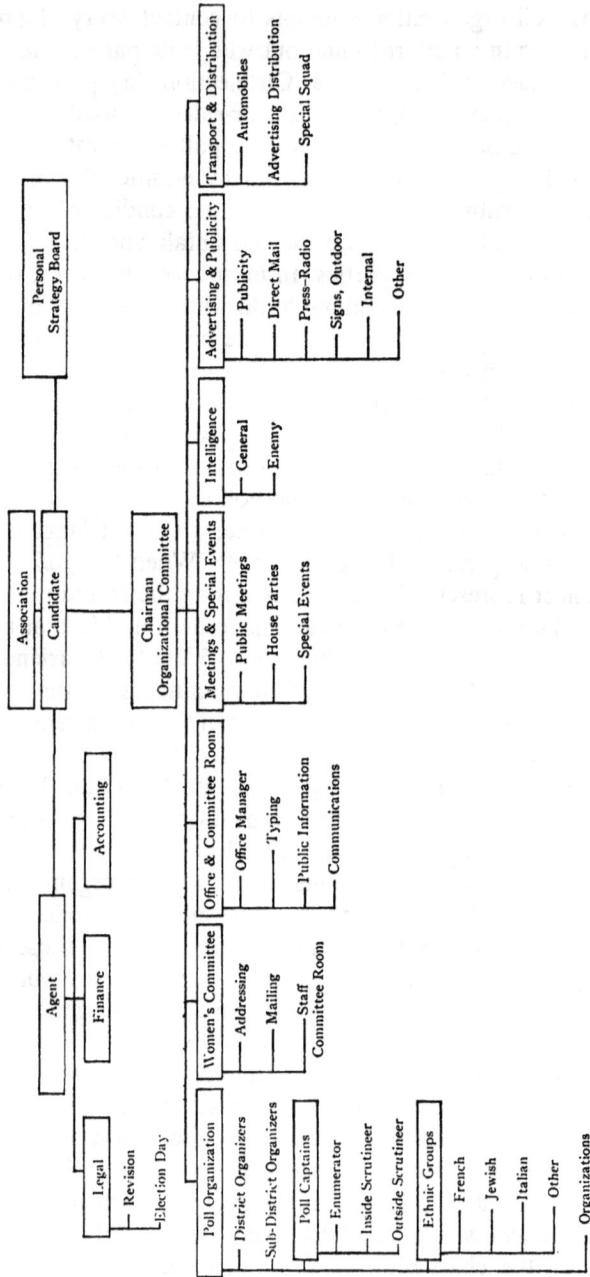

Association

Candidate

Personal Strategy Board

Agent

Chairman Organizational Committee

Legal
— Revision
— Election Day

Finance

Accounting

Women's Committee
— Addressing
— Mailing
— Staff
— Committee Room

Office & Committee Room
— Office Manager
— Typing
— Public Information
— Communications

Meetings & Special Events
— Public Meetings
— House Parties
— Special Events

Intelligence
— General
— Enemy

Advertising & Publicity
— Publicity
— Direct Mail
— Press–Radio
— Signs, Outdoor
— Internal
— Other

Transport & Distribution
— Automobiles
— Advertising Distribution
— Special Squad

Poll Organization
— District Organizers
— Sub-District Organizers

Poll Captains
— Enumerator
— Inside Scrutineer
— Outside Scrutineer

Ethnic Groups
— French
— Jewish
— Italian
— Other

Organizations

person called "Chairman, Organizational Committee" corresponds to the campaign manager and that the committee over which he presides is made up of the candidate, the official agent and the heads of the seven organizations shown directly under him.

The second chart depicts the Liberal organization in Oxford County, a mixed (rural and urban) constituency in Ontario. The chart was not prepared by the candidate, but by an outside observer. If the Conservative organization depicted in Chart I was unusually complete and effective, the Liberal organization shown in Chart II was probably less elaborate than many other Liberal campaign machines in the country. Neither of the campaign organizations outlined in the charts should, therefore, be considered typical of the election machines created by the party whose label each happens to bear.

D. R. Allan, on whose observations Chart II is based, emphasizes that although the constituency associations were theoretically at the top of the organization pyramid, in fact they were "relegated to the position

CHART II

Organization of the Liberal Party for the 1957 General Election, Oxford*

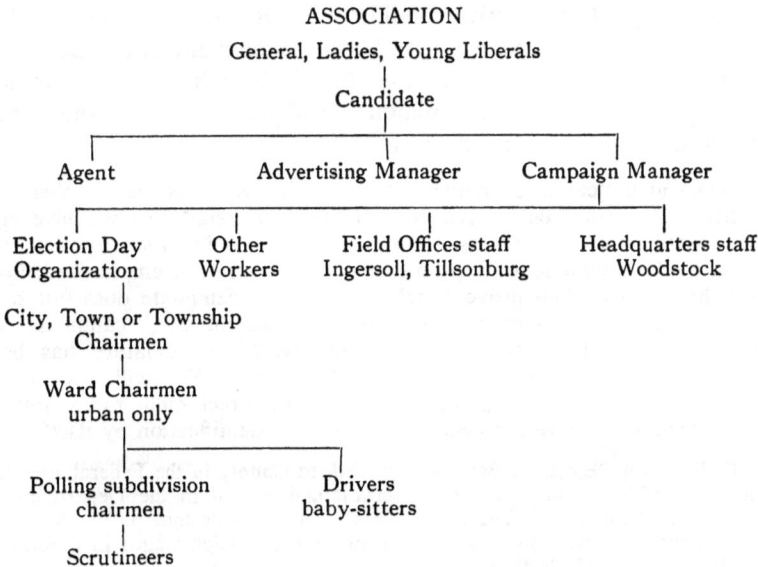

ASSOCIATION
General, Ladies, Young Liberals

Candidate

Agent   Advertising Manager   Campaign Manager

Election Day Organization   Other Workers   Field Offices staff Ingersoll, Tillsonburg   Headquarters staff Woodstock

City, Town or Township Chairmen

Ward Chairmen urban only

Polling subdivision chairmen   Drivers baby-sitters

Scrutineers

*Adapted from a chart in D. R. Allan, "Electoral Behaviour in Oxford County in the Federal Election," June 10, 1957, an unpublished B.A. dissertation deposited with the Department of Political Science and Economics, Queen's University, p.76.

of work-crew for the purpose of the election."[5] The position of the campaign manager is an interesting one. Noting that his "interview with the Liberal campaign manager distinctly revealed the lack of knowledge about what the other officials were doing," Allan observes that in this case the Liberal system seemed to be characterized by the "separation of powers."[6]

The Candidate Meets the Public

So far in this discussion emphasis has been placed only on the central aim of the constituency organization: to bring out the vote. But it is not enough to make sure that all friendly voters find themselves in a polling booth on election day. Great care must be taken that once there they know whose name to mark in order to vote for the party of their choice. This is not as easy a job as might appear at first glance. A national survey by the Canadian Institute of Public Opinion taken only a few months after the 1953 election showed that only 61 per cent of those interviewed knew the name of their Member of Parliament.[7] In Oxford County during the 1957 election, one potential Liberal supporter cast her vote for the Conservative candidate because she could not find Mr. St. Laurent's name on the ballot and because the name of the Conservative was "the only one she had ever heard of."[8] One of the campaign aids prepared by Conservative national headquarters stressed the importance of this aspect of elections as follows:

Candidate identification by name and picture is treated as the Number One objective of all campaign procedures until we feel certain that we have high name identification with voters. (Sometimes public opinion surveys are used to check.) This name identification cannot be too strongly emphasized. Polls which have been taken prove conclusively that a candidate does not have automatic identification in the minds of voters as the P.-C. candidate just because he is well-known in the community, his candidature has been announced and his picture has been in the papers. Nor will any one of newspaper advertisements, publicity, poll cards, direct mail, radio time or public meetings achieve the necessary degree of identification by itself.[9]

[5]D. R. Allan, "Electoral Behaviour in Oxford County in the Federal Election, June 10, 1957," unpublished B.A. dissertation, deposited in the Department of Political and Economic Science, Queen's University, Kingston, p. 73. Allan's is the most comprehensive study known to me of a campaign waged in a constituency during the 1957 election.
[6]*Ibid.*, p. 71.
[7]Toronto *Daily Star*, April 17, 1954.
[8]Allan, "Oxford County," p. 40.
[9]*Advertising and Publicity Hints for Candidates*, p. 3.

In addition, therefore, to getting out the favourable vote, the organizations whose general structure and functions were outlined above had to make their candidate's name known to as many potential voters as possible. Of the several techniques available for this purpose the most effective by far is thought to be the personal campaigning of the candidate himself assisted by his wife (or husband) and possibly by his older children. Some candidates like to frequent places in their constituency where they can talk to many people in a short period of time. Street corners on heavy shopping days and factory gates early in the morning are favoured by some aspiring politicians. One Liberal decided to vote for a physically handicapped Conservative candidate after he had seen him standing for hours in the snow and sleet at a bus stop, shaking the hands of possible supporters. An unusually enterprising Liberal candidate devised a startling way of addressing the voters. From the front seat of his car, parked at busy rural crossroads, his voice, amplified by a loudspeaker, blared "cheery reassurances to the local residents, their names supplied sotto voce by a campaign worker alongside."[10] Experienced campaigners recommend that candidates visit as many shopkeepers as possible, leave some literature and ask permission to say a word or two to the shoppers on the premises. Mr. Gordon Churchill was reported to have called on almost every storekeeper on Portage Avenue, the main shopping street in Winnipeg.[11] He was also indefatigable, according to press reports, in applying the most popular of the techniques used by candidates to make themselves known. He was said to have made impressive numbers of door-to-door calls soliciting votes. Dr. Vivian, a Conservative contesting the predominantly rural Durham constituency, was only one of many candidates applying this method to the country voters. His approach, as described by a newspaper reporter, was typical: "Sitting informally in back kitchens, on woodpiles or standing out in the fields, Dr. Vivian stressed John Diefenbaker's statement on agricultural policy, made to the House of Commons on April 9, and the Conservative leader's attacks on the dumping of U.S. farm surpluses. To make doubly sure the point strikes home, he leaves behind a copy of Mr. Diefenbaker's Ottawa address."[12] Rural campaigners could not, in the short time available, contact nearly as many voters as their urban counterparts. In built-up areas a fast-moving, skilled campaigner can

[10]Ronald Haggart, "If Noise Wins Votes, He Will Make History," Toronto *Globe and Mail*, June 5. The candidate in question was F. E. Dunlap in the Ontario constituency of Carleton. He was defeated.

[11]Winnipeg *Free Press*, June 1.

[12]Robert L. Gowe, "Durham Seen Pivotal Riding for June 10 Vote," Toronto *Globe and Mail*, May 20.

visit an astounding number of homes during an election campaign. Lee Grillis, the Conservative candidate in Hastings South, was said to have rung twenty-five to thirty doorbells an hour. The Liberal seeking re-election in York-Scarborough, Ontario, estimated that between April 12, when Parliament rose, and May 27 he had visited five thousand homes.[13]

In some parts of the country the weather or the ruggedness of the terrain make door-to-door canvassing particularly arduous. In certain sections of northern Saskatchewan, for example, effective campaigning in the 1957 election could only be done by air. Early in May, the Liberal candidate in Meadow Lake found that the lakes which had to be used for landing were still covered with ice. At about the same time an aircraft carrying another candidate was forced by a severe snow storm to make an emergency landing on Lake Lebarge in the Yukon. Its occupants—the pilot and the Minister of Fisheries who had made a campaign speech in Dawson City—had to find their way over thin ice to shore and then walk a distance of two miles, ankle-deep in mud, before reaching Whitehorse.[14]

One favoured method of meeting potential voters consists of contacting as many voluntary organizations as possible. Seven types of such associations are listed by one election manual, which suggests that members of the local party who belong to a non-political organization should enable the candidate to meet his or her club. On such occasions, it is suggested, the candidate need not make a politically partisan speech, but simply acknowledge with pleasure the opportunity of becoming acquainted with members of the group whose meeting he happens to be attending. Not all candidates are as fortunate as the Conservative running in Halton, Ontario, who, being a botanist, was able to address a chapter of the Imperial Order of the Daughters of the Empire on lilies, a non-political subject of mutual interest.[15] The sitting member has a great advantage in meeting local clubs, of course, since he is often invited to attend meetings of various organizations in his constituency. The range of organizations visited before the election by Mr. Nesbitt, the Conservative member in Oxford, was probably only slightly wider than that of most members of the House seeking to keep in close touch with their constituency.

[13]Toronto *Globe and Mail*, May 31 and May 27, cited in an interesting study of the election in a particularly fast-growing riding. See Paul W. Fox, "A Study of One Constituency in the Canadian Federal Election of 1957," *Canadian Journal of Economics and Political Science*, vol. XXIV, no. 2 (May, 1958), p. 235.

[14]Toronto *Globe and Mail*, May 8. Winnipeg *Free Press*, May 14.

[15]Grey Hamilton, "Halton Election Depends Upon New Subdivisions in Once Rural Riding," Toronto *Globe and Mail*, May 6.

He was able to attend a meeting of the Ingersoll Kiwanis Club, a Home and School meeting in Bright, a legion zone meeting in Beachville, a Y's Men's Club dinner in Woodstock, a meeting of the Otter Creek Conservation Authority, an Air Force Veterans' Dance, the Kiwanis Music Festival in Woodstock, a New Canadians' party and a citizenship granting ceremony, a Farmers' Union meeting, a Carpenters' Union meeting in Ingersoll, and the Oxford Fish and Game Club Stag Party. He officiated at the opening of the Woodstock Junior Chamber of Commerce Home and Industry Show; he presented the Nesbitt Public Speaking trophies for the Canadian Legion Contest; he attended a function at the Tillsonburg Polish Hall.[16]

In addition to making himself well known to members of the permanent organizations listed above, Mr. Nesbitt also sought to become familiar to more ephemeral groups. According to one report, " 'drinks on the house from Wally Nesbitt' became a byword in the beverage rooms of the country hotels and the clubrooms of the Canadian Legion."[17] Despite his assiduous efforts to meet personally as many electors as possible, Mr. Nesbitt was not able to duplicate the feat of a western candidate who boasted to a reporter: "We've had four weddings in our family in recent months. At 350 people a wedding I ought to be doing pretty well."[18]

A candidate must be careful not to give the impression that he is abusing the relationship he may have established with a particular group in his constituency. Some observers thought that a doctor, seeking election in Winnipeg, may have lost more support than he gained as the result of a letter which was sent by seven physicians and dentists to members of their profession urging them to support their politically ambitious colleague.[19]

Meetings

Although in danger of being made obsolete by television, the political meeting is still of considerable importance as a medium through which contact can be made with the voters. Three kinds of meeting were widely used in the 1957 campaign: the usual meeting addressed only by the candidate and perhaps a guest belonging to one party; the so-called contradictory meeting, at which representatives of more than one party confront one another; and the increasingly more popular coffee or tea party which is less formal than the others.

[16]Allan, "Oxford County," pp. 45–6.
[17]Ibid., p. 45.
[18]Mr. Nick Halas, quoted by Ted Byfield in Winnipeg Free Press, May 28.
[19]Ted Byfield, "Winnipeg South Centre," Winnipeg Free Press, June 1.

Both parties staged monster rallies designed to present the leader to a large crowd drawn from a number of nearby constituencies. The Conservatives' Massey Hall rally, at which Mr. Diefenbaker made his first major campaign speech and which was attended by Mr. Frost and other leaders of the Ontario government, was a quiet and restrained affair compared with that held by the Liberals in the same city towards the end of the campaign. Liberal candidates from the eighteen constituencies in the Toronto area were on the platform, flanking Mr. St. Laurent and other members of the cabinet. Each candidate had groups placed in the audience at Maple Leaf Gardens carrying banners. Some of the groups were costumed. One, dressed like Indians, performed a war dance in the aisle when its candidate was introduced. But this feathered *claque* apparently proved less popular with the electorate than a group of short-skirted blondes. There were massed bands, bagpipes, dancing girls, the Leslie Bell Singers, drum majorettes, cheer leaders, cow bells, noise-makers, Lorne Green as Master of Ceremonies, and a tandem bicycle.[20] It is difficult to tell what contribution a meeting of this sort is to make to the campaign. Since a young heckler was injured in the sight of the assembled crowd, it is likely that many participants and the general public viewed the epic with mixed feelings.[21]

Meetings arranged by single constituency organizations were, of course, considerably less elaborate. The usual procedure was to have a few speeches and sometimes a little food and coffee. It was not unusual to present some musical entertainment to relieve the tedium occasioned by too much speech-making. Compensating for the frequently questionable musical merit of these interludes, one candidate made them more attractive to some of the audience by arranging for performances by children of the district in which the meeting was held.[22] Most local organizations have not yet found a successful way of avoiding too many speeches. Instead of being presented with an address from the candidate and perhaps an outside speaker, the audiences are usually inundated by an endless stream of speakers, introducing or thanking one another or saying "a few" words on behalf of the women, the young people, the good neighbours in the adjoining constituency, or some other group. When a really important outside speaker is expected, the proceedings

[20]For an account of the Conservative rally, see the Toronto *Globe and Mail*, April 26. The above description of the Liberal rally is based on the report of the special correspondent covering the event for the pro-government Winnipeg *Free Press*. See the issue of June 8. For a hostile and satirical description see George Bain, "Minding Your Business," Toronto *Globe and Mail*, June 7.

[21]See also chap. IX, p. 185.

[22]Allan, "Oxford County," p. 49.

may be enlivened by an audience-participation programme. Before the Prime Minister arrived at a Windsor meeting, for example:

to march to the platform preceded by a piper . . . a master of ceremonies rehearsed the crowd in singing "For he's a Jolly Good Fellow" and in delivering three rousing cheers for the Prime Minister. The crowd was carefully coached on when to sing and when to cheer and it responded like a well trained troup.[23]

At another meeting the waiting crowd was entertained by a radio and television trio of performers which also coached the audience in the singing of a Liberal campaign song composed for the occasion.[24] One of the most dramatic attempts to maintain the interest of an audience was made by a Vancouver candidate who was critical of the way in which the government had dealt with drug addiction. He introduced three persons who were described as confessed drug addicts. One of the three wore a mask.[25] But even despite the occasional use of such startling methods, the formal election meeting has declined as a technique favoured by constituency parties. The only large formal meetings which still attract voters are nominating meetings when a genuine contest is in the offing and meetings attended by the national leaders.[26]

Meetings at which debates take place between representatives of more than one party are still favoured by some rural constituencies and are making a come-back in the larger urban ridings as well. During the 1957 election the Farmer's Unions in the Prairie Provinces arranged a large number of these meetings, the Saskatchewan group alone sponsoring twenty-four such gatherings.[27] The way in which these meetings were utilized by the candidates is illustrated by what occurred during an interparty encounter at Beauséjour in the Manitoba constituency of Springfield. The theme of the meeting was the government's agricultural policies, which were attacked bitterly by the Conservative, C.C.F., and Social Credit candidates. According to reports, Mr. Schulz, the C.C.F. candidate and former president of the Manitoba Farmer's Union, mounted the most vigorous offensive and was the favourite of the audience made up largely of farmers.

. . . Mr. Schulz, laying down a three point platform of parity prices, cash advances on farm-stored grain, and crop insurance—charged the federal government with "dragging the farmer down to hell". . . . Unruliest point in

[23]Winnipeg *Free Press*, June 6.
[24]*Ibid.*, May 4.
[25]C.P. dispatch from Vancouver, dated May 16.
[26]Both types of meetings are discussed below in chaps. VI and VII.
[27]C.P. dispatch from Saskatoon, dated May 24.

the stifling hot hall during the debate came when Lawrence Schlamp, Social Credit candidate, charged C.C.F.'er Schulz with being a capitalist because he owned a $50,000 . . . store in Winnipeg as well as an apartment block.

Angry audience protests on Mr. Schulz's behalf brought one of half a dozen interventions of the evening by the meeting chairman to restore order.

Val Yacula, Progressive Conservative candidate, told the meeting that in four years in Ottawa Mr. Weselak had spoken 1,000 lines in Hansard, "which means we pay him $40 a line."

Mr. Yacula, whose speech had the hall rocking with laughter, later said the Senate was used as a "sanitary disposal plant" by Prime Minister St. Laurent to dispose of "the boys who oppose him—he puts them there to keep them quiet."

Climaxing his appeal, Mr. Weselak said, "I don't care how you vote, just vote according to your opinion. I don't have to go back to Ottawa; I would be quite happy to stay home." . . . He said he had a family, and being an M.P. posed schooling problems. It also threatened his law practice in Beauséjour. 'We don't have to have a dirty campaign and its pretty bad here I don't mind telling you."

Mr. Schulz, first speaker, waving a table of statistics over his head, claimed that buying power of a bushel of No. 1 Northern was now the same as in 1930, and declared: "The only surprise to me is that you farmers are still living . . .

"If we can't sell the wheat, let's give it away," Mr. Schulz added. "We're a rich country: so rich we're giving jet aircraft away. Wheat will fill people's stomachs, and there's no better way to turn back communism.

The Liberal government had become "completely encircled by big business and by big business ideas," and this had led it to "commit many deals against the people of the country."

Here he held up a reproduction of a Free Press cartoon showing Rt. Hon. C. D. Howe, Trade Minister, loaning $80,000,000 at three per cent interest to Trans Canada Pipe Lines, and at the same time offering $1,500 loans to prairie wheat farmers at five per cent.

"Do you think one farmer will vote for a government that does that?" he asked. A chorus of noes followed. . . .

Mr. Schlamp said it was his search for information on parity prices that led him to Social Credit. Under the present economic system, parity prices were "a dream," he declared . . .

(At one point during Mr. Schlamp's speech, the noise of audience conversations and jeers grew so loud as to nearly drown out his voice, and brought an appeal by the chairman for a hearing for the speaker.) . . .

OUT IN THE COLD

Mr. Yacula said the farmer had become the "forgotten man" in the Canadian economy. Last year while other Canadians were setting records, "hitting the bull's-eye, the farmer was out in the cold, and the bulls were looking at him." Something was wrong, and he called for an investigation of the wheat marketing system. The "wheat board monopoly" had not produced a solution . . .

The Liberal government appointed its "worn-out politicians as magistrates, and gives its beaten candidates good jobs," he declared ... There had to be a change. "Who can you put in?" he asked, and replied, "the answer is me."

Mr. Yacula, a hotel-keeper, said Springfield riding had been represented "by lawyers, doctors and farmers—but never an hotel-keeper, and at least at my place you can get a beer."

Last speaker was Mr. Weselak ... He had "drawn the attention of the house to the developing cost-price squeeze in agriculture," and had urged committee study of the situation. He had urged extension of the Agricultural Price Supports Act, and opposed tariff increases which would hurt the farmer. He had pressed the government for long-term loans to young farmers, opposed any change in Crow's Nest Pass freight rates on grain, supported the senate land use probe, asked for P.F.A.A. [Prairie Farm Assistance Act] amendments to make the legislation more suitable for Manitoba, and supported removal of sales tax on municipal equipment. He had supported government payment of storage charges of grain carryovers in terminal positions, and had opposed taxes on rural insurance cooperatives ...

He said he had made himself "readily available" to constituents, and had written many letters on their behalf to obtain settlement of P.F.A.A. claims. He had supported an additional egg-grading station for Beauséjour, and had made his job of M.P. a full-time one ...

To one heckler he cried, "If you don't like what I stand for, you know what to do on election day."

Government agricultural policies were not formed on the floor of the house, but in the Liberal caucus, and there the voice of the prairie provinces was 15 members who had to fight for concessions from Liberals from all parts of the country. "If you get rid of those 15—or even some of them, God help us in the west ..."[28]

Yet another kind of meeting generated a good deal of heat and interest. At least two candidates in 1957, both of them in the West, challenged famous personages to verbal duels. By far the most sensational of the two was the debate between Mr. Ross Thatcher, the apostate C.C.F.'er, running for the Liberals in Assiniboia, and Hon. T. C. Douglas, the C.C.F. Premier of Saskatchewan. An estimated two to three thousand listeners came to Mossbank, a village of six hundred in which the debate was held. About a thousand people were able to squeeze into the hall where a heated discussion of provincial Crown corporations took place. The rest remained seated in their cars or sought protection from a steady downpour in nearby buildings, while the debate was amplified by loudspeakers.[29] It was also broadcast to an extremely wide radio audience.

To challenge the mighty seemed to have been the favourite pastime

[28]Michael Best, "Cheers, Jeers, Leers, Hotelman's Beers . . ." Winnipeg *Free Press*, May 10.

[29]*Ibid.*, May 21. See also E. N. Davis, "In the Douglas-Thatcher Ring," Toronto *Globe and Mail*, May 30.

of those who had previously changed their political affiliation. The other gauntlet was dropped by the renegade Liberal, Laurier A. Regnier, contesting St. Boniface for the Conservatives, who invited Mr. Garson, the Minister of Justice, to a verbal contest. This duel proved to be rather dull, despite receiving a great deal of advance publicity. Only about fifty people attended a quiet debate of the motion "Resolved that the present Federal administration betrayed the principles of parliamentary government in its closure procedure on the pipeline debate in the House of Commons last year." No vote was taken.[30]

The two examples cited show that any candidate, even when less skilled in polemics than the four mentioned above, has much to gain from challenging a national figure to a debate. If nothing comes of the proposal, a great deal of vote-catching publicity will have been obtained. The smaller parties, whose financial position is usually less satisfactory than that of the Liberals and Conservatives, often press for the holding of debates and contradictory meetings. It is likely, however, that they are motivated in this as much by a feeling that they have an infinitely better case than their opponents as by the desire to obtain publicity cheaply.

In eastern Canada it was not so much farm organizations as ratepayers' groups in the new suburbs who favoured meetings at which all the parties presented their views. The greatest impetus for such meetings was found in suburbs inhabited predominantly by people pursuing professional and sales occupations. Reports about such meetings emanated most frequently from places like well-to-do Applewood Acres, a large subdivision in Cooksville near Toronto, or Scarborough, another generally prosperous new satellite community near Toronto. In the latter riding, about fifteen such meetings were held, each attracting from fifty to a hundred people.[31] Not all of the panel type meetings in the East took place in the newer suburbs, however. Carleton constituency near Ottawa is said to have held at least one such meeting before every election since 1867 and in the Montreal constituency of Notre Dame de Grace six hundred were reported as having turned out to hear the candidates argue.[32]

A third type of meeting—the tea or coffee party meeting—was born almost of necessity. Tremendous impetus to hold this kind of political gathering was given the Ontario Conservatives a few years before the

---

[30]Winnipeg *Free Press*, May 9, 10, 11, 18 and 28. See also George Bain, "Minding Your Business," Toronto *Globe and Mail*, May 24.

[31]Fox, "A Study of One Constituency," p. 235.

[32]C.P. dispatch by Bernard Dufresne from Ottawa, May 30.

1957 election when scandals associated with one candidate and later with the Department of Highways made regular political meetings somewhat risky. At that time, frequent use was made of informal meetings held in homes, to which neighbours and friends were invited to meet the candidate. The same technique was successfully applied by Dorothy Downing, the Conservative federal organizer in Ontario, in a Toronto by-election in which she allegedly told the Conservative candidate, "We'll float you into Ottawa on tea!"[33] By 1957 the home meeting had become a standard and highly favoured way of electioneering. The Liberal candidate in Winnipeg North was reported as holding four to five home meetings a day.[34] Arthur Smith, running as a Conservative in Calgary, was said by one observer to have averaged about seven coffee parties a day "to the immense good, perhaps, of his own political chances, and certainly of Canadian-Brazilian trade."[35] Attendance at "informal gatherings of this sort occasionally reached impressive proportions. A tea held at an hotel in London, Ontario, attracted about six hundred women.[36] A turnout of such magnitude requires the launching of a special "invitation campaign." In Winnipeg, one candidate's organization staged "blitzes" in which as many as sixty workers descended on a neighbourhood, inviting its residents to a tea where they could meet the candidate.[37]

Up to this point we have described the campaign efforts of the constituency organizations. In this activity it is not absolutely necessary to stress a particular line or position, since the emphasis is usually on the candidate's personality, or, if that is not the case, on the ideas and record of the party taken as a whole. In the remaining activities, however, which are primarily concerned with advertising, a particular line or position must be adopted if the various efforts are not to cancel one another out. This aspect of local electioneering warrants brief consideration before resuming the description of campaign techniques.

Local Strategy

Most experienced campaigners agree that appeals made in local terms and related to local issues are the most effective. Even national or

[33]Margaret Aitken with Byrne Hope Sanders, *Hey, Ma! I Did It* (Toronto, 1953), p. 29. The technique is not unlike that described as a "cottage" meeting by H. G. Nicholas in *The British General Election of 1950*, p. 235.
[34]Winnipeg *Free Press*, May 28.
[35]George Bain, "Minding Your Business," Toronto *Globe and Mail*, May 17.
[36]London *Free Press*, May 30.   [37]Winnipeg *Free Press*, June 1.

provincial issues can best be exploited if they are related directly to the constituency and to the candidate who might be able to do something affecting them. However, two factors, more than any others, are likely to influence the general tone of a candidate's campaign. His strategy will vary depending, first, on whether or not his party is in office in Ottawa and, second, whether he himself is already in the House or is making his first bid for a seat.

Liberal candidates, who have had previous experience in the House, invariably pointed to how much they (and the government) had done for the constituency. This theme was stressed at meetings, during speeches, and in advertisements. Groups who had benefited particularly as a consequence of governmental expenditures were reminded of the fact. Towards the end of the campaign, a comprehensive statement was sometimes issued showing how effective the candidate had been in looking after his constituency. A full-page advertisement, for example, in the local newspaper on the Saturday preceding the election, asked the voters of Kingston, Ontario: "Do YOU want to change all this?" To the right of this query was a picture of the Liberal candidate, a Parliamentary veteran, with hand outstretched partly as if to greet the reader, partly pointing to the printed matter on the page. This consisted of headings and opening paragraphs from articles in the local paper which had announced governmental expenditures in the riding. A dozen items were reproduced, bearing titles such as these: "Shipyards Get Contract for RCMP Patrol Boat—W. J. Henderson Announces Award; Cost Set at $1,000,000," "Government Pays City $100,000 Sum," "Grant Made to Queen's of $124,000," "Starting Construction On Federal Building," "CLC gets $25,000,000 Government Contract." At the bottom of the page there appeared an answer to the question on the top, inquiring of the reader whether he wanted to change this. "Definitely NOT! Vote LIBERAL on Monday and be sure! Re-elect W. J. 'Bill' HENDERSON . . . and be sure!"[38]

A notably crass appeal to human cupidity was made by a Liberal senator campaigning vigorously in support of the local Liberal candidate in Hastings South in Ontario. Discussing the possibility of a new federal building being erected in Trenton, he said: "When Frank Follwell (the Liberal candidate) is re-elected, I am sure with his co-operation that the necessary funds will be provided in next year's estimates . . ." Later statements by the senator were reported as follows:

Pyrotenax of Canada located in Trenton as a result of the co-operation of C. D. Howe in arranging the export of capital from England as well as

[38]Kingston *Whig Standard*, June 8.

certain tariff adjustments and release of structural steel under quota, Sen. Fraser said. He went on: Mr. Howe was a personal friend of the chairman of the board of the firm in England and the senator gave the company 12 acres of land free on which to build the plant.

Sen. Fraser had a list of 12 such examples. Williams and Williams (Eastern) Ltd. were persuaded to build in Trenton by the senator and Mr. Howe; the firm realized, the senator said, they were among friends in a Liberal government that could assist them in many ways.

And, the senator went on, Delft Gelatin established in Trenton after it discovered it could get the required assistance from the Liberal government in Ottawa in taking the duty off raw materials. As much business as possible is being directed to Downs Coulter Ltd. from government departments requiring uniforms.

"Do not believe," the senator warned, "that I would be accepted as an adviser to a Tory government and I ask you to make sure by your ballot that Frank Follwell and Fred Robertson (Northumberland candidate) are re-elected. I will require their assistance in the future as in the past in securing the co-operation of the Liberal Government in a number of important ventures I have at present in mind—projects that will provide more labour for more people in the area."[39]

But candidates making claims on behalf of the government must take care that these do not back-fire. Mr. Howe himself, for example, suffered in this regard. Full-page newspaper advertisements in Port Arthur "stressed the millions in wages, the fleets of vessels that had come to the [local] shipyards since the political advent of the Minister." It was well known in the constituency that Mr. Howe had very close connections with Sir James Dunn and with Senator Paterson whose shipping interests were of major importance to Great Lakes navigation. Liberal advertising in Port Arthur was made to look ridiculous when the C.C.F. showed, by using figures taken from reports of the Canadian Maritime Commission, that "of all the yards under this [Dunn] control, Port Arthur's had gained the fewest ship-building contracts."[40]

It was not only Liberal candidates who took credit for some of the actions of the government. Any previously elected member could claim that such wisdom as the government had shown was the result of opposition prodding. Wallace Nesbitt, who had had one session's experience in the House, made the slogan "Nesbitt gets things done!" the main theme of his campaign. "Over and over again, the record of Nesbitt's one term in office was stressed. 'Every farmer knows what

[39]"Hastings South Gets Politics, Postoffice?" Toronto *Globe and Mail*, May 31.
[40]D. M. Fisher, "An Interesting Campaign," *Canadian Forum*, Sept., 1957, p. 143. This incident taken from an account of the Port Arthur election by the man who defeated the Trade Minister offers greater testimony to Mr. Howe's probity than to the diligence and meticulousness of his campaign committee.

R.O.P. means' found its way into advertisements many times."[41] When the government decided to protect Canadian cheese producers by banning cheddar imports, Mr. Nesbitt took a bow. Advertisements appeared in one daily and seven weekly newspapers headed NESBITT GETS THINGS DONE. Below was the newspaper clipping announcing Mr. Howe's banning of New Zealand cheese. A short paragraph followed:

Day after day he [Nesbitt] hammered away at the government—it's on the record in Hansard, March 1957—pp. 2008, 2156, 2187, 2434, 2440, 2441, 2442—and Nesbitt as usual got it done! No wonder we say "every farmer knows R.O.P." KEEP NESBITT WORKING FOR YOU.[42]

Opposition candidates who had not been members of the House of Commons were forced to take a more negative attitude. They were usually content to criticize the government, holding it responsible for local manifestations of such regional or national problems as might affect their consituency. The theme of most of the campaigns of opposition candidates was, therefore, that of attacking the Liberals on a broad front, but illustrating their case by reference to local hardships or to local discontent. Wherever possible, Liberal failure to do more for power development in the Maritimes or on the West Coast, to facilitate the disposal of surplus wheat, to increase pensions, to ease the financial burden of municipalities, to protect various industries or to permit easy borrowing of money was pointed to as an explanation of various local difficulties. By electing the Conservative candidate the local elector could help defeat the government and make sure that its inevitably Conservative successor would benefit from the advice of the local Conservative member. Frequently, the name of Mr. Diefenbaker was also associated with that of the "native son." Only rarely did purely local grievances assume a central role in the arguments of an opposition candidate.

Liberal candidates running in constituencies held by members of opposition parties usually argued that the riding's interests could be pressed more forcefully in Ottawa by a member adhering to the government party. "If you want to get warm, you've got to move near the fire" was how one campaign worker put it.[43] Since, before the election, practically everyone believed in the return of the St. Laurent government, this argument made more sense when its was presented than it does in retrospect.

An altogether different approach was adopted by constituency organizations whose standard-bearer was thought to have a promising

[41]Allan, "Oxford County," p. 52. R.O.P., according to the author, is the abbreviation for Record of Performance, a term used in evaluating the quality and quantity of milk production of dairy cattle.
[42]Ibid., p. 58.   [43]Toronto Globe and Mail, June 5.

future before him. In the case of the Liberals, for example, it would be hinted (never, of course, by the candidate himself) that a Parliamentary Assistantship was in the offing, or perhaps even a cabinet portfolio. It was widely rumoured, for example, and probably with some justification, that Mayor William Hawrelak, the Liberal candidate in Edmonton East, was to have succeeded the retiring George Prudham as the cabinet minister from Alberta. Mr. Diefenbaker, on the other hand, indicated while speaking in Kamloops, British Columbia, that Mr. Fulton would be a cabinet minister in the event of a Conservative victory.[44] While this statement could not have come as a great surprise to his audience, it was no doubt a useful indication that the leadership race had not left the Conservative party unduly divided.

One aspect of the general line adopted by a candidate concerned his own personality. It was not so much a question of what sort of pose he might strike in the course of the election—only an accomplished actor could probably get away with anything other than more or less being his natural self—as a problem of deciding which attributes to emphasize. This decision, according to one party handbook, should be made only in relation to the characteristics of the opposing candidates. If a candidate has local government experience and his rivals do not, the candidate should stress his *experience*. If, on the other hand, the candidate is a community leader, lacking the municipal experience of his opponents, then his *ability* should be played up.[45]

A comparison of Liberal (McCall) and Conservative (Nesbitt) newspaper campaigning in Oxford reveals the Liberal candidate as having made effective use of this approach. Summarizing his analysis of Liberal advertising, Allan points to

its emphasis on "the family man", "the poor boy made good", "the common touch", the honest, friendly, sincere and religious young fellow, the acquaintance with rural problems, his lack of acquaintance with the smoke-filled rooms of the professional politicians, and his support of Prime Minister St. Laurent. . . . Besides this aspect, Liberal advertising was engaged in trying to destroy the Nesbitt legend, chiefly by claiming that most of the credit belonged "to those who are too modest to boast about it". Again they implied Nesbitt was insincere, that because he was a Nesbitt he did not know what poverty, hard work or a cow was like.[46]

A candidate's occupation is sometimes exploited for political ends. Much depends on the nature of the constituency and on how well he is known in it. Since virtually all university students nowadays spend part

[44]Winnipeg *Free Press*, May 25.
[45]*Advertising and Publicity Hints for Candidates*, pp. 2–3.
[46]Allan, "Oxford County," p. 57. Nesbitt was a bachelor and came from a well-to-do family.

of the summer holidays in some gainful employment, many lawyer candidates can legitimately claim to have been farmers or labourers or to have done something which might extend their appeal in certain sections of the constituency. A well-to-do, portly lawyer, with a fair number of years in the House of Commons, was fond of pointing to the fact that he had been a miner in Canada's northland. Another candidate, contesting a seat near Ottawa, had worked for the Income Tax Department for two years between university courses. He was a barrister. But during the campaign he was often referred to as a former civil servant, no doubt so as to be more acceptable to a constituency many of whose residents were employees of the government.

It is sometimes possible for a candidate to exploit existing rumour about himself to his advantage. It was stated in the press during the 1957 campaign that Mr. Howe had taken a violent dislike to William Hamilton, the Conservative M.P. for Notre Dame de Grace in Montreal, and that, consequently, special efforts were made to defeat him in the election.[47] One correspondent mentioned that the Liberal party was prepared to spend $75,000 on the defeat of Mr. Hamilton. Whatever the source or the veracity of these rumours, Mr. Hamilton's organization did nothing to dispel them. Indeed, there are reasons to believe that it would have been disappointed had they died down. For whatever major theme Mr. Hamilton wished to adopt for his campaign, the additional one of his playing David to Mr. Howe's Goliath was certain to strengthen his position. By June, 1957, Mr. Howe had become a national bogey.

According to the C.C.F.'er who opposed the Minister of Trade and Commerce in Port Arthur, Mr. Howe also tried to use rumour in support of his re-election. On a final telecast, Mr. Howe

used the Labour-Progressives. "Would you want a young fellow down at Ottawa who was under Communist influence?" Then he spoke his democratic concern over stories abroad that union organizers were strong-arming the bush-men to vote CCF or else ... Mr. Howe wanted to give his personal assurance to the men of the camps that he would stop this in a hurry if they would get in touch with him . . . this ploy had several ironies. First, the picture of a pulp-cutter supplicating Mr. Howe, second, the reputed strong-arming took place in a region under an organizer who was less than luke-warm to me and the CCF.[48]

[47]See, for example, Robert Duffy, "Montreal PC Appears Particular Target for Liberals," Toronto *Globe and Mail*, May 10, and Langevin Coté, "Quebec Swing to PC's Seen by Diefenbaker," *Ibid.*, June 1.
[48]Fisher, "An Interesting Campaign," pp. 143–4. The Labour Progressive party supported the C.C.F. in constituencies where it ran no candidates, to the C.C.F.'s embarrassment and annoyance. Mr. Fisher was no more under Communist influence that Mr. Howe himself.

In selecting a general line for use in the campaign, the candidate is therefore likely to present his interpretation of how national issues and the national political situation affect the constituency he wishes to represent and how they affect his own position in it. In addition, he will try to create a popular image of himself—one which will contrast favourably with those of his opponents. This image may become particularly appealing if he can convince the voters that powerful outside forces are meddling in the affairs of the constituency by trying to defeat him or that unethical and unfair methods are being used against him. The line he adopts and the image of himself he wishes to create are presented to the public in his personal contacts with it, at political meetings, and by his party workers who conduct door-to-door canvasses. But these activities may prove ineffective if they are not accompanied by additional advertising. Most candidates use the following media: newspapers, broadcasting, favours, pamphlets and leaflets, items mailed directly to the electors' homes and outdoor displays of various sorts.

Newspapers

Newspaper advertising is second only to personal campaigning as the most popular means of "selling" the local candidate. In addition to publicizing local activities it is used to make the candidate's name a household word, to present the local campaign theme and to apply suitable national issues to local conditions. This type of advertising, placed in both daily and weekly publications, is designed to supplement material inserted by the national or provincial campaign organization. Sometimes the pages of the local press become the battlegrounds on which candidates argue against one another from day to day, refuting one another's claims and generally engaging in lively controversy. The advertising battle in Lincoln, Ontario, illustrates this phase of campaigning.

During the early stages of the Lincoln campaign the Conservatives and Liberals completely disregarded one another's advertising activities. The usual announcements were placed in the local press concerning nominating meetings and visits to the constituency of outside luminaries. Alleged Liberal maltreatment of Parliament and the plight of local farmers and fruit-growers were stressed by the Conservatives. On May 31, for example, an advertisement appeared in the St. Catharines *Standard*, consisting merely of the words "REMEMBER BLACK FRIDAY" in bold letters, surrounded by a black frame. In very small print there appeared the advertisement's sponsor: the Conservative Association of Lincoln County.[49] Several days later a larger advertisement presented the picture of the local candidate, Mr. John Smith, and asked the reader:

DO YOU KNOW? That Liberal policy has cost our farmers and fruitgrowers 1¢ a pound for all asparagus sold this year—due to ineffective protection and thoughtless disregard for their welfare?
JOHN SMITH and the Diefenbaker government guarantee protection by new and effective legislation.
ON MONDAY JUNE 10, MAKE A DATE WITH DIEFENBAKER AND ELECT JOHN SMITH.[50]

The name of the candidate, which happened to be the one used by the electoral officer for purposes of illustrating sample ballots, was placed in a three-sided heavy black border resembling the official ballot form. At the bottom, there appeared not only the name of the issuing organization, but also that of the official agent, followed by the words, "Fruit Grower."

All Liberal publicity material emphasized that Harry Cavers, the sitting member seeking re-election, had served the community well. His speeches in Parliament were listed, as well as Liberal welfare measures and amounts allegedly spent by the government locally on family allowances, old age pensions, and hospitals. The advertisements contained a good deal of textual material in a style that was anything but terse. One full-page advertisement, for example, contained the following *inter alia*:

To be a faithful servant of the people is no easy task ... particularly when one is big-hearted and generous minded . . . when one is so anxious to see prosperity and security and happiness prevail throughout the land ... but Cavers came through with flying colours attested by the fact that he now has more staunch friends than he had at the beginning ... a proud tribute indeed to the man himself . . . and a justification of the voters' choice eight years ago.
Eight years ago Harry Cavers made up his mind to serve all the people of Lincoln equally well regardless of who they were and what they were ... he has drawn no barrier between the factory worker and the tiller of the soil ... the shop keeper or the manufacturer ... neither race, colour or creed has swayed him from this determination.
There is only one way to judge a man ... and that is by the sum total of his works on your behalf ... with this you must agree ... and in doing so decide to once again vote for Harry P. Cavers. There can be no other choice.[51]

[49]St. Catharines *Standard*, May 31. The description of the advertising campaign in Lincoln is based largely on H. C. Organ, "Report on the Political Activities in the Riding of Lincoln," unpublished essay prepared for a course in political science at Queen's University.
[50]St. Catharines *Standard*, June 3.   [51]*Ibid.*, June 5.

At the bottom, in extremely large, red letters was the admonition "RE-ELECT CAVERS"—and below it a rather unusual item: "Vote for the first name on the ballot." A special box contained an appeal for the votes of women. Another full-page advertisement attempted to differentiate between the Liberal and other parties by emphasizing the Liberals' performance in the field of social legislation. At the top and bottom of this page there was the reminder: "HEAR the Rt. Hon. LOUIS ST. LAURENT—TONIGHT, 8.30...[52]

In addition to the familar red exhortation "RE-ELECT CAVERS," a Liberal advertisement inserted on June 1 bore the headline "RESULTS!" also in red. Below, there were photographs of buildings in St. Catharines and elsewhere in the county housing post offices and other government agencies. The page claimed to show that Mr. Cavers and the Liberal government had made certain that "the people of Lincoln were provided with adequate and up-to-date public services."

Five days later, the Conservatives reprinted six of these pictures, also in a one page lay-out. "LET'S BE HONEST!" the advertisement admonished.

The Liberals claim to have given you action and prosperity. They show you pictures of six Public Buildings as proof of this claim. Five of these buildings were built with private funds—not a nickel of the taxpayers' money nor effort by the local member of Parliament—the post offices merely rent space. "THESE LIBERAL CLAIMS ARE DELIBERATE ATTEMPTS TO MISLEAD THE VOTERS OF LINCOLN COUNTY".

The advertisement then asked: "Is the replacement of outdated post offices more important than... 1. Loss of employment. 2. Loss of farm income. 3. Loss of freedom?" A picture of some industrial buildings was placed above a paragraph listing three local concerns which, allegedly, had been "forced to close their doors to hundreds of our workers due to the lack of concern and fair protection by the present Liberal Government." A similar protectionist line was assumed with reference to decreasing farm income. The heading concerning the loss of freedom was amplified as follows:

Our local member sat in the House of Commons on June 1st, 1956 and sang "Hail! Hail! The Gang's all here ... what the h— do we care!" as Parliament was defiled and freedom of speech denied: As C. D. Howe made his charitable loan with YOUR money to Texas oil millionaires and wrecked the Parliament of Canada.

No doubt to the delight of the publishers of the St. Catharines *Standard*, the Liberal reply also took up a full page. It was inserted on

[52]*Ibid.*, June 4.

Saturday, June 8, two days before the election. The photographs of the seven buildings which had been used before appeared again, under the huge, red heading: "LET'S REALLY BE HONEST!" In addition to other material, the text said:

THE LIBERALS *HAVE* GIVEN YOU ACTION AND PROSPERITY. THESE EIGHT[53] PUBLIC BUILDINGS ARE PROOF OF THIS. At no time has Harry Cavers or the Liberal party advertising claimed that all these buildings were built with Federal funds as Tory advertising would have you believe. Such misrepresentation in the paid advertisement of Thursday, June 6, is proof of who is really being honest in this election.

Some of these public buildings were built by private capital and leased by the Post Office Department . . . proof of the tangible results produced by Harry P. Cavers, your hard working member of Parliament.

The erection of these buildings . . . demonstrates the true Liberal policy of combining Federal spending with investment by private capital.

LIBERALS BELIEVE IN FREE ENTERPRISE.

Private investors were invited to erect these buildings and lease them back to the Government . . . (at tremendous saving of the taxpayers' money by avoiding large capital expenditures from the Federal Treasury).

Some candidates created a continuous opportunity for commenting on the election by writing a newspaper column which was regularly placed in the same corner of a certain page. The space was, of course, paid for. A Conservative candidate in one of the Montreal constituencies filled such a column with all manner of interesting information, much of it unrelated to the election. One issue contained an item referring to a lexicographic project at the University of Montreal. The column raised the question what the French word is for "bulldozer."[54] The title of the column was "Egan Chambers' Ballot Box," and its relation to the election was unmistakable.

Another ingenious idea was devised by Mr. F. C. McGee, running in York-Scarborough near Toronto. He persuaded the publisher of the large-circulation Toronto *Telegram* to use him as the subject of a feature describing a day in the life of a candidate. Mr. McGee was apparently able to obtain enough free copies of the lavishly illustrated page containing this feature to provide one for every home in the constituency.[55] There is no doubt that many candidates were able to obtain newspaper publicity by somewhat similar means. It is impossible to say, for example,

[53]Neither party could or would count properly. *Seven* buildings were portrayed in both Liberal advertisements. The Conservative reply mentioned only *six*, conveniently ignoring the huge Federal Government Building erected in St. Catharines by the government. The Liberals, on the other hand, mentioned *eight* when in fact only seven pictures were printed. The eighth photograph was that of the candidate.

[54]Montreal *Daily Star*, May 24.

[55]Fox, "A Study of One Constituency," p. 236. The article appeared on June 2.

whether any given news item about the election really represented genuine news or whether it was "created" by an energetic candidate seeking to keep his name before the public. Many political meetings, reported as such in the press, were probably merely small gatherings of party workers about which an efficient campaign organization wrote a seemingly newsworthy press release. Similar techniques were applied for the purpose of obtaining publicity on the air.

Radio and Television

Radio and television were used to the same end as newspapers. Both spoken and visual appeals were employed by the parties to advertise their major electoral activities and to "sell" their candidates. The latter efforts involved the utilization of ordinary "commercials" and of speeches by the candidates. Previously elected members had an advantage in this respect: many of them had long ago adopted the habit of making periodic broadcasts to their constituents reporting on the Ottawa scene. Frequently during the campaign, local supporters also made speeches on behalf of one or the other of the candidates. Retired politicians, members of the provincial legislatures, attractive relatives, or citizens presumably representing various professions, interests, or ethnic and religious groups in the constituency were brought to the microphones and cameras in support of those seeking election. It is generally thought that "unknown" individuals are more effective "salesmen" than prominent local personages.[56] Short announcements making national appeals, endorsements by the party leaders, or similar "trailers" were used by those candidates who could afford to utilize on the local stations the services prepared by the central party organizations.

Candidates whose constituencies were close to the United States border were unable to benefit from the large listening and viewing audiences enjoyed by some of the American networks in Canada, because of Canadian regulations governing political broadcasting. A leading member of the Toronto Young Progressive Conservatives succeeded in circumventing the rule when he appeared on a Buffalo television station's programme carrying a sign bearing the words "Vote Conservative, Vote Diefenbaker!" Knowing that a crowd scene was to

[56]Allan, for example, commenting (p. 56) on the Liberal campaign in Oxford, suggests that the use of prominent local dignitaries was not particularly effective. Fisher, whose success in defeating Mr. C. D. Howe has been attributed to the skilful use of television, states (p. 142) that almost all the people appearing on his programmes were publicly unknown.

be filmed in front of the studio, he arranged to be "on location" with his sign at the appropriate time. A picture of his placard was thus transmitted to the Niagara-Hamilton-Toronto area.[57]

An equally unorthodox, if less spectacular, use of television was made by C. D. Howe. His main opponent had booked a number of television periods on the local station, including the last half-hour on the last day on which political broadcasts were permitted before the election. Wishing to have the last word, Mr. Howe persuaded the management of the station to delay the usual closing hour on that occasion for half an hour, which he utilized for a final election appeal.[58]

In general, during the campaign, radio was used most during the daytime and television, in places where it was available, in the evening. One election manual recommended that candidates buy radio time immediately preceding or succeeding the most popular news broadcast in the morning and that they persuade the station's newscaster to write and read a short bulletin, in the privately bought time, reporting on the candidate's electioneering activities. Although no evidence showing that this advice was taken by any candidates has been found, it is likely that the idea—obviously a good one—was acted upon by many of those who could afford to do so.

In the previous chapter it was shown that the national organizations of the major parties provided some assistance to candidates wishing to utilize the new medium of television. In the absence of precise information it is not possible to say how much use was actually made of this available help. The very high cost of television advertising suggests, however, that few candidates were able to use the magic screen as much as they would have liked. One candidate—the Liberal in Brandon-Souris, Manitoba—who did make extensive use of television, was obviously immensely impressed by the potentialities of the medium: his committee room was arranged like a television theatre with about fifty chairs lined up in front of a television receiving set.[59]

Other Media

Television was not the only advertising technique that cost considerable sums of money. In large constituencies outdoor displays of various kinds were also extremely expensive. It was estimated, for example, that one candidate in sprawling York-Scarborough spent around $10,000 on

[57]C.P. dispatch from Toronto, May 31.
[58]Fisher, "An Interesting Campaign," pp. 121, 143–4.
[59]Winnipeg *Tribune*, May 30.

signs alone.[60] There are about five types of outdoor advertising devices widely used in Canadian elections. The most popular are pole cards, which are usually placed on telephone poles, trees and similar places visible, so it is hoped, by large numbers of passers-by. They normally carry the name and possibly picture of the candidate and the name of the constituency. Some are treated so that they glow at night. Billboard advertising is also resorted to, particularly by candidates running in areas of high population density. A cheaper way to make the candidate known—and incidentally, when skilfully placed, to indicate widespread support—is to distribute so-called verandah cards. These are put either on verandahs or in windows by supporters at modest cost. A fourth form of display advertising, and one which seemed particularly popular in 1957, consists of car cards. These are tied or glued to various parts of motor-cars, thereby becoming perambulatory reminders of the candidates' names. Lastly, a more stationary type of display can be made up of banners placed across a busy street.

One unorthodox campaigner made extensive use of a trailer to keep his name before the public.

That thing behind Frank Dunlap's car is so plastered with red and white bunting and Liberal election signs that it is almost indistinguishable as a trailer ... Even at night ... [the] trailer does its work. A parking place along some busy highway is carefully chosen every night so hundreds of headlights will pick out its strident messages.[61]

An equally unorthodox use of outdoor advertising was applied against Mr. Diefenbaker's campaigners in Prince Albert. They had given extremely wide circulation to a pole card urging the voters to "ELECT JOHN G. DIEFENBAKER." At the top of each card someone (allegedly C.C.F. campaigners) pasted a single word: "WHY."[62]

Almost all candidates advertise by distributing various favours in their constituency. These always display in a prominent place the candidate's name, which is often accompanied by an election slogan or a short message. Blotters, book matches, and shopping bags were among the most popular of these items. Wealthy campaign organizations may distribute more expensive items. Balloons and caps are popular. In 1957 one affluent local party widely distributed T-shirts to school children in the constituency. Each shirt bore the candidate's name.[63]

[60]His opponent placed the figure at $13,000, the Toronto *Globe and Mail* at $9,000. See Fox, "A Study of One Constituency," p. 237.

[61]Haggart, "If Noise Wins Votes, He Will Make History."

[62]George Bain, "Minding Your Business," Toronto *Globe and Mail*, May 21.

[63]W. R. Brunt, Jr., "Reports of the Electoral Districts of Grey-Bruce (Federal) and Grey-South (Provincial) for the Elections of 1951, 1953, 1955, 1957," unpublished essay prepared for a course in political science at Queen's University, p. 16.

The most direct way of appealing to the voters is through the mail. Many candidates prepare their own pamphlets for local distribution, or at least add their own name to literature prepared by the national organization. Widespread use is made of letters written by candidates to their constituents. These are usually made to look as if they were hand-written or, if they are obviously typed, as if the signature were affixed in ink by the candidate. Some ambitious campaigners actually do write large numbers of personal letters to constituents, asking for their support. Sometimes the number of these personal letters reached into thousands. Here, as in so many ways, the previously elected member is at a distinct advantage. Almost all M.P.'s make a point of sending to numerous constituents suitable messages commemorating important occasions in their lives. This is a cheap and easy way of "keeping in touch"; the parliamentary franking privilege is invariably used and the names can easily be found in the local press. Recently married couples, students winning scholarships, or citizens whose names stray into local papers for a variety of other reasons may hear from their member, though they have possibly never set eyes on him. It is not always only the sitting member who conducts a long-term campaign of this sort. In the 1957 election the Liberal running in Parry Sound-Muskoka, was reported as having sent 20,000 Christmas cards to residents of the constituency he wished to represent.[64]

An effective and widely used publicity item which is mailed to the constituents' homes consists of a simple card informing the recipient of the location of his polling station. It may also include a telephone number which, if called, will bring a car on election day. Another type of card has in recent years been gaining popularity among Canadian candidates. It is a very glossy, usually thick-papered photograph of the candidate, invariably surrounded by his family. On the back the names of the children are usually given, as well as their age and an indication of what each is doing.

Only routine campaign techniques have been described so far. These are often supplemented by additional efforts prompted by particular developments in the campaign or by the inventive genius of one of the workers. Parades, hecklers or even floats may be utilized. A Liberal "Victory Rally" in Ottawa, for example, featured a "Miss Liberal." At the entrance to the hall, meanwhile, the Conservatives created a tableau ridiculing one of Mr. St. Laurent's favourite electioneering tactics: a young couple with a baby carriage could not be missed by those arriving

[64]Grey Hamilton, "Plentitude of Posters Not Necessarily Victory Sign," Toronto *Globe and Mail*, May 17.

to the meeting, for it stood under a large sign reading "DON'T KISS MY BABY".[65]

Sometimes candidates engage in activities which have no apparent relation to the election. Dances are often arranged by the parties at which the candidates may or may not speak. An unusual campaign, in this regard, was waged by the saxophone-playing Liberal seeking re-election in Meadow Lake. Eschewing speech-making to a large extent, he campaigned by leading a five-man band playing dance music in various centres in his constituency. "Dance to the music of Jack Harrison and his Parliamentary Pipeliners," his posters proclaimed. "All non-Liberals cordially invited to come to get in step with the times. Liberal admission—namely free. Closure may be enforced any time after three A.M."[66]

Campaigning in Quebec

No mention has been made in the preceding pages of electioneering techniques in the province of Quebec. Basically, these are the same as elsewhere in Canada. Federal law, including the Electoral Act, applies uniformly in all the provinces and as far as the work of the Chief Electoral Officer and of the Deputy Returning Officers is concerned, Quebec differs in no way from the rest of the country except that election instructions and all other aids must be in the French language. But general attitudes towards politics in Quebec are without doubt somewhat unique in Canada.[67] Two differences are outstanding. The

[65]Winnipeg *Free Press*, May 28.

[66]Harvey Hickey, "Saskatchewan Voters Dancing to Pipeliners," Toronto *Globe and Mail*, May 8.

[67]No adequate studies of the differences between politics in Quebec and in the other provinces exist. The reader wishing to acquaint himself with some French-Canadian criticism of Quebec politics is advised to consult the following: Pierre Elliott Trudeau, "Some Obstacles to Democracy in Quebec," *Canadian Journal of Economics and Political Science*, vol. XXIV, no. 3 (Aug., 1958), pp. 297–311; "L'Election fédérale du 10 aôut 1953: prodromes et conjectures," *Cité Libre*, vol. III, no. 8 (Nov., 1953), pp. 1–10; "Réflections sur la politique au Canada français," *Cité Libre*, vol. II, no. 3 (Dec., 1952), pp. 53–70; Gérard Dion and Louis O'Neill, "L'Immoralité politique dans la province de Québec" (a paper by two priests originally published in the bulletin *Ad Usum Sacerdotum*, circulated among the Quebec clergy, reprinted by *Le Devoir*, Aug. 7, 1956, and again Aug. 14, 1956. It has since been published as a separate pamphlet with press comments by the Comité de moralité publique de Montréal). The December, 1952, issue of *Cité Libre*, cited above, is devoted to an analysis of French-Canadian politics, particularly with reference to the Quebec provincial election of 1952. Among articles of general interest the following are particularly useful: Charles-A. Lussier,

first concerns French-Canadian nationalism which often affects the general line a candidate will take. The second is more difficult to define. It is concerned with what is usually referred to as political morality and can perhaps best be stated by saying that, on the whole, Section 65 of the Canadian Elections Act (Bribery, Treating, Undue Influence and Personation) is violated more frequently and more as a matter of course than in the other provinces. Appeals to venality are, in short, more frequent and more openly made. There are, of course, notable exceptions, and it would be wrong and foolish to conclude that *every* election in Quebec is conducted with doubtful honesty or that the campaigns in *all* constituencies outside Quebec are unexceptionable.

While Mr. St. Laurent refrained from trading on his French origins and culture when appealing to his Quebec compatriots, there is little doubt that many individual Liberal candidates tried to utilize his antecedents in appealing for votes. Towards the end of the campaign particularly, appeals to French-Canadian nationalism were not uncommon. They usually took the form of veiled or outright indications that French Canadians simply could not vote against "one of their own."[68] The Conservative candidate in Bagot St. Hyacinthe, for example, accused local Liberal speakers of attributing to Mr. Diefenbaker anti-French and anti-Catholic utterances. "Prime Minister St. Laurent goes about the country preaching national unity," he said, "while his henchmen in Quebec descend to a political level which we had hoped had disappeared from Quebec politics."[69] But the Liberals were not the only ones to exploit ethnic differences. Attempting to capitalize on the prevailing mixture of ethnic and religious sentiment, some Quebec campaigners used posters promising that Mr. Diefenbaker would give Canada a distinctive national flag and that he would appoint an ambassador to the Vatican.[70]

It would be fruitless to describe in detail the techniques used in the attempted intimidation of Quebec voters. As will be shown below,[71] the Union Nationale gave full support to a number of Conservative candi-

"Loi électorale et conscience politique," pp. 23–34; Gérard Pelletier, "D'où vient l'argent qui nourrit les partis?" pp. 35–41; Pierre Laporte, "La Machine électorale," pp. 42–6; and Marcel Rioux, "L'Election vue de l'Anse-à-la-Barbe," pp. 47–52. A penetrating study is that of Michael Oliver, "Quebec and Canadian Democracy," *Canadian Journal of Economics and Political Science*, vol. XXIII, no. 4 (Nov., 1957), pp. 504–15.

[68]Interview with a Liberal who had held a position of responsibility in his party's Quebec campaign.

[69]Montreal *Gazette*, June 7.

[70]Fred Manor, "Liberal Party's Young Turks Eager for Perch in Quebec," Winnipeg *Free Press*, June 6. The posters were seen in the constituency of Compton-Frontenac.

[71]Chap. VIII, pp. 174–6.

dates. It was fighting with the same weapons it generally favoured in the provincial elections; a lot of money, public works, payment of hospital bills, undue pressure on voters who receive certain pensions, and similar devices.[72] Where the Liberals tended to appeal to nationalism, the Union Nationale usually stressed local issues:

"You vote Conservative in federal election (sic) and you will get a bridge, a school, a road," the voters are promised. Work has begun on a number of provincial roads, and according to Liberal organizers, the municipalities are told everywhere by Union Nationale that the work will stop if the vote goes against the Tories.

In Nicolet-Yamaska ... the Conservative party is not even mentioned in the campaign. The Tory candidate here is Paul Comtois, a personal friend of Quebec's Premier Maurice Duplessis and for many years general manager of the Farmers Provincial Savings Bank.

The Union Nationale organizers are, according to Liberal and impartial sources, going from farm to farm, reminding the farmers that it is Mr. Comtois to whom they owe their loans, and warning what may happen to future loans if the vote should not go right.[73]

In fairness to M. Duplessis it must be noted that neither he nor his party were the innovators in Quebec of this type of political behaviour. The provincial Liberal party which had been in power from 1897 to 1936 showed, towards the end of its tenure in office, many of the usual gerontic symptoms of long-established administrations. Under Hon. L. A. Taschereau, who was premier from 1920 to 1936, the provincial Liberal regime had become associated with scandals and had acquired a reputation not unlike that later to be enjoyed by the Duplessis government. And in the 1957 election even Mr. St. Laurent, whose election manner seemed to some of his supporters at times almost recklessly "non-political," permitted himself the occasional appeal to Quebec parish pump politics. Referring to a new railway line extension favouring the community in which he was giving an address, he said:

It grated me to see that all this railway expansion would direct business to Toronto or Montreal. Of course we are all part of one and the same country, but we all have our own little homeland. Frankly, it is more as a Quebecer than as Prime Minister of Canada that I put my weight behind the demands of your citizens here for an extension of the project to St. Félicien in this region.[74]

[72]Pierre Laporte, *Le Devoir*, June 6. An admittedly hostile witness, *Le Devoir* is nevertheless an extremely useful source of news on Quebec politics. Unlike any other newspapers, notably the two leading English-language dailies in Montreal— the *Star* and the *Gazette*— it was consistently fearless in exposing irregularities and illegalities committed by the Union Nationale.

[73]Manor, "Liberal Party's Young Turks."

[74]C.P. dispatch from Roberval, May 29.

Cost of Local Campaign

In theory, there should be no difficulty in discussing the cost of elections at the constituency level.[75] As was indicated at the beginning of this chapter, each candidate's official agent must submit a full statement of all campaign expenditures and a summary must be published in a local newspaper.[76] It is a universally accepted fact, however, that most of the official returns do not represent anything like the real election costs incurred by the candidate and the local parties.

While reference will be made later to the candidates' declared expenses, a more realistic impression of how much it costs to seek a seat in the Canadian House of Commons is gained by looking at what the candidate must do if he wishes to conduct a reasonably effective campaign. The activities mentioned in this chapter are, for the most part, extremely expensive. A large field force and a fleet of cars must be assembled; scrutineers must be hired and office space rented; newspapers, radio, and television are now essential means of campaigning; some items should be sent by mail; pamphlets are required and so on. All this costs money, particularly since some advertising media cunningly raise their rates for election purposes. It is rare for Liberal or Conservative organizations to rely exclusively on voluntary help. Most campaign committees hire large numbers of workers, at least for the work which must be done on election day. Here, too, the law is ignored, which forbids the hiring of conveyances for the purpose of taking electors to the polls and otherwise limits the number of persons a candidate may employ without disenfranchising them.[77] Rates of pay vary from region to region, but it is probably not misleading to assume that drivers with cars cost from $10 to $30 per day, where they must be paid or compensated for loss of their normal pay. Canvassers, scrutineers, and baby sitters are somewhat less expensive, costing about $6 to $8. But in some constituencies very large numbers of these may have to be hired.

A normal election campaign in a rural constituency probably costs the Liberals or the Conservatives from $7,500 to $12,500. It is difficult to conduct a satisfactory urban campaign for less than $15,000 and a reasonably conducted fight in a metropolitan constituency can hardly be attempted for much under $25,000. There are, of course, many constituencies where considerably more or less was spent by the two leading

[75]In chap. VIII below, some discussion will be found of the costs of national campaigns. See pp. 172–3.
[76]Canada Elections Act, section 63.
[77]Ibid., sections 15, 73, 74.

parties, but the figures presented here seem reasonable ones for typical campaigns in view of what the various candidates attempted in the 1957 election.

In discussing the official statements of expenditure, it must be borne in mind that they seriously misrepresent the amounts actually spent in most

TABLE V/1

Percentage of 478 Liberal and Conservative Constituency Organizations Incurring Specified Election Expenses During the 1957 Campaign in Canada and in Five Regions

Sum spent	Canada	Maritimes	Quebec	Ontario	Prairies	British Columbia*
$2,500 or less	20	32	11	17	36	10
$2,501–$5,000	30	28	30	33	31	23
$5,001–$7,500	23	28	23	23	14	31
$7,501–$10,000	13	11	13	13	12	13
$10,001–$12,500	6	2	7	7	1	13
$12,501–$15,000	4	–	7	5	3	4
$15,001 or more	4	–	10	1	2	6
Total	100	101	101	99	99	100
Number of cases	478	54	124	162	90	48

*Includes Yukon and Mackenzie River.
Figures do not always add to 100 because of rounding.

constituencies, but that the level of distortion is probably uniform throughout the country. In any event, there are startling disparities in the amounts the parties admitted to having spent. Considering only the returns of Liberals and Conservatives, it is found that the lowest figure is $385, representing the expenses of a Conservative in Saskatchewan.[78] A Quebec Liberal spent $58,000. Table V/1 shows that half the candidates filing returns spent five thousand dollars or less and that it was considerably cheaper to run in the Maritimes and in the Prairies than elsewhere.

[78]Letter from the Chief Electoral Officer to the Under-Secretary of State for Canada, dated November 26, 1957. This letter, which is mimeographed, contains the election expenses on behalf of each candidate and the names of those candidates on whose behalf no expense returns were submitted. The Under-Secretary of State executes the wish of the House of Commons to have these returns made available in this form. The Order of the House was moved by Mr. Stanley Knowles of the C.C.F. In referring to this document it will be assumed, for brevity's sake, that the returns were accurate. This permits the avoidance of such qualifying adjectives as "alleged," "declared," "admitted," which would otherwise have to precede every use of the words "expenses," "costs," etc.

About one-third of the constituency campaigns in these areas cost $2,500 or less, whereas in Quebec and British Columbia only one of every ten electoral battles was waged for so little. Quebec and British Columbia showed the highest number of expensive campaigns. In these provinces almost one quarter of the returns fell into the $10,000 or higher category, whereas in the Maritimes and the Prairies only 2 per cent and 6 per cent of the constituency parties seemed to have spent over $10,000. Ontario comes closest to the national average for each category of expenditure. This is surprising in view of the fact that the province seemed to provide good fighting ground for both parties and that consequently fairly expensive campaigns were probably waged in a number of constituencies. The admission by only one campaign organization to having spent over $15,000 suggests that those making out the returns in Ontario and particularly in Toronto showed a self-effacing modestly with which their province and city is not usually credited elsewhere in the country.

Statements about campaign expenditures of both the major parties were available for 217 constituencies. In 138 of these the Liberals spent more than the Conservatives who, for their part, outstripped the government party in 79 cases. Table V/2 shows how many seats the parties carried or lost in relation to their relative expenditures. No sweeping generalizations can be made on the basis of this table, even if it is assumed that the figures are accurate. It appears, however, that to spend more money is by no means a certain way of gaining more seats. The Liberals spent more than the Conservatives in 138 (64 per cent) constituencies for which figures for both parties are available. But they only won 37 per cent of the seats. The Conservatives won 43 per cent of the seats while spending more than the Liberals in 79 (36 per cent) constitu-

TABLE V/2

Seats Won and Lost by Liberals and Conservatives in Relation
to Their Relative Expenses

	Won by P.C.'s		Won by Liberals		Won by others		Total	
	n	%	n	%	n	%	n	%
79 Seats in which P.C.'s spent more than Liberals	42	53	25	32	12	15	79	100
138 Seats in which Liberals spent more than P.C.'s	51	37	55	40	32	23	138	100
Total	93	43	80	37	44	20	217	100

encies. In the 79 constituencies in which the Conservatives spent more than the Liberals, they carried 53 per cent of the seats compared with Liberal victories in 32 per cent of the seats. Of the 138 seats in which the Liberals spent more than the Conservatives, 40 per cent went Liberal against 37 per cent Conservative. Both parties, therefore, won a larger percentage of seats than their main rival in constituencies in which they spent more. But whereas the Conservatives won more than half the seats in ridings in which they campaigned more lavishly than the Liberals, the latter carried only 40 per cent of the constituencies in which they spent more than the Conservatives.

While money is an essential ingredient in a successful campaign, too much of it can also constitute a hazard. Conservatives in Winnipeg South Centre, for example, thought during the 1957 campaign that the Liberal campaign there was so massive as to affect some voters adversely. An obviously extremely costly and high-powered campaign featuring 60-man blitzes and similar spectacular activities was thought to have back-fired. At a time when many believed that the government was too power-ful and too well entrenched, the opulence of the Liberal campaign was viewed as another proof of the immense power of the government.[79] Obviously neither money nor any other single factor alone determines the outcome of a constituency battle. Each struggle consists of a complex, and for the candidate a hazardous, interplay of techniques, personalities and issues not all of which are susceptible to his control.

In this chapter an attempt has been made to give something of the flavour of the 1957 campaign in the constituencies. In the absence of adequate case studies of election campaigns in various ridings it has been impossible to paint a minute and searching canvas reminiscent of a Vermeer or of the Little Dutch Painters. Rather, the foregoing treatment is a montage. It is hoped that the elements which constitute it make a kaleidoscopic pattern which as a whole presents a true picture of the constituency campaigns.

[79]Ted Byfield in Winnipeg *Free Press*, June 1.

THE CANDIDATES

6

Nomination

IT IS NOW GENERALLY HELD that the characteristics and qualities of particular candidates have only a minor effect on the outcome of an election in any given constituency. In the long run, however, the picture the public has of a party is probably influenced by the sort of candidates it nominates to represent it in successive elections. The party image must, in some measure, reflect the party's personnel. It is, therefore, of interest to examine some of the personal attributes of the candidates and to look at their political experience. In 1957 did the characteristics of the Conservative politicians support the often-heard allegation that their party was more representative of high finance than the Liberal party and that generally it has been more concerned with the preservation of privilege? Did the Liberal candidates confirm the widespread belief that their party was more hospitable to non-Protestant and non-Anglo-Saxon members of Canadian society? Before these and similar questions are considered, however, it will be well to comment briefly on the way in which candidates were selected by the major parties in the 1957 election.

There are several ways in which this is done. In the absence of thorough studies of the various methods in use, only a general impression of the most common procedures can be given. No evidence is available indicating how often a particular form of selection was applied in the 1957 election or which, of the several methods followed, was employed most frequently. On the whole, it is the provincial executive of each party which has the final responsibility for seeing that each constituency party picks a suitable candidate. As a rule, the local party organization selects the person it desires to run and its choice is accepted by the provincial party. No case is known, in the 1957 election, of a provincial executive vetoing the candidature of a person selected by a recognized constituency organization.

The most common means of selecting candidates, used almost without fail in constituencies where there is an active local organization, is to hold a special nominating meeting at which the choosing of a candidate is the main business. In most instances the executive agrees beforehand on a candidate who then secures the nomination. Many cases are known, however, of executive-sponsored candidates being turned down by the constituency organization. Considerable manoeuvring and in-fighting, concealed from the public may, in any event, precede the decision of the executive. In the majority of cases, the executive's favourite will be one of a number of persons nominated. Most of them turn out to be individuals who have no intention of running. They may be serious and hard-working members of the association who are thus being shown the respect of the local party or they may be younger men, hoping some day to be chosen but who, for the time being, are merely interested in becoming known in the local organization. In any event, the so called "courtesy candidates" decline the honour of having their names placed before the meeting until only one or a very small number of names remains. If only one name is left then the candidate has been chosen by acclamation. Usually more than one name remains and a vote is taken. Invariably the person receiving the second-highest vote moves that the election be made unanimous.

There is considerable variation in the matter of who is entitled to attend the meeting and who may vote. In some cases delegates from wards or polling subdivisions are selected beforehand. Where delegates choose the candidate, only a fixed number of votes can be cast and in that case it is certain that only members of the party actually express their view as to who should represent it in the forthcoming election. Another type of nominating meeting makes it possible for neutral persons and even opponents to select, or influence the selection of, the candidate. This may happen when an open meeting is called to which anyone who is so inclined may go. In urban centres this type of meeting is common. Sometimes the advertisements announcing the meetings specify that only party supporters are invited, but there are other instances where everyone interested is asked to attend.[1] It is a measure either of the rectitude or of the apathy of Canadian voters that no in-

[1]An advertisement in the Winnipeg *Free Press*, of April 6, for example, included the following instance of western hospitality: "Open to all residents of the constituency; come out and vote."

stances were known in the 1957 election of nominations being unduly influenced by opposition votes. Open nominating meetings of course offer ample opportunity to ambitious candidates for packing the convention with their own supporters.

In safe constituencies, where to be chosen the candidate of the locally invincible party is tantamount to being elected, the procedure is usually much less haphazard. Carleton, in Ontario, for example, is a safe Conservative seat: it has an elaborate and rigid system of selecting the Conservative candidate. In 1957 Russell Boucher, a former local member who had resigned to enable Mr. Drew to enter the House after being chosen party leader, and R. A. Bell, a former director of the Conservative national office, sought the nomination. They were ultimately joined by Miss Charlotte Whitton who added considerable colour to the race but was never a serious contender. Carleton has an unusually large Conservative Association. Of its then 4700 members 1075 were eligible to vote as delegates at the nominating convention. This figure was arrived at by permitting each of the 215 polling subdivisions established at the previous election to have five representatives. Thirty days before the convention no new members were allowed to join the Association, lest an attempt should be made to influence unfairly the selection of the candidate. Members of the Association met in each of the areas served by the 215 polling stations twenty-four hours before the convention to agree on a candidate and to pledge their delegate to support him. The delegates were issued with identification cards entitling them to the ballot papers at the convention. In the end, 1074 out of the 1075 eligible delegates cast their ballots and selected Mr. Bell.[2]

Even when candidates are selected by delegate conventions they may first have to appear before the local party executive so as to give its members a chance to make up their minds whom to support. In Scarborough, for example, the Conservative aspirants had to address a dinner meeting attended by the members of the executives of the Conservative associations in the constituency.[3]

Selection committees sometimes appoint candidates without bothering to have their choice confirmed by a meeting of the constituency party. This practice was widespread in Quebec, particularly among Conserva-

[2]Despite the carefully arranged procedure, Miss Whitton was dissatisfied with the method of selecting the candidate. She objected to the delegates being based on the 1953 polling station areas and claimed that she knew that she was bucking "a closed convention and, I am told, an absolutely water tight machine." Ottawa *Citizen*, April 17. See also the Toronto *Daily Star*, April 18, the Ottawa *Journal*, April 20, and the C.P. dispatch from Ottawa dated April 25 for full accounts of the Carleton Conservative nomination procedures.

[3]Fox, "A Study of One Constituency," p. 233.

tives in constituencies where their organization had ceased being very active. But it was employed even in some of the predominantly English-speaking constituencies in Montreal, where the Conservative organization was usually more efficient than elsewhere in the province.[4] Occasionally a clique within the party, controlling the executive, selects a candidate by calling a meeting to which only a small, carefully chosen group of members is invited. This practice is also confined to constituencies where the local organization has degenerated and where lists of members are small and probably out of date.

Provincial party executives sometimes try to influence the choice made by a local organization. These attempts are usually resented by the constituency associations and may, consequently, meet with failure. The Conservatives in Essex East in Ontario turned down the person named by the Ontario party's executive, despite the fact that he had already been announced as the Conservative candidate.[5] A more unsettling episode occurred at the nominating meeting of the Conservative party in Toronto Trinity. Provincial headquarters had arranged with a mining executive that he would receive the nomination unopposed. A token candidate was accordingly nominated and also a young man who did not really intend to contest the seat. The person selected to nominate the mining executive changed his mind between the time when he agreed to place the provincial party's nominee before the meeting and the moment when he was to make the nomination: he failed to nominate the agreed-upon candidate. The token candidate followed the pre-arranged plan and withdrew from the race. Someone moved that nominations close and the young sales clerk who had never seriously thought of running found himself chosen by acclamation. "Somewhere along the line," the mining executive was quoted as having said, "somebody goofed."[6]

A constituency organization whose candidate won the previous election sometimes finds itself in a difficult position. This happens when opposition develops against the sitting member. In safe seats, where to be nominated by the dominant party practically amounts to being elected to the House of Commons, a tense situation may arise as the result of ambitious men wishing to replace members who have held the seat for a long time. The Liberal party which, at the time of the dissolution, held more than three times as many seats as the Conservatives, was confronted by a serious problem in this regard. In Quebec, where this vexing situation became particularly acute[7] the provincial federal organi-

[4]Montreal *Star*, March 12.
[6]Toronto *Telegram*, February 16.
[5]Windsor *Daily Star*, April 27.
[7]See below chap. VIII, pp. 176–7.

zation decided to renominate all sitting members wishing to run.[8] This was resented in a number of constituencies. One of the reasons for the large number of Independent Liberals running against official candidates in Quebec was, in fact, the discontent among some local associations with their former Members of Parliament. In Richmond-Wolfe, for example, an Independent Liberal was chosen by the local party because the sitting member had not presented himself for renomination by the constituency party. The outgoing member in Drummond-Arthabaska refused to abide by the decision of the Liberal Association that he should step down. The candidate supported by the local party organization therefore ran as an Independent Liberal.[9] He won. In some constituencies, Hull for example, this situation led to there being more than one Liberal Association.[10]

Dissatisfaction with the previous representatives in Ottawa was not confined to Quebec, however, or to the Liberal party. In three Manitoba constituencies Liberal candidates were troubled by the presence of former Liberal M.P.'s who had failed to be renominated.[11] And the Conservative whip, George J. Tustin, failed to be renominated in Prince Edward-Lennox, in Ontario, after representing the constituency for twenty-two years.[12]

On the whole the Liberals nominated their candidates somewhat earlier than did their chief opponents. On May 1 it was reported that they had selected 223 of their standard-bearers to the Conservatives' 186. One month before polling day—on May 10—their number had risen to 262 whereas Mr. Diefenbaker's supporters were still forty-four short of the maximum of 265. By May 16 the slate of government candidates was complete; the Conservatives, who did not contest every constituency, picked their last candidate just before the deadline on May 27.[13]

[8]Interview by Pierre Laporte with Jaques Vadboncoeur, chief Liberal organizer for forty-eight constituencies in the Montreal area, reported in *Le Devoir*, April 16.

[9]Fred Manor, "Liberal Party's Young Turks."

[10]*Le Devoir*, April 13.

[11]In two of these constituencies—Dauphin and St. Boniface—the former members were running as Independent Liberals and in the third—Springfield—the antics of the ex-M.P. became a public comedy and scandal ending in the courts. For an informative and hilarious report of the situation in Springfield see Ted Byfield's account in the Winnipeg *Free Press*, May 10. Liberal problems in the other two ridings are discussed fully by Michael Best in the Winnipeg *Free Press*, May 11.

[12]"PC's in Lennox Split by Nomination Battle," Toronto *Globe and Mail*, June 3.

[13]All figures based on C.P. dispatches as reported in the Ottawa *Journal* from April 30 to May 28.

A candidate is, of course, not officially nominated until he has filed the nominating papers and the deposit with the returning officer at any time between the date of the Proclamation and the close of nominations.[14] In twenty-one constituencies where, because of communication difficulties, extra time is needed for the delivery of ballots and other supplies, the official nominations closed on May 13. Two weeks later, on May 27, the remainder of the candidates had completed filing their nomination papers. Altogether, 862 persons contested the election.[15] The number nominated by each party is shown in Table VI/1.

TABLE VI/1

Number of Candidates Nominated by the Parties in 1957

Liberal	265[16]
Progressive Conservatives	257[17]
C.C.F.	162
Social Credit	114
L.P.P.	10
Others (Independents etc.)	54
Total	862

Personal Attributes

As indicated in the preface, this study of the 1957 general election centres on the performance of the main parties. In what follows, therefore, the attributes of the Liberal and Conservative candidates only are considered. The personal characteristics of the C.C.F. and Social Credit candidates are described in another chapter.[18] Since in some respects

[14]*Canada Elections Act*, 2 (23).

[15]Originally, 867 were nominated, but one Conservative (Kamouraska), two Independent Liberals (Matapedia-Matane and York South), a Social Credit candidate (Davenport), and a candidate calling himself a Free (Franc) Liberal (Three Rivers) withdrew before polling day. Henry A. Hosking, the former member for Wellington South, who was again contesting the riding for the Liberals, died one week before the election. Polling in the constituency was postponed until July 15 by which time another candidate had been chosen by the Liberal party. Since the balloting in Wellington South was part of the 1957 general election its results and candidates are considered here with those from the other constituencies.

[16]Includes W. M. Benidickson (Kenora-Rainy River) who called himself Liberal Labour but who had been a Parliamentary Assistant in Liberal governments since January 24, 1950.

[17]Includes H. Courtemanche (Labelle) who called himself an Independent Progressive Conservative, but was elected as a Progressive Conservative in 1949 and after the 1957 election again dropped the Independent label. He became Deputy Speaker on October 14, 1957.

[18]See below, chap. x, pp. 219, 230.

the candidates' characteristics vary more from region to region than from party to party (particularly, of course, in so far as the two major parties are concerned) the regional distribution of the candidates is of some interest: the Liberals nominated a candidate in every constituency, the Conservatives were short one in the Maritimes, six in Quebec, and one in the prairie provinces.

It is natural to assume that the occupation of a candidate will have influenced his general outlook and his political perspective.[19] In comparing the candidates, their geographical distribution may be of some interest and also the question of whether the characteristics described were related to their success or failure in the election. Table VI/2 shows the occupations of the Liberal and Conservative candidates in relation to the regions in which they contested the election and Table VI/3 whether the candidates pursuing the various vocations were elected or defeated. Although in analysing the available information about the candidates all their known characteristics were broken down in these two ways, hereafter in this chapter the geographical distribution will be presented only when it seems to have been of some importance.

The regional breakdown of occupations seems to be of only minor interest. It reveals that an unusually heavy concentration of educationalists was to be found in the Maritimes, that Quebec constituencies were over-represented by lawyers—forty-seven (33 per cent) out of

[19]Information about the candidates was derived from a number of sources, none of them entirely satisfactory. Occupation was taken from the Chief Electoral Officer's Report, but even here it became apparent that much of the information was misleading. Was it reasonable to classify Mr. C. D. Howe as an engineer or Michael Starr as a clerk? And what to make of a practising lawyer who also bred shorthorns? While the information given in the Chief Electoral Officer's Report was used as a base for classifying the occupations of the candidates (and was in most cases not altered) additional evidence was derived from a number of other sources. These included (a) the Parliamentary Guide, particularly for 1957 and 1958, although earlier volumes were occasionally consulted, (b) information provided by the national headquarters of both parties, (c) newspaper reports of nominations and electoral battles, (d) The Canadian Who's Who and Who's Who in Canada. These sources of information, while useful, were often spotty and probably not always comparable or entirely reliable. In some cases the desired information could not be obtained. Wherever necessary, the number of candidates for whom information was not available is indicated in the accompanying tables. Information about every candidate was available only in relation to our first attribute: occupation. In each case where a candidate had had more than one occupation, that occupation was assigned to him which was held to have had the greatest influence on his political outlook. For an excellent discussion of some of the difficulties associated with assigning occupations to Parliamentray candidates see McCallum and Readman, The British General Election of 1945, pp. 77–80, and p. 272. See also Nicholas, British General Election of 1950, pp. 47–50; Butler, The British General Election of 1951, p. 40, and idem, The British General Election of 1955, p. 42.

141 in Canada—and inadequately represented by farmers—three (5 per cent) out of fifty-eight—and that only in the Prairies did this latter occupation contribute a sizeable proportion of the Liberal and Conservative candidates: twenty-seven (28 per cent) of the ninety-five nominees of the old parties in Alberta, Saskatchewan, and Manitoba were farmers. Table VI/3 sheds additional light on the farmer candidates. Of the twenty-eight Liberals claiming agriculture as their occupation, only three succeeded in getting elected. This heavy casualty rate among farmers suggests that discontent with the Liberal government was particularly intense in the Prairies and in rural Ontario—the areas which contributed an overwhelming proportion of Liberal farm candidates.

The table distinguishing between successful and unsuccessful candidates reveals that with the exception of politicians (who are here treated as being *sui generis*), it was the professional groups which suffered the lowest proportion of defeats.[20] Ninety-one (45 per cent) out of 201 candidates classified in the professional category won their contests. This compares favourably with business groups, only sixty-five (38 per cent) of whose 170 members succeeded in getting elected and even more so with farmers, only 29 per cent of whom won. The latter fact is to be accounted for in large part by the success of the C.C.F. and Social Credit candidates in the predominantly agricultural prairie provinces. Within the professional group the lawyers did a little better than the rest, 65 (46 per cent) out of 141 having gained victories. On the whole, it seems that candidates in some occupational categories had a better chance of being elected than those in others.

No relation has ever been found to exist between the occupational composition of the Canadian House of Commons and the distribution of the major occupations in the country.[21] Indeed, few would agree that such a correlation is desirable. The same lack of occupational representation is to be observed among the candidates. Some occupations were grossly over-represented and others, pursued by large numbers of Canadians, could hardly be found among the candidates. In the latter category, manual workers and clerical and white-collar workers are the most obviously under-represented group, with only five and ten representatives

[20]Generalizations of this sort are made here only about occupations represented by more than thirty members.

[21]Recent studies are L. H. Laing, "The Nature of Canada's Parliamentary Representation," *Canadian Journal of Economics and Political Science*, vol. XII, no. 4 (Nov., 1946), pp. 509–16; Norman Ward, *The Canadian House of Commons: Representation* (Toronto, 1951); and J. R. Williams, "Representation in the House of Commons of the Twenty-first Parliament: Party and Province," *Canadian Journal of Economics and Political Science*, vol. XVIII, no. 1 (Feb., 1952), pp. 77–87.

TABLE VI/2

Occupations of Liberal and Conservative Candidates by Region

Occupation	B.C.		Prairies		Ontario		Quebec		Maritimes		Canada		
	L.	P.C.	L.	P.C.	L.	P.C.	L.	P.C.	L.	P.C.	L.	P.C.	Total
Professions													
Law	6	7	11	11	24	19	27	20	7	9	75	66	141
Medicine and Dentistry	1	—	4	2	4	5	3	1	2	2	14	10	24
Engineering	—	2	1	—	—	—	2	—	—	—	3	2	5
Education	2	—	—	6	1	1	—	3	5	3	8	13	21
Miscelleous	—	—	2	2	1	1	3	—	1	—	7	3	10
Total	9	9	18	21	30	26	35	24	15	14	107	94	201
Business													
Retail	1	1	2	2	9	6	6	5	2	4	20	18	38
Insurance and Real Estate	1	3	2	1	4	6	8	9	—	1	15	20	35
Other Business Owner	3	3	3	3	12	10	10	8	3	3	31	27	58
Other Business Executive	2	1	2	1	1	3	2	7	—	—	7	12	19
Company Director	—	1	—	—	—	—	1	—	1	—	2	1	3
Accounting	—	—	—	—	3	4	2	3	—	—	5	7	12
Miscellaneous	—	—	—	—	—	1	1	1	—	2	1	4	5
Total	7	9	9	7	29	30	30	33	6	10	81	89	170
Agriculture	—	1	14	13	11	12	—	3	3	1	28	30	58
Other													
Politics	2	3	3	2	5	6	4	1	3	1	17	13	30
Clerical and white collar	1	—	1	2	3	1	1	1	—	—	6	4	10
Workers	1	1	—	—	—	—	—	2	—	1	1	4	5
Retired	2	1	1	1	4	4	1	1	2	1	10	8	18
Publishers, Journalists	1	—	1	—	3	2	1	—	2	2	8	4	12
Radio and T.V.	1	—	1	—	—	—	—	1	—	2	2	3	5
Miscellaneous	—	—	—	1	—	4	3	3	2	—	5	8	13
Total	8	5	7	6	15	17	10	9	9	7	49	44	93
Grand Total	24	24	48	47	85	85	75	69	33	32	265	257	522

Table VI/3

Occupations of Elected and Defeated Liberal and Conservative Candidates

Occupation	Liberal			Conservative			Total		
	Elected	Defeated	Total	Elected	Defeated	Total	Elected	Defeated	Total
Professions									
Law	35	40	75	30	36	66	65	76	141
Medicine and Dentistry	4	10	14	6	4	10	10	14	24
Engineering	2	1	3	1	1	2	3	2	5
Education	4	4	8	5	8	13	9	12	21
Miscellaneous	3	4	7	1	2	3	4	6	10
Total	48	59	107	43	51	94	91	110	201
Business									
Retail	10	10	20	7	11	18	17	21	38
Insurance and Real Estate	6	9	15	3	17	20	9	26	35
Other Business Owner	13	18	31	14	13	27	27	31	58
Other Business Executive	4	3	7	4	8	12	8	11	19
Company Director	1	1	2	–	1	1	1	2	3
Accounting	1	4	5	2	5	7	3	9	12
Miscellaneous	–	1	1	–	4	4	–	5	5
Total	35	46	81	30	59	89	65	105	170
Agriculture	3	25	28	14	16	30	17	41	58
Other									
Politics	7	10	17	13	–	13	20	10	30
Clerical and white collar	2	4	6	1	3	4	3	7	10
Workers	1	–	1	1	3	4	2	3	5
Retired	3	7	10	4	4	8	7	11	18
Publishers, Journalists	2	6	8	3	1	4	5	7	12
Radio and T.V.	–	2	2	2	1	3	2	3	5
Miscellaneous	4	1	5	1	7	8	5	8	13
Total	19	30	49	25	19	44	44	49	93
Grand Total	105	160	265	112	145	257	217	305	522

respectively among the Parliamentary candidates of the major parties. The professions, on the other hand, were responsible for providing 201 (39 per cent) of the 522 Liberal and Conservative candidates. Lawyers alone furnished 141 (27 per cent) of the Liberals and Conservatives seeking a seat in the House. Business and finance accounted for 170 (33 per cent) of the total, whereas agriculture, like the manual and office workers, was under-represented. According to the 1951 census, agriculture contributed about 15 per cent of the labour force,[22] whereas only about 11 per cent of the candidates could be classified under farming.

Some of these figures are misleading, however, and require modification. To prepare Tables VI/2 and VI/3 one dominant occupation was assigned to each candidate, even though he might have fitted into two or more categories. Both Mr. St. Laurent and Mr. Diefenbaker, for example, were listed as politicians although they might equally have been classified as lawyers. What was one to do with Mr. Lionel Chevrier who, calling himself a lawyer, had been in the Liberal cabinet from 1945 to 1954 when he resigned to become President of the St. Lawrence Seaway Authority, a post he also resigned to contest the 1957 election?[23] Some farmers, tabulated as such, while still running their farms, were subdividing portions of them and acting part of the time as businessmen, builders, and contractors. Other farmers also operated dairies and were, therefore, in a sense merchants. It was consequently thought desirable to tabulate the material dealing with Liberal and Conservative candidates in such a way as to show how the various occupations were represented among them. In this tabulation ninety-three candidates were counted twice. All those originally listed as politicians, those giving their occupation as "retired," a sizeable group formerly classified as businessmen, some lawyers, and some farmers made up the additional occupations.

With 235 representatives among 522 candidates the professional group appears even more over-represented than before. The professions, as is shown in the final column of Table VI/4 contributed no less than 45 per cent of all the Liberals and Conservatives running in the election. And of the professional group, lawyers constitute 166, thereby accounting for almost 32 per cent of the total number of candidates representing the old parties. The percentage of men with business interests now also has increased to almost 38. Farmers no longer appear to be under-represented, constituting over 17 per cent of the candidates, although their number—ninety-two—admittedly includes some gentleman farmers and some who, at the time of the 1957 election no longer engaged in agriculture.

[22]*Census of Canada 1951*, vol. IV, Table 4.
[23]He was put in the miscellaneous category.

TABLE VI/4

Main Occupational Groups of Elected and Defeated Liberal and Conservative Candidates

Occupational group	Liberal			Conservative			Total			Percentage of total no. of candidates (522)
	Elected	Defeated	Total	Elected	Defeated	Total	Elected	Defeated	Total	
Professions	56	69	125	56	54	110	112	123	235	45.0
Law	42	45	87	40	39	79	82	84	166	31.8
Business	41	53	94	40	61	101	81	114	195	37.4
Agriculture	8	34	42	26	24	50	34	58	92	17.6
Education	7	14	21	14	11	25	21	25	46	8.8

As suggested above, some areas of Canada exhibit distinct preferences for certain occupations among their candidates. This is not surprising in view of the fact that some regions are vitally interested in, and dependent upon, certain kinds of economic activity. Table VI/5 shows that the prairie region, in which only 18.2 per cent of the majority party candidates were nominated, provided 42.4 per cent of all the candidates having some farm experience. Ontario, with its eighty-five seats (32.6 per cent of Liberal and Conservative candidates) nominated 41.3 per cent of all old party nominees with agricultural experience. Therefore almost 84 per cent of candidates experienced in agriculture ran in the Prairies and in Ontario. The table also shows that the two central provinces, Ontario and Quebec, strongly favoured candidates with business experience: 60.2 per cent of all the candidates were nominated in the central provinces, but 72.3 per cent of those with a business background contested seats in Ontario and Quebec. Quebec also contributed a large proportion of lawyers. Only 27.6 per cent of all candidates ran in the province, but 34.3 per cent of Liberal and Conservative nominees with a legal background came from there. The previously noted low percentage of Quebec candidates with agricultural experience is again evident and constitutes a dramatic feature of Table VI/5.

TABLE VI/5

Percentage of Main Occupational Groups among Candidates of
Both Parties by Regions

Occupational group	B.C.	Prairies	Ontario	Quebec	Maritimes	Total	n
Professions	9.8	18.3	28.1	29.8	14.0	100.0	235
Law	10.2	15.1	29.5	34.3	10.8	99.9	166
Business	8.7	9.7	36.9	35.4	9.2	99.9	195
Agriculture	2.2	42.4	41.3	6.5	7.6	100.0	92
Education	8.7	32.6	15.2	15.2	28.3	100.0	46
Percentage of all candidates	9.2	18.2	32.6	27.6	12.5	100.1	

Forty-six candidates had at some time in their lives been engaged in full-time educational work, thirteen of them at the university level. Curiously, 61 per cent of the former educators ran in the Prairies and the Maritimes—two regions which between them accounted for only 31 per cent of Liberal and Conservative candidates. Tables VI/4 and VI/5 show how the some-time educators were distributed, and how they fared in the election. Like the ninety-two agriculturalists, the forty-six candidates with a pedagogic background were not necessarily engaged in education immediately before the 1957 election. Some may have taught only briefly.

It is not by accident that so far nothing has been said about the differences betwen the parties in relation to the occupational backgrounds of their candidates. The reason for this lacuna is primarily that very little can be said about them, except that they are small. Table VI/4 shows that there was a somewhat larger number of professional people among the Liberals than among the Conservatives—125 as compared with 110. The government party also included a slightly larger contingent of lawyers—eighty-seven to the Conservatives' seventy-nine. These differences are so small as to preclude their becoming the basis of any confident generalizations about the differences between the parties. Similarly, the degree to which farmers (50 to 42) and businessmen (101 to 94) were represented more fully among the Conservatives than among the Liberals is negligible.

Only in one province and in one occupational group does the difference between the parties appear worthy of special note. Of those classified as professional in Quebec, 60 per cent were Liberals, and only 40 per cent Conservatives. A similar pattern existed in Ontario, but there the bias of the government party in favour of the professional group was less marked. Quebec Conservatives were probably able to attract fewer professional people than the Liberals because of the seemingly hopeless position of their party in French Canada. In 1957 the Conservatives, whose organization in many Quebec constituencies was almost non-existent, did not always find it easy to nominate strong candidates; many of Mr. Diefenbaker's supporters in Quebec were fully aware that their chances of winning were very small indeed. It is possible, although further study is certainly required to confirm this, that under such circumstances it is easier to attract members of occupations other than the professions. The careers of some professional people—lawyers for example—may be influenced more than are those of other occupations by the degree to which their practitioners are deemed generally successful by their community.

But even the differences in Quebec and in Ontario between the number of professional people chosen by the parties are not substantial enough to call for more than a passing reference. Only if the same or larger margins were to recur in successive elections would it be justifiable to conclude that one of the older parties is definitely more hospitable to certain occupations than the other. Since this is the first attempt to analyse the characteristics of all the candidates nominated by the parties, no such conclusions can be made. Such slender evidence as is provided by the present breakdowns confirms the findings of Professor Ward about the representation in the House of Commons: on the whole, in so far as the two major parties are concerned, differences among the occupational backgrounds of Canadian federal politicians are more noticeable on the basis of region than on that of party.[24]

Even the slight occupational differences between Liberal and Conservative candidates deserve to be noted, however, for they may assume great importance when they are compared with the vocational characteristics of candidates in future elections. Of the 265 Liberals contesting the 1957 election 47.2[25] per cent had been engaged in professional occupations and 35.4 per cent in business. The comparable figures for the 257 Conservative candidates were 42.8 per cent and 39.4 per cent. There was, therfore, a small but unmistakable bias among the Liberals towards the professions and among the Conservatives towards business.

An irresistible although no doubt puckish comparison is suggested by one of the more interesting features of the 1957 campaign. It was generally thought that Conservatives were more flamboyant and aware of public relations in their tactics than were the Liberals. Was this difference reflected in a larger representation, among Conservative candidates, of men experienced in the public relations industry or in the occupations demanding well-developed powers of persuasion? Table VI/2 tells us that seventeen candidates were engaged in newspaper or broadcasting work. Of these, ten were Liberals and seven Conservatives. When all the candidates who can be said to have been engaged in verbal persuasion as a means of livelihood are considered, similar results prevail. Excluding all businessmen, among whom there were no doubt some persuasive salesmen, thirty-three candidates were thought to fall into the category of "persuaders."[26] Of these, twenty were Liberals and thirteen Conservatives. If the main opposition party really did exhibit a greater flair for good public relations, the cause must, therefore, be sought elsewhere than in the occupations of the Conservative candidates.

The candidates' educational qualifications are shown in Table VI/6 as falling into three broad categories: primary, secondary and university.[27] The Liberals are revealed as the party with a noticeably larger proportion of candidates having had a higher education. The difference

[24]*The Canadian House of Commons,* p. 135.

[25]The figures are based on the "consolidated" Table VI/4: some candidates are counted more than once.

[26]Journalists, broadcasters, publicists, auctioneers, paid party officials and one clergyman were included in this group. Educators were excluded.

[27]For a more detailed breakdown see Table VI/7.

TABLE VI/6

Numerical and Percentage Distribution of Liberal and Conservative
Candidates by Formal Educational Attainment

Education	Numbers			Per Cent		
	L.	P.C.	Total	L.	P.C.	Total
Primary*	13	17	30	5.7	7.3	6.5
Secondary†	44	74	118	19.4	31.9	25.7
University‡	170	141	311	74.9	60.8	67.8
Total	227	232	459	100.0	100.0	100.0
No information	38	25	63			

*Includes candidates who have had only a primary education as well as some additional training but none in a secondary school.
†Includes candidates who completed or had some secondary education as well as those who had additional training, but not at the university level.
‡Includes those who attended university or its equivalent: a law school or in French Canada a classical college.

between the parties is large enough to offset any possible bias introduced by the absence of information about some candidates. To the previously observed fact that in 1957 the Liberals nominated a slightly larger proportion of professional people than the Conservatives, it must, then, be added that they also had a larger number of candidates with higher education. The two differences between the parties are, no doubt, related.

The very large percentage of candidates with university education or its equivalent suggests either that constituency parties prefer to nominate formally well-educated persons or that Canadians with university training offer themselves more frequently for nomination than do individuals with secondary or other schooling. The large percentage of lawyers engaged in politics obviously swells considerably the numbers of university men nominated by both parties. Table VI/7 shows that, on the whole, among candidates with relatively little formal education the percentage elected was lower than among those with longer years of schooling.

Candidates from the Maritimes contained the highest percentage of university-trained individuals: 69.4 per cent of them had either attended a university or its equivalent. The Prairies, which had the second largest percentage (64.2) were followed by Quebec with 61.7 per cent. In Ontario, only 53.0 per cent of the candidates nominated were classified in the highest educational category. The Prairies, which, as was noted

TABLE VI/7

Formal Educational Attainment of Elected and Defeated Liberal and Conservative Candidates

Education	Liberal			Conservative			Total		
	Elected	Defeated	Total	Elected	Defeated	Total	Elected	Defeated	Total
Primary school only	4	5	9	2	10	12	6	15	21
Primary school +	–	4	4	3	2	5	3	6	9
Secondary school only	11	19	30	23	27	50	34	46	80
Secondary school +	2	12	14	14	10	24	16	22	38
University*	68	87	155	59	66	125	127	153	280
Law without university†	4	5	9	9	5	14	13	10	23
Classical college	5	1	6	–	2	2	5	3	8
No information‡	11	27	38	2	23	25	13	50	63

*Includes at least fifteen who attended university but did not complete their course.

†Includes all lawyers about whose education nothing was known. Some of these undoubtedly had attended university.

‡This group no doubt includes a number of candidates with only a few years of schooling. While nothing whatsoever was known about the educational attainment of some candidates, others were reported as having been educated in their birthplace. The latter group was classified under the "no information" rubric, although in all probability those so described (and coming from a village) attended only a primary school.

above, had the second highest percentage of university people among its candidates, surprisingly had the highest percentage in the lowest educational category. Of candidates running in Alberta, Saskatchewan and Manitoba, 7.4 per cent were classified under the primary rubric, Ontario followed with 6.5 per cent, and Quebec with 4.9 per cent. The numbers in this category are so small as to deprive them of any comparative significance. The predominance in the Maritimes of candidates with higher education assumes particular interest when it is recalled that in relation to the number of its candidates, this region had nominated an unusually large percentage of individuals who had at one time in their lives been engaged in educational work. It is tempting to conclude from these facts that the Maritimes like to be represented by a more intellectual type of Parliamentarian than the other regions, but such inference would have to be supported by considerably more evidence than is now available before it could be accepted as anything more than an intriguing speculation.

TABLE VI/8

Age of Elected and Defeated Liberal and Conservative Candidates

Age	Liberal			Conservative			Total		
	Elected	De-feated	Total	Elected	De-feated	Total	Elected	De-feated	Total
20's	–	5	5	4	7	11	4	12	16
30's	14	21	35	28	29	57	42	50	92
40's	31	41	72	28	30	58	59	71	130
50's	33	38	71	29	32	61	62	70	132
60's	18	24	42	21	19	40	39	43	82
70's	8	4	12	2	1	3	10	5	15
80's	1	1	2	–	–	–	1	1	2
No information	–	26	26	–	27	27	–	53	53
Total	105	160	265	112	145	257	217	305	522

Such information as was available about the candidates' ages indicates that the Conservatives fielded a younger group than their main opponents. Fifty-three of the candidates had to be placed on the "No information" line in Table VI/8, all of them in the defeated columns. The table might lead the unwary to conclude that the older a candidate the better his chances of election. For if the percentage of the elected candidates is calculated in each age group, results obtain as shown in Table VI/9. It looks, therefore, as if the younger candidates had heavy odds against them and as if those in their seventies had the best prospects of being sent to the House of Commons. It is likely, however, that the figures merely indicate that young persons are willing to gain publicity, experience, and the gratitude of their party by consenting to stand in hopeless constituencies and that sitting members, particularly in safe seats, are renominated and returned to the House even after they have reached old age. Of the forty-three Conservative candidates who were known to have been sixty years of age or over, for example, twenty-two ran in Ontario—the party's strongest province; five of the twenty-two, it must be admitted, failed to win.

TABLE VI/9

Percentage of Candidates Elected in Specified
Age Groups

Age	Per Cent Elected
20's	25.0
30's	45.6
40's	45.4
50's	47.0
60's	48.2
70's	66.7
80's	50.0

No marked regional differences were detected in relation to the ages of the candidates. Only two features of note appear in the relevant table (not reproduced here): (1) The fifty-three candidates about whose age no information was available were not distributed normally among the total population. Seventeen (74 per cent) of the twenty-seven Conservative "unknowns" were running in Quebec; fifteen (58 per cent) of the twenty-six similarly "obscure" Liberals contested British Columbia and Prairie seats. (2) By far the most pronounced difference between the parties—in so far as age was concerned—occurred in the Maritimes. In this region nineteen (66 per cent) of the Liberals about whose age anything was known were fifty years old or more, whereas only seven (25 per cent) of the Conservatives were in this age group.[28] The difference looks even more startling when one examines the number of Maritime candidates in the youngest age groups. Only 10 per cent of the Liberals as compared with 61 per cent of the Conservatives were in their twenties and thirties.

[28]The ages of four of the thirty-three Liberals nominated in this region were unknown and also those of four of the thirty-two Conservatives.

TABLE VI/10

Numerical and Percentage Distribution of Liberal and
Conservative Candidates by Age.

Age	Numbers			Percentage		
	Lib.	P.C.	Total	Lib.	P.C.	Total
20's	5	11	16	2.1	4.8	3.4
30's	35	57	92	14.6	24.8	19.6
Young (20's & 30's)	40	68	108	16.7	29.6	23.0
40's	72	58	130	30.1	25.2	27.7
50's	71	61	132	29.7	26.5	28.1
Middle-aged (40's & 50's)	143	119	262	59.8	51.7	55.9
60's	42	40	82	17.6	17.4	17.5
70's	12	3	15	5.0	1.3	3.2
80's	2	—	2	.8	—	.4
Old (60's–80's)	56	43	99	23.4	18.7	21.1
Total	239	230	469	99.9	100.0	100.0
No information	26	27	53			

A similar, although by no means equally pronounced, bias among the Conservatives towards younger candidates can be observed in the figures for Canada as a whole. Table VI/10 indicates the extent to which the government party had nominated a larger proportion of older candidates than their main opponents. It is at least plausible to ascribe this difference to the very much greater number of sitting Liberals than Conservatives, to the long years in office of the Liberal party, to the seeming certainty of another Liberal victory, and to the revival of interest in the Conservative party among a growing number of younger Canadians.

Before the religious denominations of the candidates are examined some indication must be given about the geographical distribution of the 103 (19.7 per cent) candidates whose religion was unknown. To the extent that adherents to certain religions are particularly numerous in some parts of Canada, the geographical distribution of the candidates whose religion is unknown may introduce an important bias into the figures. If, for example, most of the Conservatives about whose religion no information was available had come from Quebec, this would inevitably have reduced the number of Roman Catholic Conservative candidates in the accompanying tables. The distribution of candidates whose religious affiliation was unknown is shown in Table VI/11. These figures

TABLE VI/11

Geographic Distribution of Candidates whose Religious Affiliation is Unknown

	B.C.	Prairies	Ontario	Quebec	Maritimes	Canada
Liberal	10	19	10	2	4	45
Conservative	15	14	13	7	9	58

suggest that the bias caused by the relatively large number of "unknown" candidates was probably not responsible for distorting the proportion of adherents of each of the major religious denominations given in our tables.

At first glance, one of the most startling features of Table VI/12 is its revelation of the degree to which Catholic candidates fared better in the election when they fought under the Liberal rather than the Conservative banner. The explanation is, actually, simple: the Liberal party did very much better in Quebec and in other French-speaking areas and consequently a large proportion of its successful candidates was French-Canadian and Roman Catholic. The Conservatives, in these areas, were also largely Catholics and are shown in the table as having been defeated. It is not so easy to explain the reverse odds which favoured the Conservative adherents of the United Church and seemingly not their Liberal co-religionists. A study of the relation, in the 1953 Canadian election,

TABLE VI/12

Religious Affiliation of Elected and Defeated
Liberal and Conservative Candidates

Religion	Liberal			Conservative			Total		
	Elected	De-feated	Total	Elected	De-feated	Total	Elected	De-feated	Total
Roman Catholic	74	32	106	20	55	75	94	87	181
United Church	14	35	49	39	11	50	53	46	99
Anglican	7	16	23	22	9	31	29	25	54
Presbyterian	4	16	20	12	1	13	16	17	33
Protestant*	3	16	19	12	15	27	15	31	46
Other†	1	2	3	2	1	3	3	3	6
No information	2	43	45	5	53	58	7	96	103
Total	105	160	265	112	145	257	217	305	522

*Includes candidates belonging to Protestant Churches not previously mentioned and also those about whom it was known that they were Protestants but whose specific affiliation was unknown.

†Includes, among others, Jews, Greek Orthodox and Greek Catholic adherents.

between religious affiliation and voting suggests that in one constituency, at any rate, United Church voters favoured the Conservative party,[29] but it is not certain that the findings of this study would have applied to other constituencies and whether what was true in the 1953 election still prevailed in 1957. In any case, the fact that adherents of a particular religious faith prefer to vote for a given party does not necessarily mean that they will also vote more readily for candidates of their own denomination. The greater chance of election enjoyed by Protestant Conservatives as compared with Protestant Liberals must be ascribed in large part to the afore-mentioned fact that the Liberals maintained their strength in French Canada but lost a good deal of support in most other parts of the country.

TABLE VI/13

Numerical and Percentage Distribution of Liberal and
Conservative Candidates by Religion

	Numbers			Percentage			
Religion	Lib.	P.C.	Total	Lib.	P.C.	Total	Canada*
Roman Catholic	106	75	181	48.2	37.7	43.2	43.3
United Church	49	50	99	22.3	25.1	23.6	20.5
Anglican	23	31	54	10.4	15.6	12.9	14.7
Presbyterian	20	13	33	9.1	6.5	7.9	5.6
Protestant†	19	27	46	8.6	13.6	11.0	9.8
Other†	3	3	6	1.4	1.5	1.4	6.1
Total	220	199	419	100.0	100.0	100.0	100.0
No information	45	58	103				

*Based on 1951 census of Canada. Adapted from table in Dominion Bureau of Statistics, *Canada Year Book, 1956*, p. 165.
†For definition of this term see Table VI/12 above.

Table VI/13 shows the percentage of candidates contributed by the major religious denominations to each party and also the relative size of the religious denominations expressed as percentages of the total Canadian population. The information suggests that at least in so far as the major religious groups were concerned, the candidates nominated by both parties combined represented fairly accurately the Canadian population as a whole. The proportion of Protestants to Catholics among the candidates was almost identical to that prevailing among the Cana-

29See J. Meisel, "Religious Affiliation and Electoral Behaviour: A Case Study," *Canadian Journal of Economics and Political Science*, vol. XXII, no. 4 (Nov., 1956), pp. 481–96.

dian population at the time of the census preceding the election. Within
the Protestant group, the United Church and the Presbyterians seemed
to have been slightly over-represented and the Anglican Church under-
represented, but the differences were small. They suggest, however, that
studies of the degree to which the various Protestant groups are represented among the candidates might bear fruitful results.

A marked contrast appears when the two parties are compared from
the point of view of the religious denomination of their candidates: 48.2
per cent of the Liberals were Roman Catholics, the corresponding Conservative figure being 37.7 per cent. The difference is great enough to
offset possible inaccuracies caused by the absence of information about
some candidates. The impression, shared by many Canadians, that of
the two parties the Conservative has traditionally been more "Protestant"
seemed confirmed by the 1957 election at least in so far as the presence
of a disproportionate number of Protestant candidates can be held as
attesting to the more "Protestant" nature of the party. The somewhat
greater preponderance of Anglicans among Conservative candidates,
although less pronounced, also conforms to a popular notion about the
party. The former close ties in Canada between Anglicanism and Tory-
ism were thought by many Canadians to have influenced Conservative
attitudes, at any rate, until the advent of Mr. Diefenbaker as the party
leader. Table VI/13 shows 10.4 per cent of Liberal candidates to have
been Anglicans as compared with 15.6 per cent Anglicans among the
Conservatives. While the difference in percentage points is not as great
as that pertaining to the Roman Catholics it is, nevertheless, suggestive.

The traditional association of the Conservative party with Anglicanism was no doubt related to the widely-held belief that it was also the
most British of the Canadian parties. It was therefore particularly interesting to examine the ethnic composition of the candidates. Was the
proportion of British candidates greater among the Conservatives than
among the Liberals and, more important perhaps, was the number of
non-Anglo-Saxon candidates so small as to confirm the alleged Tory
intolerance of anything which was not thoroughly British?

In view of all the well-known difficulties of definition, the large number of "unknowns," and the absence of significant numbers in any except
the major categories, the candidates were divided into only three ethnic
groups: (1) Anglo-Saxon, (2) French-Canadian, (3) Other.[30] This

[30]These labels, although not very satisfactory, suit our purposes better than
others. "Anglo-Saxon" comprises all those whose ancestors came from the British
Isles and those who called themselves Canadians, all, or almost all, of whom
were of British origin. "French" includes seven candidates of French-Irish ances-
try. The "Other" category includes four candidates who came to Canada from the

breakdown shows that the Conservatives succeeded in electing only six French-Canadian candidates and that the Liberal party found itself with more than ten times that number in the twenty-third Parliament.

Table VI/14 indicates that the French made up a much larger proportion of candidates running for the Liberals than for the Conservatives and that the latter group contained a larger contingent of candidates classified as Anglo-Saxon. In interpreting these figures, it should be recalled that the Conservatives failed to nominate candidates in six Quebec constituencies and that among those about whose origin nothing was ascertained, there was probably a larger number of French Conservatives than of French Liberals.[31]

TABLE VI/14

Numerical and Percentage Distribution of Liberal and
Conservative Candidates by Ethnic Origin

Ethnic origin	Numbers			Percentages			
	Lib.	P.C.	Total	Lib.	P.C.	Total	Canada*
Anglo-Saxon	114	125	239	53.0	64.4	58.4	47.9
French	80	55	135	37.2	28.4	33.0	30.8
Other	21	14	35	9.8	7.2	8.6	21.3
Total	215	194	409	100.0	100.0	100.0	100.0
No information	50	63	113				

*Based on the 1951 census. See *Census of Canada 1951*, vol. I, Table 31.

Nevertheless, despite the need to treat it with caution, the evidence in Table VI/14 suggests that in so far as the number of French Canadians among its candidates was concerned, the Conservative party lived up to the image a large part of the public had long had of it: its candidates in the 1957 election included a smaller proportion of French Canadians than did the Liberal candidates. When it is remembered that among the twenty-one Liberal candidates whose origin was neither French nor Anglo-Saxon, four were American and, therefore, probably Anglo-Saxon,

United States and who were probably Anglo-Saxons, eight candidates classified as Slavs, seven as German or Scandinavian, the rest being either mixed (for example Czech and Austrian) or unspecified Slav, Scandinavian, and Latin. Two candidates were classified as Jewish. One or two candidates of the Hebrew faith were classified under "national" groups other than Jewish (Polish, for example) since this seemed a more realistic way of describing their cultural background.

[31]More information was available for elected than defeated candidates. Since the number of Liberals elected in Quebec was very much larger than the corresponding Conservative figure, there were more "known" Liberals than Conservatives in the provinces of Quebec.

it appears that the proportion of non-British and non-French candidates was practically the same in both parties. The Conservatives had, in addition, the distinction of being the first party in Canada to propose successfully for election a Canadian of Chinese origin. Mr. Diefenbaker's pleas for the acceptance of the idea of "un-hyphenated Canadians" and his attempts to destroy the "Blimpish" image the party presented to numerous Canadians, was paralleled by the constituency organizations, at least with regard to the ethnic origin of the candidates they chose. At any rate, the Conservatives did not noticeably lag behind the Liberals in terms of the proportion of their candidates who had themselves come, or whose forefathers had come to Canada from northern, central and eastern Europe and even from Asia.

But Table VI/14 indicates to what extent Canadians of neither British nor French origin were under-represented among the candidates chosen by the older parties. According to the 1951 census over 21 per cent of the Canadian population was of non-British and non-French stock. The ethnic origin of fewer than 9 per cent of the Liberal and Conservative candidates contesting the 1957 election was neither Anglo-Saxon nor French.

When the candidates' birthplaces are examined it becomes apparent that in this regard also the Conservatives were no more "British" than the Liberals. Table VI/15 shows that the Liberals did not nominate a larger proportion of candidates born outside Canada or outside Britain than the Conservatives. The Conservatives, in fact, nominated a slightly smaller proportion of British-born candidates and a larger number of candidates born on the Continent of Europe. The margins are so small as to be meaningless, however, particularly in view of the large number of "unknowns." No distinction between the parties can, therefore, be

TABLE VI/15

Numerical and Percentage Distribution of Liberal and
Conservative Candidates by Country of Birth

Country of birth	Number			Percentage		
	Lib.	P.C.	Total	Lib.	P.C.	Total
Canada	216	209	425	91.9	91.3	91.6
United Kingdom	10	8	18	4.3	3.5	3.9
Continent of Europe	2	5	7	.9	2.2	1.5
Elsewhere	7	7	14	3.0	3.1	3.0
Total	235	229	464	100.1	100.1	100.0
No information	30	28	58			

made in this regard. Whether a candidate was born in Canada, in Britain, on the Continent, or elsewhere seemed to have had no visible effect on his chances of election.

Candidates born in the constituency they were contesting rather than elsewhere, seemed to have had a better chance of election only if they ran as Conservatives. Table VI/16, which provides this intriguing information, also tells us that, among the government party candidates, those who were born outside their constituency, but in the province in which they were running, had a better chance of winning a seat than those born in a different province. Of all the candidates nominated by the two parties, about 40 per cent were born in their constituency, 34 per cent in their province and the rest abroad or in another part of Canada. Forty-three per cent of the Liberal candidates were born in the constituency they contested. The corresponding proportion of Conservatives was 37.9 per cent.

TABLE VI/16

Birthplace Related to the Constituency Contested by
Elected and Defeated Liberal and Conservative Candidates

Candidates	Liberal			Conservative			Total		
	Elected	De-feated	Total	Elected	De-feated	Total	Elected	De-feated	Total
In constituency	43	56	99	55	28	83	98	84	182
In province	37	40	77	33	43	76	70	83	153
Elsewhere	21	33	54	22	38	60	43	71	114
No information	4	31	35	2	36	38	6	67	73
Total	105	160	265	112	145	257	217	305	522

In British Columbia and the Prairies more than half the candidates were born outside their province. Only about one in ten candidates nominated in Quebec was born in another region of Canada. The proportion of "outsiders" was not much greater in the Maritimes. It seems that geographical mobility of prospective candidates is related to the length of settlement of the area in which they are contesting their seats. This, of course, is to be expected: the more recently settled areas contain a greater proportion of people who have come from other parts of Canada and from abroad. The greater mobility of the total population is mirrored in the greater mobility of the candidates running for public office.

Political Experience

A party which has repeatedly won large majorities in the House of Commons will obviously have a greater number of experienced Parliamentarians than one whose members have in recent years filled only about one-fifth of the available seats. But there are other ways of gaining political experience than by participating in federal politics.

Table VI/17 summarizes the political experience of candidates by showing how many of them had been elected to local, provincial and/or federal legislatures. Those who served at more than one level of government are listed under each appropriate heading and are, consequently, counted more than once. The table shows that among the Liberal candidates almost a third (33.2 per cent) had held some sort of municipal office and that almost two-thirds (64.4 per cent) had been in the federal House. Among the Conservatives there was a slightly larger proportion (34.9 per cent) of candidates with municipal experience, but, naturally, a considerably smaller ratio (22.8 per cent) of former federal M.P.'s. While municipal experience is fairly common among candidates, service in a provincial Chamber is obviously not a stepping-stone to a career in federal politics.

TABLE VI/17

Municipal, Provincial and Federal Experience of
Liberal and Conservative Candidates

Level of government at which office held	Numbers			Percentage*		
	Lib.	P.C.	Total	Lib.	P.C.	Total
Municipal	82	81	163	33.2	34.9	34.0
Provincial	16	15	31	6.5	6.5	6.5
Federal	159	53	212	64.4	22.8	44.3

*Percentages in this case are of candidates whose political experience was known. There were 247 "known" Liberals and 232 "known" Conservatives. 33.2 per cent Liberals with Municipal experience means, therefore, that among the 247 Liberal candidates 33.2 per cent had served at the local level either exclusively or in addition to having sat in a provincial legislature, the federal House, or in both.

Thirty per cent of the Liberals running in 1957 made their first bid for federal office at that time, whereas 60.1 per cent of the Conservatives were new to the federal field. In this context it is worthy of note that of the 265 Liberals contesting the 1957 election, 152 had sat in the twenty-second Parliament, nineteen contested the constituency in which they were defeated in 1953, and the remaining ninety-four ran for the first time in their 1957 constituency. Forty-eight Conservatives had sat in the previous Parliament, twenty-three fought constituencies they had contested unsuccessfully in 1953, and 186 were making their first attempt to carry the riding in which they were nominated in 1957.

Did opposition charges that the Liberals had become an old party have an adverse effect on the chances of re-election of Liberal candidates with many years' experience in the House of Commons? Table VI/17 shows that 159 Liberal candidates had at one time sat in the House of Commons. When the percentages are computed of those elected within the various periods in which the 159 entered the House it becomes apparent that the candidates who had only recently been elected for the first time fared no better than the veterans of long standing in Parliament. Table VI/18 gives the relevant figures.

TABLE VI/18

Percentages of Liberal Candidates Returned, by Period of First Entry into the House of Commons

First elected	Percentage elected in 1957
1953–56	61
1949–52	61
1945–48	57
1940–44	60
1939 and before	65

Summary and Conclusion

The following emerge as the most significant differences between the candidates of the major parties. Often, although not always, they are attributable to the strength or weakness of either party in one or more of the major regions of the country. The Liberals favoured the professions more than the Conservatives, who showed a slightly greater interest than their main rivals in candidates with business experience. The Liberals also nominated a larger proportion of candidates having had higher education. In terms of age, the Conservatives were decidedly the younger party, having both a larger contingent of young candidates and a smaller one of old ones. Politicians of the Roman Catholic faith were more numerous among Liberal candidates than among Conservatives, and the Liberals were also more hospitable to French Canadians seeking a seat in the House of Commons. Both parties included about the same ratio of candidates whose ethnic origin was neither French nor British. Over ninety per cent of candidates nominated by the major parties were born in Canada, neither party showing a greater preference for the native product than its main rival.

The Liberals had, naturally, a considerably larger number of candidates with experience in the federal House. As far as provincial and municipal office was concerned, there was little difference between the parties. The anti-government swing in the 1957 election caused the defeat of a sizable number of Liberals. Whether a former Liberal member was defeated or not seemed to have been unrelated to the length of service he had seen in the House before the 1957 election.

Indeed, the tables distinguishing between elected and defeated candidates suggest, on the whole, that with only minor exceptions, the characteristics described in the preceding pages were only slightly, if at all, related to the electoral prospects of the candidates. An observation made about the 1945 British election, which brought down the government, is applicable to the election which, twelve years later, had the same result in Canada: ". . . the electors appeared to have been little influenced by the actual record and occupations of the candidates and voted more for the party . . . it was not a candidates' election; it was not a soldiers' battle. It was rather a battle of mass manoeuvre and all substantial success went to the big battalions. Electors voted not so much for the man as for the side."[32]

It would, of course, be foolish to discount the possibility of certain attributes being of special importance in some constituencies. But when the country is surveyed as a whole, it appears that none of the characteristics examined above can be considered as particularly advantageous from the point of view of winning office. It is another matter, of course, when the question of being nominated by one of the older parties is considered. The non-Anglo-Saxon, non-French, non-professional aspirant to office was found less frequently in the ranks of Liberal and Conservative candidates than his numbers in the country might have led one to expect. Similarly, white-collar and manual workers have, in the past, failed to participate in the life of the federal Parliament in numbers corresponding to their numerical strength in the country.

An interesting question about the candidates is posed by the thesis that when it elected Mr. Diefenbaker as leader, the Conservative party had embarked on something of a revolution. Did the Diefenbaker revolution and the defeat of the "old guard" lead to a transformation of the party visible in the sort of persons selected as Conservative candidates? Obviously in constituencies where there is an active Conservative associa-

[32]McCallum and Readman, *British General Election of 1945*, p. 87.

tion the choice of candidates is made locally. But in less well-organized parts of the country—Quebec, for example, in the case of the Conservatives in 1957—it is likely that the ideas of the federal leadership about who will make a good candidate will be reflected in the local nominees. The Diefenbaker revolution came too late to affect the method of choosing candidates and the actual selection in very many constituencies. Over a longer period of time, however, the new federal leadership will no doubt influence the type of personnel gaining prominence in provincial and constituency organizations, the ways in which candidates are chosen, and in some cases the actual persons selected to contest federal elections. Studies of the 1958 election and of those yet to come will offer valuable material about the extent to which the Diefenbaker revolution may have transformed the personnel of Conservative candidatures. In the meantime we must be satisfied with conclusions based on the 1957 election. In any event, if the Conservative party appeared to the country as substantially different from that which was rejected in previous elections, the explanation must be sought not so much in the characteristics of the candidates as in the changed conditions in the country and in the new leadership. It is the latter aspect of the 1957 election which forms the subject of the next chapter.

The Itineraries

MR. ST. LAURENT AND MR. DIEFENBAKER both undertook gruelling campaign tours. As mentioned previously, the general course of the tours was determined by the respective national party organizations after they had consulted the various provincial associations. The latter were responsible for the itineraries within their provincial boundaries and for most arrangements not made locally. Their representatives also accompanied the leader on his tour through their provinces. In addition, the leaders were accompanied by a train manager, one or more public relations people, researchers and others who assisted in the preparartion of speeches, secretaries, and one or more members of their families. An army of reporters, representing the press and radio, was also provided with facilities on the trains, which actually consisted of one or two special railway cars attached to scheduled trains.

At least one major speech every evening, possibly another one at noon, with numerous smaller addresses and teas taking up additional time—such was the leader's schedule as far as the public was concerned. He also had to meet literally hundreds of candidates, party workers and sympathizers, decide broad issues of campaign strategy, keep in touch with the activities of the opposition, and prepare and deliver important radio and television speeches on behalf of his party. Often he had to travel hundreds of miles in a day. On one occasion Mr. Diefenbaker gave an evening address to about one thousand people in Minnedosa, Manitoba, after driving seventy miles from Dauphin where he had attended a supper meeting. He arrived at Dauphin by air, having flown two hundred miles from Flin Flon where he appeared at an afternoon gathering. The day had started at nine o'clock when the Conservative leader boarded a plane for the four-hundred-mile flight from Winnipeg to Flin Flon.[1]

While Mr. St. Laurent's programme was not, on the whole, nearly as strenuous as that of Mr. Diefenbaker, it was nevertheless an exhausting and arduous one for any man, but particularly for one over seventy-five years old. May 16, the day for which Mr. Diefenbaker's activities in Manitoba were just outlined, found Mr. St. Laurent campaigning in Ontario. His morning schedule called for a 25-mile drive from Owen Sound to Wiarton, where he addressed an outdoor meeting and from where he flew by chartered plane to Camp Borden. Another open-air appearance was scheduled for 1.15 in Penetanguishene, which had to be reached from Camp Borden by car. The drive back to Camp Borden was to be interrupted by stops in Elmvale and Barrie. Another plane flight was to take the Prime Minister from Camp Borden to London, where he was to address a meeting in the London Arena. According to Canadian Press observers, 2,500 people heard the speech, probably without realizing Mr. St. Laurent's well-planned day included at least two additional, unanticipated events: a scaffolding near some new construction on which he had been standing collapsed, and his car side-swept another car and went into a ditch near Barrie.[2]

Not counting a visit to Newfoundland immediately before the opening of the formal tour, Mr. Diefenbaker campaigned for thirty-nine days. Mr. St. Laurent spent twenty-eight days touring the country in search of votes.[3] He made a direct personal appeal to a little under 120 constituencies. Mr. Diefenbaker's score in this regard was higher—he spoke in or near about 130 ridings.[4]

[1]*Itinerary—John Diefenbaker—1957* (mimeo), p. 5; and Winnipeg *Free Press*, May 17.

[2]*The Prime Minister's Itinerary* (mimeo); Winnipeg *Free Press*, May 17. For additional comments on the hazards of the leaders' campaign tours see Robert Duffy, "Vote Will Tell—Liberal Workers Question Whether Present Methods Are Worthwhile," Toronto *Globe and Mail*, May 17, and Clark Davey, "Four-a-Day Schedule Hot Pace for Diefenbaker," *ibid.*, May 16.

[3]Only actual campaign days are counted. Sundays, for example, have been omitted, although the leaders were probably rarely able to devote much time to rest even then. Mr. St. Laurent, particularly, who spent one weekend in Quebec City and another in Ottawa, must have found the schedule on those two occasions as demanding as during the week.

[4]It is impossible to give precise figures because an important speech by a national leader in a metropolitan area is obviously intended for voters in more than one constituency. The large meeting held by each leader in Toronto was counted in the above figures as an appeal to eighteen constituencies, their Montreal visits added twenty-one to their scores. Addresses in smaller centres like Calgary

Winnipeg was chosen by the Prime Minister as the city in which to open his national tour. He spent three days in the Prairies and then moved to the west coast for major addresses in Vancouver and Victoria. On his way back to Ottawa Mr. St. Laurent stopped at Saskatoon and Regina. Most of the second week of the campaign was spent either en route or in Ottawa. The third week opened with an important address in Quebec City followed by intensive campaigning in Ontario, and ended with his returning for the weekend to his home in Quebec City. The next week saw four days' touring of the Maritime provinces and of eastern Quebec. After spending that week-end in Ottawa Mr. St. Laurent opened the penultimate week of the campaign by speaking to a large rally in the capital. The ensuing seven days were again devoted to the Maritimes and Quebec; this phase of the tour ended with an address to a large gathering in Montreal. The final week was spent in Ontario and came to a conclusion at the Maple Leaf Gardens rally in Toronto.

Mr. Diefenbaker had spent a good deal of time since his election as party leader addressing Conservative and other meetings in different parts of the country. The formal starting-point for his national tour was in Toronto, where he spoke at Massey Hall on April 25. The Leader of the Opposition spent only two days in Ontario on this occasion. He then moved to the Maritimes, stopping for a speech in Quebec City. The first two days of the second week found Mr. Diefenbaker touring in Quebec, after which he moved into Ontario. The two weeks following began with a short stop in Toronto but were otherwise devoted to an intensive appeal to the Prairies and the west coast. Although during the final two weeks of the campaign Mr. Diefenbaker spent the largest number of days in Ontario, the other regions were not entirely neglected —the Conservative leader appeared in Saskatchewan on two separate occasions, visited the Maritimes, and made some appearances in Quebec. He spent the election week-end in his own constituency of Prince Albert, just as the Prime Minister withdrew to his home in Quebec City.

Many factors are taken into account when it is decided which constituencies are to be visited by the leaders and which are to be by-passed. The importance of the various population centres has to be considered, as well as the personalities running in the different constituencies, local

---

or Hamilton were also considered to constitute campaigning in more than one constituency. Mr. St. Laurent's score of about 120 includes 65 constituencies appealed to in ten localitties. Mr. Diefenbaker was credited with appeals in 60 constituencies by appearing in eight cities. The two large centres visited by Mr. St. Laurent and not by Mr. Diefenbaker were St. John's, Newfoundland (2), in which the Conservative leader campaigned before the election had actually been called and Ottawa (3), which was also left out of Mr. Diefenbaker's itinerary.

conditions, and the wishes of the provincial and constituency organizations conducting the electoral battles. Geography and the shortage of
time are also important.

It was to be expected that the leaders would concentrate on marginal
constituencies. Table VII/1 shows that in all of Canada there were
fifty-three "marginal" seats and forty-seven "close" seats.[5] By no means
all of the hundred constituencies in which the margin of victory was ten
per cent or less were ridings, however, in which the Conservatives and
Liberals had been the two top contenders. The Conservatives' weakness
in some areas at the time of the 1953 election is revealed dramatically
in the fact that in only three constituencies west of Ontario had a Conservative candidate been placed first or second. There is, therefore, not
much point in comparing the number of western marginal seats in which
the leaders campaigned, nor, for similar reasons, need their performance
in Quebec be subjected to detailed scrutiny from this point of view. It
is interesting, however, that neither leader spent very much time in
Montreal where fifteen out of twenty-one seats had been won by
impressive margins. Both Mr. St. Laurent and Mr. Diefenbaker made
speeches in Notre Dame de Grace, the only constituency in Montreal
in which the two major parties had been running neck and neck in the
previous election.

Thirty-nine per cent of the Toronto constituencies were marginal and
an additional twenty-eight per cent were close. Altogether two-thirds
of the ridings in Metropolitan Toronto were battlegrounds in which
either of the major parties stood to gain or lose representatives in the
House of Commons as a result of only a relatively small swing of the
votes. Mr. St. Laurent addressed the somewhat ill-fated monster rally
staged by the Liberals towards the end of the campaign in Toronto's
Maple Leaf Gardens, but he did no campaigning in the various constituencies. Mr. Diefenbaker, on the other hand, not only spoke at a
large rally but also visited several ridings in which he made short
speeches or attended large tea and coffee parties. Elsewhere in Ontario,
the leaders' itineraries emphasized the marginal and close seats. Mr. St.
Laurent visited ten and Mr. Diefenbaker eight of the thirteen seats in
which their parties had been separated by five per cent or less of the vote.

After Toronto, the Maritimes provided the largest proportion of
marginal and close seats. Of the thirty-three ridings in this region, sixteen

[5]The term "marginal" is applied to constituencies in which the percentage
of the vote separating the winner from the runner-up in the previous election
was five or less. A "close" seat is one in which the margin was from 5.1 to 10
per cent.

TABLE VII/1

Marginal and Safe Seats

Number of constituencies in the major regions in which the winner of the election preceding that of 1957‡ was separated from the runner-up by various stated margins expressed as percentages of the total number of votes cast.

Region	Margin separating winner from runner-up*											
	5% or less		5.1%–10%		10.1%–15%		15.1%–20%		10.1%+		Total	
	n	%	n	%	n	%	n	%	n	%	n	%
Maritimes	9	27.3	7	21.2	4	12.1	2	6.1	11	33.3	33	100.0
Quebec (exclusive of Montreal)†	4	7.7	9	17.3	6	11.5	8	15.4	25	48.1	52(**)	100.0
Montreal	2	9.5	2	9.5	–	–	2	9.5	15	71.4	21	99.9
Ontario (exclusive of Toronto & Yorks)	13	19.4	12	17.9	15	22.4	11	16.4	16	23.9	67	100.0
Toronto & Yorks	7	39.0	5	27.8	3	16.7	3	16.7	–	–	18	100.2
Prairies	12	25.0	9	18.8	9	18.8	7	14.6	11	22.9	48	100.1
British Columbia	6	27.3	3	13.6	5	22.7	2	9.1	6	27.3	22	100.0
Yukon & Mackenzie R.	–	–	–	–	1	50.0	–	–	1	50.0	2	100.0

*Computed as the percentage of those who cast their ballots.
†Two acclamations.
‡Based on the results of the 1953 general election except in constituencies in which by-elections had been held subsequently. In the latter instances the by-election results were incorporated rather than those of the 1953 election.

could be so classified. The Conservative leader made speeches in twelve of these and Mr. St. Laurent in ten. In this region, the Prime Minister spoke in five constituencies in which the margin separating the parties was more than ten per cent, and Mr. Diefenbaker in only three.

There was, therefore, some relation between the leaders' campaign itineraries and the size of the margin separating the parties in previous elections. But the relationship was not a close one. The campaign managers had obviously paid greater attention to general political conditions in the various regions than to the statistics of previous elections. Circumstances in most parts of Canada had changed considerably since 1953 and the campaign managers were naturally guided by recent developments in the constituencies when they worked out the itinerary of their leader.[6]

Campaign Styles

Mr. Diefenbaker's was the more exciting of the two campaigns. He not only spoke more often than the Prime Minister, but what he said lent itself better to being played up as headline news. The manner of presenting his material, the fact that he was, in a sense, a new political personality, the outspoken attacks against the government, and the unexpectedly large crowds attending his meetings combined to make his campaign ideally suited for effective exploitation by the press. It is likely that the newspapers were, on the whole, more friendly to the Conservatives than to the Liberals, but this was probably only a minor factor in the way in which the press treated the campaigns of the two national leaders.

The Conservative leader's speeches revealed in him considerable histrionic talent. He was able, on most occasions, to sense the temper of his audience and to cast his message in a way which was in tune with it. His speaking style was somewhat old-fashioned, reminiscent of the fiery orators so popular in the nineteenth century. Indeed, Mr. Diefenbaker's oratory has been likened to that of the revivalist preacher. Certainly whatever he uttered was expressed with complete self-assurance. Despite the use of somewhat exaggerated gestures, diminuendos and crescendos, and of dramatic changes in the tempo of delivery, an overwhelming number of listeners gained the impression that the most characteristic

[6]For a related discussion of the leaders' and particularly Mr. Diefenbaker's campaign trip see John Meisel, "Analysing the Vote," *Queen's Quarterly*, vol. LXIV, no. 4 (Winter, 1958), pp. 488–91.

feature of what he said was his sincerity and the great conviction with which he held his views.

Mr. Diefenbaker's speaking style during the election was an extremely interesting one. Much of what he said would, if transcribed word for word, be virtually meaningless. The reason for this is Mr. Diefenbaker's habit, during electioneering, of frequently failing to complete his sentences and of moving freely from one idea to the next without indicating where one ends and the other begins. The concluding paragraph of the Massey Hall speech offers a good example:

If we are dedicated to this,—and to this we are,—you, my fellow Canadians, will require all the wisdom, all the power that comes from those spiritual springs that make freedom possible,—all the wisdom, all the faith and all the vision which the Conservative Party gave but yesterday under Macdonald, change [*sic*] to meet changing conditions, today having the responsibility of this party to lay the foundations of this nation for a great and glorious future.[7]

In most instances it was easy to tell what the Conservative leader was talking about and even what he was saying, but the manner of presenting his ideas was unorthodox. It had a powerful effect on his audiences, for the impression left by this type of oratory was one of great urgency. The hearer could not but conclude that Mr. Diefenbaker knew perfectly well what he was trying to say, that it was clear in his mind, but that the faith with which he held his views was so strong, the urgency to discuss them so pressing and the number of things that needed saying so great that it was impossible to compress everything into the usual form employed by public speakers.

The communication, like that of a "stream of consciousness" novel, was on several levels. Mr. Diefenbaker's speeches were full of words and expressions which undoubtedly released powerful emotions in his listeners. He often employed imagery which was highly evocative to anyone reared in the Christian faith.[8] Indeed much of what Mr. Diefenbaker said had an apocalyptic aura about it. Words appealing to the listeners' patriotism, to their hopes, to their desire to participate in

[7]Mimeo by the Conservative party.

[8]The Massey Hall speech for example, cited above, contained the words "sacred trust" more than once, referred to the "unrepentant" taxmasters, utilized the words "brotherhood," "destiny," "vision," and "faith." In its opening paragraphs, the speech contained a phrase which would have pleased Benjamin Franklin and which Max Weber and R. H. Tawney could have used as illustrations in their studies of the relation between religion and the rise of capitalism. "Well," Mr. Diefenbaker said, "last minute repentances do not pay dividends in public affairs."

national greatness, and to sacrifice something in a common effort, to their wish to be on the side of good and right—words appealing to all of these widely-felt emotions—played an important part in most of Mr. Diefenbaker's speeches. Underlying a good deal of what he said, therefore, was the assumption that Canada was on the threshold of greatness if it could only get rid of its old and inadequate government. The voter needed only to vote for the Diefenbaker party and he would at once become allied to those who were creating a dazzlingly bright and promising future. Each voter could, so Mr. Diefenbaker seemed to say, participate in an effort which would make his own dreams come true.

The type of approach just described represented only one facet of Mr. Difenbaker's oratorical style. Added to it there was the aggressive and uncompromising attack on the government and particularly on Mr. Howe. The Conservative leader was bitterly critical of virtually everything the government had done. He gave the impression that he believed that directly or indirectly the government was responsible for all of Canada's problems. Furthermore, he frequently seemed to imply that malevolence had often as much to do with alleged governmental culpability as incompetence. The government's handling of the construction of the Trans-Canada pipeline, its attitude to Parliament, to wheat disposal or provincial finances were invoked over and over again by the Conservative leader to show that it was time the Liberals were defeated. And the only alternative, he kept emphasizing, was a Diefenbaker government. This theme was repeated in endless variations at formal meetings whose attendance figures almost always exceeded expectations, at teas and coffee parties arranged by local associations and at whistle stops arranged in most parts of the country. Mr. Diefenbaker obviously enjoyed campaigning and meeting people—most of his audiences seemed to enjoy him.

Mr. St. Laurent's style was entirely different. His speeches were carefully written and constructed briefs, delivered in an unemotional and quiet style befitting an elder statesman. His manner, according to an editorial commenting on his opening address in Winnipeg, "was less that of political controversy than of the Chairman of the Board of a successful corporation reporting to a shareholders' meeting. He was reporting a record of continually rising dividends, and therefore he seemed hardly to recognize the existence of a dissident group of shareholders demanding a change in the management."[9] Newspaper comments, even from friendly reporters, suggested that sometimes he seemed to be reading speeches

[9]Winnipeg *Free Press*, April 30.

with which he was not quite familiar.[10] On occasion, when commenting on local personalities, he mispronounced their names.[11]

Many of Mr. St. Laurent's speeches contained extremely long passages describing in detail how much the Canadian economy and the people's welfare had grown and improved during the previous eight years. Since a steady diet consisting of large doses of production and population statistics tends to be heavy and indigestible the Prime Minister's campaign oratory was usually not very exciting. While his audiences were, on the whole, well disposed towards him, they found his speeches dull and lacking in sparkle. This seemed to be the case despite the fact that on occasion he managed to inject into his addresses a touch of humour and even of pleasing imagery. On one occasion for example, he compared the Liberal and Conservative programmes by saying:

Since our Liberal program, while big, has no room in it for election promises it might, to that extent, be less spectacular than an Opposition election program prettied up to attract votes.
But an election promise, after all, is a mere cream-puff of a thing—with more air than substance in it![12]

Typical of Mr. St. Laurent's subdued speaking style was his frequent repeated insistence that he had in the past done his best and that all that he and his government could promise was that they would continue to do their best in the future. The general impression left by the speeches was that this dignified gentleman had done extremely well in the past, that he knew that everyone was aware of it, and that all that he needed to do during the campaign was to assure the populace that he would be around for a little while yet to look after its affairs. This quiet approach was epitomized in an analogy which found its way into practically every speech made by the Prime Minister. Whether addressing the French-speaking population of Mont-Joli, Quebec, the cosmopolitan citizenry of Winnipeg, Manitoba, or the predominantly Anglo-Saxon audience in London, Ontario, Mr. St. Laurent stressed that his view towards the problems of state were essentially those of a family man coping with the decisions confronting any normal family.

Often, in appealing for public support, Mr. St. Laurent adopted the tone exemplified in the following extract from a speech prepared for delivery in Quebec. Recalling that the late Cardinal Villeneuve had

[10]Winnipeg *Free Press*, May 27. See also assessment by Victor Mackie, *ibid.*, May 16.
[11]See, for example, his reference to the members of the Edmonton Eskimos football team, Winnipeg *Free Press*, May 2.
[12]Vancouver, May 3 (mimeo), p. 6.

advised him, when he first entered politics in 1941, to do his best each day and trust to Providence, he said:

> I have followed this advice, I apply it to my life each day and I have the impression that it is this conviction that I collaborate with Divine Providence which enables me to carry, without tiring too much, the heavy burden of the Prime Minister of Canada.
> I will tell you another secret—which no longer is one—concerning the method I have found successful in the administration of the affairs of state.
> I have always thought that the concept of the father of a family was the best one to be applied to the management of public affairs. The adaptation of this concept to my new responsibilities enabled me to draw on my personal experience.
> I consider that all Canadians have an equal right to benefit from the advantages of belonging to the Canadian nation, just as all my children have an equal right to the affection I give them as their father. . . .
> I know that this respect for the Canadian family is shared completely by the people of Roberval and of the entire beautiful region of Lac Saint-Jean.[13]

Sometimes the family image was developed a little differently:

> I have already said several times in the course of this election campaign that, according to my view, the success of the Liberals comes from the fact that we consider all Canadians in each region and each province as being part of the same national family, and that we bring to the administration of public affairs the care of a family father who loves all his children equally and who tries to divide equally the family possessions among all its members.
> You will agree that we succeeded in the application to political life of this family concept. It is revealed in our social legislation, fiscal relations with the provinces, and in the assistance given by the federal government to provinces which have particular problems . . .[14]

Whether, in emphasizing the family so much, Mr. St. Laurent's public relations advisers were trying subtly to exploit for political purposes the fashionable father image or whether this was simply an attempt to play up his reputation as a kindly family man, he obviously enjoyed being fatherly.[15] His campaigning seemed to have been most effective when, as he did often throughout his tour, he stopped briefly to address children on some question of civics and then arranged with local authorities for school to be cancelled that day in celebration of the Prime Minister's visit. To address children, pat their heads, and be photographed with them was an important element in Mr. St. Laurent's campaign style.

[13]Roberval, May 29 (mimeo), pp. 1–2. The translation is my own.
[14]Chicoutimi, May 29 (mimeo), p. 3. The translation is my own.
[15]For hostile assessments of Mr. St. Laurent's style see George Bain, "Minding Your Business," Toronto *Globe and Mail*, June 4, and "There Are Two Louis: One on the Hustings, One in the East Block," *ibid.*, June 1. For a sympathetic view see Victor Mackie's dispatch from Ottawa in the Winnipeg *Free Press*, May 16.

Attendance at Mr. St. Laurent's meetings varied considerably. While it reached impressive proportions in some centres, on the whole it indicated that the Prime Minister's visits were stirring up less interest than had been expected by Liberal organizers.[16] In Saskatchewan the Prime Minister attracted larger crowds than the Conservative leader, but, on the west coast, Mr. Diefenbaker's reception was far more impressive and enthusiastic. In fact, as soon as the Conservative leader entered British Columbia, after a highly successful tour of the Maritimes and a somewhat less reassuring one in Ontario,[17] it became apparent that he was injecting into the campaign a degree of excitement and interest which no one seemed to have anticipated. His audiences were usually highly attentive and enthusiastic.

The Prime Minister, unlike the Leader of the Opposition, was heckled frequently. No evidence has come to light proving that the heckling and other disturbances at Mr. St. Laurent's meetings were the result of a carefully planned campaign. The regularity of their occurrence, however, and the intensely provocative behaviour of the otherwise politically apathetic boy who mounted the podium of Maple Leaf Gardens and slowly and deliberately tore up a photograph of the Prime Minister as the latter was speaking,[18] make it difficult to rule out completely the possibility that the heckling was the result of one or more organized attempts to discomfit the Prime Minister. During the campaign his opponents had made frequent attempts to destroy what they believed to have been an invention of the Liberals' public relations advisers: the Uncle or Papa Louis myth.[19] To provoke Mr. St. Laurent at public meetings and so make him appear in an irritable rather than in an

[16]Reluctance of voters to attend his meetings was particularly noticeable in Quebec. In Quebec City his organizers were unable to fill an even medium-sized movie theatre and in Sherbrooke, Quebec, seven hundred people filled only half the seats provided for the meeting. Mr. St. Laurent was said to have been irritated by the low turnout. See Robert Duffy, "Quebec Voters' Apathy to Federal Campaign Worries Both Parties," Toronto *Globe and Mail*, May 17, and C.P. dispatch from Sherbrooke, May 24.

[17]See Clark Davey, "Diefenbaker in Algoma Hits Housing Policies; Tough Week Faces Him," Toronto *Globe and Mail*, May 13, and "Four-a-Day Schedule a Hot Pace for Diefenbaker," *ibid.*, May 16.

[18]See Victor Mackie's dispatch from Toronto, Winnipeg *Free Press*, June 8.

[19]Mr. Hees, for example, who was, after Mr. Diefenbaker, the most ubiquitous of the Conservative leaders, made frequent hard-hitting attacks on the Prime Minister. Sometimes he suggested that Mr. St. Laurent was too old and would retire after the election; on other occasions he attempted to weaken the general popularity of the Liberal leader. A speech delivered at Napanee was characteristic of Mr. Hees' offensive. Mr. St. Laurent, he was reported as having said, sent Canadians mere platitudes. Suddenly the Liberal bosses had realized that "the people of Canada were bored by Dear Old Uncle Louis. Panic reigned in Liberal circles and Uncle Louis reacted like a fading Beauty Queen confronted by a

avuncular mood must have seemed an attractive and easy way to counter the Uncle Louis legend.

As the campaign developed Mr. St. Laurent's campaign style became more aggresive. During his opening address in Winnipeg, he referred to the Liberal party or to his government fifty-five times and to the opposition not once. During the middle of his tour he began to mention the opposition more and more frequently so that in a prepared text for a speech delivered in Windsor, Ontario, on June 5, he referred to his own side thirty times, while using the words Tory, Tories, Conservative, Progressive Conservative, Diefenbaker, and Diefenbaker party altogether forty times. As his speeches became somewhat more controversial, they probably became more interesting. But on balance, even towards the end of the campaign, the interest created by the Prime Minister lagged behind that aroused by Mr. Diefenbaker. Press comments on the two campaign tours illustrate and partly explain the different reception accorded the two leaders in their appeals to the people. Mr. Harvey Hickey, after accompanying him on most of his tour, described the Prime Minister's manner as follows:

No one could quarrel with the Liberal slogan, Peace, Prosperity and Security, and from Prime Minister St. Laurent down, the Liberals are trying their best to keep the campaign limited to that uncontroversial statement.

Conservative Leader John Diefenbaker has charged that the Prime Minister has already made election promises which would cost the country hundreds of millions of dollars. However, a careful reading of Mr. St. Laurent's speeches will show that he has been cautious in the extreme . . .[20]

The newspaper which printed this comment on the Liberal campaign carried on the same day an article by its reporter who had accompanied Mr. Diefenbaker on his tour. He wrote:

The Conservative Party has been reborn in the image of John Diefenbaker who, with a superhuman effort, has tried to win this 1957 election on what is basically a spiritual issue.

He has made his campaign a crusade for freedom. He used the pipeline debate of 1956, particularly the House of Commons scenes of Black Friday, to dramatize his claims that only a change of government can restore to the Canadian people their freedom to govern themselves through Parliament.[21]

---

younger, more fascinating rival. He became waspish and petulant. He complained to his own people that they were not filling the halls, that he disliked speaking to half-empty auditoriums . . . .The mythical benign gentleman disappeared and suddenly the country was confronted by a petulant, irritable old man who was willing to create national disunity in order to win at any cost." C.P. dispatch from Napanee, June 4.

[20]Harvey Hickey, "Prime Minister Found Cautious in Extreme," Toronto *Globe and Mail*, June 1.

[21]Clark Davey, "P.C. Leader's Campaign Likened to a Crusade," *ibid.*

Both of the comments on the leaders' tours just cited appeared in a newspaper whose editorial policy was friendly to the Conservatives and bitterly hostile to the government. To counter any possible bias, the final illustration is taken from the Winnipeg *Free Press* which hoped for a Liberal victory. Commenting on the leaders' campaigns after Mr. Diefenbaker's triumphal performances in British Columbia, an article on the editorial page stated that

the government had adopted a calculated posture of confidence, almost of indifference. Mr. St. Laurent had travelled through British Columbia obviously determined to say as little as possible in speeches written by a discreet ghost. In fact, he said practically nothing. The strategy of refusing to argue issues, relying on the Prime Minister's personal prestige and scorning the enemy had worked well in 1953. Why change it?

After giving an inconclusive answer to this query, the paper turned to Mr. Diefenbaker, saying that he had made his campaign as noisy and gaudy as possible.

Actually the contents and delivery of his speeches were somewhat below his average, for he arrived tired from a long national tour with all his ideas already spent. He had nothing to offer but the old promise of more spending and less taxes, lower interest rates, an end of inflation, the revival of parliament and the development of resources.

All these themes he touched lightly without any explanation of policy or any coherent argument. Facts were overwhelmed with sound, passion substituted for arithmetic, moral indignation pumped up to the bursting point. But Mr. Diefenbaker provided the liveliest show of the election . . . and many listeners undoubtedly failed to notice that he was saying even less than the Prime Minister, though saying it more shrilly and with evangelistic fervour. . . .

The Prime Minister's speeches . . . had form and organization but no fire. Mr. Diefenbaker's had no organization or form but they were flaming hot . . . Mr. Diefenbaker has chosen instead to cast himself as the humble man in a mood of protest, the common Canadian outraged by Liberal prosperity, the little guy fighting for his rights.

So far as the crowds mean anything, that posture is a brilliant success at one night stands . . .[22]

Broadcasts

Important though the personal appearances of the leaders no doubt were to the parties' campaigns, their effect on the outcome of the election was probably no greater than Mr. Diefenbaker's or Mr. St. Laurent's talks on the radio and particularly on television. Political meetings are attended

[22]Winnipeg *Free Press*, May 27.

in large part only by the converted; normally their major effect is to kindle enthusiasm among party workers and to obtain publicity. Broadcasts not only attract audiences whose numbers far exceed the total attendance of political meetings; the proportion of opposed, uncommitted, and undecided voters listening to them is also incomparably greater. By 1957 television had become a more important medium than radio for purposes of national political broadcasting in Canada. The leaders' television scripts were also made to serve for their radio appearances. In the ensuing discussion of their broadcasting activities, therefore, only television will be considered.

Eight so-called free-time television network broadcasts were made available by the C.B.C. in each language to the Liberal party; the Conservatives were allotted seven such free periods. Mr. St. Laurent spoke on three occasions in each language whereas Mr. Diefenbaker appeared four times in English and made only a minor contribution to his party's French television broadcasts. The Conservative leader occasionally appeared with a candidate who could be counted on to make a direct appeal to certain sections of the electorate. In a Quebec broadcast, for example, he introduced and thanked Mr. Léon Balcer, who had been so publicly opposed to him at the time of the national convention. In a telecast from Winnipeg, Mr. Diefenbaker performed the same service for Mr. Regnier, a former prominent Liberal, contesting a Manitoba seat for the Conservatives. The leader also appeared on a panel with two Conservative ladies who had been elected to the House of Commons.

It is, of course, difficult to compare with exactitude the effectiveness of two television performers, but there was general agreement among impartial observers that Mr. Diefenbaker did better than Mr. St. Laurent. The Prime Minister made few concessions to the new medium. He tended to read his script as he would have in a radio broadcast. Even the use of a teleprompter failed to make his performance more relaxed. He was unable to overcome his objections to make-up or ever to feel really at home before the television cameras. He, therefore, appeared somewhat wooden, and unexciting.

Mr. Diefenbaker, on the other hand, took well to the new medium. He had no objection to being made-up and was otherwise prepared to adopt any measure or device which would contribute to the effectiveness of his performances. On the whole his television manner was rather restless, exhibiting numerous personal mannerisms, but these did not seem to detract from the effectiveness of his speeches. He appeared more relaxed than the Prime Minister and his television broadcasts seemed to have been as convincing to his viewers as his personal appearances had been to those attending his meetings. Conservative organizers thought that Mr. Diefenbaker's television appearances were a decided asset in their campaign; Liberals had some doubts about the effectiveness of their leader's programmes. Mr. St. Laurent made dignified and restrained speeches on the air, but they were lacking in the sort of magnetism which many viewers seemed to find in the more flamboyant television manner of his Conservative opponent.[23]

What has been said above about the general campaign styles of the two leaders applies equally to their broadcasts. Mr. Diefenbaker's argument on the air, as on the hustings, was more belligerent and aggressive, Mr. St. Laurent's more restrained. While Mr. Diefenbaker's speeches seemed to follow a line which was in no way affected by what the Liberals did in the campaign, Mr. St. Laurent's talks contained attempts to answer some opposition arguments. The Prime Minister was, therefore, occasionally on the defensive and this even when he was attacking the Conservatives.

[23]Something of the essential flavour of the leaders' campaign arguments can be detected in their television appeals. A summary of their major television speeches is, therefore, placed in Appendix C, for those who wish to obtain a more detailed view of the campaign oratory than can be presented in the main text of this book.

THE CAMPAIGNS COMPARED

8

General Strategy

IN THE 1953 ELECTION the Liberals won 173,[1] or 65 per cent, of the seats in the House of Commons. Their main rivals only carried fifty-one (19 per cent) of the constituencies, and the C.C.F. and Social Credit parties twenty-three (9 per cent) and fifteen (6 per cent) respectively. Three independents were also elected on that occasion. At the time of the dissolution in 1957, there were seven vacancies in the House, but otherwise the relative strength of the parties had not changed materially in the period between the two elections. The Liberals had about 120 more seats than their nearest rivals. Almost everyone, therefore, expected, in the spring of 1957, that they would again be returned on June 10. But even the staunchest Liberal supporters admitted that their party would be doing extremely well if it held its own. True, the Conservative leadership convention had made it almost certain that the Liberals would again be able to count on a solid nucleus of Quebec seats, perhaps around sixty-five in number. Newfoundland also seemed to have remained fairly safe. But elsewhere in the country the main Liberal task would be to prevent any serious losses in the number of seats held by the party's sitting Members.

No spectacular election strategy had been devised for the purposes of maintaining Liberal strength. The pre-election budget had been a model of restraint and caution. The government was obviously not going to bribe the electorate by spending public funds recklessly. Liberal

[1]The figure includes two Independent Liberals and one Liberal-Labour member.

strategists appeared convinced that on the whole the public still supported their party and that no drastic measures were required to ensure
the government's return. To the extent that any over-all plan of the
campaign was formulated at all, it seemed to consist of the notion that
nothing dramatic was to be attempted, that a quiet campaign was desirable, and that the most effective thing the party could do was to discredit the opposition.

Two incontrovertible facts confronted the Conservatives responsible
for planning the campaign. First, their party had in recent years repeatedly polled about thirty per cent of the popular vote and no more.
A hard core of Conservatives had clearly remained loyal to the party
even when its representation in the House seemed almost to disappear.
The Conservatives had equally clearly failed to appeal effectively to
many individuals outside this solid core of Tory voters. Secondly, the
party had repeatedly been unable to attract any appreciable support in
the province of Quebec. And, without Quebec, everyone kept saying, a
Parliamentary majority in Ottawa was out of the question. From the
recognition and examination of these two facts emerged, in the beginning
of 1957, the strategy which was to guide the election campaign of the
Diefenbaker party.

The problem of Quebec had occupied the party for many years, of
course. Mr. Drew had made several attempts to build up some support
among the French-Canadian population, and it will be recalled that the
chief of Mr. Fleming's claims to the leadership of the party was that
he was popular in Quebec. But the position the Conservative party took
vis-à-vis French Canada was influenced to a large extent by a westerner
—Mr. Gordon Churchill.

Early in 1954 Mr. Churchill wrote a memorandum[2] based on an
exhaustive analysis of the relation between votes and seats in the House
of Commons obtained by the major parties in past elections. He argued
that to secure a working majority the Conservatives would have to win
137 seats. At the time of writing they had fifty; from where were the
remaining eighty-seven seats to come? The traditional answer had always
been that a good proportion would have to be won in Quebec. Mr.
Churchill, after his painstaking analysis of earlier elections, doubted
whether the Conservative party was wise in expecting support from that
quarter sufficient to carry it into office. If twenty more seats were won
in Quebec, instead of the four the Conservatives then held, sixty-seven
seats would still have to be gained in Ontario, the Maritimes and the
West. But to double the seats the Conservatives had in 1953 in these

[2]Gordon C. Churchill, "Forming the Government," unpublished memorandum, Jan., 1954.

areas would only give them an additional forty-six members, still twenty-one short of the quota. What was required, therefore, was victory in 60 per cent of the constituencies in these areas, or 75 per cent of them in Ontario and 50 per cent in the Maritimes and the West. This would give the Conservatives 116 Members in the House, who, if joined by twenty-four from Quebec, would control the Chamber. Mr. Churchill concluded: "It appears . . . that the major effort of the Conservative Party must be made in Ontario and to an almost equal degree in the Maritimes and the West. In these areas the Party has formerly had considerable strength whereas in Quebec it has had very little strength since 1891 and practically none at all since 1935."

Some of Mr. Churchill's critics have claimed that in his analysis he exhibited a typically Tory anti-French attitude. In a second memorandum,[3] restating his case, Mr. Churchill took account of his critics: "The statement is frequently made that 'you cannot govern the country without Quebec' and to this statement there is no serious disagreement, for in the interest of national unity all parts of Canada should be represented in the government." Repeating the argument presented in the previous memoir, Mr. Churchill insisted that "Quebec should not be ignored but it is extremely doubtful that Quebec will be decisive. The military maxim 'reinforce success not failure' might well be considered as applicable to political strategy." At the time of writing, Mr. Churchill found that if the Liberals lost sixty seats to the Conservatives, the latter, while not in a clear majority, would be the largest party in the House, would form the government and could probably endure with the support of the "splinter" parties. Where could the Conservatives find these sixty seats?

Surveying the by now familiar terrain, Mr. Churchill found that in the Maritimes, Ontario and the West there were 141 seats not held by his party.

Our major effort should be directed towards obtaining 60 of those 141 seats. This would not represent a greater change than occurred in 1878 when 64 seats changed, nor in 1925 when 57 changed, nor in 1935 when 83 changed. In these three elections 80%, 91% and 82% of the changes occurred in the areas represented by Ontario, the Maritimes and the West.

If 60 seats are won in that good fighting territory, a minority government can be formed. If Quebec produces a gain of 20 seats a government with an overall majority would be assured.

Mr. Churchill's recommendation that the party "reinforce success not failure" constituted a revolutionary precept in so far as recent prac-

[3]"Conservative Strategy for the Next Election," unpublished memorandum, Jan., 1956.

tice was concerned. In the previous election, almost half the funds of the national organization were spent in Quebec, with only four seats to show for it. The new leadership of the party accepted Mr. Churchill's analysis and his recommendation: Quebec was not to be treated as a special case, the major effort was to be made in Ontario, the Maritimes, and to a somewhat lesser extent in the West.

Out of the realization that in recent elections only about thirty per cent of the voters had supported the Conservative party grew the second important element in the 1957 election strategy: an all-out effort would be made to appeal to normally non-Conservative voters. Fifteen to twenty per cent of the electorate, if they joined the traditional Conservative voters, would assure the Liberals' defeat. It was assumed that the traditional party supporter would again vote Conservative, provided a reasonably acceptable candidate were running, and that the major effort would have to be directed at the new voters, the uncommitted, and at the disgruntled followers of the other parties.

Underlying the Conservative campaign, therefore, was the decision not to weaken the efforts of the party elsewhere by over-emphasizing the struggle for Quebec. Secondly, there was the realization of the obvious but seemingly often forgotten fact, that success depended on the votes of a substantial number of the electorate who had probably never before voted for a Conservative federal candidate. Given these two points of departure, it was not to be marvelled at that the 1957 Conservative campaign stood in marked contrast to previous ones, and that on the whole the efforts of Mr. Diefenbaker and his supporters sometimes seemed unorthodox. By comparison, Liberal campaign strategy made for a more static and traditional type of electoral campaign.[4]

The Strategy Applied

Because of the nature of the Liberal campaign little can be said about it that has not already been suggested. The most effective means of keeping an election reasonably quiet and of not stirring up undue excitement is to do as little as possible that is out of the ordinary or in any

[4]Exceptions can be found to almost every generalization made in this chapter about the parties' campaigns. This is inevitable in a highly decentralized party where in a sense even a national election consists of a series of by-elections fought by a variety of individuals in a variety of circumstances. But the conclusions reached here seem valid nevertheless: they are the result of careful observation of not only the national offices and the national leaders, both of which impose certain uniformity on the campaigns, but also of the activities in large numbers of constituencies.

way exciting. The Liberal campaign, whether by design or accident, failed to arouse more than routine interest among the voters or the correspondents. It was devoid of subtle ploys, unexpected turns, or sensational developments. The means employed in appealing to the public were well tried and simple: Mr. St. Laurent—considered the most valuable asset of the party—was linked to the generally good conditions in the country. Uncle Louis—this time, as was shown above, ever more frequently and openly emphasizing the family image—was identified with Canada's development and prosperity. And Uncle Louis was, of course, linked inseparably to the Liberal party.

No issues were admitted to exist, no alternative to the Liberals acknowledged, no reason for discontent credited. Canada had done exceedingly well under the Liberals: why should anyone change the government? The calm reply to opposition onslaughts was in keeping with the unruffled tones of the earlier Liberal speeches: promises made by the other parties were irresponsible and could not be kept, the Conservative leader had entered into an unholy alliance with the premier of Ontario, the Conservatives could not possibly win enough seats to be elected— to avoid a stalemate a vote for the Liberals was essential.

Conservative efforts to capture the support of new groups took many forms. The most obvious of these was the continuous emphasis on Mr. Diefenbaker and on the Diefenbaker party. The support of traditional Conservatives was taken for granted regardless of what the party was called in the advertisements or on the air. But there were many, it was thought, who wanted to vote against the Liberals, who liked Mr. Diefenbaker, but who would have preferred to overlook the fact that they were voting Conservative. Hence the stress on the Diefenbaker party. It made it possible for many to vote Conservative without apparently doing so. The slogan "It's time for a Diefenbaker government" had the additional advantage of stressing the theme that the government had been in power too long, while simultaneously providing a "non-partisan" alternative. And Mr. Diefenbaker proved himself a campaigner of unexpected popularity.

In addition to the label, the text, too, was changed. The transformation of the public image of the Conservative party, begun at the leadership convention, was continued during the election. One of the most serious handicaps of the Conservative party in its bid for national support had been its association in the popular mind with the wealthy and supposedly reactionary interests of Ontario and Quebec. Mr. Drew's retirement removed one link with the well-to-do Toronto Conservatives. Mr. Diefenbaker took the party further from the stereotype it had previously formed in the public mind by stressing the progressive element in the programme. Conservative election promises placed the party well ahead of the Liberals in terms of proposed welfare payments. While assuring everyone that, if elected, the state would revert to its proper status of servant, Mr. Diefenbaker's promises left no doubt that the servant would do more for the people under his orders than under those of his predecessors. Traditional Conservative distrust of the state had disappeared from the party Mr. Diefenbaker was presenting to the voters, and with this disappearance, presumably, much of the public's identification of the party with eastern financial interests.

One of the reasons for the abandonment of the convention resolutions was precisely that one of these resolutions left some ambiguity about whether the Conservatives wished to attach a means test to the old age pension.[5] The resolutions were considered another link with the "old guard" and as such were suppressed.[6] The new leaders' judgement in not using the resolutions was confirmed, as far as they could see, when an old-line Conservative editorial writer of a Toronto financial paper strongly urged them to play up the conventions' doubts about the old age pension. This, to the "progressive" element among the leaders, was exquisite proof of the fact that it would have been politically foolish to release the resolutions.

Actually there were additional reasons for this seemingly unwarranted censorship on the part of the new leaders. Mr. Diefenbaker was reluctant to enter the election campaign with a well-formulated programme or a short manifesto. These, he probably thought, would reduce the area within which he might manoeuvre. Greater flexibility was achieved by working out his programme or promises as he travelled from region to region. In addition to not tying him down to a virtually irrevocable stand, which their publication would have entailed, the withholding of the resolutions also conferred some tactical advantages on the Conservatives. The Liberals were, no doubt, taken in by Conservative promises of an early release of the resolutions. They were, therefore, probably preparing to fire at a target which in fact never materialized.

[5]"A Progressive Conservative Government in agreement with the provinces will provide increased benefits under the Old Age Assistance Act. . . . Similar increased benefits will be extended to recipients of Old Age Security (i.e. Old Age Pensions) *where necessitous."* Progressive Conservative Party of Canada, *What the Progressive Conservative Party Stands For,* Report of the Committee on Resolutions and Policy as Adopted by the National Convention, Dec. 14, 1956, p. 14 (italics added).

[6]They did not, in fact, reflect the views of the "old guard" as was shown in chap. II above.

More important, however, the piecemeal publication of the Conservative programme succeeded in creating front-page news not once, but on several occasions. Many of the resolutions adopted by the convention were incorporated, sometimes verbatim, into Mr. Diefenbaker's programme. But they were released only a few at a time and in such a way as to be given the maximum amount of publicity in the areas of the country in which they would be most effective. Furthermore, had they been published as the party resolutions, they might have been rejected or at least suspected by those easily offended by the Conservative label. Announced by Mr. Diefenbaker, they were identified with him more than with the party and—a consideration of great importance not only to the leader himself but to the general plan of the campaign—they helped to place Mr. Diefenbaker's speech on the front pages of the newspapers. The suppression of the convention resolutions was, therefore, another instance of the party attempting to acquire a new physiognomy and of the campaign being linked to the Conservative leader more than to the party.

Ample evidence was presented in previous chapters of Conservative attempts to undermine public confidence in the government and in the Liberal party. One phase of the campaign to appeal to the previously anti- or non-Conservative voters was connected in a particular way with these attacks on the party in power. It was no doubt assumed that Mr. St. Laurent's following was often so loyal that nothing the Conservatives said could drive a wedge between the Prime Minister and many of his supporters. It was therefore argued that Mr. St. Laurent was too old to remain in office long and that he would resign soon after the election. The choice confronting the voter, according to this argument, was not between Mr. Diefenbaker and Mr. St. Laurent, but between Mr. Diefenbaker and an as yet unknown Liberal leader.

It was suggested above that the Conservative campaign had a somewhat unorthodox aspect, compared with earlier campaigns. Among the reasons for this was the fact that national headquarters had been taken over from the so-called "old guard" practically on the eve of the election. Mr. Grosart and his staff introduced a number of innovations, the most notable of which was the decision to decentralize many of the party's activities. As was stated above, the Conservatives' national organization had always been more highly centralized than the Liberals'. One of the consequences has been that their election machinery has tended to be more rigid. The new leaders, partly perhaps out of choice and partly because, being new to the job, they had no other alternative, decided to reverse this trend and to decentralize much of the decision-making within the party. For practical purposes this meant that the provincial parties were able to adapt their campaigns to local conditions and to utilize local issues and local grievances in a highly effective manner. Since all sections of the party recognized the strong appeal of Mr. Diefenbaker, the common and frequent use of the leader's name and picture gave considerable uniformity to a variety of activities which were local in inspiration and scope. Co-operation between the provincial and national organizations was harmonious as the result of the operation of the decentralization principle.

Campaign Costs

In one sphere this co-operation proved of particular benefit. It enabled the leaders to reduce the allocation of funds to Quebec on grounds which were unexceptionable—that all provinces must be treated alike. In the past, the national office had interfered in a number of important ways with the spending by provincial and constituency parties of moneys derived from the national campaign funds. This had been inevitable but frequently created friction. In 1957 a new way of allocating the bulk of the party's war-chest was devised, to the satisfaction of most provincial party treasurers.

A quota of $3,000 was assigned to every constituency by the national party. But this three thousand dollars was not paid to the constituency organization. Each provincial committee was given a lump sum equal to $3,000 multiplied by the number of constituencies in the province. Ontario, with eighty-five constituencies, received $255,000; Manitoba, with fourteen ridings, obtained $42,000 from the national treasury. Each provincial party could decide how to allocate the sum it received from Ottawa. If it wished to spend the whole amount on only a small number of constituencies it could do so. Or if it preferred, it was able to divide its grant equally among all constituency parties. At least two important consequences followed from this new practice of allocating resources: money was spent more effectively because each provincial committee was able to assess local conditions better than the national organization had been able to do in the past. Secondly, Quebec received its grant on the same basis as everyone else and was not particularly favoured over the other—and, according to the Churchill memorandum, more promising—areas. Its allocation was about $200,000—a sum which, when related to previously obtained results, was a more reasonable portion of the available funds than that which had been allocated to that province in the past.

Altogether, the provincial parties received about three quarters of a million dollars from the national office for distribution among Conservative constituency organizations. In addition, the Ottawa headquarters also helped to defray part of the expenses incurred by the provincial parties in the course of the campaign. Printing costs, advertising outlays, the national leader's tours, and its own administrative expenses constituted the other major items for which the national organization assumed financial responsibilities. The total amount spent by the Conservative national office was about $1,700,000, which is a relatively small sum considering other national campaigns. It reflects the great difficulties encountered by the Conservative party in raising an adequate campaign fund. One of the curious features of the 1957 campaign was that despite the serious impecuniosity experienced during the campaign, contributions of considerable magnitude were made to the Conservative party in the three or four days immediately preceding the election. This last-minute financial aid suggests that towards the end of the campaign the business community was beginning to have doubts about the outcome of the contest.

About half the cost of the Conservative national campaign was borne by the national office. Provincial parties and constituency organizations raised the rest of the money and paid for a number of expenses incurred by themselves. The total cost of the Conservative campaign was probably between three and three and a half million dollars.[7]

The activities and consequently the costs of the Liberal campaign were on a much grander scale than those of the Conservatives. But it was unfortunately impossible to obtain first-hand information about the financial aspects of Liberal campaigning. The government party probably spent two to three times as much as its main rivals. In the absence of more information it would, however, be useless to speculate about the detailed costs of the Liberal campaign. It is no doubt safe but not greatly enlightening to conclude that the national, provincial, and constituency organizations of the Liberal party spent between six and ten million dollars in the course of the 1957 election.

[7]For an excellent discussion of the financing of Conservative campaigns in the past see Williams, *The Conservative Party of Canada*, chap. v. I am indebted to the frankness of Mr. A. Grosart for the information on the financial aspects of the 1957 Conservative campaign.

Campaign Strategy in Quebec

Conservative politicians in Quebec were at first greatly disturbed by their party's policy on the allocation of national funds, referred to above. The reason was not merely that the amounts to be spent in Quebec were drastically reduced compared to previous elections. The decision to treat their province like any other seemed to them, para-doxically perhaps, to be highly discriminatory: it had always been recognized in the past that electioneering was considerably more expensive in French Canada. Not to acknowledge this was to misunder-stand Quebec, to treat it shabbily and, indeed, to make the position of French-Canadian Conservative politicians extremely awkward compared with their colleagues elsewhere in the country. Conservative leaders refused to consider Quebec as a special case, however, and insisted that basically French Canadians are not very different from their English-speaking fellow-citizens. Nevertheless, it was inevitable that the party's plans should reflect conditions prevailing in that province.

Conservative strategy was influenced by two factors: the decision of the national party to avoid heavy involvement in the province and the absence, to all intents and purposes, of an effective provincial organiza-tion. With one or two exceptions, notably some of the English-speaking areas in Montreal, the constituency parties were in a lamentable state of decay. The appearance of strength given by the absence of acclamations and the presence of sixty-nine Conservative candidates in Quebec, out of a possible total of seventy-five was, therefore, rather illusory. Some of the Conservative standard-bearers were largely token candidates without effective organizations to back them. The party seriously contested only about twenty-five constituencies in which, for one reason or another, it seemed worthwhile to do so.

Union Nationale support was one of the best reasons for the serious contesting of a Quebec riding by a Conservative candidate. Mr. Duplessis maintained his customary official neutrality in the election and the Union Nationale did not, as such, participate. But about half a dozen provincial cabinet ministers and a larger number of Union Nationale members of of the provincial legislature did intervene in opposition to Liberal candi-dates.[8] The reasons for Union Nationale support vary. In some instances

[8] The following members of the Duplessis ministry took an active part in the election: Hon. John S. Bourque, Minister of Lands and Forests; Hon. J. D. Begin, Minister of Colonization; Hon. Antonio Talbot, Minister of Roads; Hon. Antoine Rivard, General Solicitor and Minister of Transportation and Com-munications; Hon. Arthur Leclerc and Hon. Jacques Miquelon, Ministers without Portfolio. Others may also have intervened without receiving as much publicity

relatives of prominent members of the provincial administration were nominated as Conservative candidates. More frequently the reason was that attempts were made to settle old debts with the Liberals. In the 1956 provincial election a number of prominent federal Liberal members and particularly cabinet ministers intervened on behalf of provincial Liberal candidates against nominees of the Union Nationale. The latter party now retaliated against these disturbers of a previous gentlemen's agreement which had kept federal Liberals out of provincial contests.[9]

In the partly English-speaking constituencies of Montreal intensive organizational work had been done for a long period of time. Some of these ridings, particularly Notre Dame de Grace, St. Lawrence–St. George, St. Antoine–Westmount, and Jacques Cartier–LaSalle, therefore offered good fighting ground and were seriously contested. Some additional constituencies were selected for determined battle because a Conservative held it (Dorchester and Quebec West), because a good candidate had come forward, because results in the previous election had been reasonably close or because Liberal disunity seemed to offer a promising opportunity for a Conservative candidate.

But most Quebec contests were fought in earnest because Union Nationale support was forthcoming for the Conservative candidate and the outcome did not, therefore, seem completely hopeless. It would be misleading, however, to assume from this reliance on the Union Nationale that an alliance had been reached between Mr. Diefenbaker and the Quebec nationalist party. No such alliance or axis, as agreements with Mr. Duplessis were inevitably called, was in existence in 1957. As so often happens in politics, all that occurred was that it suited both the Conservatives and the Union Nationale in a number of constituencies to work together in a limited way and for a limited purpose. It was the same identity of interests which induced the Conservatives not to nominate candidates in a few constituencies where the Union Nationale thought it could help defeat a Liberal by backing an Independent in a straight fight against a government candidate. Small-scale electoral pacts between members of M. Duplessis' party and the Conservatives were in fact

as those listed here. The information contained in this section of the chapter is based on dispatches about the election in *Le Devoir*, the Winnipeg *Free Press*, and the Toronto *Globe and Mail*. I also discussed the campaign in Quebec with Conservative officials.

[9]While it was not always possible to say with complete confidence whether Union Nationale support was being given to Conservative candidates, newspaper reports indicated that it was forthcoming in at least the following constituencies: Bellechasse, Bonaventure, Brome-Missisquoi, Charlevoix, Compton-Frontenac, Dorchester, Gatineau, Hull, Laval, Lotbinière, Nicolet-Yamaska, Pontiac-Temiscamingue, Portneuf, Saint-Hyacinthe-Bagot, Sherbrooke, and Three Rivers.

paralleled by local agreements between the Union Nationale and some Liberal candidates. In St. Jean–Iberville–Napierville and in Beauharnois–Salaberry, for example, the official Liberal candidates were backed by Union Nationale organizers. These instances were, however, less typical than the Conservative–Union Nationale pacts.

Conservative strategy in Quebec was, therefore, largely determined by the relationships that developed locally with the dominant provincial party. For the student of the election, Union Nationale backing of a number of Conservative candidates was of particular interest because of the effect it had on the financing of the Conservative campaign in Quebec. Some of the new Conservative leaders have expressed their pride in having treated Quebec like any other province; they deprecate the idea that Quebec is unique and supports a political life quite different from that of the other provinces. The Conservative record in Quebec subsequent to the first application of the new formula for dividing national funds is invoked as one of the proofs of the "Quebec is just like any other province" theory. But this particular prop in the argument is knocked out of position when the role of the Union Nationale in the 1957 election is recalled. For wherever the local Union Nationale organization did oppose a Liberal candidate it did so lavishly and in a manner which has made notorious the electioneering techniques employed by M. Duplessis' party.[10]

Union Nationale support for some Liberal candidates was one of the factors which complicated Liberal campaign strategy in Quebec. The party was almost certain of winning an overwhelming number of seats, but it was not free from difficulties. The problem lay in the large number of Independent Liberal candidates who presented themselves to the electorate, invariably running not only against other parties but also against official Liberal standard-bearers. There were twenty-four such Independent Liberals causing annoyance and apprehension among the provincial party leaders.

Some of the Independent Liberals offered themselves to the public in protest against the allegedly infamous alliances between the Liberals and the Duplessis forces. This was the case in Saint Jean–Iberville–Napierville where one of the bitterest struggles in the province was waged between an officially backed Liberal and a candidate challenging the party hierarchy. In a number of constituencies opposition developed against the sitting member with consequent mounting pressure to select a new candidate. Indeed, some of the attempts to field Independent Liberal candidates reflected growing restiveness resulting from the

[10]See above, chap. v, pp. 114–15.

tendency of the provincial officials to overlook the wishes of the local associations.[11]

Another reason for the large number of Independent Liberal candidates was to be found in the strong position of the Liberal party in Quebec. Since the election of a Liberal candidate was assured in a number of constituencies, it was tempting for those with political ambitions to try their luck as a Liberal candidate, albeit an Independent one. It was assumed (and in view of earlier Liberal practice not without reason) that once elected, it would be only a matter of time before an Independent Liberal would become acceptable as a *bona fide*, full-fledged Liberal Member of Parliament. A number of Independent Liberals presented themselves to the voters, therefore, in hopes of benefiting from the popularity of Mr. St. Laurent and from the party's position in office, at the expense of sitting Liberals whom they thought they might defeat.

The main strategy of the Liberal party in Quebec was, of course, to capitalize on the popularity of its French-Canadian leader. Secondly, its efforts were designed, in so far as this was possible, to prevent the atomization of Liberal votes among official and Independent candidates. The method most relied upon was for Mr. St. Laurent to make a number of strong pleas on behalf of the official Liberal candidates. On the whole this proved to have been sufficient—only two Independent Liberals were elected and in none of the other constituencies where the Liberals failed to win could their defeat be ascribed to the division of the Liberal vote among several candidates.

Neither party thought it necessary to wage a particularly intensive battle in the French-speaking province. The Liberals were too sure of victory, the Conservatives too certain of defeat. The province was divided by the Conservatives into three regions—Montreal, Quebec, and an area centring around Three Rivers—and by the Liberals into only two—the Montreal and Quebec areas. In each of these regions the routine campaign activities were deployed. But the certainty of the outcome had clearly relegated Quebec to the position of a secondary battlefield. Almost all election reports emanating from that province testified to the seeming apathy of the Quebec voters. Under the circumstances, this apathy was probably the condition upon which were predicated the local campaign strategies of both the major parties.

[11]See also above, chap. VI, pp. 123–4.

THE CAMPAIGNS ASSESSED

9

Efficacy

AN OVERWHELMING MAJORITY in the House of Commons and a long series of successful elections gave the Liberal party immense confidence as it embarked on the campaign. Being in office and seemingly having every prospect of returning to power, the party attracted considerable financial support from those individuals and corporations whose donations constitute the campaign funds of the parties. In addition to attracting private support, the party derived the usual benefits associated with being in office: it controlled public spending, had access to the knowledge and skill of the civil service, and its leaders, as ministers of the Crown, were well known in all parts of the country. Despite the likelihood that the government would suffer some electoral setbacks in the forthcoming contest, its assets seemed so massive as to preclude the possibility of defeat.

So impressed was everyone with the credit columns of the Liberal balance sheet that to a large measure the liabilities went unnoticed. And yet, as subsequent events have shown, they were considerable. At the provincial level the party had been losing support steadily and it is to be surmised that most provincial Liberal organizations were in a weak state. At the time of the 1949 election the party was in office in five provinces and participated in the coalition government of a sixth. By 1953 it formed the government in only four provinces, and in 1957 it held office in only Newfoundland and Prince Edward Island, provinces whose populations were represented in the House of Commons by only eleven members, and in Manitoba where, as we have seen, the provincial organization did not give the federal party much support. Furthermore, some ministers, though well known were no longer well liked. Mr. Howe was the most outstanding but by no means the only leading Liberal who had been receiving an increasingly bad press and who, whatever else he may have been, probably had ceased being an electoral asset to the government. The economy, while giving the country general prosperity, nevertheless creaked in some sectors and thus caused hardship and anxiety in certain regions of Canada. Most important, perhaps, the party was not being given vigorous national leadership. The various ministers minded the affairs of their departments, but there seemed to be no unified and dynamic force leading the cabinet.

This absence of leadership in the cabinet became increasingly apparent and led to the identification of the government with some of its less popular ministers, notably Mr. Howe and Mr. Pickersgill, rather than with the better-liked Mr. St. Laurent. Lack of unity and dynamic over-all leadership affected not only the government but also the conduct of the election. National headquarters went through the motions which had proved successful in earlier elections (with the exception of its television activities which were, of course, new) but, given the general line of the campaign, its efforts proved unexciting. The various leaders seemed to be performing their routine electoral tasks well enough, but the Liberal campaign gives the impression that there was no high command regularly examining the party's strategy and tactics, comparing these with the efforts of the opposition, and providing the central leadership which would give the party the flexibility and dynamism required to counter effectively the activities of its opponents.

It is possible, of course, that the above assessment made by an outside observer fails to do justice to the real efforts that were being made by the Liberal leaders. But some of the details of Liberal activities given below strengthen such a view and confirmation of it is to be found in the recollections of a well-informed Liberal campaigner. "All during the period, from the beginning of the year right to the date of the election," he wrote, "various incidents brought confirmation to my mind of the opinion, which I had formed some time before, that there was no real co-ordination of efforts or team play amongst the party leaders."[1]

If only hindsight now enables us to detect the extent of the weaknesses affecting the Liberal party in 1957, the handicaps confronting the Conservatives were plain for everyone to see at the time. Having failed in five successive elections to win power, and apparently completely devoid of support in some important regions of the country, the party appeared

[1]"The Election of 1957," an unpublished memoir by Senator Power.

destined for another crushing defeat. The new leader seemed unacceptable to French Canada, was disliked by many of his colleagues, and probably was also unpopular with the eastern financial backers of the party who had supported it even during its long years of adversity. Times seemed good and such anti-government sentiment as there was in the country was again likely to be neutralized by being scattered among C.C.F., Social Credit, and Conservative voters. If to these drawbacks were added the inexperience at the head of the party of the new leader and some of his advisers, the youthfulness of many Conservative candidates, and the apparently unshakable habit among large numbers of Canadians of voting only Liberal in federal elections, it seemed most improbable that the Conservatives would do more than pick up a few additional seats and so endure another Parliament in forlorn opposition.

Mr. Diefenbaker, if his self-confident manner was taken at face value, seemed totally unaware of the apparent odds facing him. Or if aware of them, he chose to ignore them. It was, indeed, one of the factors favouring the party that it had selected a leader who was either convinced that he would lead it to power or who at least acted as if he held this conviction. But the confidence, vigour and appeal of the new leader was not the only asset enjoyed by the party. While he and his closest advisers— Mr. Hees, Mr. Churchill, and Mr. Grosart—injected a new spirit into the campaign, the provincial organizations in the Maritimes and in Ontario and, as it appeared later, also in British Columbia and the Prairies, were providing the traditional organization and plodding campaign efforts without which no election can be won. The skilful improvization of the national leaders was therefore complemented by the painstakingly built-up and laboriously maintained organizations in the provinces and in the constituencies which antedated the advent of Mr. Diefenbaker to the party leadership.

Whereas the Liberals were suffering from the gradual decline of their party organizations in most provinces, the Conservatives were undergoing something of a revival in the Maritimes and in parts, at least, of the Prairies. Mr. Diefenbaker and his friends could therefore draw on the strength, support and popularity of Mr. Flemming and Mr. Stanfield, the successful premiers of New Brunswick and Nova Scotia, and of Mr. Roblin, the rising young Conservative leader in Manitoba. Further strength was given the Conservative campaign by the unqualified and invaluable support of Premier Frost who had previously avoided extensive involvement in federal elections. But while these Conservative assets made the situation of the party less hopeless than it seemed to many, they nevertheless were far from assuring its electoral victory.

It is impossible to say to what extent the Conservative and Liberal campaigns affected the outcome of the election. It would be most surprising, however, particularly in view of the closeness of the result, if the activities of the parties during the campaign had not had a decisive effect on it. And whereas the Liberal campaign was characterized by the almost placid confidence of the cabinet, Conservative efforts were dominated by the sense of urgency and crisis imparted by Mr. Diefenbaker's astoundingly tireless and vigorous campaign. The difference is epitomized by what each of the leaders did just before the formal opening of the campaign.

Mr. Diefenbaker, unburdened by the responsibilities of a prime minister, campaigned vigorously from the moment of his selection as leader. During much of the time in which Mr. St. Laurent attended to government business, the new leader of the opposition, quite properly, criss-crossed the country, making himself known to the people in his new capacity as the most serious challenger for the prime ministership. Early in March, he visited British Columbia, making some important speeches. Later he met about a thousand supporters in Montreal, and campaigned in Newfoundland, Nova Scotia, Manitoba, and Saskatchewan. It was to be expected that the Liberal leader would counter this feverish activity of Mr. Diefenbaker by making some widely advertised and heralded speeches as soon as his government duties permitted it. But those Liberals who had hoped that their leader would attempt to offset the effects of his chief adversary's early start were to be disappointed. At a press conference held a few days after dissolution Mr. St. Laurent announced that he would go to his home in Quebec for Easter and return to Ottawa on April 27.[2] This meant, in fact, that the Liberal leader was absent from Ottawa and out of the limelight for well over a week at a time when the Conservative leader was already well launched on his national campaign.

Mr. St. Laurent may have spent this time preparing for his forthcoming nation-wide trip or in some other way working on the election. After a strenuous Parliamentary session the Prime Minister no doubt welcomed a little respite prior to undertaking the gruelling campaign tour. Indeed, for a man of his age a holiday was probably essential. It may even be argued that the kind of campaigning undertaken by Mr. Diefenbaker is too tiring and was wisely not copied by the Liberal leader.[3] These, however, are not questions which concern us here: the

[2]Winnepeg *Free Press*, April 16.
[3]See Robert Duffy, "Vote Will Tell—Liberal Workers Question Whether Present Campaign Methods Are Worthwhile," Toronto *Globe and Mail*, May 27.

matter is emphatically not raised in a spirit critical of Mr. St. Laurent. But it illustrates the different approach to the election adopted by the two major parties. At a crucial stage in the campaign nothing was heard of the Liberal leader for ten days during which Mr. Diefenbaker was getting front-page national news-coverage. During this short interval the Conservatives seized the initiative in the campaign which the Liberals never really recovered.

Despite its slow start, however, and its ill-starred course, the Liberal campaign should not be written off as incompetent. In many of its aspects it was impressive, better conceived and better organized than the Conservatives'. Liberal efforts to canvass the service vote were more extensive, thorough and vigorous than those of their opponents. Unlike the Conservatives, the government party fought with more or less equal intensity in all provinces and its campaign was, therefore, more national in scope. Circumstances had forced the Conservatives to stress some areas more than others and so, to a certain extent, to confirm the accusations of its opponents that it was not a truly national party. Its greater resources enabled the Liberal party to campaign more widely in another sense: in the extensive use of posters, billboards, newspaper and magazine advertisements, radio and television, nationally-known speakers, leaflets, pamphlets and all the other media of advertising, it presented its case more often and within view of a larger number of voters than the Conservatives (not to mention the other parties) who, because they were less affluent, could by comparison make only sparing use of some of the seemingly effective techniques provided by the advertisers.

It would also be misleading to underestimate the effectiveness of Mr. St. Laurent. While Mr. Diefenbaker indubitably provided the more eye- and ear-catching performance and while he was the more exciting campaigner, he did not rob the Prime Minister of all his appeal. Mr. St. Laurent's personality as revealed during his public appearances and in Liberal publicity was among the greatest assets of the party. Mr. Pearson's informative talks on foreign policy questions and his wit and charm also were appealing features fully exploited by the Liberal campaign.

It was shown in chapter VI that the Liberal candidates were older than the Conservatives, that they included a larger number of University-educated people and also a more numerous contingent of those whose occupations were classified under the professions. As a group, the Liberal candidates were therefore somewhat more senior and well established than the Conservatives. In Alberta, for example, the mayors of Edmonton, Calgary, and Medicine Hat were all contesting seats as Liberal candidates.[4] Among the impressive aspects of the Liberal campaign must be listed the prominence and respectability of many of its candidates. It will be argued later that certain drawbacks were also attached to the type of candidate often favoured by the Liberal party. For the present, however, it is worth noting that the old cliché about success breeding success had some relevance in so far as the choice of Liberal candidates was concerned. The success of the government attracted many successful men to the Liberal party and they in turn gave an aura of success to the local campaigns waged by the constituency organizations.

Its tradition of successes was, in fact, one of the Liberal party's most useful assets. Everyone knew that it had triumphed in a series of elections and, that in many constituencies, for anyone to vote other than Liberal was to vote for a certain loser. And the view is not uncommon in Canada, that it is foolish to vote for anyone who does not have a chance of winning.[5] The desire to be represented by a member sitting on the Government side of the House and not to "throw away one's vote" probably prompted an appreciable number of voters to support the Liberal candidate. Seeming Liberal invincibility was therefore an asset of the government party and as such was fully exploited during the campaign.[6]

Past Liberal successes strengthened the party's electoral campaign in yet another way: as has been suggested above, its main theme was that the government had done very well and that there was absolutely no need for a change. This approach gave the Liberal campaign a defensive and static character, but it also proved of undoubted value. For no matter how much justification there might have been for criticizing certain of the government's actions, it was difficult to deny that on the whole the country had been doing well and that the Liberal party had for a long time provided Canada with good government. There was enough truth in Liberal speakers' catalogues of past achievements to give a compelling air of authenticity to their whole argument, even to

[4]For a description of their campaigns see the Winnipeg *Free Press*, May 20.

[5]This was one of the unpublished findings of a study of voting in the 1953 general election in Kingston, Ont. Cf. "Electors like their votes to count one way or another; they do not like to feel that they are casting waste paper into the ballot box." McCallum and Readman, *British General Election of 1945*, p. 118.

[6]This argument was often associated with the claim that the Conservatives could not possibly win a majority. That many voters supported the Liberals in part because they were likely to be re-elected is suggested by the wholesale desertions of former Liberals in the 1958 election, when the Conservatives obtained 54 per cent of the votes compared with 39 in 1957. Two months after the 1957 balloting the Gallup poll indicated that 47 per cent intended to vote Conservative.

those parts of it for which there was much less justification. By the same token, the effectiveness of some of the well-earned attacks of the opposition was reduced by the tendency of its speakers to subject the government to wholesale and unqualified condemnation. The heavy emphasis placed by Liberal campaigners on the party's achievement in the past cannot, therefore, be written off without qualification as having been ineffective. It did not, it is true, enable the party to return to power; but it may have prevented an even more serious defeat. Under the circumstances it was a sound line to have taken, but its effectiveness would certainly have been increased had it been complemented with something more positive—an indication, for example, that the Liberal party had produced some exciting ideas and plans for the future.

When compared with the electioneering of the Conservatives, Liberal efforts appear to have been heavy-handed and lacking in imagination. The Liberals received disastrous publicity, for example, as the result of a political meeting at Morris, Manitoba, at which Mr. C. D. Howe's conduct conformed perfectly to the unflattering descriptions of him so often and so gleefully depicted by opposition speakers. He was arrogant and autocratic.

Earlier speeches by the Minister of Trade and Commerce had impressed many western farmers as having been unsympathetic to their plight. The audience he confronted at Morris was consequently rather hostile. From the beginning the Minister was subjected to a steady stream of criticism, jeers, boos, and catcalls. At one point during the uproar a man made his way to the front of the hall and asked the chairman whether he could speak from the platform. Mr. Howe saved the chairman the trouble of replying by telling the man that he could not have the floor. "When your party organizes a meeting," he was reported as having said, "you'll have the platform . . . and we'll ask the questions." The man then revealed that he was the President of the Morris Provincial Liberal Association. When he was given the floor, he was bitterly critical of Mr. Howe and the government. One embarrassing incident followed after another until the Minister withdrew to the wings, claiming that he had to return to Ottawa. But he was unable to leave the hall and had to face the hostile crowd once again. His attempts to answer the numerous barbed questions failed to satisfy the audience and placed the Minister in a steadily worsening light.

At one point, he said that aircraft which Canada was giving to her allies were obsolete. Asked whether he thought that this was all right, he offered the questioner a revealing insight into his conception of cabinet responsibility. The government, he suggested, was guided in these matters by the Department of External Affairs. "I don't decide who gets the planes," he added. "I just make them." The little drama ended no better than it had begun. As Mr. Howe was leaving the meeting one of the audience approached him saying that he still wanted an answer to a question he had put earlier. According to the Winnipeg *Free Press*, Mr. Howe replied as follows: "Look here, my good man, when the election comes why don't you just go away and vote for the party you support? In fact, why don't you just go away?"[7]

A number of circumstances no doubt conspired to make this meeting a particularly unfortunate one for the Liberal party. It was fully reported in all parts of the country and received mention in one of Mr. Diefenbaker's television talks. Prairie discontent with the government was well known and it was therefore to be expected that difficulties might be encountered by Liberal speakers addressing western agricultural audiences. Under the circumstances it would have been wiser to have kept Mr. Howe away from the centres of agrarian discontent. As evidenced by the two or three incidents cited above, Mr. Howe was not particularly skilled in winning back the support of alienated farmers. A less prickly campaigner would have served the Liberal cause better.

The incident in which a young heckler was knocked off the platform while Mr. St. Laurent was addressing a crowd of 12,000 in Toronto may be ascribed to bad luck. But Liberal bad luck during the campaign was frequently the product of bad management. One is tempted to ask whether a party organizing an extravaganza like the Liberal Maple Leaf Gardens rally is not inviting trouble and also to query the relation between a government election and such circus-like political meetings.[8]

Failure of the Liberals to use television as effectively as the Conservatives cannot be attributed to lack of planning by the national organization. It will be recalled that headquarters had established an impressive scheme for the preparation of television programmes and for familiarizing the candidate with the required techniques. Nevertheless, the self-assurance of the government party probably led many Liberal campaigners to approach the new medium without adequate preparation. Only one cabinet minister—Mr. Campney—had availed himself of the opportunity to perfect his television technique provided by the garage-studio at national headquarters. At any rate, many Liberals were insufficiently relaxed before the cameras and unfamiliar with the pitfalls associated with television broadcasting. On one occasion a minister—

[7]Ted Byfield, "Jeers, Boos, Catcalls Tear Rally to Pieces," Winnipeg *Free Press*, May 20.
[8]For a description see above, chap. v.

Mr. Garson—was unable to cope effectively with the failure of the television prompter during his final telecast from Winnipeg. The breakdown was obviously a piece of bad luck for which the party cannot be held responsible. But greater foresight on the part of the Minister and his advisers would have prevented the affair from becoming what press reports described as a fiasco.[9] Mechanical difficulties with the teleprompter were common enough to justify being prepared for their occurring in the course of an important political speech. The matter was, of course, relatively unimportant; it illustrates the point that much of the bad luck of the Liberals during the campaign could have been prevented or mitigated had the party been more alert.

One feature of the Liberal campaign can certainly not be ascribed to bad luck, having been the product solely of bad judgment. In frequently and loudly ridiculing the Conservatives for advertising themselves as the Diefenbaker party the Liberals probably won more friends for their chief opponents than for themselves. At any rate, they spent their own resources—time, energy and advertising funds—in giving currency to the main opposition slogan. "It is time for a Diefenbaker government" was a cry the Conservatives were sure would appeal to the many voters who, while disgruntled with the Liberals, might hesitate before voting Conservative. Often, no doubt, by being repeated at Liberal meetings and in Liberal publicity material, the slogan reached audiences that would otherwise have paid very little attention to it.[10]

Past Liberal success in discrediting the reputation of leaders of the opposition may have led the government party to adopt an ineffective approach in 1957. Previous covert and overt efforts had obviously succeeded in discrediting Mr. Drew and in contributing to his unpopularity. By applying the same tactics against Mr. Diefenbaker, however, the Liberals had misjudged the temper of the Canadian public. Whereas many had in the past been willing to accept an unfavourable picture of Mr. Drew, Liberal attempts to discredit Mr. Diefenbaker met with little success. It is, in fact, likely that Liberal attacks on the new Conservative leader backfired. It would probably have been more effective to have spoken well of Mr. Diefenbaker, but to have portrayed him as the prisoner of the Old Tory party.

Another argument used by the Liberals probably redounded to their disadvantage. Repeated attacks on the C.C.F. and Social Credit parties

[9]Winnipeg *Free Press*, June 6.

[10]For an interesting example of this, and the way in which the Conservatives exploited it, see the comments by Mr. Allister Grosart at the Mount Allison Summer Institute in 1959, in J. G. Greenslades, ed., *Canadian Politics* (Sackville, N.B., n.d.), pp. 30–1.

associated with the claim that only the Liberals and Conservatives were national parties were more likely to help the Conservatives than the Liberals. It might have been possible for the Liberals to remain in office after the election had the seats they lost been divided only a little more evenly among the three other parties. In that event the Liberals would have had the largest number of seats and a better claim to remain in power. To have said "the only political party that can possibly be regarded as an alternative to the Liberal Party is the Progressive Conservative party,"[11] may have been accurate, possibly even public-spirited, but from the point of view of electoral strategy it was unwise.

Finally, the effectiveness of the Liberal campaign suffered from the high incidence of intra-party squabbles. Reference has been made in preceding chapters to disunity in Quebec and in the Prairies. These disagreements found tangible expression in the large number of Independent Liberal candidates and in the lack of co-operation between federal and provincial parties, as in Manitoba. Unresolved differences were also apparent in the cabinet. Mr. Howe, for example, flatly contradicted some statements by Mr. Sinclair about federal proposals to assist power development in British Columbia.

A retrospective view of the campaign suggests that the Liberals often adopted an ill-advised course and that, in addition, they were frequently pursued by bad luck. The Conservatives, on the other hand, seemed to have been more fortunate and, perhaps because their campaign was less elaborate, they made fewer errors of judgment. The campaign started badly for them with regard to Quebec, since obviously the leadership convention did not augur well for the party's chances in French Canada. But, as the campaign proper developed, the Conservative cause seemed to be gaining momentum without the candidates and leaders making any serious errors. The mood of the country was obviously well disposed towards the opposition parties, and particularly the Conservatives.

Among the imperfections in the Conservative campaign some were obviously the result of faulty organization or carelessness. An effort depending on as many individuals as participate in election campaigns inevitably produces a number of slip-ups. This was as true of the Conservatives as of the Liberals; the various small mishaps which befell the parties need not be illustrated in detail. It is only fair to point out, however, that the television difficulties encountered by Mr. Garson referred to above could at least be attributed to a cause over which the party had no control. No such *deus ex machina* excused the non-appearance of Mr. Diefenbaker on a scheduled television programme. Accord-

[11]Mr. St. Laurent on the C.B.C. television network, June 5.

ing to newspaper reports, Mr. Diefenbaker was made to interrupt a car-trip through northern Ontario several times to shake hands with relatively small numbers of people. By the time he had arrived in Sault Ste Marie from where his talk was to originate he had missed his broadcast —probably the most important engagement of the day.[12]

A serious deficiency of the Conservative campaign was the seemingly reckless charges it levelled at the Liberal administration. An opposition party must, of course, attack the government and do so vigorously, but many Conservative accusations were so exaggerated that those who heard them and were familiar with the problems in question must have doubted either the sincerity or the knowledge of those making them. Who, for example, could really believe that "the St. Laurent government must bear the full responsibility for the unbuilt schools, inadequate roads, overcrowded mental and other hospitals, and deficiencies in the supply of home and housing services throughout Canada"?[13] Was it possible that Mr. Diefenbaker meant it when he said that "the real causes of inflation in this country are over-spending by the Federal government and too-high taxes"?[14] Election results show that a great many voters were not put off by this type of exaggeration or over-simplification. But it is likely that a small yet influential section of the population questioned the seriousness of the Conservative party as a consequence of the somewhat intemperate tone of its campaign. However, while the failure of this group to be convinced by the Conservative party may possibly affect its long-term prospects, it did not prevent the party from enjoying an immediate and rousing success in the 1957 election.

A related problem concerns Conservative promises. Well-informed voters knew that the Conservatives could not fulfil all their election promises unless they provided for substantially increased government revenues. The party's assertions, therefore, that it would increase spending and reduce taxes must have been suspected by some at least of the voters. It is of course possible that many of them thought that increased government spending was desirable and that the party could reduce taxes for a short time by adding to the national debt. Viewed this way, Conservative claims that they would increase government spending while reducing taxes appeared strictly speaking true, but they smacked of sophistry. This, too, seemed to have little effect on its chances of immediate success, but may influence future elections. Many voters probably switched to the Conservatives because of a desire to censure the

---

[12]Toronto *Globe and Mail*, May 16.
[13]*Federal-Provincial-Municipal Relations*, "Talking Points" series, p. 5.
[14]Speech in Truro, May 1. See Halifax *Chronicle Herald*, May 2.

Liberals rather than because they were particularly attracted to Mr. Diefenbaker's party. The intensity and duration of the Conservative appeal will depend less and less on the actions of the St. Laurent government and more and more on the impression created by the Diefenbaker party. And this may be influenced by long-term factors among which the 1957 actions of the party cannot be discounted. In defence of the Conservatives, it should, however, be added, that opposition parties have traditionally campaigned in the manner criticized in this paragraph and that the voters are more likely to judge a government party on the basis of its performance in office than on the way in which it conducted the previous election.

Throughout the campaign Mr. Diefenbaker showed what has since been confirmed as an impressive ability to gauge public opinion and to sense what issues can be exploited with political profit. It is therefore surprising that towards the end of the campaign he launched what looked like a last-minute scare—one he could not sustain. A week before polling day, speaking in Liverpool, Nova Scotia, he accused the government of having made a list of service personnel available to the Liberal party and not to the others. He referred to a letter, signed by the Prime Minister, which had been sent to all members of the armed forces and which urged them to vote Liberal. The implication clearly was that the Prime Minister had abused his official position to influence the service vote. Mr. Diefenbaker, who produced a copy of the offending letter, obviously felt greatly injured by it. He said about the incident that "No more serious thing had been done in my political experience," and the press, particularly pro-Conservative papers, gave the episode front-page, large-headline treatment. No more came of the whole matter, however, since the Prime Minister's letter had been printed on National Liberal Federation of Canada stationery, was not signed by him in his capacity of Prime Minister, and was a perfectly proper election document. More important, the Chief Electoral Officer, whose integrity and impartiality had never been questioned, announced that all parties had had equal access to the lists of service voters.[15] Since Mr. Diefenbaker's account, therefore, turned out in the end not to have been based on facts, it probably damaged the prestige of the Conservative party and of its leader.

Despite some features of the Conservative campaign which reduced its effectiveness, the results, as has repeatedly been argued, indicate that the campaign had succeeded in achieving what it had set out to do: the party scored a surprising victory. Liberal electioneering, which was

[15]Winnipeg *Free Press*, June 4.

on a larger scale that that of the Conservatives, considerably more elaborate and vastly more expensive, failed to secure the return of the government. And yet on the whole the 1957 Liberal campaign does not appear
to have been radically different from the party's successful ventures of
1953 and 1949. Does the comparison of the Liberal and Conservative
campaigns of 1957 then confirm what D. E. Butler suggests both electoral statistics and party officials in Britain show, namely, "how little
the behaviour of the voter seems to be determined by ordinary campaign
activities and arguments?"[16] This question is considered in a broad context in the concluding part of this study. At present a provisional answer
can be attempted by examining the public opinion surveys undertaken
by the Canadian Institute of Public Opinion—the Canadian "Gallup
Poll."

TABLE IX/1

Percentages Supporting Liberal and Conservative Parties in Selected
Surveys Conducted by the Canadian Institute of Public Opinion Prior
to the 1957 Election

Date of Survey	Liberal	Conservative	Undecided and no answer
October, 1956	49.0	32.7	15.1
November, 1956	50.6	31.7	19.8
January, 1957	48.2	31.4	24.6
March, 1957	46.0	32.9	26.2
May 4–10, 1957	46.8	32.9	14.7
May 28–June 1, 1957	43.3	37.5	12.8
C.I.P.O. Forecast June 8	48.0	34.0	
Election result*	42.3	39.0	

*As listed by the C.I.P.O.

Table IX/1 shows the support received by the Liberals and Conservatives in surveys conducted from October, 1956, to June, 1957. The
percentage of those who refused to answer and who were undecided
is also given. In each survey the following question was put to 1,200 or

[16]*The British General Election of 1951*, pp. 3–4. Cf. the finding of the Elmira
study in the United States: ". . . the time of the final decision, that point after
which the voter does not change his intention, occurred *prior* to the campaign
for most voters—and thus no 'real decision' was made *in* the campaign in the
sense of waiting to consider alternatives." Bernard R. Berelson, Paul P. Lazars-
feld, William N. McPhee, *Voting* (Chicago, 1954), p. 18.

more persons: "If a Dominion election were being held today which party's candidate do you think you would prefer?" The percentages given are those adjusted by the Canadian Institute of Public Opinion to allow for a certain measure of distortion which the Institute has found more or less constant during many years of interviewing in the various provinces by comparing the interview results with the outcome of elections. The final forecast was obviously fairly wide of the mark even if it is borne in mind that the Institute usually allows itself a four per cent margin of error. But the excellent record of the Institute over a long period of time justifies the ensuing speculation based on the above figures.

If the final forecast is set aside, it is found that during the period from Mr. Drew's resignation to the eve of the election Liberal support declined by 5.7 percentage points and that Conservative support rose by 4.8 percentage points. The Conservative leader's resignation was followed by a considerable increase in the number of undecided voters, accompanied by a drop in Conservative support. The first poll after the Conservative convention showed a further slight decline in the percentage of respondents indicating they would vote Conservative. This decline, as was to be expected, was of considerable proportions in Quebec. By March, however, the Conservative party recovered and it appears extremely likely that the swing towards it grew in strength particularly during the last days of the campaign. Indeed, the C.I.P.O. claims that one of the reasons it underestimated the number of Conservative votes actually cast was a pronounced last-minute increase in Conservative support.[17] The poll suggests, therefore, that many voters—certainly enough of them to affect the outcome—finally decided how to cast their ballots in the course of the campaign, possibly fairly close to polling time. If this conclusion (admittedly based on somewhat uncertain evidence) is correct, then it is extremely likely that the campaigns influenced the outcome of the election. It is possible that many people decided how to vote while the campaign was going on without actually being influenced by it. But it would be surprising if their decision had been unaffected by the general election talk and by newspaper, radio, and television accounts of the activities of the parties and of the leaders.

[17]Wilfrid Sanders, "How Polls Like That Happen," *Canadian Commentator*, vol. I, no. 6 (June, 1957), pp. 14–15. Also Canadian Institute of Public Opinion, "What Happened to the Gallup Poll?—An examination of the Report on party standings for the Federal Election as published, June 8th, 1957" (mimeo). The adjusted figures in Table IX/1 were kindly provided by the Canadian Institute of Public Opinion and differ slightly from the figures released in the newspapers, since they relate to single interviewing periods.

The campaigns must, therefore, be held to have had some effect on how the voters assessed the Liberal record, the likely performance of the parties in the future, and the personality of the new Conservative leader.

Education of the Electorate

So far in assessing the major parties' campaigns, their effectiveness in producing votes has been considered. But this, of course, is only a partial view. A party may win an election and yet do untold harm to the political structure in which it operates. A British election, as H. G. Nicholas has pointed out, "is generally expected to do three things: return a government, provide a 'mandate', and educate the electorate by the processes of public debate."[18] The criteria are applicable to Canada, where the 1957 election clearly failed to produce very satisfactory results with regard to the first two functions. How well did it fulfil the third?

To attempt an answer to this question is to risk being misunderstood. Criticism of the parties is likely to be attributed to partisanship and to subject the author to charges of academic insularity and of failure to live in the "real" world. Before attempting to answer the above question, it will, therefore, be useful to cite a comment made by one of Britain's leading students of elections:

In the overheated atmosphere of the election things are said and done which are considered by many to be reprehensible. The student of politics must beware of too moralistic an approach; it is not necessarily helpful to sit on the academic sidelines and censure contestants whenever the level of discussion drops below that of a disinterested search for truth. Politicians are seeking votes; unless and until it has been proved that absolute fairness in argument is in fact more rewarded by the electors than partisan contentiousness, the latter will continue to flourish, and no particular good will be achieved by railing against it. However, the student of politics can render useful service by helping to clarify the nature of election tactics. The more people are able to recognize the stunt and the insincere approach, the less it will be worth employing them.[19]

If the degree to which the parties tried to inform, elucidate, explain, and enlighten is considered the standard according to which they are to be judged, then neither Canadian party is entirely above reproach. They can both, in fact, be charged with a certain measure of irresponsibility. Each proved irresponsible in a different way: the reader can

---

[18]*The British General Election of 1950*, p. 303.
[19]Butler, *The British General Election of 1951*, p. 3.

decide for himself which form of irresponsibility seems more damaging to the political health of the country.

Conservative speakers, by attacking the government so indiscriminately, tended to conceal the difference between real and illusory issues. While many of the points raised by the opposition were important and, so to speak, legitimate, numerous others were either imaginary or not really within the powers of any government, and certainly not a Canadian government. After the election, when they were in office, Conservative ministers must often have recalled with mixed feelings some of the things said during the campaign about their predecessors. Conservative campaign oratory, by blaming the government for every ill encountered by the country, often misled the public as much as it enlightened it. Evidence supporting this assertion can be found in the preceding pages, notably in chapter III and in Appendix C. Some additional examples will illustrate more specifically what is meant.

Speaking in Quebec on May 7, Mr. Diefenbaker blamed some Canadian agricultural difficulties on heavy imports into Canada of United States farm products. This was a reasonable position to take, but Mr. Diefenbaker went on and made fun of the government's inability to come to some agreement with the United States about the settlement of these and other American-Canadian problems. "The ride the Canadian farmers are getting from this government is nothing like the ride Mr. St. Laurent got at the hands of President Eisenhower."[20]

In the middle of a campaign in which he promised to extend government spending in a wide variety of fields, the Conservative leader referred in the following terms to a Liberal publication listing alleged social security spending by the government in each constituency: "That's Pied Piper philosophy; they gave nothing but what they took from you and me. That type of Roman holiday at the expense of the people will ruin democracy."[21] When the Canadian Wheat Board announced in mid-May its final payment on the 1955–6 wheat crops Mr. Diefenbaker's "heavily-accented sarcasm left no doubt that he felt the payment was just a bid to buy Liberal votes from Western farmers."[22] The accuracy of the innuendo can be gauged from the fact that in the previous year the corresponding announcement was made on May 18, and in 1955 on May 16.[23]

To what extent Conservative campaigners abdicated their right and

[20]C.P. dispatch from Kazabazua, Que. See Winnipeg *Free Press*, May 8.
[21]C.P. dispatch from Brockville in Winnipeg *Free Press*, May 9.
[22]Winnipeg *Free Press*, May 16.
[23]*Ibid.*

opportunity to educate the public by refusing to discuss issues seriously and by over-simplifying them is illustrated in their treatment of the problem of inflation. Credit controls were attacked frequently and vigorously, but always by pointing to their irksome features without mention of the real nature of the problem. Economists were beginning to question at the time of the election the wisdom of applying some of the controls, and a legitimate case could be made for the time having become ripe for their relaxation. Not once, as far as one could ascertain, was the attack on the government based on these legitimate doubts about the wisdom of continuing governmental restrictions on spending at a time of possibly growing unemployment. The level on which the problem was usually treated is shown by Mr. Diefenbaker's reference to it in his television talk of May 14. "The cost of home owning is going up," he said, allegedly quoting married couples who wanted to buy or build a home, "because the government says we can't be trusted to borrow money."[24] Another illustration is to be found in the treatment of the housing shortage at Elliot Lake by Mr. Hees. He was reported as having said on May 25 that Mr. Pearson's alleged failure to intercede with the Central Mortgage and Housing Corporation on behalf of his constituents in Elliot Lake was "a good example of the arrogance of cabinet ministers."[25] Mr. Pearson had in fact taken the matter up in Ottawa, and the Central Mortgage and Housing Corporation later reversed its ruling that it had had no authority to approve loans in Elliot Lake. Mr. Hees' response was contained in a speech made in the constituency of Algoma East. He was reported as having said that "the only reason Central Housing and Mortgage agreed suddenly to back mortgages . . . in the Elliot Lake . . . area is that Mr. Pearson's seat is threatened.[26]

To accuse the Liberals of arrogance for not taking a particular action and then, when that action was taken, to ascribe it to politically mercenary motives was not a particularly instructive or constructive way of campaigning against Canada's Minister of External Affairs. The incident is as enlightening about Liberal campaigning, however, as it is about that of the Conservatives. Approval by the C.H.M.C. of the loans *was* granted only after strong cabinet intervention and, therefore, showed that the Liberals were prepared to press a Crown corporation into an action strongly suggesting electoral expediency.

On the whole, however, their campaign was remarkably free from

[24]Mimeo, p. 3.
[25]C.P. dispatch from Oakville, Ont., Winnipeg *Free Press*, May 27.
[26]See Gray Hamilton, "Pearson Battles on Home Front," Toronto *Globe and Mail*, June 3, and C.P. dispatch, dated June 2, from Sudbury.

the type of quasi-bribery modern governments sometimes engage in by passing legislation or making administrative decisions favourable to certain aggrieved sections of the population. There were at least two notable exceptions: towards the end of May the government banned the imports of Cheddar cheese and early in the same month it had announced that it would place supports under the price of fowl. Even the friendly Winnipeg *Free Press* found it necessary to criticize the latter concession to a particular interest. Terming the decision "an electioneering move," the *Free Press* said that its primary motive was "to shore up not fowl but the government's candidates, especially in rural Ontario."[27]

Accusations by Mr. Diefenbaker to the contrary, the Liberal campaign was generally free of promises designed to appeal to voters in particular regions. Mr. St. Laurent did on occasion mention proposed governmental projects or expenditures—such as a railway spur line in northern Alberta or a possible causeway linking Prince Edward Island with the mainland.[28] These lapses were, generally, rare.

A more serious flaw in the Liberal campaign, if it is thought that a party should clarify rather than confuse issues, concerned the treatment by some Liberals of the economic difficulties of the thirties. The Speaker's Handbook referred to the "Bennett depression"[29] and Mr. St. Laurent himself was not above resorting to the bogey of the great economic crisis.[30] This argument seemed to have been used more frequently towards the end of the campaign than at the beginning. In the final broadcast made by a cabinet minister other than Mr. St. Laurent, Mr. Sinclair revealed, when resorting to the depression theme, that to get votes the government party was prepared to reduce economically complex situations to the point of absurdity:

In the dreadful days of the depression of the thirties, we had the same hard working resourceful Canadian people as today, we had the same bountiful resources in the nation, but nevertheless we wallowed in a depression which found almost one third of our people unemployed, found our young men herded into relief camps guarded by the army.

The difference was in governments. Then we had a Conservative government headed by R. B. Bennett—a government unable to combine the labour and resources of Canada into full employment.[31]

---

[27]Winnipeg *Free Press*, May 1.

[28]These promises were made by Mr. St. Laurent in Edmonton and Moncton on April 30 and May 21.

[29]*Liberal Action*, p. 331.

[30]In a speech in Montreal, on June 3, he reminded his listeners of "the nightmare of the 1930–1935 Tory Government" in contrast to the good times provided by subsequent Liberal governments.

[31]Broadcast over C.B.C. Trans-Canada network, June 6 (mimeo), pp. 1–2.

Oversimplification of this sort certainly matched many of the irresponsible charges made against the government by the Conservatives. In its treatment of some of Canada's economic problems, the Liberal party revealed itself clearly unwilling to explain the reasons for some of its policies. No really serious effort was made to impress upon the public the necessity for imposing credit restrictions. If the Conservatives were able to win votes as the result of the tight money policy and if they were able to get away with making irresponsible charges against the government about them, the fault lay in part with the Liberals. They simply did not bother to explain repeatedly and lucidly why the government had had to take some of its unpopular measures. Many regionally resented economic policies of the government, some of the unpopular measures of the last budget, the desirability of accumulating surpluses, all these could have been defended in a well-planned campaign of enlightening the public about the economic problems confronting the country. On the whole, Liberal speakers touched only lightly or not at all on these matters and in that sense they, too, conducted an irresponsible campaign.

Apart from the failure to utilize fully the educational potentialities of the campaign, and apart from the other blemishes mentioned above, however, the Liberal campaign was carried out on a high plane. The budget introduced by Mr. Harris, which must be considered as an integral part of the election, was an extremely honest and courageous one. The government had obviously resisted the pressure to embark on a politically rewarding spending spree at a time when it believed that to have done so would have been economically unsound. The restraint of the party in this regard, and the almost equally restrained tone of its campaign, speak very highly for the integrity of the Liberal leaders. The Conservative campaign lacked some of the restraint exhibited by the Liberals and on the whole made it difficult for future governments to impose necessary but unpopular measures, particularly in the fiscal sphere. As subsequent events have shown, the Conservatives themselves have had to adopt or continue many of the measures and policies for which they castigated the government. Many of the bitter accusations they hurled at the Liberals could subsequently have been levelled at themselves.

But having criticized some of the methods used by the Conservatives, it is well to recall that it is the task of parties to get themselves elected and that the Conservatives obviously found an approach to this problem which proved acceptable to the Canadian public. And while its campaign was shrill and exasperated to the point, sometimes, of being irresponsible, it was highly responsible in one important aspect.

The impartial student of Canadian politics cannot escape the conclusion that the Liberal party had come to treat Parliament in a way which reduced its effectiveness. The debates about the amendment to the Defence Production Act and the Trans-Canada pipeline were dramatic instances revealing what had probably become an unconscious disregard, among many Liberals, of the importance of a lively and virile Parliament. By relentlessly hammering away at the importance of Parliament and at Liberal abuses of it, Mr. Diefenbaker and his party performed a valuable service to Canadian politics. Furthermore, it is likely that the very shrillness and flamboyance of the Conservative campaign was one of the main factors in the public having shown such a very great interest in the election. That a so much higher proportion of eligible voters actually cast their ballots in 1957 than in 1953 must in part be attributed to the effective stimulus of the Conservative campaign and not to the quiet efforts of the Liberals. In extending interest among the Canadian public in what the government was doing, and in persuading large numbers of citizens to do something about it, the Conservative campaign added something of great value to the political life of the country.

THE C.C.F.
AND
SOCIAL CREDIT
PARTIES

10

The Co-operative Commonwealth Federation

IN ADDITION TO THE LIBERALS AND CONSERVATIVES, seven other parties nominated candidates in the 1957 election. Of these, the Canadian National Democrats, the Capital-Familial Party, and the National Credit Control can be ignored: they were not really political parties in the generally accepted sense of the term. One candidate ran under the banner of each. Réal Caouette, a one-time Social Credit M.P., was the sole candidate to contest a constituency under the label "candidat des électeurs." The Labour Progressive party nominated ten candidates, seeking to capture seats in Montreal (three), Toronto (two), Winnipeg, Regina, Vancouver (two) and a rural area of Alberta (Vegreville). Beside the Liberals and Conservatives, therefore, only the C.C.F. and Social Credit parties enjoyed sufficient support, and made a large enough electoral effort, to merit consideration in a general study of the 1957 election. The geographical distribution of their candidates is shown in the accompanying table.

Only the C.C.F. had nominated enough candidates to give it at least a theoretical chance of gaining a majority in the House of Commons. At dissolution, it had twenty-three members in Parliament, from five provinces. The Social Credit party was represented by fifteen members, all of them from British Columbia and Alberta. Moreover, while it could hardly claim national support, the C.C.F. was represented in six provincial legislatures, whereas Social Credit held seats in only four provinces, none of them east of Manitoba.

But it was not so much the number of its elected representatives which

TABLE X/1

C.C.F. and Social Credit Candidates by Province and Region

	C.C.F.	Social Credit	Seats
Newfoundland	1	—	7
Prince Edward Island	3	—	4
Nova Scotia	6	1	12
New Brunswick	2	2	10
Maritimes	12	3	33
Quebec	22	4	75
Ontario	60	39	85
Manitoba	14	14	14
Saskatchewan	17	16	17
Alberta	15	17	17
Prairies	46	47	48
British Columbia (Incl. Yukon and Mackenzie River)	22	21	24
Canada	162	114	265

gave the C.C.F. its importance as the influence the party had had in Canadian politics during the previous quarter century. This influence can be attributed chiefly to two factors: the quality of its leading members and the degree to which it had pushed the Liberal party towards the adoption of welfare state policies. The vigorous participation of the C.C.F. group in the activities of the House of Commons gave the party much publicity despite the almost universal editorial hostility of the Canadian press. The words and actions of the party's major spokesmen, J. S. Woodsworth, M. J. Coldwell, T. C. Douglas, and Stanley Knowles had for many years been received with a degree of attention out of all proportion to the C.C.F.'s electoral strength.[1]

Its social democratic ideology had consistently led the C.C.F. to demand the extension of governmental activities. The party had therefore pressed for a variety of social services long before the old-line parties thought it prudent even to mention them. Consequently the C.C.F. took credit for driving the Liberal party to implement a number of welfare

[1]Note, for example, what J. W. Pickersgill has called "a remarkable and moving reference to J. S. Woodsworth" in Mackenzie King's speech in the House of Commons on September 8, 1939, urging Canada's participation in the war. *The Mackenzie King Record* (Toronto, 1960), vol. I, p. 19.

policies. The party no doubt contributed to the forming of a climate of opinion favouring the extension of governmental services. This changing attitude among the Canadian voters was observed and acted upon by the Liberal party. The booklet, *The Liberal Party of Canada*, for instance, refers to the September, 1943, Gallup poll which showed that each of the old-line parties was supported by 28 per cent of those interviewed who gave a party preference, and that the C.C.F. received 29 per cent of the "votes," slightly more support, in other words, than any of its rivals.

The time had come [the booklet states] for the Liberal party to adopt a new political policy. Accordingly, Mr. King asked Honourable Norman McLarty ... to call a meeting of the Advisory Council as early as possible ... The Council adopted fourteen resolutions, constituting a program of reform and a plan for postwar reconstruction of far-reaching consequences ... When the session concluded on August 14 [*sic*] the Liberal administration had placed on the Statutes of Canada most of the measures suggested by the Advisory Council . . . Thus the Liberal Administration laid plans to protect the well-being and prosperity of the Canadian people in the postwar years.[2]

The programme presented to the Canadian electorate by the C.C.F. in 1957 had its inspiration in three different but related sources. The first of these was natural to a party which prided itself on being actuated by a coherent set of principles derived from a well-defined view of society. The basic principles of the C.C.F. were drawn up at the party's founding convention in 1933; they founded the party's charter which is usually referred to as the Regina Manifesto[3] and which is based on the traditional principles of social democracy. The general position of the party was therefore similar to that of the British Labour party.

By the middle fifties, however, many C.C.F.'ers had come to believe that the political philosophy underlying the Regina Manifesto was no longer adequate for Canadian conditions. In January, 1956, the C.C.F. national council consequently resolved that a new statement of principles and policies be drawn up. Accordingly four of its members were charged by the national executive in February to draft an appropriate document.[4] The first version was discussed and amended by the national executive in June and July. When the national council met at the end of July it was presented with a draft *Statement of Principles and Policies*, ten foolscap pages in length. The council decided that it would be advisable

[2]*The Liberal Party of Canada: Liberal Policies are creating a better life for all Canadians* (1957), p. 53.

[3]For a discussion of the convention and the manifesto see Dean E. McHenry, *The Third Force in Canada: The Cooperative Commonwealth Federation, 1932–1948* (Berkeley, Calif., 1950), *passim*.

[4]They were David Lewis, national chairman; Morden Lazarus; Michel Chartrand; and Lorne Ingle, national secretary.

to prepare a much shorter version. The committee was therefore asked to draft a concise document embodying the party's principles and to treat policy matters as resolutions submitted to the forthcoming fourteenth national convention. The new principles were therefore recast in the form of a manifesto, and as such were presented to the convention which met in Winnipeg in August, 1956. After due discussion and the passing of half a dozen amendments, the convention approved the party's new Manifesto and entitled it *1956 Winnipeg Declaration of Principles of the Co-operative Commonwealth Federation (Parti Social Democratique du Canada)*. The themes of the short, four-page statement are indicated by the titles given the various sections: "Canada Still Ridden by Inequalities," "The Folly of Wasted Resources," "The Challenge of New Horizons," "Capitalism Basically Immoral," "Social Planning for a Just Society," "Building a Living Democracy," "Basis for Peace," "Support of UN," "Confidence in Canada," and "Socialism on the March."

In addition to bringing the Regina Manifesto up to date, the Winnipeg Declaration changed the general tone of the party's creed. The different emphasis is best illustrated by the contrast between an extract from each of the two documents. The final paragraph of the Regina Manifesto states unequivocally:

No C.C.F. Government will rest content until it has eradicated capitalism and put into operation the full program of socialized planning which will lead to the establishment in Canada of the Co-operative Commonwealth.

Twenty-three years later, the Winnipeg Declaration adopted a considerably milder tone:

The C.C.F. has always recognized public ownership as the most effective means of breaking the strangle-hold of private monopolies on the life of the nation and of facilitating the social planning necessary for economic security and advance. The C.C.F. will, therefore, extend public ownership wherever it is necessary for the advancement of these objectives.

At the same time, the C.C.F. also recognizes that in many fields there will be need for private enterprise which can make a useful contribution to the development of our economy. The co-operative commonwealth will, therefore, provide appropriate opportunities for private business as well as publicly-owned industry.

The second source of the 1957 election programme may also be found in the proceedings of the 1956 convention. The national council meeting in conjunction with the convention "resolved that the national executive be authorized to publish various resolutions passed at this convention or previous conventions."[5]

[5]Minutes, C.C.F. National Council meeting, Aug. 4, 1956.

Lorne Ingle, the national secretary, and Kenneth Bryden, a member of the national executive, were asked by the executive to prepare a federal platform in accordance with the wishes of the council. Their labours, as revised by the national council, resulted in a closely printed eight-page pamphlet entitled *Share Canada's Wealth: (The National CCF Program)*. The national council agreed that although the comprehensive programme "could and would be used during the election in instances where a more complete statement of CCF policies was required it was not intended as an election document for mass distribution."[6] Its nature is also described in a boxed statement at the very beginning:

This is the official national program of the Co-operative Commonwealth Federation, drawn up by the CCF National Council in January, 1957, on the basis of resolutions approved at CCF National Conventions. It is supplementary to and in elaboration of the "Winnipeg Declaration of Principles" which outlines the basic philosophy of the CCF.

In the main body of the pamphlet the reader could find, in great detail, the policy of the C.C.F. on every issue that could conceivably arise in the election. The subheadings of the seven sections indicate the scope of the document and something of the drift of the argument.

I. Economic Democracy
   (a) Basic Economic Planning
   (b) Canadian Capital for Canadian Development
   (c) Finance and Credit
   (d) Taxation according to Ability to Pay
   (e) Planned Immigration
II. New Economic Horizons
   (a) Sharing the Benefits of Automation
   (b) Atomic Energy for Peace
   (c) A National Fuel and Energy Policy
III. Security for Primary Producers
   (a) Agriculture
   (b) Fisheries
   (c) Bigger and More Secure Markets
IV. Security for Labour
V. More Abundant Living for All
   (a) Social Security
   (b) Comprehensive Health Services
   (c) Low Cost Housing
   (d) Federal Aid for Education
   (e) Recreation and the Arts
VI. Basic Rights and Freedom
VII. A Policy for Peace

---

[6]Minutes, C.C.F. National Council meeting, Jan. 12 and 13, 1957.

While the Winnipeg Declaration and the National Programme were of undoubted importance in shaping the C.C.F.'s election argument, they were not exclusively election documents. They provided a theoretical base and a programme for the party's campaign, but nevertheless, did not single out the issues which could advantageously be exploited in the spring and summer of 1957. The third source of the election programme arose directly out of the exigencies of the campaign and the need to establish a line of argument which would present the party's programme in the best light during this particular election.

At its meeting in November, 1956, the national executive appointed a committee consisting of the national secretary, the research director, and three M.P.'s to be chosen by the parliamentary caucus, "to discuss election issues and bring recommendations before the next meeting of the national council."[7] The committee was specifically asked by the executive to consult Premier Douglas of Saskatchewan.

When the national council met in January of the following year, the national secretary, Lorne Ingle, reported on behalf of the special committee:

The committee recommended that heavy emphasis be placed on the egalitarian aspects of the CCF programme. While great economic development was taking place in Canada, with new areas being opened up, new resources tapped, industries and construction expanding, this increase in wealth was not being fairly shared by all Canadians. In the first place, the workers who helped produce the increased wealth were not obtaining their fair share of the increase. Even more was this true of the people on fixed incomes, particularly pensioners, etc. People in the Atlantic provinces and those engaged in agriculture as well as some other occupations had actually seen their income decline in recent years. Inflation and increasing prices which were accompanying the economic boom wiped out even the comparatively small gains which were being made in the way of increased income to various groups of workers. It was suggested by the committee therefore that the whole CCF programme be presented in this context.[8]

Members of the council discussed the recommendations at some length, having expressed general agreement with the theme suggested by the committee. A great many other points were considered as possible election issues favourable to the C.C.F. In the end it was resolved "That the table officers be guided by this discussion in the council in the emphasis they give to various points during the course of the campaign, insofar as C.C.F. literature, press releases, broadcasts, T.V. programmes, speeches, etc. are concerned."[9]

[7]Minutes, C.C.F. National Executive meeting, Nov. 24 and 25, 1956.
[8]Minutes, C.C.F. National Council meeting, Jan. 12 and 13, 1957, p. 4.
[9]*Ibid.*, p. 5.

In many instances C.C.F. criticism of the government was similar to that of the other opposition parties, particularly that of the Conservatives. But there were numerous important differences, most of them stemming from the C.C.F.'s basically hostile attitude to many features of the private-enterprise system. The distinctive flavour of the dish offered the electorate by the C.C.F. was traceable to the party's philosophy, as stated at the opening of the Winnipeg Declaration: "The aim of the Co-operative Commonwealth Federation is the establishment in Canada by democratic means of a co-operative commonwealth in which the supplying of human needs and enrichment of human life shall be the primary purpose of our society. *Private profit and corporate power must be subordinated to social planning* designed to achieve equality of opportunity and the highest possible living standards for all Canadians."[10]

In its election campaign the C.C.F. did not undertake to nationalize or socialize any specific industry in the event that the party would find itself in power. The party did, however, advocate making tax changes which, if implemented, would certainly have led to a considerable redistribution of income in Canada. It proposed to increase the exemptions from income tax, to abolish sales and special taxes on the necessities of life, to recognize all medical expenses as deductions from income for tax purposes, to abolish special tax exemptions for income received from corporation dividends, to increase taxation on higher income groups and on corporations, and to see that full municipal taxes were paid on all federal property located in organized municipalities.[11] Mr. Coldwell summarized the C.C.F.'s attitude to taxation in a broadcast on May 15:

We cannot, as the Tories do, promise to expand social security measures, to build causeways and canals and so on and, at the same, reduce the over-all level of taxation. Any tax reduction should be confined to the lower income groups. And the special tax concessions to privileged groups . . . should be eliminated.[12]

Some of the measures proposed for the reform of the tax system were also expected to combat inflation, which was considered by the C.C.F. as one of the important issues of the election campaign. The Liberal

[10]Italics added. This difference was stressed frequently by C.C.F. speakers. The passage quoted was, for instance, cited by Premier Douglas in his Dominion Network broadcast for the C.C.F. on May 16.

[11]*Share Canada's Wealth*, p. 2. These points were also discussed in a number of C.C.F. speeches and broadcasts.

[12]Co-operative Commonwealth Federation, Woodsworth House, Ottawa, Press release, May 15, p. 1. The party issued a large number of such press releases. In what follows they are cited as Press release, with the appropriate date.

government, the C.C.F. proclaimed, did little to deal with this problem because "inflation really benefits nobody but a few privileged groups"[13] and it was precisely these groups which influenced the policies of the Liberal party:

> ... the economically strong and powerful groups, the wealthy corporations, have much more influence with the Liberal government, than the economically weak have. They finance the Liberal party and pay its campaign expenses. And they don't do it because they think the Liberal leaders are nice fellows. They do it because they know full well that "he who pays the piper calls the tune." And just to be on the safe side they finance the Conservative and Social Credit parties as well.[14]

Unbeholden to wealthy party contributors, the C.C.F. proposed to lower interest rates immediately, to impose a direct tax on the undistributed profits of all corporations having taxable income of more than $20,000 a year, to defer depreciation allowances on newly acquired assets of large companies not directly engaged in the expansion of productive capacity, to establish a National Investment Board "to channel the huge accumulations of wealth under the control of financial and other corporations into socially desirable projects," and "to end profiteering" and curb monopolies and combines.[15]

Regionally, the C.C.F.'s greatest strength lay in the west, particularly in the prairies. It was therefore not surprising that agricultural policies received considerable emphasis in the party's campaign. Government support of farm prices was one of the issues over which the parties' programmes differed most emphatically. Mr. Coldwell's bid to appear as the only genuine friend of the farmers, as expressed in a Saskatchewan speech, was typical of many such C.C.F. appeals:

> I am sorry that Mr. Diefenbaker for the Conservatives had seen fit to denounce a programme of full parity or 100% parity for the farmer as a "delusion" and has attacked the CCF agricultural programme. I am sure that Canadian farmers will be sorry and angered that both the Conservatives and Liberals voted against the CCF motion for a 100% parity programme. Farmers know that 30% or 50% or 60% of parity is just not good enough. After all, anything less than 100% of parity is not real parity at all. Those, like the Liberals and Conservatives, who voted against the motion for 100% of parity, were saying that the farmer should be satisfied with something less and that the farmer should be satisfied to be a second-class citizen. The CCF emphatically disagrees. The big business supporters of the Liberal, Conservative and Social Credit parties are realizing much more than parity profit.

[13]M. J. Coldwell, broadcast, May 6. Press release, May 6, p. 2.
[14]Ibid.
[15]Ibid., pp. 3–5.

We don't see why there should be this opposition to the expression of the CCF conviction that the farmer should receive an income at full parity with the rest of the economy.[16]

In addition to promising parity prices, the C.C.F.'s farm programme proposed the following: establishment of national marketing boards, where requested by producers, for all farm products entering into inter-provincial and export trade; cash advances for farm-stored grain; long- and short-term credit for farmers at low interest rates; comprehensive crop insurance; and removal of monopoly control of farm machinery, fertilizer, chemical, meat-packing, flour-milling, and other supply and processing industries.[17] Of the several measures recommended in support of Canadian fisheries, three differed somewhat from the programmes of the other parties. The C.C.F. undertook to provide adequate unemployment insurance coverage for fishermen, to encourage fishermen's co-operatives, and to initiate special measures for the relief of Atlantic coast fishermen. These ranged from guaranteeing forward prices and paying cash advances at the beginning of the fishing season to establishing government stores and depots to supply salt, twine and other equipment at "much lower prices."[18]

In a previous chapter it was noted that one reason for Canadian agricultural problems was the difficulty experienced by many primary producers in selling their produce abroad. Agricultural policies were therefore often discussed during the campaign in relation to trade policies. The C.C.F. shared the widely held view that one of the most important reasons for Canada's inability to sell her agricultural surplus was the dollar shortage experienced by many overseas countries. Accordingly, the party advocated the diversion to non-dollar countries of "a substantial proportion of the government orders and contracts now placed in the United States, long-term commodity agreements, special credit arrangements, barter and direct exchange of goods, acceptance of sterling in part payment for Canadian produce sold to sterling area countries and foreign exchange control." The party also advocated the establishment of export and import boards "to regulate and expand Canada's trade in all fields."[19]

While the C.C.F. emphasized economic development of the north less than the other parties, its whole programme assumed and stated that if

[16]Speech in Butte, Sask., May 1st.
[17]Share Canada's Wealth, p. 4. Fuller statements may be found in speeches by Mr. Coldwell and Mr. Douglas. See Press releases for May 1, 18, 31, and for June 7.
[18]Share Canada's Wealth, p. 5.
[19]Ibid.

more planning were done by the government, the country could be developed more rapidly and more equitably than had been the case before. The party's election programme stressed the opportunities afforded by automation and the peaceful uses of atomic energy. More than any of its rivals, the C.C.F. attempted to present to the voters the problems imposed by what was termed "a second and greater industrial revolution" and to suggest a broad programme of action designed to cope with the anticipated technological revolution. "Wisely planned," the national election programme asserted, "these developments will make possible an unprecedented increase in standards of living and leisure time and the end of drudgery, poverty and insecurity."[20]

Since its inception the C.C.F. had pressed relentlessly for the extension of social services in Canada. The 1957 election afforded a new opportunity to present to the public the party's social programme. *Share Canada's Wealth!* devoted almost two of its eight pages to an explicit cataloguing of the C.C.F.'s welfare policies, and the other pages were liberally sprinkled with implicit references to the need for the extension of social services. While some of the proposals were extremely vague, such as that, for example, which promised "adequate provision for Canada's veterans," many were quite specific. An old age pension of $75 per month was advocated for everyone over 65 years of age. Family allowances of $8 per child were proposed for children up to five years of age and proportionate increases for older children. The party also promised sickness benefits "to maintain a basic family income during illness of the breadwinner," and to increase benefit rates and widen the coverage of the unemployment insurance scheme.

With regard to health services, the C.C.F. considered that the Liberal programme had been introduced much too late and that it was inadequate. Mr. Coldwell was prompted by the government's scheme to produce the following exercise in electoral arithmetic: ". . . the federal government will be paying for only one-third of hospitalization costs which are themselves one-third of total health costs. This means that after 38 years of promises, the Liberal government is providing for only one-ninth of a national health plan. At that rate it would take a Liberal government another 304 years to implement a full national health plan."[21] Its own election promise was to establish "a nation-wide health insurance plan to provide every man, woman and child in Canada with full medical, hospital, nursing, dental, optical and other health care, with the federal government paying 80 per cent of the cost and the

[20]*Ibid.*, p. 3.
[21]Speech in Regina, June 3. Press release, p. 2.

provinces the remaining 20 per cent."[22] The plan was to feature "decentralized administration in co-operation with the provincial governments, and with full freedom for everyone to choose his own family doctor."[23]

The C.C.F. also undertook to initiate an extremely ambitious housing programme, to provide "generous financial assistance to the provinces for education"[24] and to establish a National Labour Code guaranteeing labour minimum wage and adequate working conditions.

In general, the C.C.F. programme differed markedly from that of the older parties in the length to which the party was prepared to go to create the welfare state and in the items emphasized. Much more attention was devoted to labour, for example, or, to take another example, in dealing with education the party specifically mentioned the need to "train technicians, engineers, scientists, economists, teachers, and social and welfare workers needed for Canada to take full advantage of the era of automation and atomic energy."[25] The party also stressed much more than its rivals the need for government support for recreational activities and for the arts. Alone among Canadian parties, the C.C.F. went out of its way to express support for the C.B.C. in its election programme, urging the "maintenance and expansion of the Canadian Broadcasting Corporation as a major medium in the development of a distinctive Canadian culture."[26]

Like Mr. Diefenbaker, the C.C.F. advocated a Canadian Bill of Rights. In foreign policy the C.C.F. differed only in emphasis from the other parties. It stressed the need for increased efforts in achieving well-being in the underdeveloped countries and urged that Canada do more in this field. The party also advocated the creation of a World Food Pool. Like the Conservatives, the C.C.F. opposed the manner in which the Liberal government had handled Parliament during the discussion of the pipeline issue. The importance which the C.C.F. attached to this issue was indicated by Mr. Knowles, speaking in British Columbia: "Economic issues are of great importance in this election. But no issue is any more important than the need to re-establish parliamentary democracy."[27] As was to be expected, the C.C.F. made much of the large profits some individuals stood to make as the result of the way in which the whole matter was handled by the government. Premier Frost was also criticized for his part in the construction of the Ontario link in the pipeline system. The C.C.F. gave unequivocal support to a publicly

[22]*Share Canada's Wealth*, p. 6.
[24]*Ibid.*
[26]*Ibid.*
[23]*Ibid.*
[25]*Ibid.*, p. 7
[27]Kelowna, B.C., May 10. Press release.

owned pipeline and was critical of all schemes which enabled private owners to control this utility.

In its attitude towards dominion-provincial relations the C.C.F. was more sympathetic to the poorer provinces than to the wealthy giants of central Canada. This attitude was no doubt due to the party's close connection with Saskatchewan and also to its general sympathy for the underdog. Mme. Casgrain, speaking in Nova Scotia, outlined an ambitious programme to aid the maritime economy. Its unique feature, in terms of what the other parties proposed, was the readiness to assume public ownership of the steel industry.[28] With regard to the fiscal arrangements between the federal government and the provinces, Mr. Coldwell gave strong support to the tax rental agreements. He was perhaps somewhat unfair to the government when he accused it of "minimizing the tax-rental agreements and encouraging the richer provinces to stay out."[29]

In addition to its legislative programme, the C.C.F. emphasized two special issues during the election campaign. The first arose out of the party's fear of being confused with the Labour Progressive party. The second was imposed on it by the oft-repeated argument that a vote for the C.C.F. was, in fact, a wasted vote, since it was virtually certain that Canada's social democratic party would fail to get anything like a majority of seats.

An election platform drawn up by the Labour Progressive party's national executive committee and published in the party's *National Affairs* in April, asked Canadian Communists to support C.C.F. candidates in the forthcoming election.[30] The party faithful were encouraged to vote and work for C.C.F. candidates in all constituencies where the L.P.P. did not nominate its own standard-bearers. This decision by the L.P.P. executive, like similar ones in the past, was a source of embarrassment to the C.C.F. which had, from its inception, to contend with the charge that a vote for the C.C.F. was a vote for the Communists. The L.P.P. announcement was, therefore, met with a vigorous declaration issued over the name of Mr. Coldwell. In addition to tracing the twists pursued by Communist policy in Canada over the years, the statement also stressed the fundamental differences between the C.C.F. and the Communists. Mr. Coldwell's statement emphasized that "the C.C.F. will have nothing to do with the L.P.P. or any other Communist organization and will not collaborate with them in any way, direct or indirect."[31]

Social Credit and the C.C.F. were not likely to be confused with regard to their respective attitudes and policies, but the two parties were

[28]Halifax, May 14. Press release.　　[29]Regina, June 1. Press release.
[30]Winnipeg *Free Press*, April 18.　　[31]Press release, April 23.

competitors for the votes of those who were reluctant to vote for either of the older parties. While C.C.F. spokesmen did not make an anti-Social Credit stand an important election issue they did on occasion attack the party led by Mr. Low. Mr. Coldwell, for example, speaking in the heartland of the Social Credit party, expressed shock at "the slavish manner in which the Social Credit members supported every move made by the government to stifle debate" when Parliament dealt with the pipeline. Mindful of the tinge of anti-semitism associated with the Social Credit party and some of its M.P.'s Mr. Coldwell continued:

Most of you will recall however that this was not the first, nor the last, occasion upon which Social Credit has shown its contempt for elementary freedoms. Indeed, just a few months ago, in opposing the establishment of the Canada Council, Social Credit members lashed out at UNESCO, . . . One Social Crediter quoted with approval a rabid American publication which flayed UNESCO's "alien racist agitation". So long as we have individuals in Canada, let alone political parties, which preach the doctrine of racial superiority the CCF insists we need a Bill of Rights . . .[32]

Vigorous efforts were made by the C.C.F. to refute the charge that to cast one's ballot for the C.C.F. was to waste a vote. The C.C.F. was presented as a party entirely different from the old parties. Free from the influence of business contributors, the C.C.F. was described as the only group capable of defending the interests of the Canadian voters.[33] A vote for either of the older parties was portrayed as a wasted vote, since there was so little to choose between the Liberals and Conservatives. "Certainly no vote could be more useless," said Premier Douglas, "than one cast in support of a government which has used its large majority to rubber-stamp policies of lethargic drift and complacent arrogance. Equally wasteful is a vote for any opposition party which offers no distinct difference in basic political philosophy from that of the Liberals."[34] Premier Douglas, on another occasion attempted to counteract the "wasted vote" attack on his party:

In this constituency you are being told that you will be wasting your vote by voting CCF. The fact remains that over the past quarter of a century every important economic reform and every piece of progressive social legislation has been popularized by the CCF and has been forced upon a timid and reluctant government. The Liberal Party does not need a bigger majority. What it needs is to be shaken out of its complacency and indifference.

Mr. Diefenbaker is reported to have said in Ontario—"Every vote cast for

[32]Edmonton, May 24. Press release.
[33]See, for example, Mr. Coldwell's C.B.C. television broadcast, May 2. Press release.
[34]C.B.C. Dominion Network broadcast, May 16. Press release.

a third party will be an innocuous vote in the final result." It is significant that Mr. Diefenbaker's appeal against what he called "third parties" was made in Ontario. However, west of Ontario it is Mr. Diefenbaker's party which is a third party. . . . if the people of Western Canada are to heed Mr. Diefenbaker's injunction to eliminate third parties, then it is the Progressive Conservative party which will have to go and not the CCF.[35]

Not only its arguments, but also the scope and nature of the C.C.F.'s organization differed markedly from those of the Liberals and Conservatives. The party's campaign expenditures, as will be seen shortly, were an insignificant fraction of those of its more affluent rivals; this fact alone precluded the use of many electoral devices and the recourse to many campaign techniques customarily associated with Canadian politics. And yet, the party had to operate in the same political environment as its opponents, and its candidates had to appeal to much the same sort of voters. It is, therefore, not surprising that the campaign organization of the social democratic party resembled in many particulars that adopted by the more capitalistically oriented parties. The chief differences were related to the magnitude of the C.C.F. efforts and to the amateur status of the party workers. The C.C.F. could not afford anything like the heavy expenditures of its rivals. On the other hand, it benefited from the virtual absence of paid party workers and the concomitant reliance on volunteers. On the whole, the latter were probably more effective than paid workers. In any event, a common basic outlook on social, economic, and political problems naturally contributed to a spirit of solidarity and comradeship among the party's election fighters. The C.C.F.'s impecuniosity and paucity of supporters in some constituencies, were, therefore, offset in some measure by greater cohesion and ideological commitment of its leaders and many workers.

In addition to three or four typists and a typist-receptionist-librarian, headquarters could boast only three "political" officers. These were Mr. Lorne Ingle, the outgoing national secretary, Mr. Carl Hamilton, his successor, and Mr. Russell Bell, the research director. The campaign also benefited from the part-time services of Mr. Harry Howit, who helped with publicity as well as being the Co-operative Press representative in Ottawa.[36] In planning the electoral campaign and in laying down the broad outlines of campaign strategy, the party bureaucracy worked closely with the various elected leaders of the C.C.F. Chief of these was,

[35]Prince Albert, Sask., June 5. Press release.
[36]Most of the information on the operations of the national office was obtained by talking to Mr. Hamilton and by perusing the party files dealing with the 1957 election.

of course, the national leader, Mr. M. J. Coldwell. Mr. David Lewis, national chairman, was also an extremely influential member of the party not only by virtue of his current office but also because he had for many years served as national secretary. Other members of the executive who played prominent roles in the planning of the election campaign and in its execution were the two vice-chairmen, Mme. Th. Casgrain and Mr. Stanley Knowles, Mr. Andrew Brewin, national treasurer and chairman of the finance committee, Messrs. Hazen Argue, Kenneth Bryden, Morden Lazarus, Michel Chartrand, and Premier Douglas. The latter and Mr. Bryden served on the national executive in their own right, not by virtue of their positions at the provincial level.[37]

Election plans were first discussed by the national executive at its meeting late in November, 1956.[38] The national secretary presented the meeting with tentative plans for the campaign, including a draft budget, proposals for election literature and advertising, and an estimate of how many candidates would have to be provided with deposits. After a long discussion, the executive decided that Mr. Ingle should discuss these proposals in detail with the various provincial sections and that final plans should be placed before the next national council meeting. The executive also established the committee, mentioned above, which was to advise it on election issues.

It was at its January, 1957, meeting that the national council gave final approval to the election plans as proposed by the national secretary, after he had discussed them with the various provincial organizers and executives. The issues to be emphasized, literature, advertising, the number of candidates to be nominated, the activities of the national leader and the contributions to be sought from the provincial party organizations were all discussed by the council. Provision was made for the preparation of French-language publications. The whole campaign thereafter consisted essentially of the interpretation, elaboration, and execution of these plans by the national office staff, sometimes in consultation with the leader.

Before the election campaign proper started, the national office assisted the various provincial organizations, particularly in areas where the party was weak, in finding suitable C.C.F. candidates and in guaranteeing deposits where this was necessary. The national organizer, Mr. Carl Hamilton, had travelled across Canada in an effort to strengthen the party's organization. In addition, M. Michel Chartrand and Mr.

[37]Premier Douglas was, of course, the Saskatchewan leader, and Mr. Bryden was the secretary of the Ontario C.C.F. organization.
[38]Minutes, C.C.F. National Executive meeting, Nov. 24 and 25, 1956, p. 5.

Howard Pawley were charged with doing special organizational work in Quebec and Manitoba respectively.

About three months before the election, C.C.F. candidates were provided with excerpts from speeches given by Mr. Coldwell on a large number of current issues. They also received copies of the Winnipeg Declaration and of the national programme, with instructions regarding the purchase of these documents in bulk from the provincial party organizations. Candidates in constituencies in which the C.C.F. was entitled to appoint one of the enumerators were urged to prepare a list of suitable individuals so that the returning officers could receive the suggested names as soon as the election was called.

In the middle of April, headquarters distributed a number of additional aids to the constituency parties. Draft scripts for five-minute radio broadcasts dealing with old age pensions and taxation were mailed and additional scripts promised. An election time-table, prepared by the Chief Electoral Officer, and a Scrutineer's Manual were also provided. A popular item sought by the candidates was the mimeographed booklet, *Speakers' Notes*. Drawing on debates in Parliament, official statistics, newspaper accounts and similar sources, this slim volume provided the candidates with ammunition required to support their election arguments. The record of how the parties had voted during the previous session of Parliament was also sent out. Throughout the campaign, the national office also issued candidates (and the press) with a flood of *Press Releases* containing passages selected from speeches made by the party leaders. Some of these campaign aids were also provided in French.

By far the most important item of campaign literature, planned by the headquarters staff, and executed by Ganes Productions, a firm of commercial artists, was a so-called "illustrated booklet" entitled, like so much of the C.C.F. material in this election, *Share Canada's Wealth*. Tabloid sized and printed on newsprint, this was set up like a four-page comic strip, presenting the highlights of the party's programme in story form. The comic book appearance of this item was reputedly embarrassing to some of the members of the party hierarchy, hence its official title of "illustrated booklet." However designated, it was so popular with the constituency organizations, that more than a million copies were purchased from the national office. Part of the final page was left blank, permitting individual candidates to insert their own names and brief messages.

In addition to the illustrated booklets, headquarters, with the assistance of A. L. Barkes, an advertising artist, prepared mats and layouts for a number of additional leaflets and advertisements to be used by campaign committees at the provincial and constituency levels. But the 1957 campaign differed from earlier ones in that only one main item of campaign literature—the illustrated booklet—was designed and given extremely wide distribution. In a report based on returns to a questionnaire distributed to candidates after the election, Mr. Hamilton expressed the view that "both the content and appearance were acclaimed by the vast majority of candidates" and that reliance on one main item, of similar design, was desired for the next election.[39]

To a party suffering from a chronic shortage of funds the free national broadcast time made available by the C.B.C. was of particular importance. The C.C.F. was allocated ten radio and five television broadcasts on each of the French and English networks. The former were handled by the Parti Social Democratique in Montreal and the latter were the responsibility of the national office staff. Mr. Coldwell, an extremely persuasive and effective radio and television performer, delivered most of the English addresses. Premier Douglas, Mme. Casgrain, Mr. Knowles, and Mrs. Marjorie Cooper, a member of the Saskatchewan Legislative Assembly, also broadcast on behalf of their party. Mme. Casgrain and Michel Chartrand were the C.C.F.'s chief spokesmen on the French network.

In addition to planning the party's programmes, the national office also advertised them. Indeed, with only one exception, all newspaper and periodical advertising placed by headquarters was published in conjunction with the radio and television broadcasts over the C.B.C. The exception consisted of some advertising in the ethnic press arranged by the national office in co-operation with the Ontario party. The broadcast and ethnic advertisements were largely paid for out of the party's national campaign fund.

The planning of broadcasts had to be related to the campaign tours of the leaders, particularly that of Mr. Coldwell. It was the responsibility of the national office to arrange the speaking engagements of the leaders. In drawing up the itineraries every effort was made to benefit from the high reputation some of them enjoyed in the country. Mr. Coldwell's heart ailment seriously curtailed the extent of his activities, although not the vigour with which he tackled his responsibilities in the campaign. In addition to making ten free-time television and radio broadcasts, the natonal leader embarked on a speaking tour in central and western Canada. Mr. Coldwell left Ottawa on April 26 for his own constituency

[39]*Acting National Secretary's Report to the National Council on the Federal Election, 1957.*

of Rosetown-Biggar. On May 10 he opened his campaign tour in the east by addressing a meeting at Timmins in northern Ontario. He spent two days campaigning in Toronto and then moved west speaking in and around Saskatoon, Vancouver, Edmonton, Winnipeg, and Regina, before returning to his own riding for the final days of the campaign.[40]

Considerable thought went into the planning of Mr. Coldwell's speeches. Owing to the state of his health, only eight major campaign addresses were given by the C.C.F. leader, but care was taken to explore the major issues in these eight speeches and to secure for each of them wide national publicity. One theme of each of Mr. Coldwell's addresses, taking about five minutes of an hour-long talk, was written out and made the subject of a special press release. The releases became the basis of much free publicity for the party. The remainder of each of Mr. Coldwell's speeches was not based on a prepared, fully written out text. The C.C.F. leader's chief lieutenant on his campaign tour was Mr. Carroll Weenas, his executive assistant, who looked after local travel arrangements and assisted in the preparation of speeches. Similar assistance was rendered by Mr. Bell, and to a lesser extent by Mr. Ingle and Mr. Hamilton. These officers had held a conference with Mr. Coldwell early in the campaign and discussed with him the main themes of his speeches and what issues were to be emphasized in the various centres visited by Mr. Coldwell.

Mme. Casgrain assumed, on behalf of the national organization, the main burden of campaigning in Quebec and in the Maritime provinces. The west coast was visited by Mr. Knowles; Premier Douglas made a speaking tour of Ontario. Several members of Parliament and provincial cabinet ministers also made isolated sorties into neighbouring constituencies or farther afield, to address C.C.F. meetings. The speaking tours of Mr. Coldwell, and of the other nationally known party chiefs, were an extremely effective campaign activity organized by the national office. For regardless of the size of the audiences the speeches given on these occasions received national coverage. Publicity so obtained served a dual purpose: it presented the C.C.F. view to many who would otherwise never have been exposed to it and it indicated that the party was of sufficient *national* interest to merit being "covered" by the national media of communication.

The efforts made by the national organization were, of course, complemented by the campaigns of the provincial parties. In Saskatchewan, British Columbia, and Ontario the provincial bodies waged extremely vigorous campaigns which were probably more effective than the elec-

[40]"M. J. Coldwell Itinerary," C.C.F. National Office files.

tioneering of the national party. In provinces where the C.C.F. was weak, however, the local campaigners usually depended heavily on the assistance provided by the Ottawa office.

Repeated references have been made to the meagre financial resources of the C.C.F. compared with those of the Liberals and Conservatives. The party was not only less lavishly endowed, but also less secretive about the magnitude and sources of its funds. A confident estimate of the cost of its election campaign can, therefore, be given. The national office spent about $31,000 on the election campaign, about $12,000 of which it recovered through the sale of the picture booklet to provincial and constituency parties. A special fund to assist in its general organizational work had been established previously, but its expenditure can, in a sense, be considered as being related to the election. About $11,000 was spent on the salaries and expenses of general field organizers under the National Organization account. The 1957 federal campaign, therefore, cost the national office about $30,000. Where did this money come from? Two sources account for practically all the expenditure incurred by the national organization; contributions from provincial parties, particularly the Ontario and Saskatchewan sections, and contributions from trade unions, particularly the United Packinghouse Workers and the United Automobile Workers. The provincial parties raised their funds in various ways, primarily through individual and trade union contributions and occasionally through special efforts, such as, for example, the C.C.F. Action Fund in British Columbia.[41]

Provincial organizations not only contributed to the national fund, of course, but also spent money on their own provincial campaign. A wealthy organization, like the Saskatchewan party, spent about $100,000 on the 1957 federal election. The Ontario C.C.F. also made a sizeable contribution in support of the federal candidates. Some constituency parties were able not only to support themselves, but in addition, to contribute to less wealthy C.C.F. organizations in nearby constituencies. The C.C.F. organization in Winnipeg North, for example, made $600 available for deposits elsewhere, and Winnipeg North Centre gave financial assistance to its sister organization in Winnipeg South Centre.

When all these outlays are taken into account, it appears that the total sum expended on behalf of the C.C.F. by the federal, provincial and constituency sections of the party, was not much in excess of $200,000 and certainly less than $250,000. The Liberals obtained roughly 3.8 times as many votes as the C.C.F. and the Conservatives about 3.6 times, but even the Conservatives, whose total campaign ex-

[41]See *C.C.F. News*, Vancouver, vol. XXI, *passim*.

penditure was modest compared with that of the Liberals, spent at least twelve times as much as did the C.C.F.

Trade unions played an important role in the financing of the C.C.F. campaign; and this fact raises the question of the nature of the relations between the party and the trade union movement. At the federal level, the degree of interaction and day-to-day contact was surprisingly slight. Beyond contributing to the campaign fund, the unions took practically no interest in the activities of the national office. Some trade unionists were, of course, active members of the party hierarchy, but in each case this was the result of personal interest rather than of trade union policy. And although some unions officially recognized the C.C.F. as their political arm, they did not participate in the electoral activities of the national party. In this connection it is interesting to note that when the national executive met immediately after the election on June 14 and 15, four trade union representatives attended the meeting and conducted a post-election analysis with the members of the party's executive.[42]

That all four were Ontario trade union officers may be attributed in large measure to the fact that the meeting was held in Toronto, but it cannot be explained entirely in terms of a fortuitous geographical circumstance. For although there was no formal connection between the C.C.F. and the trade unions at the national level, there was a very close relationship between the Ontario C.C.F. and the Ontario Federation of Labour. A co-ordinating committee constituted by the two organizations ensured that formal machinery existed for continuous and intimate consultation. Informally, daily contact was maintained between the leaders of the Ontario party and the Ontario Federation of Labour. Such intimate contact had not developed in the less industrialized provinces, or in Quebec.

There was also a good deal of collaboration at the local levels in constituencies where the trade unions were well organized. Many C.C.F. party workers in industrialized ridings were trade unionists and in some instances local unions formally endorsed the C.C.F. candidates. In Winnipeg, for example, the District Labour Council (C.L.C.) issued 15,000 copies of a pamphlet entitled *Let's Support Our Friend*, backing the seven C.C.F. candidates in Manitoba who were trade unionists.

Three of these seven candidates, Messrs. Bryce, Manchur, and Schultz, were classified as unionist by virtue of their membership in the

[42]They were Mr. Cleve Kidd, president of the Ontario Federation of Labour, Mr. Bert Gargrave, Political Action Committee chairman of the Toronto and District Labour Council, Mr. Dave Archer, secretary of the Ontario Federation of Labour and Mr. Lloyd Fell, Political Action Committee director of the Ontario Federation of Labour. Minutes, C.C.F. National Executive meeting, June 14 and 15.

Manitoba Farmers' Union. This may be a generous application of the term unionist, for in many respects the attitudes and interests of farm organizations tend to diverge fundamentally from those of organized industrial labour. In view of this difference it is necessary to consider the question of whether the C.C.F. received the same support from labour and farm unions.

In Saskatchewan, C.C.F. strength had always rested to a significant extent on the support the party enjoyed among the farm population. But there is no evidence that this support was translated into an institutional pattern corresponding, for example, to the formal support received by the Ontario C.C.F. from the Ontario Federation of Labour. Farm organizations in Canada have been more reluctant than some of the trade unions to ally themselves with certain political parties. The C.C.F. has, therefore, not been able to draw on the support of the influential farm organizations, even in provinces like Saskatchewan, where the party is well entrenched. But while the C.C.F. received no formal aid from these organizations, there is little doubt that both in Saskatchewan and Manitoba many farmers and officials of farm organizations were favourably disposed towards the C.C.F.

Another group which was sometimes thought to provide a pool from which the C.C.F. could be expected to draw considerable support was that of the so-called New Canadians. Many of them were one-time supporters of social democratic parties and were, therefore, thought to be favourably predisposed towards the C.C.F. Insufficient evidence is available for the evaluation of this hypothesis. Some New Canadians, as refugees from Communism, were violently hostile to any form of socialism, whether democratic or not. But the C.C.F. felt that it could usefully appeal to those voters who had recently arrived from Europe. In addition to the advertisements in the ethnic press, mentioned earlier, the C.C.F. made special appeals through its non-Anglo-Saxon M.P.'s and candidates to that section of the electorate which did not think of the British Isles as "the Old Country." Messrs. Ancevich, Sefton, Lewis, Kedzierzykowski, and Zaplitny were among those who made special efforts to woo the New Canadians. Mr. Coldwell also talked to editors of the ethnic press in Winnipeg during his campaign tour in the west.

A notable exception to the C.C.F.'s generally friendly attitude towards the less favoured minorities in Canada was noticeable in the campaign of one of its western candidates. Erhart Regier, the Mennonite C.C.F. Member for Burnaby-Coquitlam, published a weekly newsletter during the campaign. The issue of May 20 dealt with immigration and included the following recommendation: "That a greater share of the immigrants be from western and northern Europe, from the Scandinavian countries and from the United Kingdom."[43]

C.C.F. campaign tactics, at the constituency level, differed little from those adopted by the other parties. Two unique local efforts deserve special notice. J. P. Griffin, contesting McLeod in Alberta, published a long pamphlet, entitled *We Are Not Ashamed of the Gospel*, resting the C.C.F. case squarely on Christian foundations. And in British Columbia, C.C.F. women advertised that they would be glad to visit the sick in hospital, if they wished it.

An examination of C.C.F. candidates shows that they differed from those of the other parties in some interesting respects.[44] In the first place, the number of trade unionists was, of course, considerably greater. At least forty per cent of the party's nominees belonged to a labour organization. Only sixteen per cent of the C.C.F. candidates belonged to the professions; exactly the same proportion was engaged in business. This was to be expected in a party espousing a moderate socialist philosophy. More surprising, in view of the C.C.F.'s strength in the prairies, was the low percentage of candidates engaged in agriculture: a mere twelve per cent were classified as farmers.

The educational qualifications of C.C.F. candidates were somewhat lower than those of the older parties. About half of those for whom this information was available had attended university. The percentage of those who had not had any schooling beyond the primary level was higher than among the older parties, but this group of C.C.F.'ers included a number of individuals who were self-taught in many fields of knowledge. One highly literate candidate, for example, had left school after third grade.

On the whole the C.C.F. slate of candidates included a larger proportion of younger people, and a smaller ratio of those in their sixties and seventies than was true for the other parties. Adherents of the United Church formed a relatively larger contingent of candidates, as did also Unitarians. At least nine of the latter were to be found among the C.C.F. nominees. With only twenty-one candidates running in Quebec, the C.C.F. nominated considerably fewer French Canadians than the Liberals and Conservatives. But its ranks included a somewhat larger proportion of other non-Anglo-Saxons.

The foregoing description of the C.C.F. campaign indicates that the

[43]*Burnaby-Coquitlam Newsletter* (mimeo), p. 1.
[44]It was, unfortunately, impossible to secure the biographies of all the candidates of the minor parties. Under most of the categories considered in this discussion, information was available for fewer than 70 per cent of the C.C.F. candidates. The occupations of all candidates were known. See note 19, chap. VI.

party differed from its older rivals in a number of respects, the chief of which was its ideology. The C.C.F. approach to Canadian problems, while far from being Marxist, was nevertheless clearly rooted in the socialist tradition. The party's aim was not only to replace the government, but to transform much of Canadian society.

The Social Credit Party

If the C.C.F. was the main party of the Left, the Social Credit party must be placed on the extreme right of the traditional political spectrum. The principles underlying the party's proposed election programme were said to "demand that Government get out of business and make way for private enterprise; they re-state the fundamental belief in the dignity and God-given rights of the individual man; they denounce all government-inspired schemes to degrade man and make him subservient to the state or any monopoly."[45] Indeed, the party's opposition to state intervention in the day-to-day working of the economy was stressed infinitely more, in the course of the campaign, than any of the monetary teachings normally associated with Social Credit.[46] Reference to Social Credit theories were in fact remarkably rare, except in the most general terms, on the part of Social Credit candidates. It is difficult to say whether this slighting of the party's theoretical foundations was due primarily to the difficulty of expounding a complex theory in the course of an election, or to a growing opportunism on the part of the leaders.

Throughout the campaign there were persistent rumours of disagreements between the so-called doctrinaire and opportunistic wings of the party.[47] The latter group was said to have formed primarily around the British Columbia leaders, many of whom were relatively recent converts to Social Credit, and who were allegedly less orthodox and less devoted to its principles than the national and Alberta parties, represented primarily by Mr. Low and Mr. Manning. The party programme to be used in the election was actually prepared in British Columbia by a campaign committee, established at the instigation of Mr. Low, the

[45]"How Does Social Credit Know What Canada Wants?" *Canadian Social Crediter*, Special Edition no. 1, March 15, p. 6.

[46]The reader who wishes to examine the theoretical basis of Social Credit economics is advised to consult a standard work, such as Maurice Colbourne's *The Meaning of Social Credit* and to examine C. B. Macpherson's brilliantly succinct summary in his *Democracy in Alberta* (Toronto, 1953).

[47]See, for example, George Bain's "Minding Your Business" from Vancouver in the Toronto *Globe and Mail*, May 10, and May 14.

national leader, but under the chairmanship of Mr. R. W. Bonner, the Attorney-General of British Columbia. The platform, as drafted by this western-based committee, was to be presented to the party and the public at a monster rally in Massey Hall in Toronto. Mr. Low did not see the draft until just a few hours before its unveiling and was said to have been irate over the absence in it of any references to Social Credit principles. The whole document had to be revised at the last minute, and then only in the face of determined opposition from the party's public relations adviser.

An article in the *Canadian Social Crediter* asserts that the party programme had been "Tailored expressly to the written and spoken demands of countless thousands of . . . citizens."

Here is how it was done. Our National Leader, Solon E. Low, sent out many thousands of questionnaires to Canadian voters. The individuals who received them were invited to list ten of the most important problems standing in need of immediate attention.

Needless to say, a great number of people were glad to avail themselves of this chance to tell a Great National Movement just what they considered the ten most important problems of the day.

Out of the great mass of replies that came in, Social Credit leaders formulated a set of principles on which to build a platform of government action. These are no flimsy "planks" suspended by straws, or resting on empty gas barrels. They are concrete proposals from people, on which to build a foundation for the Canada they desire. These principles are embodied in a program of action.[48]

It is conceivable that the absence of emphasis on Social Credit principles in the party programme was the consequence of a similar neglect on the part of the respondents to the questionnaire, assuming, of course, that it was possible to deduce any principles from the listing, by a number of citizens, of the ten most important problems of the day. In fact, it has proven impossible to confirm the existence of the questionnaires referred to in the *Social Crediter* article.

Mr. Low enunciated the principles on which the party's platform was to be based, and the general line of the Social Credit argument, in a statement contained in the first special election issue of the *Canadian Social Crediter*. Emphasizing the necessity for political parties to adhere to principle, Mr. Low pointed to the reliance on expediency allegedly exhibited by the Liberals. The new Conservative programme was characterized as a slightly modified Liberal one, "a sort of auction sale by which [the Conservatives] hoped to outbid the Liberals." The C.C.F. was accused by Mr. Low of having allowed its hunger for office to

[48]"How Does Social Credit Know What Canada Wants?" p. 6.

compromise its principles when the Winnipeg Declaration was created to supersede the Regina Manifesto. "Moreover, the Liberals have swiped so many socialist policies for their own programme that there is no alternative in the C.C.F." The only effective alternative confronting the Canadian voter, according to Mr. Low, was the programme shortly to be announced by the Social Credit party. This programme would be based on a number of fundamental principles. The enunciation of these principles comes closer than any other election document to linking the party with some of the monetary theories of Social Credit. For this reason, and also because the principles reveal something of the general ethos of the party, they are reproduced in their entirety:

1. Government should keep out of business—let private enterprise, not socialist or State enterprise, prevail.

2. Every person shall be free to manage his life, free to speak, to assemble, to work, to worship, to choose, to live, provided only that he or she allow all others the same privilege.

3. The people's elected representatives in Parliament shall be supreme within the sphere of their jurisdiction as a means of ensuring that the people can get the results they want from the management of their affairs.

4. Every Canadian shall be afforded the opportunity to obtain an equitable share of Canada's national production.

5. Government by the people themselves at the "grass roots" level, shall be made more and more possible and actual, by decentralizing administration and by spreading the truth about things as they really are.

6. Canadians will be encouraged by every means to produce in Canada more and more of their vital needs of shelter, clothing and food, as well as tools to make them; and in so doing, shall, by the use of Canada's credit, be shielded from unfair foreign trade practices such as dumping and the like.

7. Canada's natural resources shall be developed in Canada for CANADIANS of today; and shall be husbanded and preserved for CANADIANS of tomorrow.

8. Full and free access to the courts will be guaranteed to all including "little people" as well, regardless of financial cost, by providing not only crown "prosecuting" attorneys but also crown "protecting" attorneys.

9. What is physically possible and desirable shall be made financially possible.

10. It shall be recognized positively that every people on earth shall have the right to self-determination and every nation shall have the right of unimpaired sovereignty, provided only that in exercising its own self-determination or sovereignty, such people or nation shall not interfere with the same rights of other peoples or nations.

11. Man's right to think and act independently does not transcend his obligation to law.

12. The means to even a desirable end are never justified where fundamental principles are compromised, or where truth is ignored, or where human liberties are set aside.

13. Only by recognizing our dependence upon the help of God and by humbly seeking to know His will can we possibly find our way through the perplexities that beset us, and into a state of peace and happiness at home and through the world.[49]

While not being excessively specific about the way in which Social Credit principles would be applied to the Canadian economy, there was, at least, in some items (4 and 9, for example) a reference to some of the party's traditional economic arguments. The platform itself, on the other hand, could have been the product of any non-socialist party contesting the election. If taken out of context, its connection with the Social Credit movement could not have been suspected. As presented in the party's chief electoral booklet, it read as follows:

Social Credit proposes the immediate introduction of these measures:
—An increase in the Old Age Pension payments designed to bring them to $100 a month.
—A financial policy designed to keep purchasing power in balance with Canada's production.
—Dropping of the present impractical experiments with "tight money".
—A national health plan designed to meet the standards of all provinces.
—An increase in income tax exemptions to meet higher living costs.
—A national housing programme designed to make home-ownership possible for every Canadian family.
—A vigorous, enlightened trade policy designed to widen markets for Canada's surplus production involving a two-price system for the sale of farm products, barter deals, and acceptance of the currency of other countries.
—Low interest loans for small businesses and farmers.
—Federal financial assistance for construction of all arterial highways.
—A new foreign policy, broader than military power alone, which would be based on the distribution of our surplus farm products and output of our factories to the less favoured nations of the world.
—A national security policy based on defence, not aggression and the elimination of inefficiency and waste.
—Bring about much-needed reforms in the Senate.
—Keep government out of private business.
—SOCIAL CREDIT believes Canada must have a planned and vigorously executed policy to bring people to this country and place them where they are needed.
—Canada's northland will be developed and made an integral part of our expanding nation by a SOCIAL CREDIT government.
—Superannuation benefits for wage earners to be transferable.[50]

There were some interesting differences between various versions of the platform. The regular May issue of the *Canadian Social Crediter*

[49]Solon E. Low, "National Leader Outlines Social Credit Principles," *Canadian Social Crediter*, Special edition no. 1, March 15, pp. 4–5.
[50]The National Social Credit Campaign Committee, *It's Your Canada*, pp. 1–2.

reported that the platform was presented at the party's opening election rally in Massey Hall and reproduced it in a box at the centre of the page. The thirteen items of this version omitted the planks listed above dealing with trade policy, security policy, the Senate, and immigration. The promise that government would be kept out of business was also excluded. A specific reference was added to the availability of mortgage funds at low interest rates and to parity prices for farmers. Neither item was mentioned in the campaign booklet. The latter merely indicated that the party favoured higher income tax exemptions, without specifying the amounts. The boxed platform in the *Canadian Social Crediter*, on the other hand, stated that the exemption would be raised from $1,000 to $1,500. The booklet omitted to add to the foreign policy plank the following sentence: "To encourage them to develop their own natural resources" which was placed in brackets in the *Canadian Social Crediter* version. The platform was also reproduced in the third special edition of the party's newspaper, but here the paragraph dealing with foreign policy read:

—A new foreign policy, based on the broadest human sympathy and understanding, and involving:
(a) scrupulous honesty in our dealings with other nations;
(b) recognition of the sovereign rights of nations and right of self-determination of all peoples;
(c) sharing our rich blessings with less fortunate sections of the human family.[51]

These and other differences are relatively unimportant. They indicate, however, that no serious objection existed to making changes in the number and wording of the platform planks when this suited the purpose at hand.

Another interesting feature of the Social Credit platform was that it omitted reference to a number of topics which played an important part in the party's arguments during the campaign. Chief among these was an intense dislike of, and vigorous attacks on, the C.B.C., the Canada Council, the government's actions at the time of the Suez crisis, and the United Nations. Social Credit candidates made frequent references to these issues in their indictment of the Liberal administration. The Canada Council, the C.B.C., and the National Film Board were attacked on the grounds that the government should first solve economic problems before spending tax money on the arts and also on the general ground that state interference is undesirable. It has already been mentioned that Mr. Low

[51]*Canadian Social Crediter*, Special edition no. 3, May 15, p. 3.

had accused Mr. St. Laurent of threatening Britain at the time of the Suez crisis. The party's ire on this issue may have been aroused in part by a generally pro-British sentiment as well as by the deep-seated suspicion it has traditionally displayed towards any international organization.

Of all the campaign organizations discussed so far, that of the Social Credit party was least influenced by the activities of the national office. The minor role accorded to headquarters was due in part to the high degree of decentralization prevailing in all Canadian parties, and in part to a number of circumstances peculiar to the Social Credit party. Its M.P.'s had, on the whole, played a much less important role in Parliament than those, say, of the C.C.F., and with the exception of Mr. Low, none of them had established a national reputation. Secondly, the party had forged a strong link with the province of Alberta—its first and most impressive base—and the national movement had never seemed to develop anything like the sort of national identity which the C.C.F. assumed apart from its base in Saskatchewan. Thirdly, having seized power in a second western province—British Columbia—the prestige and resources of *two* provincial governments tended to detract from the importance of the handful of federal M.P.'s and of the national party's small Ottawa office. This state of affairs was accentuated by the energy, ambition, and dynamism of the British Columbia premier who took an active part in the national campaign. Fourthly, the national office had never had as large, or as politically powerful a staff as the C.C.F. Mr. David Lewis, for many years the C.C.F.'s national secretary, had been one of the ablest and most influential leaders of his party, a fact which could not but enhance the importance, in the party's organization, of the Ottawa headquarters. No corresponding officer was ever attached to the Social Credit's national office. And finally, virtually all the financial resources of the party were raised by and spent with the consent of the Alberta and British Columbia organizations, thereby depriving the national office of the kind of autonomy which would have enabled it to play a more influential role in the election campaign.

The campaign was lacking a vigorous central leadership for the reasons just mentioned, and also because of disagreements and antagonisms at other levels within the party. It had at one time been planned, for example, that a party of British Columbia and Alberta cabinet ministers visit Manitoba as part of a high-powered Social Credit "blitz" of the province. In the end only a B.C. contingent participated in this invasion, apparently because disagreements had developed between the British Columbia and the Alberta groups.

Dissent weakened the election organization and the campaign in other respects as well. In Manitoba, for example, Mr. Keith Hunter, the former provincial organizer, was suspended shortly before the election campaign started. This episode produced arguments about a debt the party owed Mr. Hunter, charges of communism, and an appeal by the aggrieved Mr. Hunter to the national leader. As an aftermath to this quarrel, two members of the provincial executive also resigned.[52] In addition, a number of Social Crediters nominated to contest seats for their party in widely scattered parts of the country resigned their candidatures amid undisguised local squabbles. Such resignations occurred in Skeena, in Essex East, and in Essex South. Medicine Hat was contested by an official and an "independent" Social Crediter. In Quebec there were bitter arguments between the party and its one-time affiliate, and later foe, the Union des Electeurs.

In Alberta and British Columbia, the party's campaigns were virtually completely under the control of the provincial organizations. They were well financed and conducted according to the traditional methods elaborated by the old-line Canadian parties. Perhaps because of the general hostility of the press towards Social Credit, greater use was made of privately bought radio and T.V. time than one might have expected of a minor party. But in Alberta and British Columbia, the party was not the underdog it appeared to be in other parts of the country and, unlike the C.C.F., it benefited from large financial contributions of business donors.

The national organizer, Mr. Orvis Kennedy, made only infrequent and brief appearances at the Ottawa office. He had in fact resigned his position as national organizer in the autumn preceding the election, and was only filling in the post he had vacated in the absence of a successor. He spent practically all of the time in the west, leaving the national office in the hands of a skeleton staff consisting of Miss Irene Watts, the national secretary, Mr. Bazil Kuglin, and Mr. Ed. Parisien. The latter two were responsible for organizing in Ontario, Quebec, and the Maritimes. Mr. Parisien also acted as national treasurer. Mr. Kuglin later became the chairman of the party's National Action Committee, as well as office administrator and director of research, but his role during the campaign in 1957 was essentially to give such assistance to the candidates as the national office was equipped to provide and to act as field organizer in eastern Canada.

The task of the national office was made more difficult than that of the other parties by the unusually high degree of decentralization of

[52]See Winnipeg *Free Press*, May 1, and May 2.

the Social Credit party's organization and by the location of the campaign committee in the west. Nevertheless, headquarters co-ordinated the plans for Mr. Low's campaign tour and made the arrangements for his free-time political broadcasts and television appearances. It also attempted to arrange for some of the party's M.P.'s to speak in constituencies other than their own, but met with little success in this regard. Mr. Bonner's campaign committee had no staff and the Ottawa office therefore provided information, research, and some of the clerical services required by the campaign committee. Some literature, campaign aids to candidates and newsletters were also sent from the Ottawa office to the constituency organizations and to those on its mailing lists. Organizing in eastern Canada—finding suitable candidates, making sure that the necessary deposits were provided and helping to run the individual campaigns—was probably the most important contribution of the national office.

On the whole, and in its essentials, the work of the national office was similar to that of its counterparts among the other parties. This was even more the case for the various provincial offices operated by the provincial Social Credit Leagues in Alberta and British Columbia. In the capitals of provinces where the party was weak, the offices were extremely modest. The Toronto office, for example, was opened only a short time before the campaign and was, in some respects, merely a branch of the Ottawa headquarters. Nevertheless, the party succeeded in organizing a number of Social Credit schools during the early months of 1957 in various Ontario centres.

The electoral techniques of the Social Credit organization resembled those of the other parties. However, a few differences in emphasis may be noted. Reference has already been made to the likelihood that in proportion to its total campaign expenses, the party spent more on radio and television advertising than the other parties. Another unique feature of the party's campaign was the sortie of the British Columbia cabinet ministers into the Prairies. It is not common for Canadian provincial ministers to campaign in this fashion during a federal election. Mr. Frost, for example, who gave his party large-scale and invaluable assistance in Ontario, played a negligible role in other provinces. It is not unknown, however, for federal cabinet ministers to become heavily engaged in provincial elections when these appear to affect national policies.[53]

The Social Credit party also sent a large number of letters, over the signature of Mr. Bonner, to individuals on a special mailing list in

[53]Note, for example, the Quebec election of 1939 when the Quebec members of the King government became deeply engaged in winning their province's support for the war effort.

eastern Canada. While advocating the Social Credit programme, it also assured the recipients that the party would, if elected, take a cautious "go slow" approach to implementing its policies. A large-scale mail campaign of this sort was unusual in the 1957 campaign.[54]

Huge election rallies held a particular fascination for the Social Credit organizers. The party's national campaign was opened, as has been noted, at a widely publicized rally at Massey Hall in Toronto. The lavishness of this enterprise, and its location in Toronto, were probably intended to show the leaders' expectations of massive Social Credit gains in eastern Canada.[55] The Massey Hall rally was to inaugurate officially the party's on-to-Ottawa movement. In view of Social Credit's great strength in Alberta, it was natural to hold a huge rally in Edmonton, but a party with a lesser predilection for large-scale meetings would probably not have risked holding one in Winnipeg where its strength was problematical. It is at any rate doubtful whether the Toronto and Winnipeg rallies really were successful, although the one held in Edmonton appeared to have been so. The press described the Massey Hall affair as a failure.[56] The attendance was good at the Winnipeg rally, held early in June with musicians and drum majorettes, and with Mr. Bennett as the star attraction. But there were several mishaps, chief of which was the circulation by university students of a poem mercilessly lampooning the Social Credit movement.[57]

At the local level, the party performed the usual election rites in the same manner as its rivals. In the east, the number of paid helpers was exceedingly small, and such electioneering as was done was invariably carried out by volunteer workers. In this respect the otherwise quite incompatible C.C.F. and Social Credit parties had something in common. The only unique local party activity which has come to my attention, was employed in Vancouver East. The Social Credit Association in this constituency had for a number of years conducted a Christmas Tree celebration at which presents were distributed to children and draws held for prizes offered by the members. In 1956, according to one estimate,

[54]Winnipeg *Free Press*, March 11.

[55]The cost of the rally must have been considerable, although the estimate of one journalist (P. Laporte in *Le Devoir*, May 8) that fifty thousand dollars was spent on it seems overly generous.

[56]See, for example, the Winnipeg *Free Press*, April 19, and the Toronto *Globe and Mail* (George Bain's column), May 14. For a different view, see Alice Low, "The Toronto Conference," *Canadian Social Crediter*, Special edition no. 3, May 15, 1957, p. 5.

[57]Winnipeg *Free Press*, June 6.

no fewer than three hundred people attended, about half of whom were children. The latter group provided the entertainment, apparently to their own satisfaction and also that of the parents.[58]

Catchy slogans seemed to appeal to the Social Crediters more than to campaigners of the other parties. The ambition to become a national party was reflected in the general campaign slogan which proclaimed "On to Ottawa!" and which was used even when, at the close of the nominations, it became apparent that Social Credit could not have won the election, even in the inconceivable event that all of its candidates were successful. Another slogan, favoured by the party journal, proclaimed "Social Credit Offers Most Coast to Coast." "What is Physically Possible Is Financially Possible" was a classic catch-phrase of the movement and was used frequently in the course of the campaign.

As in previous campaigns, Social Credit speakers were prone to assume, and sometimes state, that they represented a movement rather than a party. The implication was virtually always, of course, that there is something degrading or immoral about political parties, something which the right-thinking and high-minded Social Credit movement has avoided, even while holding political office. A Vancouver sign, for example, read: "Vote Social Credit Progress (Not Politics)."[59] This seemingly anti-political attitude harmonized admirably with the frequency with which religious sentiments were introduced into Social Credit campaign utterances. This emphasis on a non-temporal justification for its position was to be expected in a party which was the legatee of the political instrument fashioned by William ("Bible Bill") Aberhart.[60] But the religious emphasis was by no means confined to the western wings of the party. At the annual convention of the New Brunswick Social Credit League, for example, held in October, 1956, three of the four major addresses were given by clergymen and a devotional period was conducted by a lay member of the League.[61] The degree to which this meeting emphasized the cloth was perhaps not typical of all party gatherings, but it was indicative of something clearly present in the Social Credit atmosphere, even in areas far removed from the Calgary Prophetic Bible Institute.

Given the presence, in the Social Credit party, of this definite religious flavour, it is not surprising to find that among its 113 candidates, there

[58]"News from the Provinces, British Columbia," *Canadian Social Crediter*, vol. IX, no. 3 (March, 1957), p. 4.
[59]Toronto *Globe and Mail* (George Bain's column from Vancouver), May 10.
[60]Cf. John A. Irving's admirable study, *The Social Credit Movement in Alberta* (Toronto, 1959).
[61]"News from the Provinces, New Brunswick," *Canadian Social Crediter*, vol. VIII, no. 11 (Nov., 1956), p. 6.

were no fewer than eleven clergymen or lay preachers.[62] Another interesting feature of the party's slate of candidates was that the proportion of those engaged in business of one type or another was higher than in any other party. Forty-three per cent were classified under the business category on the basis of the occupations listed in the Chief Electoral Officer's Report. (The corresponding figures for the other parties were: Conservative, 39 per cent; Liberal, 35 per cent; C.C.F., 16 per cent.) The percentage of professional people and of farmers among the Social Credit standard-bearers was identical to that found among the C.C.F.'ers: sixteen and twelve per cent respectively. Only a small number of trade unionists contested the election under the Social Credit banner.

As a group, the Social Crediters had a lower degree of formal education than the candidates of the other parties. Only about a third had attended university or its equivalent, and about fifteen per cent had not progressed beyond primary school. The party had the highest proportion in Canada of candidates whose formal education ended at the secondary school level.[63] Anyone familiar with the theories of Major Douglas and his disciples will, however, recognize that candidates who have espoused, and presumably honestly examined, the doctrines of Social Credit, must have spent a good deal of time engaged in earnest study, regardless of the extent of their formal education.

The age composition of the Social Credit candidates was similar to that of the Conservatives. As a group they were, therefore, younger than the Liberals and a little older than the C.C.F.'ers.

Of all the parties contesting the 1957 election, Social Credit contained the smallest proportion of United Church adherents. The number of Catholics was also small; this was partly the consequence of having nominated only four candidates in Quebec. Almost a quarter of the Social Credit candidates belonged to various sects: adherents of about a dozen small religious groups were represented among them.[64] The party

[62]The denominations were represented as follows: Baptist, 2; Church of Christ, 1; Church of Nazarene, 1; Methodist, 2; Mormon, 1; Pentecostal, 3; Salvation Army, 1.

[63]Under most of the categories considered in this discussion, information was available for about 80 per cent of the Social Credit candidates.

[64]Among the religious denominations listed by the Social Credit candidates who returned a questionnaire submitted to them, there were the folowing: Ukrainian Greek Orthodox, Christian Science, Scotch Covenant, Church of Christ, Evangelical United Brethren, Salvation Army, Mennonite, Church of Latter Day Saints, Brotherhood of Faithists, Fundamentalist Sect of the Church of Nazarene. Larger groups, such as Methodists, Ukrainian Catholics, and Lutherans were, of course, also represented.

had also nominated a Jewish candidate. This fact was, curiously, not mentioned whenever the leaders insisted that the accusations of anti-semitism levelled against the party were false. The number of French-speaking Canadians nominated was, of course, exceedingly small. On the other hand, the proportion of Social Credit standard-bearers who belonged to the other non-Anglo-Saxon European ethnic groups was higher than among the older parties.

It was in the ethnic composition of their candidates that the C.C.F. and Social Credit parties exhibited their greatest similarity. They seemed to differ in almost every respect, except one: while they were both unalterably opposed to the older parties, they saw in each other the greatest menace to Canadian politics.

Part III

THE RESULTS

THE ELECTION
AND
ITS OUTCOME

11

TO PREVENT THE TREES FROM HIDING THE FOREST, Part III of this study is divided into four distinct sections, one of which has been banished to an appendix. The results are presented and grouped under various headings in the statistical tables in Appendix D.[1] The present chapter contains a survey of the election outcome without going into elaborate detail and without reproducing the minutiae tabulated in the Appendix. Some of the points mentioned briefly in this chapter are taken up again at greater length in chapter XII, which analyses some of the more interesting features of the results. The final chapter tries to answer some of the questions posed earlier and to offer some explanations for the unexpected outcome of the election.

Election Day

Election day fell on June 10. In accordance with the recommendations of the Electoral Act, the day chosen was a Monday and polling took place then in all constituencies where this was possible.[2] Balloting in Wellington South had to be postponed to July 15 because of the death of the Liberal candidate and the acclamation of C. W. Carter gave the Liberals a gratuitous victory in Newfoundland.[3] On election day contests were therefore held in 261 constituencies. All of them except Halifax

---

[1]See below, pp. 290–302.
[2]Canada Elections Act, sec. 7.
[3]The results in Wellington South have been incorporated with those of the other constituencies.

(Nova Scotia) and Queen's (Prince Edward Island) elected one member. Each of the exceptions had two representatives in the House of Commons.

The provisions of the electoral law are readily available and have been condensed in a number of reference works.[4] It is consequently not necessary to summarize them here. The main features of the electoral system are the franchise, open to virtually every Canadian citizen (or other British subject) aged at least twenty-one and in full possession of citizenship rights,[5] and the principle of representation based on population and apportioned by provinces. Constituency boundaries are revised after each decennial census.[6] No revisions were made between 1953 and 1957, the population changes revealed by the 1951 census having been taken into account during the 1952 redistribution.[7]

A high turn-out of voters was indicated not only by the generally good weather prevailing in the country on June 10, but also by a public opinion survey conducted about a month before the election. The Gallup Poll reported that a larger proportion of those interviewed in 1957 expressed an interest in the election and the intention of voting than a corresponding sample of the population questioned in 1953.[8]

The pollsters were more accurate in forecasting the increased percentage of voters than in predicting the outcome of the election. It was shown earlier that the Gallup Poll predicted a larger Liberal vote than was actually recorded and that it under-estimated Conservative strength.[9]

In its final report the Canadian Institute of Public Opinion showed that it had found a two percentage point drop in Liberal support and a Conservative increase of three percentage points. In addition to this national forecast (qualified in the usual manner) the Institute reported

[4]The Chief Electoral Officer, *General Instructions for Returning Officers*; Dawson, *The Government of Canada* (Toronto, 1954), chap. XVI; Ward, *The Canadian House of Commons: Representation*, chap. VIII–XV.

[5]For the exact terms see Canada Elections Act, secs. 14 to 16. It is to be noted that some Indians ordinarily resident on a reserve were not enfranchised. See sec. 14, (2), (b).

[6]British North America Acts, 1867–1952, sec. 51.

[7]For an account of this redistribution, see N. Ward, "The Redistribution of 1952," *Canadian Journal of Economics and Political Science*, vol. XIX, no. 3 (Aug., 1953), pp. 341–60.

[8]Canadian Institute of Public Opinion, "Expect Larger Turnout More Voting Interest," Toronto *Daily Star*, May 30.

[9]See above, chap. IX, p. 190, particularly Table IX/1. The percentage of votes actually received by the parties, as given by the Gallup Poll, differs slightly from those given in this chapter and in Appendix D because most Independent Liberals and Independent Conservatives are here placed under a separate category in the "Other" column, and because the figures in this volume are final ones, whereas those given by the Gallup Poll were provisional.

that "during the campaign a trend towards the Conservative party developed in Ontario but appeared to lose some of its steam in the latter days."[10] The final Ontario figures were: Liberal, 43 per cent; Conservative, 45 per cent; C.C.F., 10 per cent; Social Credit, 7 per cent. The Quebec forecast gave the Liberals 70 per cent of the votes and the Conservatives 24 per cent. In underestimating the swing from the Liberal to the Conservative party, however, the Institute was by no means alone.

As indicated on several occasions above, almost everyone in Canada, while expecting the Liberal losses, was sure that the Government's mandate would be renewed. This reading of the political situation was by no means confined to Liberals and their sympathizers. "An examination of the pre-election files of such Conservative newspapers as the Toronto *Globe and Mail*, the Montreal *Gazette*, and the Ottawa *Journal* indicates, too," wrote one political scientist, "that their reporters had perceived many of the signs of political upheaval, but had generally interpreted them to mean no more than insubstantial losses for the Liberals. Mesmerized, like almost everyone else, by the feeling that the government was invincible, they were altogether too cautions . . ."[11]

Indeed, the general failure of the laymen and experts alike to predict the outcome resembled the events associated with re-election of President Truman in the United States in 1948. The public, the pollsters, and the press were ill-prepared for the results announced late on June 10. Even the gaffe committed by *Life* Magazine in releasing an issue the cover of which bore the likeness of "President" Dewey was paralleled by Canada's *Maclean's*. Its post-election editorial commented on the Liberal retention of power, albeit with a reduced majority.

Because of the division of Canada into seven time zones the polls closed in the Maritimes about five hours before balloting ceased in the furthermost western area. The earliest returns were therefore announced while some electors were still voting.[12] Early news from the Maritimes was at first not startling. Everyone had expected some Liberal losses in this area and it did not come as a complete surprise that Mr. Milton Gregg, the Minister of Labour, was defeated. It was known that he was going to have a hard struggle to hold his New Brunswick seat of York-

[10]C.I.P.O., "Tories Up 3 Points Liberals Off 2 since 1953, Survey Reveals," Toronto *Daily Star*, June 8.

[11]J. M. Beck, "The Election of 1957 and the Canadian Electoral System," *Dalhousie Review*, vol. XXXVII, no. 4 (Winter, 1957), p. 331.

[12]To prevent western voters from being influenced by the results elsewhere, no announcement about the counting in the earlier time zones is made in any area in which the polling booths are still open.

Sunbury. But Mr. Gregg was not the only minister who failed to be re-elected. It had soon become apparent that Mr. Winters, the Minister of Public Works, had lost Queens–Lunenburg in Nova Scotia. These two led a long list of cabinet defeats, dramatizing the disaster which was befalling the government.[13] By the time the reports from the west started to come in, and before the evening was over, it was apparent that Mr. St. Laurent would have to dispense with the services of a number of former colleagues, provided that he remained in office. Nine ministers—almost half the cabinet—were rejected by their constituencies. Mr. Howe was among them, as were also Mr. Harris, the Minister of Finance, Mr. Campney, the Minister of Defence, and Mr. Garson, the Minister of Justice.[14]

No doubt the first reaction of countless Canadians to the severity of the Liberal set-back, as they clustered around their radio and television sets on the evening of June 10, was that of extreme astonishment. But surprise must soon have given way to speculation about the ultimate outcome. It was certain that the voters had registered a protest against the government: how strong this protest had been could not be told until practically all the results were known. Gradually, as more and more seats formerly held by the Liberals were listed in the Conservative column, it seemed inevitable that the Liberals, though they might still retain the largest number of constituencies, would fail to secure the minimum of 133 seats required for an over-all majority.

Results: Seats

When the final figures became known, including the armed forces vote, the result of recounts and of the delayed election in Wellington South, the Liberal party found its strength in the House reduced from 171 to 105. The Conservatives now held 112 seats (as compared with fifty-one previously), the C.C.F. twenty-five (twenty-four before), the Social Credit party nineteen (a gain of four), and various Independents four (no change).[15]

[13]For the losses suffered by members of the cabinet see Table XII/5 on p. 260 below.

[14]Mr. Lapointe, Mr. McCann, and Mr. Hellyer were also defeated.

[15]Mr. Benidickson (Kenora–Rainy River) and Mr. Courtemanche (Labelle) are counted as a Liberal and a Conservative respectively. For a summary of the results showing the seats won and lost, as well as the percentage of votes obtained, see Appendix D below, particularly Tables D 2 and D 3.

As in most recent elections, the Liberals won a sweeping victory in Quebec, taking sixty-two of its seventy-five seats. In Newfoundland also, their former supremacy was not seriously threatened: they carried five of the seven constituencies in Canada's newest and most easterly province. New Brunswick divided its ten seats evenly between the two major parties. The situation in eastern Canada was not, therefore, completely hopeless for the government party. But there were some severe losses. The Conservatives won all four seats representing Prince Edward Island and in Nova Scotia they elected ten of the possible twelve members. Here the strength of the Liberals was reduced from ten to one. In the Maritimes as a whole, therefore, Liberal strength declined from twenty-seven to twelve seats; Conservative representation from this region grew from five to twenty-one.

Quebec sent nine Conservatives into the twenty-third Parliament, compared with four previously. In the other of the two central provinces, however, the party led by Mr. Diefenbaker scored a decisive victory. Sixty-one of Ontario's eighty-five constituencies favoured Conservative candidates, compared with thirty-three in the previous election. All but one of the eighteen Toronto ridings elected Conservative candidates. The Liberals' strength was here reduced from nine to one. In the province as a whole Mr. St. Laurent's party elected only twenty-one members, compared with fifty-one previously.

The so-called third parties won their greatest number of seats in the Prairies, the C.C.F. carrying fifteen constituencies in this region (the same number as before) and the Social Credit party thirteen (compared with eleven). This left twenty seats for the major parties. Six of these were won by the Liberals (sixteen before) and fourteen by the Conservatives, who had won in only six Prairie constituencies in 1953. Liberal strength remained unchanged in Saskatchewan, but dropped from eight to one in Manitoba and from four to one in Alberta. The Conservatives increased their representation in Manitoba from three to eight, in Saskatchewan from one to three and in Alberta from two to three.

The Liberals retained the two far northern ridings of Yukon and Mackenzie River, but they saw their strength in British Columbia fall from eight to two.[16] The Conservatives elected seven M.P.'s in the most westerly region where, in 1953, they had won only three contests.

[16]In Yukon, the Liberal, J. A. Simmons, was declared the winner by sixty-four votes over E. Nielsen (P.C.), after a recount had taken place before a judge. The Yukon Territorial Court later declared the result void. A new election was held on December 19, 1957, and won by Mr. Nielsen. See below, p. 000.

Results: Votes

Despite the Conservative success in obtaining a larger number of seats in the House of Commons, the Liberals received more votes than their main rivals.[17] The Liberal margin in this respect came to almost 130,000 votes. And although the Liberals lost sixty-six seats, they received only 48,700 fewer votes than in 1953. But the electorate had increased by half a million in the period between the two elections.[18] The Liberal vote may have declined by less than 50,000; Conservative strength increased by over 800,000 votes.

Expressed in percentages, the Conservatives obtained 38.5 per cent of the popular vote to the Liberals' 40.5 per cent. The Maritimes and Ontario proved the strongest Conservative regions, although neither gave Mr. Diefenbaker's party a clear majority of its votes. Only Quebec expressed a majority verdict: 56.8 per cent of the votes were cast for official Liberal candidates with another 4.7 per cent supporting Independent Liberals. The Conservative party received its lowest vote in the Prairies, the Liberals in British Columbia.

That in the country as a whole the proportion of the vote obtained in 1957 by the Liberal party differed from the proportion it obtained in 1953 by 7.8 percentage points—exactly the same number of percentage points as the increase in the Conservative proportion—might lead the unwary to assume that all the votes lost by the Liberals were cast for Conservative candidates. Even a casual inspection of the tables in Appendix D shows that such a conclusion is not supported by the facts.

Table D/2 indicates that the government suffered its greatest losses in British Columbia (10.1 percentage points), Ontario (9.5 percentage points) and the Prairies (9.2 percentage points). The proportion of votes received by the Liberals in the Maritimes was 6.8 percentage points lower than that it obtained in 1953. The Quebec loss was one of 3.5 percentage points.

The Conservative increase was greatest in British Columbia (18.3 percentage points), next came the Prairies (11.5 percentage points), and thirdly the Maritimes (9.0 percentage points). The proportion of the votes the Conservative party received in Ontario was 8.2 percentage points higher in 1957 than in 1953. In Quebec its proportion of the vote rose by only 1.7 percentage points. In those areas where the increase in the proportion of the Conservative vote was greater than the Liberal loss

[17]The relation between votes and seats is discussed at greater length in the following chapter. See pp. 262–5.
[18]See Table D/1 in Appendix D.

the difference is accounted for by changes in the votes received by the minor parties or by independents.

Table D/3 shows how the parties did in each province. The decline in the proportion of the vote obtained by the Liberals in the Maritimes was greatest in Nova Scotia. Then, in descending order, came Newfoundland, New Brunswick and Prince Edward Island. Conservative gains were greatest in Nova Scotia and smallest in Prince Edward Island. In all Maritime provinces except Prince Edward Island the increase in the proportion of the vote received by the Conservatives was greater than the Liberal decline. Of the three Prairie provinces, Manitoba showed the greatest swing away from the Liberals. The decline of 13.9 percentage points in the proportion of votes obtained by the government was in fact greater than in any other province. Conservative gains in the Prairies were greatest in Alberta and Saskatchewan.

To discuss party strength almost exclusively in terms of the change in the proportion of votes has its dangers, however. It suggests great Conservative strength in regions where the party may have staged a remarkable revival since 1953 but where it still was relatively weak in 1957. The increase of 18.3 percentage points in the Conservative proportion of British Columbia votes may give the erroneous impression that Conservative strength on the Pacific coast was immeasurably greater than, say, in Quebec, where the increase amounted to only 1.7 percentage points. But in fact, the party led by Mr. Diefenbaker received 32.5 per cent of the votes cast in British Columbia and 30.7 of the Quebec votes. The difference lies in the great weakness of the Conservatives in some regions prior to the 1957 election.

Turnout

Over seventy-four per cent of the eligible voters cast their ballots in the 1957 election. This was an increase of more than six percentage points over the turnout in 1953. In that year, the relatively low turnout was attributed to the election date—August 10—when many people were alleged to have been on holidays. There is very little evidence to support this contention. But whatever may have caused the low turnout in 1953, the high vote in 1957 was probably the consequence of an increased interest in the party strife, occasioned in large part by the bitter Parliamentary struggles preceding the election and by the vigorous campaigning of the Conservative leader.

In the Prairies, 75.9 per cent of the people on the voters' list cast their ballots. In all other regions except Quebec the turnout was 74.0 per cent or more. In Quebec only 72.3 per cent voted. Table D/3 shows that the lumping of provincial results into regional totals conceals some interesting variations in the proportion of eligible voters actually exercising their franchise. The Maritime total of 74.3 per cent, for example, hides the extremely high turnout in all the east coast provinces except Newfoundland. In the latter province under 52 per cent of the eligible voters cast their ballots, thus distorting the total Maritime percentage. For everywhere else in the region over eighty per cent voted. The Prairies' total conceals the unusually high turnout in Saskatchewan.

When the turnout in the 1957 election is compared with that in 1953 it becomes apparent that the Prairies experienced the greatest resurgence in political interest. The turnout in this region increased by more than ten percentage points. Quebec and the Maritimes, on the other hand, exhibited a relatively minor increase in the percentage voting. In Newfoundland the proportion voting actually declined by 5.5 percentage points.

The Canadian Forces Vote

Special regulations govern the vote of members of the Canadian Armed Forces and of veteran electors "receiving treatment or domiciliary care in certain hospitals or institutions."[19] The regulations are designed to facilitate the voting of members of the forces serving abroad, or lacking a permanent domicile, and of veterans otherwise prevented from casting their ballots at the regular polling booths. In 1957 voting by the Canadian Forces and "Veteran electors" began on June 3 and ended on June 8. The counting of ballots was completed on June 15 and showed that the members of the armed forces had reacted to the government somewhat differently from the civilian population.

Almost 65 per cent of those voting cast their ballots for Liberal candidates and less than one-quarter supported the Conservatives. Table XI/1 indicates how the service vote varied regionally. As was to be expected, the Liberals won their largest majority in Quebec, where their portion was over 80 per cent. The Conservatives received only 13 per cent of the vote in French Canada. They did best in the Maritimes, but even here they polled less than one-third of the votes. The Liberals failed to obtain a clear majority of the Canadian forces votes

[19]The Chief Electoral Officer, The Canadian Forces Voting Regulations (Ottawa, 1957), p. 7.

TABLE XI/1

Canadian Forces Vote

Region	Percentage obtained by		Total votes cast
	Liberals	P.C.	
Maritimes	65.7	30.3	17,840
Quebec	81.0	13.0	10,978
Ontario	66.2	28.0	24,597
Prairies	57.1	19.9	13,063
B.C.*	49.7	22.6	7,943
Canada	64.9	24.3	74,421

*Includes Yukon and Mackenzie River.

only in British Columbia, where they fell short of getting half the votes by only three-tenths of one per cent. In both the Prairie region and on the west coast almost all the votes not received by the major parties were divided by the C.C.F. and the Social Credit party.

Irregularities

In his preliminary report on the election the Chief Electoral Officer informed the Speaker of the House of Commons that "the general election appears to have been satisfactorily conducted in accordance with the procedure laid down in the Canada Election Act."[20] There were relatively few instances of blatant irregularities, but a few convictions were imposed by the courts as the result of illegal acts committed in connection with the election.

In addition to a number of offences which came to light in the province of Quebec, and which will be referred to below, there was only one major scandal arising out of the contravention of the electoral laws. Upon receiving information that an attempt was being made in the Toronto riding of St. Paul's to pad the voters' list with the names of non-existent individuals, the Chief Electoral Officer appointed a Commissioner to conduct an inquiry into the alleged offences. His report proved highly damaging to the Liberal candidate who, although no court action was taken against him, appeared to have been implicated in the illegal activities which eventually led to the conviction in the courts of several Liberal campaign workers.

[20]Report of the Chief Electoral Officer Under Section 58 of the Canada Elections Act, Oct. 10, 1957.

The Chief Justice of the High Court for Ontario, who acted as Commissioner in the case, found that the Conservative and C.C.F. parties, although occasionally not following the letter of the electoral law in presenting names to the courts of revision, were not guilty of fraudulent practices. Mr. Justice McRuer's report included the following indictment of Mr. Rooney, the Liberal candidate:

All of the 474 names added to the list of electors which, on investigation, showed that either no such person existed or that no such person or address existed, were added by agents for Mr. Rooney...

The evidence clearly shows that there was a well-planned scheme carried out in and through Mr. Rooney's campaign headquarters to place a large number of fictitious names on the list of electors through the process of the revision of preliminary lists. On the evidence Miss Nora Conacher would appear to have been the chief instrument in the execution of this scheme...

Nora Conacher has taken the whole responsibility for the plan and execution. I cannot find that she is a reliable witness and my conclusion is that it is inconceivable that she was the only one responsible...

If Mr. Glancy (the campaign manager) and Mr. Downey (chairman of the campaign committee) had no knowledge of the corrupt practices that were being carried on... they were more naive than one would expect from men of their experience and training. It is conceivable, but hardly conceivable, that they were only imposed on by others. I think the only conclusion from the evidence is that Miss Conacher was engaged by Mr. Rooney in a special capacity to do some special work at his headquarters, and, notwithstanding his denial of all knowledge of the character of her operations, I think it is incredible that any plan to have 474 or more fictitious names added to the list of electors, and to have persons at the polls to vote in those names, could be laid out or carried into execution without Mr. Rooney's knowledge...[21]

Four Liberal workers in St. Paul's were ultimately convicted in the courts. Their sentences ranged from one month in jail and a fine of $300, to a sentence of six months. The charges were either those of forging and uttering under the Criminal Code of Canada or of personation under the Canada Elections Act. Miss Conacher was also found guilty on two charges of perjury.

It had also been "made to appear" to the Chief Electoral Officer (to use his own justifiably cautious wording) that other violations of the electoral law occurred in Beauce, Chambly-Rouville, Hull, Longueuil, Quebec South, Hochelaga, Laurier, Ste Anne, Saint-Jacques, Sainte-Marie,

[21]Hon. J. C. McRuer, *Report of the Commission of Inquiry* into alleged offenses in the Electoral District of St. Paul's riding during the Election for which a writ was issued on April 12, 1957, pp. 9 and 18. The Report constitutes Appendix A to the *Report of the Chief Electoral Officer Under Section 58 of the Canada Elections Act*, May 8, 1958.

St. Lawrence–St. George, and Saint-Jean–Iberville–Napierville. Enough evidence of a suspicious nature was collected by the R.C.M.P. to justify prosecutions in Beauce, Laurier, Longueuil, St. Lawrence–St. George, and Sainte-Marie. The charges included opening a ballot box, taking ballots from a ballot box, supplying ballots, possession of ballots, stuffing a ballot box, forgery, and making use of forged documents (by adding names to the poll book), adding fictitious names to lists of electors, and taking a false oath. In addition to the four people convicted in Ontario, twelve were found guilty by the Quebec courts. It is highly unlikely that any of the various illegal practices which were investigated or even those which never came to light altered the outcome of the election in a single seat.

The election of J. A. Simmons, in Yukon, was voided by the Yukon Territorial Court when it heard a controverted election petition by E. Nielsen, the narrowly defeated Conservative candidate. The court found that four persons had voted who were not ordinarily resident in the Yukon when the writ was issued, and that one person who was under 21 had illegally cast his ballot. More serious, the court stated that it was clear that "the number of persons who purported to vote . . . but who were not, in fact, ordinarily resident on polling day in the polling division where they voted was large enough to affect the result of the election." In voiding the election, the court emphasized that no stigma must attach to Mr. Simmons. The matters complained of by the petitioner were held to have been irregularities on the part of voters and election officials, over which Mr. Simmons had had no control.[22]

[22]Nielsen v. Simmons (1958) 25 W.W.R. 68–77.

THE RESULTS
EXAMINED

12

The Electorate

THE RAPID EXPANSION OF CANADA'S POPULATION and its increasingly industrial and urban nature were reflected in the voters' lists. In the period of less than four years intervening between the 1953 and 1957 elections, the number of eligible voters grew by more than half a million or by six per cent, if 1953 is taken as the base year. But the increase was not spread evenly across the country: it was proportionately greatest in the two most westerly provinces and in central Canada. The Maritimes and the Prairies (with the exception of Alberta) showed only a modest growth in the electorate, Prince Edward Island actually experiencing a decline.[1] The 1957 electorate in this, Canada's smallest province, had shrunk by 2.3 per cent.

The increase in Newfoundland, Nova Scotia, and New Brunswick was between one and two per cent, whereas in Saskatchewan it amounted to only 0.8 per cent. The electorate in Quebec and Ontario grew by 6.0 and 7.1 per cent respectively, in Alberta by 7.7 per cent and in British Columbia by almost 10 per cent. These figures are closely related to the uneven growth of economic activity in Canada, since the end of the Second World War. The central provinces, British Columbia and Alberta have all experienced greater expansion and a more rapid rate of development than the other provinces. They have attracted large numbers of immigrants and also of Canadians migrating from areas undergoing a slower process of economic growth.

An examination of the 1953 and 1957 electorates and of the percentage change in the various constituencies[2] indicates that the greatest

[1]See Table D/3 in Appendix D.   [2]See Table D/6 in Appendix D.

rate of growth occurred in two types of riding. One is to be found in the recently urbanized areas near the rapidly expanding metropolitan areas, and the other is closer to the periphery of settlement where mining development or other forms of economic expansion have created new communities. The first type is exemplified by constituencies like York-Scarborough, York Centre, Mercier, or Laval at the outskirts of Toronto and Montreal. In these four ridings, for example, the percentage increase in the number of eligible voters was 86.9, 39.6, 42.6 and 51.0 per cent respectively. Algoma East represents the other type of constituency experiencing unusual growth. The uranium development at Elliot Lake and similar new communities were responsible for an increase in the electorate of 50.3 per cent.

Constituencies undergoing the greatest numerical decline were to be found either in the still predominantly rural areas in the Maritimes or the Prairies or in the old and long-established centres of the great cities. The migration from the heart of the cities to the suburbs is reflected clearly in the changes in the electorates in the metropolitan areas of Toronto and Montreal. Spadina and Davenport in Toronto and Saint-Jacques and Ste Anne in Montreal are good examples. It can be seen from Table D/6 that the drop in eligible voters in these constituencies amounted to 21.3, 14.2, 14.1, and 13.6 per cent respectively. Although all the Prince Edward Island constituencies and nine of the fourteen Manitoba seats experienced a decline in population, it was nowhere as great as in the centres of the eastern metropolitan areas. Twelve of the seventeen Saskatchewan constituencies had "shrunk" but only one of these—Mackenzie—suffered a decline comparable to the greatest losses of Toronto and Montreal. Its number of eligible voters fell by 10.2 per cent.

An intriguing question is posed by the possibility that the increase in the Conservative vote varied with the rate of population growth: that the greater the population increase in any riding, the more pronounced the shift to the Conservatives. To test this idea, the hypothesis was made that there was *no* connection between an increase in the size of the electorate in the constituency and the increase in the Conservative vote. When it was submitted to the *chi* square test it was proven to be untenable. The chances are nearly 99 to 1 that the two factors were causally connected. The hypothesis that the Conservatives did better in the rapidly expanding constituencies is based on the probability that Mr. Diefenbaker's aggressive campaign style and Conservative promises of a vigorous developmental policy had a greater appeal to the more expansionist and "go ahead" communities than to the sleepier and less alive ones. It has also been argued that the greatest hardship was being caused by the government's credit restrictions in areas of new settlement and large-scale building activity. But whatever the reasons, there is little doubt that, in general, Conservative gains were related, among other factors, to the growth in the size of the electorate.[3]

Turnout

Slightly less than three out of every four eligible voters cast their ballots in the 1957 election. This was a marked improvement over the performance in 1953 when less than 68 per cent bothered to vote. The 1957 figures equal those for 1949 but are below those of 1945. In that year post-war enthusiasm and presumably heightened awareness of civic responsibility had led to a turnout of 76 per cent.

Iles-de-la-Madeleine—whose population lives on an isolated island in the Gulf of St. Lawrence—had the highest turnout in Canada. It was the only constituency in which more than 90 per cent of the eligible voters cast their ballots. The record at the other end was held by Bonavista-Twillingate where only 43.5 per cent voted. In three other ridings (two in Newfoundland and one in Montreal) less than half of those whose names were on the voters' lists took the trouble to vote. The percentage turnout was in the 50's in six constituencies, in the 60's in forty-eight, in the 70's in 129, and in the 80's in seventy-four constituencies. The greatest increase in turnout over that registered in 1953 took place in St. Jean–Iberville–Napierville where it amounted to 20.6 percentage points. The greatest drop—one of 9.5 percentage points—occurred in Grand Bay–White Falls–Labrador.

On the whole, the percentage voting was lowest in scarcely populated, outlying areas like Newfoundland, northern Quebec, or northern Saskatchewan where communications conditions are difficult, and in the crowded sections of the metropolitan areas. It is possible that the greater geographical mobility of those normally living in the downtown

[3]This analysis of the vote contradicts an earlier, more limited attempt to establish a positive relationship between the growth of the electorate and of the Conservative vote. See J. Meisel, "Analysing the Vote," *Queen's Quarterly*, vol. LXIV, no. 4 (Winter, 1958), pp. 491–3.

A fuller statistical analysis of some of the questions considered in this chapter, based in large part on the 1957 election, is contained in John Meisel and Gilles Paquet, "Some Quantitative Analyses of Canadian Election Results," a paper presented to the Canadian Political Science Association Conference on Statistics, 1962, at McMaster University, Hamilton. Mimeographed copies are available on request from the author.

rooming-house areas of Montreal and Toronto makes for greater inaccuracies in the voters' lists in these areas, thus exaggerating the appearance of an already low turnout.

The higher turnout in most regions of Canada in 1957 than in 1953 can in large part be attributed to the appeal of the Conservative party to electors who had not bothered to vote in the previous election. In a number of constituencies lost by the government party the total Liberal vote was only slightly or not at all smaller than in 1953; the sitting member's defeat was brought about by the larger turnout and the general increase in the population.

That a positive relation exists between the degree to which turnout increased and the revival of the Conservative party on the one hand and the decline of the Liberals on the other can be demonstrated by relating the median increase in turnout to the changes in the proportion of votes received by the major parties in 1957 and in 1953.

The figures in Table XII/1 show that the median increase in turnout was only 1.4 per cent in constituencies where the Conservatives actually received a lower proportion of the vote in 1957 than in 1953. In constituencies where the Conservatives had registered a gain of up to 5 points the median increase in turnout was 4.7 per cent. The increase in turnout keeps growing as the Conservative position improves, until it drops slightly for constituencies in which the Conservatives' portion of the vote was greater in 1957 by 20 percentage points or more. The *chi* square test confirms the evidence presented in the table. It shows that the chances are considerably better than 99 to 1 that the increase in Conservative gains was related to an increased turnout.

TABLE XII/1

Turnout and Conservative Gains

Conservative gain*	None	0–4.9	5–9.9	10–14.9	15–19.9	20+
Median percentage increase in vote	1.4	4.7	6.4	8.6	9.1	8.7

*The gain is measured in percentage points showing the difference in the percentage of votes obtained by the Conservative party in 1957 and 1953.

As is shown in Table XII/2, the greater the increase in turnout the greater was the Liberal party's loss. The median percentage increase of those voting was only 1.4 in constituencies in which the Liberals obtained a larger share of the vote in 1957 than in 1953. In constituencies in which the government's share of the vote declined by not more than five per cent the median increase in eligible voters casting their ballots was

4.2 per cent. For each subsequent greater loss suffered by the Liberals the median percentage increase in the vote was greater until in the final column of the table we see that the increase came to 13.6 per cent in the constituencies in which the Liberal proportion of the vote was by 20 percentage points lower in 1957 than in 1953.

TABLE XII/2

Turnout and Liberal Losses

Liberal loss*	None	0–4.9	5–9.9	10–14.9	15–19.9	20+
Median percentage increase in vote	1.4	4.2	6.1	7.9	9.1	13.6

*The loss is measured in percentage points showing the difference in the percentage of votes obtained by the Liberal party in 1957 and 1953.

It follows from this that the increase in turnout was also associated with anti-government sentiment. Since the Conservatives benefited by far the most from this sentiment we are safe in assuming that anti-Liberal feelings were for the most part accompanied by friendliness towards the Conservatives. This, at least, is a logical inference from the election results. We cannot, of course, tell, and few voters could themselves tell, what was really uppermost in their minds when they voted Conservative—liking for the Conservatives or dislike of the Liberals.

The median increase in turnout in all seats won by the Liberals was at any rate 3.6 per cent, as contrasted with 7.5 per cent in all the seats captured by the Conservatives. The median turnout in all Liberal seats was 74.7 per cent, the corresponding Conservative figure being 77.4 per cent.

Such evidence as is provided by the 1957 Canadian general election does not support the theory that turnout tends to be highest in constituencies contested by large numbers of candidates. The theory is, of course, based primarily on the assumption that potential C.C.F., Social Credit, L.P.P., or other supporters may abstain from voting if their favourite party does not nominate a candidate. It is impossible to guess at the number of such disappointed voters in constituencies not contested by all the parties. But a look at the median turnout in constituencies fought by different numbers of candidates suggests either that their number is small and/or that the absence of their most favoured party's candidate does not deter many from voting.

One constituency was contested by only one candidate, 67 by two, 74 by three, 102 by four, and 17 by five candidates. The highest number of candidates was six and only two constituencies nominated that number. One of the ridings in which six candidates ran was Halifax. Like Queens, it elects two members. The median turnout in constituencies contested by the various numbers of parties is shown in Table XII/3. It reveals that the highest turnout was registered in constituencies staging a straight fight. The turnout was higher in ridings contested by two, three and four candidates than in those sought by five candidates.

TABLE XII/3

Turnout and Number of Candidates

Number of candidates per riding	2	3	4	5	6
Median turnout	80.3	75.4	75.0	73.2	79.0
Number of ridings	67	74	102	17	2

It would not be surprising to find that the turnout was highest in marginal constituencies. The closeness of the previous contest is likely to add excitement to the subsequent election and to bring out voters who might otherwise not bother to vote. The 1957 data were submitted to the *chi* square test which showed a probability of better than 99 to 1 that the two factors—closeness of the previous contest and turnout—were associated.

Bases of Party Strength

If one had to summarize the results of the election in one sentence, the least misleading statement one could make would be that it had turned into an unmistakable expression of anti-government sentiment. This was the case despite the fact that the Liberals received a larger number of votes than any other party. A glance at the figures tells a clear story: their proportion of the vote in 1957 was lower by almost eight percentage points than in 1953. The *number* of votes polled by the C.C.F. increased by almost 11 per cent but its proportion of the votes was smaller by 0.6 percentage points, and the Social Credit's proportion was only 1.1 percentage points greater than in the previous election.[4] The Conservatives found themselves the chief beneficiaries of Liberal losses, experiencing a 7.8 percentage point increase in the portion of votes cast for them.

More serious even than its reduced strength in the House, however, was the composition of the Liberal party's group of M.P.'s. The Liberal

[4]The *number* of votes polled by the Social Credit increased by over 40 per cent.

parliamentary group, representing a party that had long prided itself on being the only truly national party, had a distinctly lopsided appearance. Out of their 105 members sixty-two came from Quebec. Indeed, some students of Canadian politics were asking themselves whether the election had not indicated that a profound realignment was taking place among Canadian parties. Was there a parallel between the changes affecting the Canadian parties and those which the Democratic and Republican parties were apparently undergoing in the United States? Was something akin to the break-up of the Roosevelt coalition affecting the party once led by Mr. King and more recently by Mr. St. Laurent? Changes of this sort are usually concealed from the view of contemporary observers; they become apparent, as a rule, long after they have taken place. Often new conditions are recognized as having come into being only after they too have begun to disappear. It is therefore difficult to elicit from the results of a recently held election the pattern of a new party alignment, even if such a pattern is in fact emerging. But, on a more modest plane, some pointers about shifts in the sources of party support can be obtained from looking at the 1957 election results.

Generally speaking, the Conservatives gained seats in every part of the country except in traditionally unassailable Liberal outposts. We can therefore ignore the small gains of the C.C.F. (two seats) and the Social Credit party (four seats) and concentrate on the areas of special Liberal strength. Is it possible to detect any uniformities in the constituencies held by the Liberals? A careful examination of the results indicates that the 105 Liberal M.P.'s in the twenty-third Parliament came from constituencies falling into three categories. In the first place, Liberal strength was rooted firmly in French-speaking ridings, not only in Quebec but also elsewhere. Secondly, a number of Liberals were returned in "frontier," far northern constituencies. The third group— the smallest—was made up of ridings in which local factors conspired to assure Liberal victories. Some constituencies, of course, exhibited more than one of these characteristics.

Seventy-five of the 105 Liberal seats can be placed in the French category. Not all of them represented completely French constituencies, but in each the French-speaking population was large enough to constitute a decisive political factor. Sixty-two of the seventy-five were in Quebec. Both of the Liberal constituencies in Nova Scotia contained a very large number of voters of French-Canadian or Acadian origin. In Inverness–Richmond where, incidentally, the Liberal candidate, A. J. MacEachen, fought an unusually vigorous campaign, about 40 per cent of the population was of French origin, and in Shelbourne–Yarmouth–

Clare there were overwhelmingly French areas. About 90 per cent of those living in Clare were Acadians. Four of the five Liberal victories in New Brunswick were won in ridings containing French majorities or important minorities of French descent. They were Gloucester, Kent, Northumberland–Miramichi, and Westmorland. In Ontario, Liberal victories in Cochrane, Ottawa East and Ottawa West, Russell, Stormont, in one of the two Essex ridings and in some additional northern areas were won in constituencies containing significant numbers of French-speaking voters. St. Boniface, the only seat won by the Liberals in Manitoba, was also inhabited by a large French minority.

Another sixteen Liberal ridings were situated at the fringes of settlement. Five were in Newfoundland where the traditional loyalty to the party which was held responsible for the benefits gained by the recent accession to Canada was probably combined with the popularity of Premier Smallwood to keep the Conservatives out of the running everywhere except in St. John's. Yukon and Mackenzie River are also outposts in the far north, largely dependent on a variety of services provided by the government and therefore perhaps likely to confuse government and Liberal munificence. As shown by the electoral map, the two Algomas, Fort William, Kenora–Rainy River, Nickel Belt, Sudbury, Nipissing (all in Ontario), Meadow Lake in Saskatchewan and Athabasca in Alberta are all ridings in the north. They are inhabited primarily by people employed in extractive industries—mining, logging, acting as guides to American tourists—whose forefathers or who themselves have in most instances come to Canada from places other than the British Isles. In many of these constituencies there are large French-speaking minorities, but there is also a liberal representation of Scandinavians, Slavs, and peoples of other ethnic backgrounds.

Of the fourteen remaining Liberal constituencies little of a general nature can be said by way of explaining their continued loyalty to the St. Laurent government. Local factors cannot be ignored in the consideration of constituency results. In Charlotte, New Brunswick, for example, fishing is by far the most important industry and the fishermen had traditionally voted Liberal.[5] Kingston and Renfrew North, in Ontario, both contain large military establishments; this fact certainly helped the Liberals, although it was probably not a decisive factor in either constituency. Kent has a sizeable French settlement, Waterloo North is overwhelmingly German. In Welland and in Toronto Trinity, the people whose origin was in the British Isles are in a minority and

[5]H. G. Thorburn, *Politics in New Brunswick* (Toronto, 1961).

this may have influenced the outcome, although more light needs to be shed on this aspect of Canadian voting behaviour before any firm conclusions can be reached about the voting preferences of any ethnic group other than the French.

The personal appeal of the candidates (or its absence) no doubt accounted for the loss or retention of some of the seats held by the Liberals before the election. Two of their Saskatchewan seats, for example—Melville and Rosthern—probably remained Liberal because of the popularity and influence of the government candidates: both Agriculture Minister Gardiner and Walter Tucker were not only prominent in federal politics but had been leaders of the provincial Liberal party. Mr. Tucker's re-election was aided by the absence of a Conservative candidate. In British Columbia the personal popularity of Fisheries Minister Sinclair may have prevented a Liberal loss in Coast–Capilano. In Kingston, Ontario, where one in every four voters was a Roman Catholic, the Conservative candidate was a prominent member of the Orange Order.

As was to be expected, Conservative areas of strength contrasted sharply with those of the Liberals. The party led by Mr. Diefenbaker won its greatest victories in non-French, Protestant, Anglo-Saxon constituencies, sweeping areas where it had previously been strong and making heavy inroads into many territories where it had been faring badly since the thirties. Despite its failure to carry many of the constituencies containing large populations of non-Anglo-Saxon origin, the party improved its standing in non-British settlements sufficiently to lose much of its earlier reputation of being primarily a British party. Names like Quinto Martini, John Kucherepa, Nicholas Mandziuk, W. H. Jorgensen, and Douglas Jung among its newly elected Members no doubt contributed to the party's "new look."[6]

It has been argued that one of the causes of the Liberal defeat was the hostility engendered by the government's policy during the Suez crisis in areas where the population was predominantly of British origin. Those taking this view suggest that Canadians of British origin were more prone than others to be resentful on this score. Eighty-two of the 112 Conservative Members came from Ontario and the Maritimes—predominantly British regions. This indicates, so it is argued, that the Suez crisis played an important part in the government's defeat. Did the Conservative vote not increase by as much as 26.5 percentage points in Victoria, the most British constituency in all Canada?

[6]For a fuller discussion of this point, see J. Meisel, "After June 10," *Canadian Forum*, July, 1957, p. 73.

The proof is by no means conclusive, although Suez may have been important. Ontario is no longer as predominantly British as it once was. The swing towards the Conservatives was as great as elsewhere in the city in those Toronto constituencies where the recently enfranchised New Canadians and others of non-British origin could have affected the outcome. While the Conservative increase in Victoria was substantial, it was greater in four constituencies in the British Columbia region which are not as British as Victoria is held to be. In four others it was almost as marked as in Victoria. In any case, there is no evidence to suggest that New Canadians reacted differently to Suez than older settlers. Those who have escaped from communism may have favoured a tough anti-Nasser policy. While the argument does not, therefore, prove that Suez was a factor in the Liberal defeat, it does point to the relative predominance of Ontario and Maritime representatives among Conservative Members of Parliament.

E. E. Schattschneider has suggested that the United States was witnessing what he termed "the nationalization of politics."[7] This "nationalization" is envisaged as the spread of two-party competition into an increasing number of areas. It is accompanied, according to Professor Schattschneider, by a relatively frequent alternation of parties in power. In a thoughtful comment on the 1957 election in Canada and on that which followed it less than a year later, Dennis H. Wrong has raised the question of whether the same process was not taking place in Canada.[8] The results of the 1957 election do not offer a clear-cut answer to this question. To the extent that the Conservatives extended their basis of support even in areas still dominated by the minor parties, the "nationalization of politics" may be said to be taking place in Canada. But much depends on what will happen to the Liberals and minor parties: at present, the results of the 1957 election simply indicate the loss of considerable support by the Liberals.

The C.C.F. and Social Credit Parties

The defeat of the formidable C. D. Howe in Port Arthur was probably the C.C.F.'s greatest triumph in the election. Mr. Douglas Fisher, a high school teacher, new to federal politics, achieved this feat in a brilliantly

[7]"United States: The Functional Approach to Party Government," in Sigmund Neumann, ed., *Modern Political Parties* (Chicago, 1956), pp. 194–215.

[8]Dennis H. Wrong, "Parties and Voting in Canada," *Political Science Quarterly*, vol. LXXIII, no. 3 (Sept., 1958), pp. 397–412.

waged campaign. He was one of the three C.C.F. candidates from northern Ontario who helped to increase the party's representation in the House to twenty-five, two more than the number of seats it won in the previous election. The other two Ontario victors were Mr. Arnold Peters, in Timiskaming, and Mr. Murdo Martin, in Timmins. The party lost its one Toronto seat—York South—to a Conservative. Its other losses were in Nova Scotia (Cape Breton South), Saskatchewan (Saskatoon), both being won by Conservatives, and one in British Columbia, (Okanagan–Boundary), which was captured by a Social Crediter. The C.C.F. gained, in addition to the Ontario seats already mentioned, Selkirk and Springfield in Manitoba, and Skeena in British Columbia. Selkirk had first been won in a by-election in 1954. All of the C.C.F.'s new seats had previously been held by Liberals.

The C.C.F. had therefore found itself deprived of its sole seat in the Maritimes and in Toronto, but it had gained three in northern Ontario. Elsewhere in the country, its position remained largely unchanged. Despite having seen its portion of popular vote drop slightly (by 0.6 percentage points), therefore, the C.C.F. had cause to be reasonably pleased with the results. Its greatest disappointment was caused by the fact that the Conservatives had staged an impressive comeback, thereby making it highly questionable whether the C.C.F. would, in the near future, become the chief opposition party.

Social Credit gained four seats, bringing its total to nineteen. Edmonton–Strathcona and Vegreville, in Alberta, had been represented by Liberals, as had the party's third new conquest: Burnaby–Richmond in British Columbia. Okanagan–Boundary, also in that province, was taken from the C.C.F. The Social Credit party's proportion of the popular vote rose by 1.1 percentage points, showing the greatest relative increases in Manitoba and Saskatchewan. In Alberta, the party lost a little ground. The three percentage point decline of strength in that province was less severe, however, than the C.C.F.'s loss of 8.1 percentage points in Saskatchewan.[9]

Of the C.C.F.'s 162 candidates, 112 (69 per cent) lost their deposits.[10] The Social Credit's percentage was almost identical: 68 per cent, or 77 of its 114 candidates failed to recover their $200.[11]

In view of our meagre knowledge of this problem, little can be

[9]The results of the C.C.F. and the Social Credit Party are listed with those of the other parties in Appendix D.

[10]It will be remembered that each candidate must deposit the sum of $200 which is forfeited if he fails to obtain a number of votes equal to at least half the number polled by the winner. Canada Elections Act, 21, (9b), (13).

[11]The Conservatives' percentage was 21, that of the Liberals 13.

gained by speculating about how the intervention of the "third" parties affected the outcome. Neither of them succeeded in making large gains as the result of the widespread disenchantment with the Liberals. But they divided the anti-government vote and to that extent helped the Liberals. On the other hand, it is probably safe to assume that a large proportion of C.C.F.'ers was more hostile to the Conservatives than to the Liberals, and that the presence of C.C.F. candidates tended to reduce the Liberal vote in many constituencies. The C.C.F. candidates, therefore, probably helped the Conservatives, whereas the intervention of a Social Krediter may have enhanced the chances of the Liberal candidate. In constituencies seriously contested by both the C.C.F. and the Social Credit parties as well as by the Liberals and Conservatives, almost any candidate could win a seat with a relatively small number of votes. This was particularly noticeable in British Columbia, where the party strength was fairly evenly distributed. Under these circumstances the conduct of the local campaign and the performance of the candidate no doubt assumed particular importance.

The Canadian Forces Vote

Why did the Canadian forces voters remain so loyal to the Liberal party? Electoral statistics shed no light on this subject; the answer must be sought in the general conditions prevailing in the country, particularly as they affected the service voters.

It is possible that members of the armed forces in the older liberal democracies are generally predisposed towards supporting the existing government, since any new policy affecting defence might upset their routine and lead to undesirable upheavals in their lives. This inherent conservatism is likely to be particularly marked under a system of voluntary recruitment when the members of the forces are satisfied with the way they are treated by the government. In Canada, there were special reasons for military personnel being apprehensive about a change of government. The opposition had been severely critical of the Liberals' alleged "waste and extravagance" with respect to the armed forces. The Department of National Defence loomed large in Conservative promises of introducing greater economy into the administration of the country. It is therefore likely that many members of the services feared a Conservative government.

An interesting but unsubstantiated theory providing an additional explanation of the 1957 forces vote is suggested by the fact that the two groups which behaved atypically in the election were the French-speaking Canadians and the service voters:

> Both of the groups which remained loyal to the Liberals live, in a sense, in isolation. The French Canadians are isolated from many of the cultural themes of the overwhelmingly English-speaking North American continent. In their educational and legal systems, in languages, family life and in many respects in general outlook they are different from the rest of Canada. These and other differences . . . give them, as a group, a sense of non-participation in the activities of the rest of the country. In a way, they may have become so isolated from national political developments as to be outside what we might call the main Canadian political community. The same may be true of the service voters. It is well known that service personnel and their families tend to form strong attachments to one another not only in their official but also in their private activities. The sense of community and of belonging imposed by compound life often persists even when the compound is no longer physically present. The service people may therefore resemble the French Canadians in being, and in feeling themselves to be, excluded from the main stream of Canadian life.
>
> It seems likely that groups which are segregated in this way respond not at all or perhaps more slowly to the political forces which agitate the rest of the community. They may have the same rights and duties as everyone else, but they may respond differently to the social, economic and political stimuli to which they are exposed.[12]

The Importance of the Candidate

In his study of the 1955 British general election, D. E. Butler found that in 1955 "sitting members had a small but appreciable advantage."[13] The criterion applied by Mr. Butler was to see whether the swing against Labour was smaller in constituencies held by Labour than in those held by the Conservatives. This test cannot fruitfully be applied to conditions prevailing in Canada in 1957. The uniqueness of Quebec politics, the importance of Quebec constituencies among those held by the Liberals, and the small number of constituencies won by the Conservatives in 1953 would make suspect comparisons similar to those made by Mr. Butler. What can be attempted is to compare Liberal performance in seats which were contested by previously sitting members with seats in which new candidates were running for the Liberal party.

This comparison also must be attempted with caution. The test is only valid if the assumption is correct that a sitting member is better known in the constituency than a new candidate and that this makes him a

---

[12]Meisel, "Analysing the Vote," pp. 494–5.
[13]*The British General Election of 1955*, pp. 203–5.

stronger contender. It is always possible that he is unfavourably known, in which case such notoriety as he may possess probably constitutes a handicap. But most politicians seem to believe that it does not matter much in what context a name is known and that the more people recognize it on the ballot, the better are the chances of its bearer. Secondly, new candidates are usually running in constituencies where the party had been unable to win the previous election: the two groups of constituencies may therefore not be strictly comparable and there may be a bias in favour of the sitting members.

For Canada as a whole, the median loss suffered by the Liberal party was smaller in constituencies contested by sitting members than by newcomers. But, as is shown in Table XII/4, there were some regional variations in this regard. Sitting members fared worse than their inexperienced colleagues in the Maritimes and in Quebec. They did better in the Prairies and in British Columbia and came out about the same in

TABLE XII/4

Median Liberal Losses in Constituencies Contested by Previously Sitting Members and by New Candidates*

Region	Sitting M.P.	New candidate
Maritimes	−5.1	−4.9
Quebec	−4.0	−1.7
Ontario	−8.6	−8.7
Prairies	−9.3	−10.1
British Columbia	−7.6	−10.7
Canada	−7.6	−8.0

*The losses are measured in percentage points showing the difference in the percentage of votes obtained by the Liberal party in 1957 and 1953.

Ontario. The explanation for the regional variation may be that on the whole Liberal members from the Maritimes were a somewhat older group than their colleagues from other parts of the country and that they had acquired the reputation of not pressing hard enough for increased federal aid to the region they represented. In Quebec there was considerable criticism of several Liberal candidates and some of the Liberal vote was diverted to Independent and Indepedent Liberal candidates. In both cases, men who had not yet been to Ottawa may have escaped some of the criticism levelled at the previously elected candidates.

This raises the possibility that Liberal back-benchers, members who had been little identified with the cabinet, suffered smaller losses than those "compromised" by intimate associations with the ministry. Cabinet ministers certainly benefit from receiving a tremendous amount of publicity; they are well known in their constituencies. They also bring prestige to the riding they represent and presumably are in a good position to induce their cabinet colleagues to treat their constituents well, both collectively and individually, if the need arises. On the other hand, they have less time to "nurse" their constituencies and in 1957 may have suffered particularly from the charge that they were arrogant and haughty. Nevertheless, on the whole one would expect them to do better than their less exalted colleagues. To show that they did not do better would throw some doubt on the previously mentioned view that notoriety automatically bestows electoral advantages.

Of the eighteen cabinet ministers who fought the election, twelve suffered losses greater than the median of all their previously sitting back-bench colleagues running in the same region; the losses of two equalled the median loss for the region; and four obtained results which

TABLE XII/5

Losses Suffered by Members of the Ministry

Ministers	Loss	Regional median*	Parliamentary assistants	Loss
Maritimes		−5.1		
Gregg	− 4.6		Dickey	− 8.6
Pickersgill	+ 7.5		Kirk	− 8.8
Winters	− 7.0		MacNaught	− 4.1
Quebec		−4.0		
Chevrier	− 9.4		Blanchette	− 8.3
Lapointe	− 8.3		Bourget	− 0.3
Lesage	− 8.0		Cardin	0.0
Marler	− 1.9		Langlois	− 3.3
St. Laurent	− 6.7			
Ontario		−8.6		
Harris	−18.0		Benidickson	− 9.1
Hellyer	−11.0		McCubbin	− 5.6
Howe	−11.9		Robertson	− 6.9
McCann	− 8.6			
Martin	− 9.6			
Pearson	−13.8			
Prairies		−9.3		
Gardiner	− 9.3		Weir	−20.3
Garson	−22.0			
British Columbia		−7.6		
Campney	−16.2			
Sinclair	− 6.2			

*These are the medians of losses suffered by previously sitting Liberal members. See Table XII/4.

were better than the relevant regional median for former Liberal M.P.'s. It can be seen from the right-hand side of Table XII/5 that Parliamentary assistants did considerably better than ministers. Only four of the eleven seeking re-election suffered losses greater than the median for the group of previously sitting Liberals taken as a whole in each region. Parliamentary assistants were not, as such, terribly exalted individuals, and it is likely that many of their constituents did not really associate their Liberal candidate with the ministry. On the other hand, the service a Parliamentary assistant could render his constituents was no doubt better than that an ordinary M.P. could provide. In any event, a glance at Table XII/5 indicates that ministers on the whole suffered greater losses than ordinary back-bench members, and that Parliamentary assistants did slightly better than formerly sitting, back-bench Liberal candidates. A visual inspection of the table leads to the conclusion, therefore, that in 1957 there had been a greater anti-Liberal government sentiment in the country than an anti-Liberal party one, although the distinction may not be a valid one. The *chi* square test, however, comparing ministers' losses with those of all other previously sitting Liberal M.P.'s, prevents us from ruling out the possibility that the difference in performance between ministers and others was due to chance.

Although no general conclusions can be based on isolated cases, the experience of one Parliamentary assistant is worthy of particular notice. J. H. Dickey was first elected in the two-member Halifax constituency in 1947. He had the same Liberal running-mate in both the 1953 and the 1957 elections. In 1953, after he had been a Parliamentary assistant for only a little over a year, he received a silghtly larger (0.5 percentage points) percentage of votes than his colleague, Mr. Balcom. In 1957 their position was reversed—Mr. Dickey trailing by less than one per cent. The change is very small and may possibly reflect a shift in the religious composition of the constituency, but it is conceivable that Mr. Dickey's closer ties with the government caused the somewhat greater decline in his vote.[14]

The foregoing examination of the election results justifies the conclusion that the personal experience and characteristics of candidates have some effect on the outcome of the contest, even in an age in which centralization and mass media of communications enhance the roles of the national leaders. This conclusion is reinforced by the results which can be observed in a number of individual constituencies. It is not altogether fortuitous, for example, that of the five prairie constituencies in which the Liberals' proportion of the vote was slightly higher in 1957

[14]Tradition in Halifax dictates that each party nominate one Protestant and one Catholic candidate. Mr. Dickey was the Catholic nominee.

than in 1953, four were contested by unusually strong candidates. In Saskatchewan the two constituencies in which the Liberals improved their relative standing were Assiniboia and Yorkton. In the former riding their candidate was Ross Thatcher, the former C.C.F. M.P. who had received tremendous national publicity when he crossed the floor of the House, and also when he engaged in the Douglas-Thatcher debate in the course of the campaign. In Yorkton, a constituency in which people of British origin are in a distinct minority, the name of the Liberal candidate in 1957 was Hluchaniuk. The 1953 standard bearer was called O'Dwyer—a fact that might have been responsible for the small change. Edmonton East and Calgary South both gave the Liberals a greater percentage of votes in 1957 than in 1953. In each case the government candidate was a popular mayor probably known to practically every voter in the constituency.

Not unnaturally, mayors seem to enjoy a particular advantage—and this not only in the West. In Quebec, for instance, the Liberals wrested Chicoutimi from an Independent, the Liberal candidate being the mayor of the city. More surprising perhaps, the Conservatives won Jacques Cartier–LaSalle from the Liberals. One of the elements in this upset was, no doubt, the fact that their candidate was the mayor of Dorval. As was to be expected, the ethnic characteristics of the candidate are also important in Quebec. In Ste Anne an Independent Liberal won against the official candidate allegedly because the formerly dominant Irish population had recently been outnumbered by the French, giving an ethnic flavour to the internecine fight of the Liberals. Gerard Loiselle therefore enjoyed a clear advantage over William James Hushion.

The Relation of Seats to Votes

In 1957, for the second time in Canadian history, a party which received the largest number of votes failed to win a majority of seats.[15] The Liberals obtained almost 130,000 more votes than the Conservatives but their representation in the House was seven short of that of their chief rivals. The bias in the electoral system which had for a long time favoured the Liberals was eliminated and replaced by one benefiting the Conservatives.

Two main causes are responsible for the distortion inherent in the Canadian electoral system: the unequal size of constituencies and the enormous margins with which some ridings are won. The Liberals benefited from the former but suffered as a consequence of the latter

[15] A similar situation prevailed in 1926.

cause. The party whose support is usually concentrated in less populous constituencies will, *ceteris paribus*, have a distinct advantage over its rival. It will require fewer votes to obtain the same number of seats. In this respect the Liberals were favoured in the 1957 election largely because of their greater success in northern constituencies.

TABLE XII/6
Average Size of Liberal and Conservative Constituencies*

Liberals	Region	Conservatives
25,788	Maritimes	29,729
33,765	Quebec	33,967
36,461	Ontario	36,860
25,883	Prairies	38,356
21,366	B.C.	40,498
32,543	Canada	35,705

*Computed as the arithmetical mean.

In every region indicated by Table XII/6, the electorate was greater in constituencies won by the Conservatives than in ridings captured by the Liberals. The disparity was particularly wide in British Columbia and the Prairies, but the number of Liberal constituencies in these regions was so small as to rob the extremely wide margins of much significance.

But if the Liberals were favoured by the relative size of the constituencies they won, they were at a distinct disadvantage with respect to their margins of victory. Their strong position in some of the Quebec constituencies gave the Liberals a great many votes which were, in a sense, wasted. Table XII/7 indicates the degree to which the Liberals

TABLE XII/7
Liberal and Conservative Margins of Victory

Victor's margin*	Liberal†	Total	Conservative‡	Total
0.0–1.0	0	0	3	3
1.1–2.0	3	3	8	11
2.1–5.0	15	18	11	22
5.1–10.0	17	35	18	40
10.1–15.0	13	48	12	52
15.1–20.0	14	62	15	67
21.1–30.0	16	78	29	96
30.1–40.0	8	86	9	105
40.1–50.0	8	94	5	110
50.1–60.0	6	100	0	110
60.1–70.0	3	103	0	110
70.1–80.0	1	104	0	110

*Margin separating winner from runner-up, in percentage points.
†Excludes Burin–Burgeo.
‡Halifax and Queens are counted as one constituency each.

were at a disadvantage as the result of winning some ridings with huge majorities. Their chief opponents won ten seats with margins of two per cent or less, whereas the government party carried only three constituencies with so small a margin. On the other hand, the Conservative candidate found himself ahead of his runner-up by 40 per cent or more in only five constituencies, whereas the Liberals had an edge of 40 per cent or more in eighteen ridings. In no case did the Conservative margin exceed 50 per cent; the Liberals won by 50 per cent or more in eleven constituencies.

Despite the fact that the Liberals won a great number of Quebec seats by extremely wide margins, the old pattern they had established in that province prevailed even in 1957: they made such a thorough sweep of the constituencies that the percentage of votes they obtained was smaller than the percentage of seats. This has traditionally helped to give the Liberals impressive majorities in the House of Commons, even when the popular vote was less one-sided than might have appeared at first glance. The Liberals won 56.8 per cent of the Quebec votes but occupied 83 per cent of the Quebec seats. But in 1957 this traditional Liberal advantage was wiped out and, indeed, far outweighed, by comparable Conservative advantages in other parts of Canada. Table XII/8 shows the percentage of the vote each major party polled in the various provinces and regions and the percentage of seats it won in the corresponding areas.

If the two numercially small seats of Yukon and Mackenzie River are disregarded, it is found that the Liberals won a greater percentage of seats than votes only in Newfoundland, New Brunswick, and in Quebec. In Nova Scotia, Prince Edward Island, the Prairies and British Columbia, on the other hand, they were at a very great disadvantage, piling up a not inconsiderable number of votes with relatively little profit in terms of seats. The Conservatives, with only modest margins in the popular vote, won large numbers of seats in Ontario (72 per cent of the seats with 48 per cent of the vote), Nova Scotia (83 per cent of the seats with 50 per cent of the votes), Prince Edward Island and, to a lesser extent, in British Columbia and Alberta. The Conservative advantage outside Quebec, therefore, more than compensated for the Liberals' favourable position in that province.

In Nova Scotia, Prince Edward Island, Ontario, Manitoba, Alberta, and British Columbia, the Conservatives polled 393,427 votes more than the Liberals, thereby winning 66 more seats. The considerably greater margin of 472,998 amassed by the Liberals in Quebec only gave them 53 more seats than the Conservatives. Taking Quebec and the six

TABLE XII/8

Percentage of Votes and Seats Won by Parties

	Liberal		Conservative	
Area	Vote %	Seats %	Vote %	Seats %
Newfoundland	61.3	71	37.4	29
Prince Edward Island	46.4	0	52.0	100
Nova Scotia	44.9	17	50.1	83
New Brunswick	47.5	50	48.1	50
Maritimes	47.7	36	48.2	64
Quebec	56.8	83	30.7	12
Ontario	36.6	25	48.1	72
Manitoba	25.8	7	35.5	57
Saskatchewan	30.2	24	23.0	18
Alberta	27.6	6	27.4	18
Prairies	27.9	13	28.4	29
British Columbia	20.4	9	32.4	32
Yukon & Mackenzie River	57.2	100	40.4	0
British Columbia	20.9	17	32.5	29
Canada	40.5	40	38.5	42

provinces just listed together, we find that the Liberals won 79,571 more votes than the Conservatives, but thirteen fewer seats. "That," according to Professor Beck, "was the deciding factor in the election of 1957."[16]

Summary

In this chapter we have noted the great rise in the electorate between the 1953 and the 1957 elections. We have found that the Conservatives benefited from it more than the Liberals. An increase in the percentage voting can also be related to the national shift away from the Liberals and towards the Conservatives. But, while the increase in turnout varied

[16]J. M. Beck, "The Election of 1957 and the Canadian Electoral System," *Dalhousie Review*, vol. XXXVII, no. 4 (Winter, 1957), p. 333. Because of the different manner of treating Independent Liberals and because Mr. Beck used preliminary figures, the calculations in the article are slightly different from mine.

directly with the size of the shift towards the Conservatives and with the decline of the Liberal vote, the turnout did not seem to have been noticeably higher in constituencies contested by a large number of parties than in those sought by only two candidates. The turnout was clearly higher in constituencies in which the previous contest had been close than in ridings where the winner had been separated from the runner-up by a wide margin.

In addition to obtaining an impressive proportion of the service votes, the Liberals' areas of special strength were French Canada, "frontier" constituencies, and those in which the population was not predominantly of British origin. The Conservatives consolidated their traditional strongholds, particularly in Ontario, and scored impressive gains in almost all other sections of the country. The increase in their strength was greatest in the metropolitan areas (except in Quebec), in Nova Scotia, British Columbia, and the Prairies, although in this region the third parties remained in a strong position. On the whole, the appeal of the Conservative party was greatest in non-French, Protestant, and British constituencies, although many areas containing non-Anglo-Saxon and non-French majorities gave Mr. Diefenbaker strong support.

The uneven shift away from the Liberals and towards the Conservative party suggests that regional factors are still important in Canadian politics. The variation in the shift within regions and provinces, while not extreme, nevertheless indicates that local conditions are of some importance in Canadian elections.

Conservative candidates, for the first time in many years, were favoured by the electoral system. Liberal advantage, derived from winning in smaller constituencies than the Conservatives, and from winning a higher percentage of seats in Quebec than votes, was offset by a bias operating in favour of the Conservatives elsewhere. In Ontario, the Maritimes, British Columbia and Alberta, the Conservatives won a larger percentage of Parliamentary seats than of votes. The Liberals, on the other hand, piled up a sizeable number of votes in the Prairies and elsewhere without winning a commensurate number of seats.

CONCLUSION | 13

SO FAR IN OUR DISCUSSION we have been concerned primarily with *what* happened and *how* it happened. We must now tackle the question of *why* it happened. What, in other words, caused the defeat of the Liberals and the revival of the Conservative party?

A general election is a complex and elusive affair. Voters and non-voters alike forever manage to escape enshrinement in the categorical niches reserved for them by social science. What has been said of the British electorate in 1945 fits most appositely the Canadian voters of 1957:

> They give their votes under every variety of circumstances and from innumerable motives. They may be impressed by the party, by its leader, by the local candidate. They may be moved by hope or fear for the public good or for their own material interest; they may be exalted by ideals or inflamed by rancours or hatreds. The discomfiture of opponents may be a more powerful incentive than loyalty to their own colours. Every consideration of class, creed, or family tradition may make its influence felt by attraction or antagonism. Many will follow the general course of their families, friends, or fellow workers, while others may be moved more by reaction against their nearest associates. Public opinion, as a matter of study, remains a mystery and in seeking to understand it one must be content with approximations to truth and imperfect deductions from infinitely complex evidence. One thing is certain about such an event as a general election. It is not simple.[1]

To seek the causes underlying the electoral upset of 1957 is therefore fraught with danger. This notwithstanding, a search for these

---

[1]McCallum and Readman, *The British General Election of 1945*, p. xi.

causes will be attempted in the ensuing pages; the benefits accruing from a probe into the reasons for electoral unheavals justify this hazardous undertaking, provided its limitations are never forgotten.

Long-Run Determinants of the Outcome

We have noted earlier that the long tenure of office enjoyed by the Liberal party constituted one of its electoral assets. Repeatedly suffering defeats, the opposition became dispirited; the public, on the other hand, could hardly conceive of a government that was not Liberal. By 1957 about half of the electorate had never known any other rule. But this longevity also had its drawbacks. One of these was the continuous drain of many of the most talented party supporters into various government jobs and more important, perhaps, to the bench.

The individuals who became judges or members of government boards and commissions probably continued to support the Liberal party, although the judges could no longer vote for it. But in most instances they ceased being active in politics and certainly did not become Liberal candidates in elections. The many appointments made by the Liberal government during its period of office therefore weakened the party in an important way: they deprived it of a large number of able men who would have made excellent candidates and presumably M.P.'s.

Liberal candidates were not always of the highest calibre. It is true that many of those who had in recent years come forward to contest the election under Liberal colours were well-established men of substance. But among them, few appeared to be outstanding. It was difficult to escape the conclusion that they would join the large army of government backbenchers without bringing either shame or glory to themselves or their constituencies.

Indeed, one received the impression that an increasing number of Liberal candidates had decided to enter politics primarily because they hoped to gain some advantage from establishing contacts in Ottawa. It is not suggested that they expected to benefit from bribery or graft, but that they hoped that their connections with the government would enable them to engage in profitable transactions not so easily open to ordinary mortals.

The advantage of running as a government candidate had therefore attracted some well-established citizens who could pay part of their election expenses and on whose behalf useful campaign contributions could be collected from local sources. But they probably failed to be the most effective vote-getters in a period when the government was under fire for having become complacent and overbearing. If elected, they were not likely to "pepper up" an aging party. Often, these respected aspirants for office were less willing than younger men, just embarking on a career, to engage in the personal kind of campaigning that allegedly gathers the most votes.

Liberal success also discouraged some first-class young men from seeking the party's nomination. The large government majority, the well-filled Liberal benches and the numerous loyal and patient M.P.'s with claims on possible cabinet vacancies made it certain that anyone entering the House in 1957 would have to wait many years before obtaining political advancement. The Liberal backbench had a lethargic appearance; it lacked glamour and failed to attract men of outstanding ability. Younger men of talent, who might have wished to pursue a political career and who thought of themselves as Liberals, were therefore deterred by the length of time they would have had to spend leading the dull existence of a backbencher of a party dominated by a powerful cabinet and boasting a huge contingent of supporters in the House of Commons.

These factors all combined to lower the quality of Liberal M.P.'s and candidates. Over the years the party had been losing some of its ablest men and had attracted a group which, on the whole, seemed less impressive. This judgment, like the reading of the facts on which it is based, is, of course, a personal one. The quality of an M.P. or of a candidate, cannot be measured. But some supporting evidence has been given in the preceding chapters. The greater age of Liberal candidates confirms our view, for example, as does the appointment of Mr. Chevrier to the cabinet, particularly as a Quebec M.P. But the point must not be carried too far. Obviously, many first-class Liberal standard-bearers contested recent elections. Some were mentioned in earlier chapters.

Two other consequences of having been long in office made it particularly desirable that the party recruit excellent new candidates. The growing reliance on the civil service for ideas about governmental policy and the tendency of cabinet ministers to lose touch with the public deprived the Liberal party of some vitality and of some appeal. A young, slightly rebellious group of M.P.'s could have done much to revitalize the party and to inject new ideas into its programme. More important, perhaps, such a group might have introduced some idealism, a characteristic not particularly noticeable among the cabinet leaders. The Liberal party had forgotten that efficient administrative performance may not be all that matters to the electorate. Had the party attracted a different type of candidate, its leaders might have been less derisive about some of the Conservatives' romantic ideas concerning the development of Canada's northland—ideas which appealed to the voters.

Finally, Liberal longevity caused some and probably most leading party members to become complacent. We have referred to several instances of cabinet behaviour lacking in humility. The point need not be laboured. Senator Power, in reviewing the 1957 election campaign, pointed to one of the most telling consequences of the long Liberal reign: " . . . lately I have read, in the life of Bonar Law, the following description of the state of mind of Neville Chamberlain . . . 'Like many before him and many after him, Chamberlain was suffering from the occupational malady which so often besets politicians—the hallucination of indispensability.' This phrase could properly be applied to . . . almost all of the Canadian Ministerial coterie, prior to the election of 1957."[2]

Overconfidence, failure to produce new ideas, loss of idealism and of contact with public sentiment, and the deterioration in the quality of its candidates and M.P.'s were, therefore, among the long term determinants of the Liberal defeat. All of them were the consequence of being in office for so long and in a sense of being so successful. The very success of the government therefore finally contributed to its downfall. Paradoxically, among the long-term causes of the Conservative revival was the growing fear, particularly among many people generally friendly to the Liberals, that Liberal permanence in office and a further decline of the opposition were highly undesirable.

A more positive achievement of the Conservatives in preparing for the 1957 election was to a great extent the work of Mr. Drew and some of his colleagues interested in party organization. During Mr. Drew's term of office as leader vigorous attempts were made to revive the party in Quebec, special efforts were devoted to winning some support among the new Canadians and the Parliamentary group was provided with an able research organization associated with the national headquarters. All these developments increased public confidence in the party and should not be overshadowed completely by the monumental contribution made to the Conservative revival by Mr. Diefenbaker. Mr. Drew's leadership of the party during the Defence Production Act Amendment and pipeline debates was also of great importance in rehabilitating the reputation of his party.

In addition to these developments at the national level, a Conserva-

[2]"The Election of 1957," p. 8.

tive revival took place in some of the provinces. A slow but perceptible shift in opinion was taking place in several regions of the country away from the Liberals and towards the Conservatives.

As causes for the 1957 election outcome, however, the long-run determinants of the Liberal decline were, on the whole, more important than the secular factors contributing to the Conservative revival. Mr. Diefenbaker's great contribution was that he succeeded in manoeuvring his party into becoming the chief beneficiary of the government's weakness.

Short-Run Causes

It was suggested in chapter II that the Diefenbaker Revolution was thought to have been one of the main causes of the Conservative revival. As we have seen, Mr. Diefenbaker's victory in the contest for the leadership inaugurated a marked change in the party. The "old guard" was defeated and replaced by a new group of leaders. These applied the latest public relations techniques to the conduct and management of the campaign.

The Diefenbaker Revolution had made it easier for the Conservatives to adopt one of the tactics formerly employed by the Liberals: to propagate a programme which would appeal to so wide a group of electors as to prevent the growth of the minor parties. It was often difficult to distinguish between C.C.F. and Conservative criticism of the Liberals. This great flexibility changed the physiognomy of the party. Under Mr. Diefenbaker's leadership the Conservative party ceased being identified with eastern financial interests, it professed to have become the champion of the underdog, and it made a much stronger appeal to Canadians whose origin was neither British nor French.

Whether this transformation can properly be called a revolution is a question of semantics.[3] The real nature of the changes introduced by the new leaders will become more apparent after the party has been in office for some time. But in bringing Mr. Diefenbaker to the leadership, the so-called Diefenbaker Revolution certainly constituted one of the main causes of the Conservative victory in the 1957 election. In addition to effecting the changes in the public image of the Conservative party mentioned in the preceding paragraph, Mr. Diefenbaker proved himself a most successful campaigner. He gave the party a strong faith in vic-

[3]For a discussion of the dangers of loosely using the term see McCallum and Readman, *The British General Election of 1945*, p. 270.

tory. More important perhaps, he succeeded in making people believe in Conservative promises. Many of the "progressive" features of the Conservative programme had been used by Mr. Drew, but few voters seemed to have believed that they would be carried out. Mr. Drew had promised to increase public spending and at the same time to lower taxes. No one believed him and Mr. St. Laurent succeeded in making him look ridiculous. The same tactics applied to similar promises by Mr. Diefenbaker seemed to boomerang—Mr. Diefenbaker's pledges were taken seriously. It is likely that without Mr. Diefenbaker the anti-government vote might have been shared more evenly by the opposition parties than was the case.

The enthusiasm injected into the Conservative campaign by Mr. Diefenbaker was matched and partly perhaps echoed by a group of aggressive candidates. They were less experienced than the Liberals and, as we have seen, younger. They lacked the standing many Liberals had in the constituencies they were contesting, but they often made up for this by vigorous campaigning. The interest generated in the campaign by the new leader, the unexpectedly large crowds at his meetings, the greater decentralization of the Conservative party all aroused unexpected enthusiasm among many Conservative candidates who had originally entered the contest without expecting to do very well. Lastly, among the short-run causes of the Conservative revival, we must refer to the conduct of the campaign. Although less massive than that of the Liberals, it seemed to be more effective.

In appealing to the French-speaking voters largely through the person of Mr. St. Laurent, the Liberals chose a fruitful approach. One of the reasons for their doing so well in some parts of the country was obviously the personality of the Prime Minister. It would have been astonishing had he been abandoned by his fellow French Canadians. The Liberals were also wise in cultivating the service voters, for they harvested a rich reward among them.

But the general campaign line adopted by the Liberal party was a mistaken one. The quiet unobtrusive campaign emphasizing the party record and the general prosperity in the country proved inadequate to placate a rather hostile electorate in many regions of the country. And since the whole of the Liberal campaign was dominated by this strategy, much of it was probably ineffective.

One of the consequences of the long-run decline in the Liberal party had therefore made itself felt among the short-run causes of the defeat: the leaders were no longer able to estimate how the public would respond to their actions. No incident illustrated this better than Mr.

St. Laurent's jocular reference to the pipeline debate. No act of omission was more costly than the failure to "sell" credit restrictions.

Among the chief short-run factors influencing the election outcome we have noted the change in the Conservative party brought about by the emergence of the new leadership. Particularly, we noted the electrifying performance of Mr. Diefenbaker. The different type of candidate and the highly skilled campaign management were also held to have contributed to the party's success. The Liberals, on the other hand, misjudged the public's mood and consequently their activities were considerably less effective than in other recent elections. They adopted the right note only in the type of appeal made in French Canada and among the military voters.

Given the general conditions in the country and given the long-run factors discussed above, could different campaign styles have led to different results? Could the Liberals, for example, had they radically altered their strategy, have averted their defeat? To answer this question we must consider the role of campaign issues.

The Issues and the Campaign

A public opinion survey conducted after the election indicated that no single issue was responsible for the substantial Conservative gains.[4] Its author reported that about a quarter of the voters were influenced in their choice to vote Conservative by the pipeline debate, about 30 per cent by the government's policy on the old age pension, a little over a third by a variety of issues lumped under the category "Time for a change," and a little under eight per cent by Suez. For those who had voted Liberal in 1953 and Conservative in 1957, these issues were alleged to have been important in the following proportions: Suez, 5.1 per cent; pipeline debate, 38.2 per cent; old age pension, 26.7 per cent; and "Time for a change," 30.0 per cent.

Even assuming that issues can be isolated in this manner (a doubtful assumption) the figures are misleading because of the way in which they are presented. Under the old age pension heading, for example, the author includes not only the six-dollar pension increase but also payments to immigrants, perquisites granted Members of Parliament, and credit restrictions. The pipeline rubric includes displeasures with the

[4]H. D. Johns, "Why Canadians Voted Conservative," pp. 7, 38–9. About 1,200 people were interviewed in this survey, but the author does not indicate how he chose his sample.

cabinet in general, criticism of Mr. Howe, cabinet arrogance and related issues, some of which are again presented in the "Time for a change" item. This category comprises such diverse factors in the Liberal defeat as the feeling of neglect experienced by farmers, anti-Catholic prejudice directed at the French members of the cabinet, displeasure with local candidates, and the anti-arrogance, anti-cabinet dictatorship, and anti-Howe sentiments also present under the pipeline heading.

Saturday Night's poll therefore fails to identify one or two specific issues to which can be attributed the Conservative victory, although it pretends to be doing so. It is nevertheless useful. The impression that the pipeline and the old age pension were given as reasons for voting Conservative by more than half of those interviewed was created only at the cost of listing several causes under one heading. If the proper headings are applied to the results, it appears that the major cause of the Liberal defeat was a widespread feeling that the government had become too powerful, too arrogant and careless in its relations with Parliament, and that governmental fiscal policies had aroused considerable hostility. The poll also indicates that in addition to these two causes there were many others reinforcing the trend towards the Conservative party.

Everything points to the fact that late in 1956 and in 1957 there was general dissatisfaction in Canada with the government on the grounds that it had become overbearing, convinced of its infallibility and contemptuous of its critics. It is, therefore, likely that the issues which proved most immediately effective were those which were linked to the view that the government had been in office too long and that it had become insensitive to the wishes of the Canadian people. The pipeline, the old age pension, the government's treatment of Parliament, the need to strengthen opposition in the House, were probably all instrumental in detaching the votes of former Liberal supporters and in inducing new voters to support Conservative candidates. Added to these factors were a number of smaller and often regional issues, such as wheat disposal, for example, reinforcing the trend away from the Liberal party.

Could a different kind of Liberal campaign have minimized the appeal of some at least of these issues, sufficiently to alter the election outcome? It is possible that the frank admission of having made a mistake in imposing closure and in its relations with the Speaker might have offset some of the hostility aroused by the pipeline issue. President Grover Cleveland, after all, probably benefited in the long run from admitting the charge made against him in the middle of a presidential campaign that he had sired an illegitimate son and that he regretted having erred as a young man. The offences of the Liberals were of a different kind, however, and could certainly not have been blamed on youthful exuberance and irresponsibility. A radical reorganization of the cabinet before the election, including the retirement of Mr. Howe, the assumption of the leadership by Mr. Pearson, and the elevation to cabinet rank of a number of younger men, might have reduced the effectiveness of the Parliamentary issue particularly had it been accompanied by a programme designed to make greater use of Parliamentary committees and to introduce a "permanent," non-party Speaker. But this is mere speculation, of course. More votes might have been lost than gained by doing all this. Equally tenuous is the argument that a vigorously conducted campaign explaining the need for preventing inflation would have forestalled some Liberal losses, or that the nomination of a number of younger candidates might have altered the results.

But the conclusion that these and other measures might have had far-reaching consequences is extremely tempting in view of the close election outcome. Had the Liberals prevented the loss of only four seats which went to the Conservatives, they would have had a plurality in the House and would perhaps have stayed in office for another short term before a new election would have had to be called. It is therefore hard to banish from one's thoughts the possibility that a differently conducted campaign or a different budget might have given the Liberal party a reprieve. Our knowledge of electoral behaviour is however inadequate to provide a certain answer.

The fairly wide variation in the shift from the Liberals to the Conservatives in various regions, and more particularly within regions and provinces, is suggestive, however. There is enough evidence in the foregoing chapters pointing to the importance in the election of local conditions, the personality and reputation of the candidates, and the different appeals of the leaders to justify the tentative conclusion that a differently waged campaign, a different approach to the issues, and possibly different personnel could have prevented the Liberal defeat.

Had they remained in power, but without a Parliamentary majority, would they have benefited from the opportunity offered them to rebuild the party while still holding office? Such reorganization of the party as would have been needed to rejuvenate and revitalize it would have had to be attempted in a short period of time, probably in about a year, and while the party was governing with a minority government. Under such circumstances, the leaders would have been fully occupied by a difficult Parliamentary situation and the rank and file would have had to fight a trend in the country favouring the Conservatives. It would have been miraculous to have quickly rebuilt and revamped the party in these conditions. The difficulties of doing so would have been aggravated by the increasing confidence of the Conservatives and the growing prestige they would have derived from being so near to office.

The doubts expressed in the previous paragraph about the possibility of the Liberal party's come-back presupposed its continuance in office as a minority government. We may be underestimating the effects of a different approach to the issues and of a differently waged campaign. To win a bare majority in the House the Liberals would have had to capture an additional twenty-eight seats. A working majority would have required at least another ten to fifteen victories. In view of the strong appeal of Mr. Diefenbaker it seems doubtful that the party could have done anything in 1957 which would have prevented the loss of the forty-odd seats required to give them another term in office of normal duration. Anything less than forty seats would have led to only a short respite. But even if the Liberals had succeeded in winning a majority, the chances are not great that the party would have survived in power for very much longer. For as we have seen in examining the long-run causes of the surprise outcome of the 1957 election, there were weaknesses in the party which were the result of its long tenure in office and which could have been removed only with the greatest of difficulty.

Theoretically it is possible that a party which has suffered the normal consequences of being in office for more than two decades should, when brought up short by a sharp fall in support, do all the right things required for its revival. In practice this is an extremely rare course of events. Certainly conditions in Canada were not conducive to a Liberal revival and the very developments affecting the party described above preclude the likelihood of its taking place. The party had lost the knack of critical self-scrutiny. It had failed to attract many candidates and members particularly adept at producing novel ideas or at giving the party a new enthusiasm and sense of purpose. Most ministers had become too settled in their routine to produce the desired changes and in any case, the best of them were probably tired and not particularly interested in rebuilding a party. Finally, no French-speaking successor to Mr. St. Laurent seemed to have emerged as the leader of the Quebec federal politicians.

We must conclude, therefore, that the above analysis does not indicate that the Liberals would have benefited greatly from a reprieve— even had they been granted one. And this conclusion contains one of the most interesting features of the 1957 Canadian general election. For the election and the events that preceded it offer a textbook example of what supposedly happens in a liberal democratic Parliamentary system. A party long in office eventually shows the corrupting influences of power. Self-satisfied and complacent, it ultimately ceases to satisfy the electors and is replaced by another party which, if it remains in office for too long, itself ultimately becomes subject to the same corroding process.

The very success of a party becomes a cause of its decline. Strong and able leaders, good relations with the civil service, large majorities in the House of Commons, an attraction to well-established individuals seeking advantage through a political career—all these add to the strength of a party and ultimately assist in its downfall. The opposition, like the chorus in an ancient tragedy, intermittently comments on the gloomy performance on the political stage. Its comments become increasingly menacing as the government ages and begins to make more and more mistakes. In the end the terrible forebodings of the downfall become realized and the chorus itself undergoes a metamorphosis: it appears on the stage as the principal actor.

This pattern was followed to the letter by the Canadian parties. In undergoing these well-known processes they behaved in a manner expected of them by students of democratic politics. The only surprising feature of the reversal of roles between the Liberals and the Conservatives was its timing. The Liberals had won so often that the suspicion had begun to grow that their charmed life would never end. But almost everyone had forgotten the apt characterization of Canadian parties given many years before by one of the country's most eminent editors. J. W. Dafoe's comments on Laurier, published in 1922, contained a fitting epitaph on the 1957 Canadian general election:

Parties, in reality, are organized states within the state. They have their own dynasties and hierarchies; and their reason for existence is to clothe themselves with the powers, functions and glory of the state which they control. Their desire is for absolute and continuing control in which they come to think they have a prescriptive right; and they never leave office without a sense of outrage . . . their real desire is the mastery of the state and the brooking of no opposition or rivalship.

Nevertheless, the people by a sure instinct compel a change in administration every now and then; but they move so slowly that a government well entrenched in office can usually outstay its welcome by one term of office.[5]

[5]J. W. Dafoe, *Laurier: A Study in Canadian Politics* (Toronto, 1922), p. 51.

APPENDICES

*By-Elections, 1953–1957**

Date	Constituency	Province	Percentage voting	Percentage change in vote†				Who won	
				L.	P.C.	C.C.F.	So. Cred.	1953	By-election
22/3/54	Elgin	Ont.	70	+ 1	− 1	–	–	P.C.	P.C.
22/3/54	Gatineau	Que.	46	− 4	− 5	–	–	L.	L.
22/3/54	Peel	Ont.	61	n.c.‡	+ 2	–	–	P.C.	P.C.
22/3/54	Mtl. Verdun	Que.	52	−36	− 3	–	–	L.	L.
8/11/54	Mtl. St. Antoine	Que.	57	+ 2	n.c.‡	–	–	L.	L.
8/11/54	Mtl. St. Laurent-St. G.	Que.	37	− 6	+ 6	–	–	L.	L.
8/11/54	Selkirk	Man.	67	−12	+14	+5	–	L.	C.C.F.
8/11/54	Stormont	Ont.	80	−14	+14	–	–	L.	L.
8/11/54	Tor. Trinity	Ont.	43	− 2	− 2	+6	–	L.	L.
8/11/54	Tor. York West	Ont.	52	n.c.‡	+ 5	−5	–	P.C.	P.C.
20/6/55	Battle River-Camrose	Alta.	66	+15	–	+6	−9	S.C.	S.C.
26/9/55	Restigouche-Madawaska	N.B.	72	− 6	+24	–	–	L.	L.
26/9/55	Quebec South	Que.	70	−19	+18	–	–	L.	L.
26/9/55	Bellechasse	Que.	70	− 7	+ 7	–	–	L.	L.
26/9/55	Témiscouata	Que.	75	+ 2	+ 4	–	–	L.	P.C.
24/10/55	Tor. Spadina	Ont.	45	−26	+10	–	–	L.	L.
19/12/55	St. Jean-Iberville-N.	Que.	76	−42	+ 3	–	–	L.	L.

*Based on *Report of the Chief Electoral Office: By-Elections and Northwest Territory Election held during the Year 1954; Ditto, for 1955;* and *Report of the Chief Electoral Officer: Twenty-second General Election, 1953.*

†A change is, of course, indicated only when a party nominated candidates both in 1953 and in the by-election. The C.C.F. fought by-elections in four constituencies it did not contest in 1953. Its vote in these was negligible except in Toronto-Spadina where it polled 15 per cent of the votes cast. Independent candidates are omitted from this table.

‡n.c. stands for "no change."

Summary of the Resolutions adopted by the Progressive Conservative National Convention, December 14, 1956

THE RESOLUTIONS[1] WERE GROUPED roughly under headings corresponding to the subcommittees of the Resolutions and Policy committee.[2] They opened with a short statement of principle, attempting to summarize the philosophy of the Conservative party. It expressed the party's belief in freedom of worship, speech and assembly, in the rule of law, and it affirmed its loyalty to "the Queen of Canada." Vigilance over parliamentary institutions was thought to be the best guarantee of freedom. The state was conceived as the servant of the people. This belief was contained in the same paragraph which affirmed the party's support of "a competitive economy" which, however, accepted "its social responsibilities." Progress and stability, it was asserted, could best be achieved "by building on the firm foundations of those things proved good by experience." Canada was thought of as "a nation of many creeds and many cultures, united . . ." and willing to accept its international obligations. A plea for the defence and restoration of provincial rights and a guarantee that a Conservative government would bring about an equitable distribution of taxation between the federal and provincial governments closed the summary statement of principles adopted by the convention.[3]

In its resolutions dealing with foreign affairs the convention reaffirmed the party's loyalty to or belief in the Queen, the sovereignty of Canada and its democratic form of government, the Commonwealth, N.A.T.O., and the United Nations. It supported the establishment of permanent machinery for a United Nations Police Force. Recognition of Canada's senior position in the Commonwealth "both historically and economically" was accompanied by the advocacy of increased Colombo Plan aid. A number of resolutions clearly constituted the aftermath to the Suez crisis: the Commonwealth and N.A.T.O. seemed to be given some precedence over the United Nations; a resolution concerning the Middle East was somewhat anti-Egyptian in tone; a Conservative government, it was promised, would seek to use Canada's understanding of the United States to compose differences between the United States, Britain, and France. As for the Communist world, the party regretted the enslavement of people in eastern Europe and

[1]Progressive Conservative Party of Canada, *What the Progressive Conservative Party Stands For*. Report of the Committee on Resolutions and Policy as adopted by the National Convention, December 14, 1956. (Second version. The resolutions, as drafted by the committee, but before they were amended by the convention, were mimeographed under the same title.) mimeo.

[2](1) External Affairs and Defence; (2) Agriculture; (3) Labour; (4) Natural Resources; (5) Welfare and Veterans; (6) Taxation and Trade.

[3]*What the Progressive Conservative Party Stands For*, p. 1.

undertook to use its authority and influence in the United Nations Organization to "lead them back to their rightful freedom".[4] If elected, a Conservative government would, according to the resolutions dealing with national defence, review defence policy to ensure that the Navy, Army, and Air Forces would be adequately equipped and organized and brought to required strength. Reserve forces, it was promised, would be revitalized and Civil Defence improved. Greater control would be exercised over expenditure in the Department of National Defence. The convention tacitly expressed a touching faith in the value and effectiveness of ancient colours and devices by placing a resolution dealing with the flag under the rubric of National Defence. The resolution supported the immediate adoption of a distinct Canadian flag.[5]

A number of resolutions concerned the machinery of government. A dominion-provincial conference was promised for the purpose of reforming the Senate. The influence of the debates on the Defence Production Act amendment and on the pipeline was evident in a number of resolutions designed to restore to Parliament the "rights and attributes which the [St. Laurent] government has denied." Federal-provincial relations were to be restored "to a healthy balance." Several recommendations were made with the avowed purpose of improving the financial position of the provinces.[6]

Several tax concessions were promised by the convention. Basic personal income tax exemptions were to be increased for both married and single persons and for dependents, the self-employed were promised the right to deduct from earned income payments into pension funds, and municipalities were told that under a Conservative government they could expect relief from a number of existing irksome federal tax policies. In general, the convention undertook to reduce taxes and to eliminate government surpluses. The party approved of foreign investment in Canada, but observed that the share of Canadian industry owned outside the country was rapidly increasing. It undertook to promote Canadian industry, but was not explicit about the way in which this was to be done. Trade with all countries was to be increased, and vigorous resistance was promised to "abuses of existing trade agreements by other nations which damage Canada's commercial markets abroad." A commitment was made to call a Commonwealth trade conference "in order to re-establish Canada's traditional Commonwealth markets for agricultural, primary products and manufactured goods." The party recommended the establishment of a board independent of the C.B.C. and of the independent stations to regulate radio and television in Canada.[7]

In the field of agriculture, the party promised a policy designed to dispose of agricultural surpluses in the export market and to give farmers "proper encouragement in the domestic field." More specifically, the Conservatives pledged themselves to develop "a flexible price support programme for various products announced well in advance of the production period, as required." Losses incurred in disposing of agricultural surpluses abroad at prices below those current domestically would, the Conservatives promised, not be borne by the producer alone. Other planks dealing with agriculture included a pledge to extend and ease farm credit, a statement that Western

[4]*Ibid.*, pp. 2–3.
[6]*Ibid.*, pp. 5–7.
[5]*Ibid.*, p. 4.
[7]*Ibid.*, pp. 8–10.

wheat should be marketed through the Wheat Board, an endorsement of the principle of advance payments on Western wheat when it was suitably stored on farms, the assurance that assistance to meet freight costs related to feed grains would become a permanent policy of the federal government, and a pledge to co-operate with the provinces in establishing a national soil and water conservation programme. A very vague set of resolutions promised aid to fisheries.[8]

Veterans were assured that their pensions would be raised and that the number of individuals eligible for them would be enlarged. A future Conservative government was also committed to raising the amounts those receiving pensions were permitted to earn. In the field of housing the party undertook to extend existing schemes for government-guaranteed low-interest loans to those wishing to buy old homes. Some assistance was also promised to persons of moderate incomes "to ensure good housing on a rental basis." The belief was expressed "that actions taken to curb inflation should not be allowed to discriminate against the low cost housing programme."[9]

Canadian pensioners, like most people in Western countries living on a fixed income, were hard pressed by inflation. Two resolutions offered them some relief: "A Progressive Conservative Government in agreement with the provinces will provide increased benefits under the Old Age Assistance Act, which is applicable to persons between the ages of 65 and 70. Similar increased benefits will be extended to recipients of Old Age Security (i.e., Old Age Pensions) where necessitous." The period of residence required to qualify under the Old Age Assistance legislation was to be reduced from the existing twenty years to ten years.[10] The party also remembered potential voters at the other end of the life span: it stated that it would continue to pay family allowances.

As well as promising to permit the deduction from taxable income of payments to voluntary hospital insurance plans and medical and dental expenses generally, the party undertook to negotiate with the provinces about the establishment of a joint plan for diagnostic services and hospitalization. Wherever possible, voluntary or provincial hospital insurance plans were to be utilized in the proposed scheme.[11]

The convention committed the party to the position that "the welfare of the Canadian people requires the adoption now of a National Development policy which will develop their natural resources for the maximum benefit of all parts of Canada, encourage more processing of those resources in Canada, foster the widest financial and other participation by Canadians in the development of [the] resources, and promote greater opportunity and employment for a steadily increasing population." The following were among the more important steps promised by the party under the National Development policy: joint investment by the federal and provincial governments in power and other self-liquidating projects; construction, with the provinces, of railways, highways, and access-roads; encouragement of and assistance to research necessary for national development; study of possible changes in personal and corporate taxation designed to encourage a greater degree of Canadian investment in Canadian mines and industry; promotion

[8]*Ibid.*, pp. 11–12, 18.   [9]*Ibid.*, p. 13.
[10]*Ibid.*, pp. 14–15.   [11]*Ibid.*, pp. 14–15.

of the tourist trade; through appropriate tax measures encouragement of the early exploitation of northern Canada's mineral resources; development of facilities at all of Canada's ports. More specific attitudes and measures were listed, appealing to certain regions or special interests. Thus, for example, the party pledged itself to revise the railway freight rates structure in the Maritimes and it went on record as favouring the fullest possible use of the port of Churchill. In the same category was a resolution which (though it did not mention the Trans-Canada Air Lines) in effect promised to institute a survey of Canada's "air traffic potential" to ascertain when "an orderly introduction of competition" (i.e., with T.C.A.) "may be instituted at the national level."[12]

The resolutions dealing with labour affirmed the party's view that Canadian labour fares best under "the free enterprise system coupled with effective free trade unions." The Conservatives committed themselves to a policy of maintaining full employment, to a review (in consultation with representatives of labour, management, and government) of all national labour legislation and, among other changes, in particular to revise conciliation legislation, to co-operate with the provinces to promote uniformity of labour legislation, and to enact legislation providing minimum wages, hours and vacations with pay for all workers under federal jurisdiction. The party also promised to provide adequate representation for labour on all government boards and commissions dealing with labour's interest. Finally, an undertaking was given to liberalize (if this word may be used in the present context) Canada's unemployment insurance legislation.[13]

The last subject tackled by the convention was immigration. The party welcomed to Canada people seeking refuge from tyranny and oppression. It advocated a vigorous immigration policy "consistent with (Canada's) ability to absorb." The recommendation was made that an effective publicity programme be instituted so that prospective immigrants obtain a true picture of Canada. It was also recommended that machinery be established providing for the review, by an independent board and then by the courts, of certain decisions by the Department of Immigration. Lastly, the party said that it would co-operate with the provinces in bringing to Canada "immigrants whose skills are neded for (the) Nation's development."[14]

[12]Ibid., pp. 16–17. [13]Ibid., pp. 19–20.
[14]Ibid., p. 21.

APPENDIX C

Summary of Mr. St. Laurent's and Mr. Diefenbaker's Telecasts

Mr. St. Laurent made the first party political broadcast on April 29. He began by reminding his audience that on June 10 it would decide whether it wanted the Liberal government to "keep up the kind of work that has helped make these past four years such really outstanding ones."[1] In discussing the Liberal party, he first considered the opening word in the party's slogan, "Unity, Security, Freedom." Canada had achieved a united, dynamic economy and the speed of Canadian progress—"particularly in the four record-breaking years we have just come through"—had given "solid substance to the dreams of the Fathers of Confederation." Canada was a wonderful land to live in. It was not surprising that so many immigrants had chosen to come there. He was glad to have them and their help in building a greater Canada. They were not the only people who had confidence in the country's future. It was the same faith as theirs which had led the flood of investment money, particularly from the United States.

Mr. St. Laurent did not claim for the government all the credit for the country's progress; the lion's share belonged to the people of Canada, but what the government had done had no doubt helped. "Good times and good government have a habit of going together." Looking back over his eight and a half years as prime minister, he found satisfaction in what he saw. The Liberal party was a truly national party, with a national rather than a regional outlook. After again returning to the theme of Canadian unity he reminded his audience that it was not only important to vote but also to think seriously before voting. While doing this the voters, he was sure, would not be disappointed, "if your Liberal candidates have no election promises for you! Except the one which we made in 1953 and kept: to do our best—and to do our best means to get on with the job of increasing opportunity in all parts of Canada for all Canadians. If, on June 10th, you give the present Government a mandate to carry on, we will try hard to surpass the record of what, over these past four years, we have already helped to achieve by working with you."

In his first broadcast, held a day after Mr. St. Laurent's, Mr. Diefenbaker sandwiched the meat of his remarks between humble expressions of thanks to the C.B.C. for so generously making available free broadcast time and to his listeners and viewers for "allowing me this short visit with you in your own home." The Conservative leader also reminded his audience that on June 10 it would decide whether to return "the present government, which has been in power for 22 years," or whether to entrust the government to

[1]This and all the following quotations from the televised speeches by the leaders are taken from mimeographed copies provided by the Liberal and Conservative national offices.

the Conservative party. He pointed to the fact that his party was the only one, beside the Liberals, which had ever held office in Canada before and briefly reviewed what he considered some of its main accomplishments when it had been in office. The Liberal government, he argued, had been in a minority in 1953 and was returned to power only because the opposition to it was splintered among several parties.

The voter, Mr. Diefenbaker insisted, had the right to be shown evidence of "the dangerous decay in the record of the Government in office" and of the fact that his party had a programme and the personnel to carry it out. On the first point, he claimed that "the danger of maintaining the present administration in office for another term is the very real threat that Canada would become a One-Party State." Indeed, he argued that "all the evils and the symptoms and the dangers of One-Party domination have already developed under the St. Laurent Government." To support this statement he invoked Black Friday and other occasions "when Parliament was deliberately and defiantly denied." By creating Crown corporations and state monopolies the government had placed millions of dollars beyond examination by Parliament. It had refused to take action on behalf of the farmers, to reduce income tax, provide adequate pensions for the aged and for veterans and civil servants, it had deprived the provinces and municipalities of their rightful sources of revenue "and the results are apparent in your municipality —a shortage of schools, inadequate roads, streets, the lack of essential services for housing developments—these are all due to the needlessly high level of federal taxation."

What would the Conservative party do about these things? It would reverse the whole trend of centralization of authority in Ottawa, restore the rights of Parliament, allow the provinces and municipalities a greater share of the tax dollar, review the operating method of every state monopoly with a view of withdrawing the state from unnecessary competition, it would think of the humble men and women, and replace the "present laissez-faire policy towards development of . . . national resources."

We will have a national resources development plan to give the fullest effect to provincial planning to the development of those areas that have lagged behind the nation as a whole. We will give young men and women a new concept—a concept of a new Canada in which they can contribute—in which they will be the architects and builders of that destiny which will be Canada if we but carry out our responsibilities.

Yes, my friends, we have a program for Canada . . . you will hear it unfolded as the campaign progresses. It is a program . . . for a united Canada, for one Canada, for Canada first, in every aspect of our political and public life, for the welfare of the average man and woman. That is my approach to public affairs, and has been through my life. And I believe it was that which elected me to the Leadership of this great party—to do something on behalf of the average man and woman across the country, and to carry out a development policy for the benefit of Canadians as a whole. A Canada, united from Coast to Coast, wherein there will be freedom for the individual, freedom of enterprise, and where there will be a Government which, in all its actions, will remain the servant and not the master of the people.

The next time a national leader of one of the major parties appeared on the C.B.C.'s free time political broadcasts was two weeks later, when Mr.

Diefenbaker addressed the nation from Winnipeg. On this occasion he was introduced by Mr. Duff Roblin, the Manitoba Conservative leader. Mr. Diefenbaker in turn introduced Mr. Regnier, the former Liberal running in 1957 as a Conservative. Mr. Diefenbaker took up most of the broadcast period. Noting that a pro-Conservative trend had for some time been evident in the country, he said that in this election the trend was assuming "something of the nature of a crusade." Again referring to the danger of the one-party state he attacked the government for being arrogant and power hungry. Specifically he accused it of concentrating power upon itself by over-taxation, of denying basic democratic rights, and of callously disregarding the needs of all those who were in its power. Credit restrictions, and the size of the old age pensions again came under attack, as well as, this time, the failure of the government to protect the textile industry. In castigating "the dictators in Ottawa" he referred to Mr. Howe's notorious phrase "If we wanted to get away with it, who would stop us?"

My fellow Canadians, I hope *you* will, for nobody else can. I believe this tremendous ground swell of protest has reached the stage when history will repeat itself and the many, small or weak though they may be individually, will rise in righteous indignation, and in unity find strength.

Mr. Diefenbaker then again dwelt at some length on Black Friday and told his audience that it was this episode which had led Mr. Regnier to change his political allegiance. Mr. Regnier spoke for about a minute and then the Conservative leader returned to close the programme. Mr. Regnier, he suggested, was not the only former Liberal who now supported the Conservative party. "All across this country, men and women who previously supported other parties are coming forward to say to me and many of our Candidates, *'This time* I am voting Conservative.'"

Mr. St. Laurent's second broadcast was made in the middle of the campaign period. Accusing the Conservatives of putting their party's interest above that of the nation, he ridiculed their promises, saying that their cost had soared well beyond the billion dollar level. Estimating that opposition promises would cost the average tax payer eleven ten-dollar bills, Mr. St. Laurent said: "These parties ask you, on June 10th, to make your mark on a ballot but afterwards it's your name you would have to write on a cheque."

Turning to opposition accusations that the government was "spendthrift," he examined the possibilities of cutting expenditures. Out of each hundred dollars spent by the government, Mr. St. Laurent said, $13 went to the provinces, $30 for social security, $34 for defence, $10 for interest on the national debt, leaving about $13. If this portion were tampered with, numerous essential services would suddenly disappear. The Prime Minister referred to the Royal Canadian Mounted Police, the mail, harbours and airports, and immigration. He then turned to the first department which is considered in the annual appropriations bill; the Department of Agriculture. Would the Conservatives reduce the services the government was providing in this field?

Where, then, did the Liberal party stand in the election?

There is, first of all, no Tory "spend more—tax less" hokum about our stand. You know our policy because you know Liberal action. And from what I have been hearing from Central Canada to the Pacific, a pretty good percentage of Canadians like what they see of Liberal action. Let me set it out briefly for you.

The government had, Mr. St. Laurent said, reduced taxes and the national debt whenever it was possible, it had cut defence cost when it was safe to do so and it had increased tax-rental payments to the provinces. The Liberal party stood for provincial rights and opposed centralization, it believed that Canadians should have the power to amend their own constitution. In trade, the Prime Minister claimed, the government had tried successfully to go after new markets and to keep the old ones. It had continued and extended floor prices and other federal programmes for farmers and for fishermen. Full employment, social security measures, transportation, the development of natural resources, encouragement of University education, vocational training and cultural development—all were linked by the Liberal leader to his government's past performance. Painting a rosy picture of Canada in 1980, he concluded by cautioning his audience:

You know, since elections were first invented election promises have fogged the issues. But wise men and women know this truth that Tories never tell: a government must tax to spend—and tax *more* to spend *more*. That Tory election promise to spend more and tax less—is just plain ridiculous!

As far as we Liberals are concerned, we invite you to commission us to go on doing our best, under all circumstances, and for all the people, and to stick to our "no nonsense—no promises" programme. Good night.

In his third address the Conservative leader again argued that an increasing number of Canadians were turning in righteous indignation against the government. He repeated the charge that the government had become arrogant and complacent. But despite its attempts to encourage electoral apathy the people were getting excited about the election. A great ground-swell was moving against the Liberals and the only alternative to them was the Conservative party. "We have become, by a wholly understandable turn of the wheel of fate, the party of the people." Among the reasons why the Canadian people thought it sensible to vote Conservative was the fact that good government, democracy, and economic interests demanded it. As in the other broadcasts the theme of the government having been in office for twenty-two years was stressed and also the oft-repeated accusation that the Liberal government sought "unbridled power," that it was influenced by the "power lust of a few men" and that control had become "more and more absolute."

The Conservatives would cope with the country's problems because they were aware of them. In this connection Mr. Diefenbaker referred to press reports quoting Mr. Howe as expressing amazement upon hearing that there was much talk about lost markets. Parliament, the old age pension, and the tax surplus were emphasized as they had been in the earlier talks.

Both leaders made their final television appeals on June 5. Mr. St. Laurent argued that it was essential that one party obtain a parliamentary majority. The C.C.F. and Social Credit parties could not possibly do so. That left the Conservatives as the only possible alternative to the Liberals. They claimed that it was time for a change. But what sort of change did they envisage? The Liberals, because of Canada's becoming richer, had been able to reduce taxes, over the years, and to increase services. No government could keep the promises made by the Conservatives. How could any government pay more to the provinces without raising taxes? The Prime Minister defended his government against the charge that it had maltreated Parliament. The Liberal majority in the House supported the government's pipeline policy: did the Conservatives think that they had a veto power? "Do the Canadian people believe that a minority in Parliament—after three and one-half weeks of debate, mind you, should be able to prevent the majority from carrying out what it believes to be the will of the people?" In any event, the building of the pipeline was essential and no time was to be lost in getting started. The Prime Minister concluded by trying to show that to win a working majority the Conservatives would have to gain a number of seats no one thought remotely possible. If the Liberal party were to fail in winning a majority no other party certainly would do so.

Is a Parliament where no party has a majority the kind of change that would be good for Canada? Do we want a Parliament, like the French Parliament, where bargains have to be made between various groups in order to form unstable majorities and where governments change every few months?

Canadian voters were also warned by Mr. Diefenbaker against diluting their votes among third parties. In his final broadcast he again noted the existence of a groundswell of opposition against the "power-mad men" in Ottawa. As in all other broadcasts, Black Friday played an important role in his last appeal, as did also the old age pension, agriculture, credit restrictions, and over-taxation. A brief allusion to foreign affairs by Mr. Diefenbaker constituted the only incursion into this field by either leader in their series of broadcasts.[2] When talking about the government's alleged maltreatment of Parliament, he referred briefly to the Norman case and to "Canada shipping, or permitting the shipment of war munitions to Egypt." Having earlier stated that the election was not a battle between the Liberal and Conservative parties, but rather a struggle of "the People of Canada against a ruling caste," the Leader of the Opposition appealed to the men and women of all parties for support. He concluded by admitting that sometimes in the future he might be wrong, "but I'll never be on the side of wrong, and this party, so long as I am its leader, will not be on the side of wrong."

The appeals made by Mr. St. Laurent to his French-speaking compatriots were essentially the same as those he made in English. Except for a brief reference to federal attempts to aid university education without interfering in provincial affairs and except for the occasional mention of Laurier and Ernest Lapointe, no arguments were deployed for special consumption by French-speaking audiences. Only the first of Mr. St. Laurent's three French broadcasts differed in tone from his English ones and the difference was merely one of emphasis. The general argument was somewhat more philosophical; Mr. St. Laurent tried to say something about the political beliefs of his party. The Liberals, he claimed, were concerned above all with the freedom of the individual and with a social philosophy based on the precept "Love thy neighbour as thyself."

[2]Except for a passing reference by Mr. Diefenbaker on May 29 to Mr. Pearson's "bumbling of External Affairs."

APPENDIX D: STATISTICAL TABLES

TABLE D/1

Summary of Votes Cast 1953 and 1957[a]

Year	Electorate	Votes cast	Lib.	P.C.	C.C.F.	So. Cred.	Other	Rejected ballots
1953	8,401,691	5,701,963 100.1%	2,751,307 48.3%	1,749,579 30.7%	640,769 11.2%	305,551 5.4%	194,066 3.4%	60,691 1.1%
1957	8,902,125	6,680,690 100.0%	2,702,573 40.5%	2,572,926 38.5%	707,659 10.6%	437,049 6.5%	188,510 2.8%	74,710 1.1%

Notes to this and following tables are at the end of this Appendix.

TABLE D/2

Election Results Canada and Regions[a]

Region	Electorate (in '000s)		Percentage voting	Change in % voting	Members elected (1953 numbers in brackets)						Percentage of votes obtained by parties (1953 % in brackets)[c]					Change in vote 1953-57[d]	
	1953	1957	1957	1953/57	Total	Lib.	P.C.	C.C.F.	So. Cred.	Other	Lib.	P.C.	C.C.F.	So. Cred.	Other	Lib.	P.C.
Maritimes	919	928	74.3	+ 2.9	33	12(27)	21(5)	—(1)	—	—	47.7(54.5)	48.2(39.2)	2.5(4.7)	0.4(0.1)	0.4(0.7)	— 6.8	+ 9.0
Quebec	2,353	2,510	72.3	+ 1.4	75	62(67)	9(4)		—	4(4)	56.8(60.3)	30.7(29.0)	1.8(1.5)	0.2(—)	9.2(8.0)	— 3.5	+ 1.7
Ontario	2,894	3,101	74.0	+ 7.0	85	21(51)	61(33)	3(1)	—	—	36.6(46.1)	48.1(39.9)	11.9(10.7)	1.6(0.3)	0.5(1.7)	— 9.5	+ 8.2
Prairies	1,495	1,550	75.9	+10.9	48	6(16)	14(6)	15(14)	13(11)	—	27.9(37.1)	28.4(16.9)	21.3(25.0)	21.1(17.6)	0.5(2.2)	— 9.2	+11.5
B.C. and Northwest	742	814	74.3	+ 8.4	24	4(10)	7(3)	7(7)	6(4)	—	20.9(31.0)	32.5(14.2)	22.2(26.0)	23.2(25.7)	0.4(2.3)	—10.1	+18.3
Canada	8,402	8,902	74.1	+ 6.2	265	105(171)	112(51)	25(23)	19(15)	4(4)	40.5(4.83)	38.5(30.7)	10.6(11.2)	6.5(5.4)	2.8(3.4)	— 7.8	+ 7.8

TABLE D/4

Election Results: Provinces and Areas within Some Provinces[a]

Area	Electorate (in '000s)		Percentage voting	Change in % voting	Members elected (1953 numbers in brackets)						Percentage of votes obtained by parties (1953 % in brackets)[c]					Change in vote 1953-57[d]	
	1953	1957	1957	1953/57	Total	Lib.	P.C.	C.C.F.	So. Cred.	Other	Lib.	P.C.	C.C.F.	So. Cred.	Other	Lib.	P.C.
Newfoundland	195	198	51.9[j]	− 5.5	7	5(7)	2(—)	—	—	—	61.3(66.5)	37.4(27.8)	0.4(4.6)	—	—	− 5.2	+ 9.6
Prince Edward Island	56	54	85.4[j]	+ 1.9	4	—(3)	4(1)	—	—	—	46.4(50.9)	52.0(47.8)	1.0(0.8)	—	—	− 4.5	+ 4.2
Nova Scotia Halifax	98	108	75.2[j]	+11.7	2	—(2)	2(—)	—(1)	—	—	47.0(55.2)	50.4(40.6)	2.2(3.9)	0.2(—)	—(0.4)	− 8.2	+ 9.8
Rest	283	276	83.7	+ 9.4	10	2(8)	8(1)	—(1)	—	—	43.4(51.3)	49.9(39.4)	5.9(8.3)	0.1(—)	—(0.2)	− 7.9	+10.5
Total	381	385	81.3[j]	+ 9.7	12	2(10)	10(1)	—(1)	—	—	44.9(52.7)	50.1(39.9)	4.3(6.7)	0.1(—)	—(0.2)	− 7.8	+10.2
New Brunswick St. John-Albert	53	54	77.6	+ 4.9	1	—	1(1)	—	—	—	45.8(47.5)	52.8(48.9)	—(2.4)	1.2(0.5)	1.6(2.3)	− 1.7	+ 3.9
Rest	235	238	82.3	+ 2.7	9	5(7)	4(2)	—	—	—	47.9(53.2)	47.1(39.9)	1.0(3.1)	—	—	− 5.3	+ 7.2
Total	288	291	81.4	+ 3.0	10	5(7)	5(3)	—	—	—	47.5(52.2)	48.1(41.5)	0.8(3.0)	1.0(0.4)	1.3(1.9)	− 4.7	+ 6.6
Quebec[g] Northern Quebec	24	31	64.4	− 1.1	1	1(1)	—	—	—	—	57.3(49.8)	41.1(47.6)	—	—	11.3(10.6)	+ 7.5	− 6.5
Gaspesia-South Shore	183	183	76.7	+ 1.6	8	5(8)	2(—)	—	—	1(—)[g]	53.5(51.9)	34.2(36.4)	—	—	28.9(34.9)	+ 1.6	− 2.2
Saguenay-Lake St. John	97	107	84.2	+ 1.6	4	4(2)	—	—	—	—(2)[g]	55.1(43.1)	15.1(21.1)	—	0.6(—)	5.3(6.1)	+12.0	− 6.0
Quebec	307	324	79.8	+ 3.0	11	9(8)	1(2)	—	—	1(1)[g]	59.4(58.8)	32.5(29.9)	—	—	1.1(4.2)[e]	+ 0.6	+ 2.6
Three Rivers	150	158	79.0	− 1.2	5	3(4)	2(1)	—	—	—	53.4(55.8)	41.3(30.8)	3.5(—)	—	0.8(6.4)	− 2.4	+10.5
Eastern Townships	229	235	77.8	+ 4.0	8	7(8)	—	—	—	1(—)[g]	52.5(61.5)	37.7(36.6)	0.2(0.9)	—	8.8(—)[e] —(6.2)[e]	− 9.0	+ 1.1
Montreal Region	290	308	73.1	+ 5.9	10	8(10)	2(—)	—	—	—	58.3(72.6)	28.8(25.8)	—(0.4)	—	10.4(—)[e] —(0.1)	−14.3	+ 3.0
Metropolitan Montreal	926	1,013	64.5	+ 4.5	23	20(21)	2(1)	—	—	1(1)[g]	59.9(62.7)	28.1(25.5)	3.9(3.7)	—	1.3(—)[f] 2.1(2.1)	− 2.8	+ 2.6
Northwestern Quebec	148	151	78.9	+ 7.0	5	5(5)	—	—	—	—	47.1(63.0)	29.7(29.0)	1.6(1.3)	2.0(—)	4.5(4.6)[e] 6.8(5.3) 11.7(—)[e]	−15.9	+ 0.7
Total	2,353	2,510	72.3	+ 1.4	75	62(67)	9(4)	—	2(3)	2(1)[f]	56.8(60.3)	30.7(29.0)	1.8(1.5)	0.2(—)	4.2(4.2) 4.7(3.7)[e] 0.3(0.1)[f]	− 3.5	+ 1.7

TABLE D/3

Election Results: Provinces and Regions[a]

Province and Region	Electorate (in '000s) 1953	1957	Percentage voting 1957	Change in % voting 1953/57	Members elected (1953 numbers in brackets) Total	Lib.	P.C.	C.C.F.	So. Cred.	Other	Percentage of votes obtained by parties (1953 % in brackets)[c] Lib.	P.C.	C.C.F.	So. Cred.	Other	Change in vote 1953–57[d] Lib.	P.C.
Newfoundland	195	198	51.9[i]	− 5.5	7	5(7)	2(—)	—	—	—	61.3(66.5)	37.4(27.8)	0.4(4.6)	—	—	− 5.2	+ 9.6
Prince Edward Island	56	54	85.4[j]	+ 1.9	4	—(3)	4(1)	—	—	—	46.4(50.9)	52.0(47.8)	1.0(0.8)	—	—	− 4.5	+ 4.2
Nova Scotia	381	385	81.3[j]	+ 9.7	12	2(10)	10(1)	—(1)	0.1(—)	—(0.2)	44.9(52.7)	50.1(39.9)	4.3(6.7)	0.1(—)	—(0.2)	− 7.8	+10.2
New Brunswick	288	291	81.4	+ 3.0	10	5(7)	5(3)	—	1.0(0.4)	1.3(—) / —(1.9)•	47.5(52.2)	48.1(41.5)	0.8(3.0)	1.0(0.4)	1.3(—) / —(1.9)•	− 4.7	+ 6.6
Maritimes	919	928	74.3	+ 2.9	33	12(27)	21(5)	—(1)	—	—	47.7(54.5)	48.2(39.2)	2.5(4.7)	0.4(0.1)	0.4(0.7)	− 6.8	+ 9.0
Quebec	2,353	2,510	72.3	+ 1.4	75	62(67)	9(4)	—	—	2(3) / 2(1)•	56.8(60.3)	30.7(29.0)	1.8(1.5)	0.2(—)	4.2(4.2) / 4.7(3.7)• / 0.3(0.1)f	− 3.5	+ 1.7
Ontario	2,894	3,101	74.0	+ 7.0	85	21(51)	61(33)	3(1)	—	—	36.6(46.1)	48.1(39.9)	11.9(10.7)	1.6(0.3)	0.5(1.4) / —(0.3)•	− 9.5	+ 8.2
Manitoba	465	474	74.2	+14.8	14	1(8)	8(3)	5(3)	—	—	25.8(39.7)	35.5(26.7)	23.4(23.3)	13.0(6.2)	0.5(2.4) / 0.7(0.4)•	−13.9	+ 8.8
Saskatchewan	481	484	81.0	+ 6.8	17	4(4)	3(1)	10(11)	—	—	30.2(37.5)	23.0(11.7)	35.8(43.9)	10.4(5.3)	0.1(1.1)	− 7.3	+11.3
Alberta	549	591	73.0	+10.4	17	1(4)	3(2)	—	13(11)	—	27.6(34.7)	27.4(14.4)	6.3(6.9)	37.5(40.5)	0.3(2.8)	− 7.1	+13.0
Prairies	1,495	1,550	75.9	+10.6	48	6(16)	14(6)	15(14)	13(11)	—	27.9(37.1)	28.4(16.9)	21.3(25.0)	21.1(17.6)	0.3(2.0) / 0.2(0.1)•	− 9.2	+11.5
British Columbia	731	802	74.3	+ 9.2	22	2(8)	7(3)	7(7)	6(4)	—	20.4(30.6)	32.4(14.0)	22.6(26.4)	23.6(25.9)	0.4(2.3)	−10.2	+18.4
Yukon and Mackenzie R.	11	12	74.8	+ 5.6	2	2(2)	—(—)	—	—	—	57.2(52.6)	40.4(26.1)	—	—(13.5)	—(5.7)	+ 4.6	+14.3
British Columbia	742	814	74.3	+ 8.4	24	4(10)	7(3)	7(7)	6(4)	—	20.9(31.0)	32.5(14.2)	22.2(26.0)	23.2(25.7)	0.4(2.3)	−10.1	+18.3
Canada	8,402	8,902	74.1	+ 6.2	265	105(171)	112(51)	25(23)	19(15)	2(3) / 2(1)•	40.5(48.3)•	38.5(30.7)	10.6(11.2)	6.5(5.4)	1.4(2.3) / 1.4(1.1)•	− 7.8	+ 7.8

TABLE D/4 (cont'd)

Area	Electorate (in '000s) 1953	Electorate (in '000s) 1957	Percentage voting 1957	Change in % voting 1953/57	Members elected (1953 numbers in brackets) Total	Lib.	P.C.	C.C.F.	So. Cred.	Other	Percentage of votes obtained by parties (1953 % in brackets)[c] Lib.	P.C.	C.C.F.	So. Cred.	Other	Change in vote 1953-57[d] Lib.	P.C.
Ontario																	
Eastern Ontario	327	348	79.3	+3.4	11	5(7)	6(4)	—	—	—	47.1(52.7)	46.0(40.9)	1.6(2.3)	2.1(0.4)	4.1(4.3)e	−5.6	+5.1
Lake Ontario	217	227	78.3	+2.3	8	1(4)	7(4)	—	—	—	38.6(43.1)	54.3(49.6)	3.2(3.6)	2.8(−)	—(3.5)	−4.5	+4.7
Metropolitan Toronto	921	1,016	69.7	+10.0	21	1(9)	20(11)	—(1)	—	—	29.1(39.3)	50.8(39.6)	16.6(17.5)	1.6(0.2)	0.3(1.5)	−10.5	+11.1
Niagara	336	360	72.8	+8.4	8	2(5)	6(3)	—	—	—	33.9(44.4)	46.6(36.5)	16.2(15.9)	1.6(0.3)	—(1.7)	−10.5	+10.0
Lake Erie	227	236	77.8	+8.1	7	—(3)	7(4)	—	—	—	32.3(45.5)	57.4(46.1)	7.5(6.8)	1.7(−)	—(0.7)	−13.2	+11.3
Southwestern Ontario	223	233	72.4	+8.0	6	3(5)	3(1)	—	—	—	47.6(55.8)	38.9(36.1)	9.6(5.1)	2.2(−)	—(1.5)	−8.2	+2.8
Upper Grand River	186	193	76.4	+3.8	6	1(3)	5(3)	—	—	—	36.2(46.5)	51.1(43.0)	10.2(8.3)	1.7(1.4)	—(−)	−10.2	+8.1
Georgian Bay	168	170	80.4	+7.6	7	—(4)	7(3)	—	—	—	38.3(48.5)	58.4(46.5)	1.8(3.3)	—(0.7)	1.5(1.0)e	−10.2	+11.9
Northeastern Ontario	199	221	73.3	+4.9	8	6(8)	—	2(−)	—	—	44.3(52.2)	32.6(26.9)	20.6(18.6)	0.5(−)	—(0.2)e	−7.9	+5.7
Lakehead and North	92	99	74.6	+4.0	3	2(3)	—	1(−)	—	—	40.6(52.4)	27.4(25.0)	30.8(18.7)	—	0.2(1.7)	−11.8	+2.4
Total	2,894	3,101	74.0	+7.0	85	21(51)	61(33)	3(1)	—	—	36.6(46.1)	48.1(39.9)	11.9(10.7)	1.6(0.3)	0.2(−)e	−9.5	+8.2
Manitoba																	
Winnipeg	234	248	72.9	+14.8	5	1(1)	2(2)	2(2)	—	—	24.7(34.4)	34.1(26.3)	30.8(33.9)	7.6(−)	9.8(3.8)	−9.7	+7.8
Rest	232	226	75.7	+14.9	9	—(7)	6(1)	3(1)	—	—	27.0(44.8)	37.0(27.0)	15.6(13.1)	18.7(12.3)	0.6(−)e	−17.8	+10.0
Total	465	474	74.2	+14.8	14	1(8)	8(3)	5(3)	—	—	25.8(39.7)	35.5(26.7)	23.4(23.3)	13.0(6.2)	0.5(2.4)e	−13.9	+8.8
Saskatchewan																	
Regina City	44	50	81.7	+9.1	1	—	—	1(1)	—	—	30.3(40.6)	25.6(9.2)	35.4(45.8)	7.2(3.2)	0.8(0.9)	−10.3	+16.4
Saskatoon	39	45	75.0	+10.1	1	—	1(−)	—(1)	—	—	20.0(27.9)	38.0(18.5)	35.4(47.8)	5.9(3.9)	—(1.1)	−7.9	+19.5
Rest	398	389	81.6	+6.3	15	4(4)	2(1)	9(9)	—	—	31.2(37.9)	21.1(11.3)	35.8(43.4)	11.3(5.6)	—(1.1)	−6.7	+9.8
Total	481	484	81.0	+6.8	17	4(4)	3(1)	10(11)	—	—	30.2(37.5)	23.0(11.7)	35.8(43.9)	10.4(5.3)	0.1(1.1)	−7.3	+11.3
Alberta																	
Calgary	96	112	71.7	+9.3	2	—	2(2)	—	—	—	22.5(28.1)	53.4(39.1)	3.2(5.1)	19.7(25.2)	—(1.3)	−5.6	+14.3
Edmonton	124	149	71.3	+12.6	3	—(2)	1(−)	—	2(1)	—	32.1(38.2)	27.0(15.9)	6.1(8.2)	33.9(34.9)	—(1.8)	−6.1	+11.1
Rest	329	331	74.1	+10.1	12	1(2)	—	—	11(10)	—	27.4(35.3)	19.1(6.9)	7.4(6.9)	44.9(46.7)	0.6(3.5)	−7.9	+12.2
Total	549	591	73.0	+10.4	17	1(4)	3(2)	—	13(11)	—	27.6(34.7)	27.4(14.4)	6.3(6.9)	37.5(40.5)	0.3(2.8)	−7.1	+13.0
British Columbia																	
Vancouver City	236	238	72.2	+9.8	6	—(3)	4(1)	2(2)	—	—	17.3(29.1)	41.6(18.1)	21.3(26.6)	17.9(23.2)	0.9(2.3)	−11.8	+23.5
Vancouver Hinterland	114	143	75.5	+9.5	3	—(1)	—	1(1)	2(1)	—	19.1(29.4)	21.4(7.0)	27.9(30.5)	30.2(29.5)	0.6(3.1)	−10.3	+14.4
Rest	382	422	75.1	+8.7	13	2(4)	3(2)	4(4)	4(3)	—	22.4(31.9)	31.1(13.6)	21.5(25.1)	24.4(26.5)	—(2.0)	−9.5	+17.5
Total	731	802	74.3	+9.2	22	2(8)	7(3)	7(7)	6(4)	—	20.4(30.6)	32.4(14.0)	22.6(26.4)	23.6(25.9)	0.4(2.3)	−10.2	+18.4
Yukon and Northwest Territories	11	12	74.8	+5.6	2	2(2)	—	—	—	—	57.2(52.6)	40.4(26.1)	—	—	—(5.7)	−4.6	+14.3

TABLE D/5

Election Results: Largest Cities[a]

City[k]	Electorate (in '000s)		Percentage voting	Change in % voting	Members elected (1953 numbers in brackets)						Percentage of votes obtained by parties (1953 % in brackets)[c]					Change in vote 1953-57	
	1953	1957	1957	1953/57	Total	Lib.	P.C.	C.C.F.	So. Cred.	Other	Lib.	P.C.	C.C.F.	So. Cred.	Other	Lib.	P.C.
Montreal Island	866	942	63.8	+ 4.3	21	18(19)	2(1)	–	–	1(1)[e]	60.0(62.4)	27.7(25.6)	3.9(3.4)	–	2.1(1.8) / 4.7(5.0)[e] / (0.3)[f]	– 2.4	+ 2.1
Toronto and Yorks	803	872	68.7	+ 9.7	18	1(9)	17(8)	–(1)	–	–	29.3(39.5)	50.8(38.5)	16.2(18.3)	1.7(0.2)	0.3(2.1)	–10.2	+12.3
Vancouver	236	238	72.2	+ 9.8	6	–(3)	4(1)	2(2)	–	–	17.3(29.1)	41.6(18.1)	21.3(26.6)	17.9(23.2)	0.9(2.3)	–11.8	+23.5
Winnipeg & St. Boniface	234	248	72.9	+14.8	5	1(1)	2(2)	2(2)	–	–	24.7(34.4)	34.1(26.3)	30.8(33.9)	7.6(–)	0.9(3.8) / 0.6(–)[d]	– 9.7	+ 7.8
Ottawa	167	180	79.0	+ 3.9	4	3(3)	1(1)	–	–	–	51.8(57.1)	41.2(36.5)	3.1(3.7)	2.5(0.9)	–(0.2)	– 5.3	+ 4.7
Quebec	115	119	77.7	+ 6.1	3	3(2)	–(1)	–	–	–	61.5(60.3)	33.0(25.2)	–	1.4(–)	2.8(12.1)[e]	+ 1.2	+ 7.8
Hamilton	136	139	72.2	+10.1	3	–(2)	3(1)	–	–	–	29.9(40.1)	42.5(35.4)	23.1(20.7)	2.5(0.7)	–(1.5)	–10.2	+ 7.1
Edmonton	124	149	71.3	+12.6	3	–(2)	1(–)	–	2(1)	–	32.1(38.2)	27.0(15.9)	6.1(8.2)	33.9(34.9)	–(1.8)	– 6.1	+11.1
Windsor	102	107	70.3	+11.9	2	2(2)	–	–	–	–	49.6(58.8)	29.1(25.0)	18.2(10.4)	1.1(–)	–(3.5)	– 9.2	+ 4.1
Calgary	96	112	71.7	+ 9.3	2	–	2(2)	–	–	–	22.5(28.1)	53.4(39.1)	3.2(5.1)	19.7(25.2)	–(1.3)	– 5.6	+14.3
Halifax	98	108	75.2[j]	+11.7	2	–(2)	2(–)	–	–	–	47.0(55.2)	50.4(40.6)	2.2(3.9)	–	–	– 8.2	+ 9.8
London	85	89	75.4	+ 8.7	2	–	2(2)	–	–	–	30.3(38.7)	59.4(48.4)	8.8(10.5)	18.7(25.6)	–(1.2)	– 8.4	+11.1
Victoria	50	51	78.7	+10.3	1	–(1)	1(–)	–	–	–	27.2(40.3)	44.5(18.0)	9.2(13.2)	–	–(2.1)	–13.1	+26.5
St. John	53	54	77.6	+ 4.9	1	–	1(1)	–	–	–	45.8(47.5)	52.8(48.9)	–(2.4)	–	–	– 1.7	+ 3.9
St. John's	61	65	60.2	– 3.9	2	–(2)	2(–)	–	–	–	44.8(46.9)	53.3(40.4)	0.8(11.5)	–	–	– 2.1	+12.9

TABLE D/6

Election Results: Constituencies[a]

Constituency	Change[b] in electorate	Percentage voting 1957	Change in % voting 1953–1957	No. of candidates	Percentage of votes obtained by parties[c]					Change in vote 1953–57[d]	
					Lib.	P.C.	C.C.F.	So. Cred.	Other	Lib.	P.C.
Newfoundland											
Bonavista-Twillingate	0.0	43.5	−9.0	2	86.6	12.7	—	—	—	+7.5	−7.4
Burin-Burgeo[l]	−13.1	—	—	1	—	—	—	—	—	—	—
Grand Falls-White Bay-Labrador	+0.3	46.3	−9.5	2	74.7	24.4	—	—	—	+2.4	−2.0
Humber-St. Georges	+3.3	54.7	−4.9	2	66.3	32.8	—	—	—	−10.6	+10.6
St. John's East	+9.7	59.7	−6.2	2	46.2	52.4	—	—	—	+4.1	+18.5
St. John's West	+4.2	60.6	−1.7	3	43.4	54.1	1.6	—	—	+8.6	+7.0
Trinity Conception	+2.2	44.0	−1.5	2	68.9	30.6	—	—	—	+2.7	+8.6
Prince Edward Island											
Kings	−2.9	87.4	+0.1	3	46.6	51.6	1.0	—	—	−5.1	+3.9
Prince	−2.5	85.7	−0.1	3	47.9	49.3	2.1	—	—	−4.1	+5.3
Queens[m]	−2.0	84.3	+4.2	5	45.7	53.1	0.6	—	—	−4.4	+3.6
Nova Scotia											
Antigonish-Guysborough	+4.6	82.8	+14.7	2	48.8	50.5	—	—	—	−17.8	+17.6
Cape Breton North and Victoria	+1.7	82.3	+15.1	3	44.2	46.1	8.9	—	—	−15.9	+6.9
Cape Breton South	+5.0	85.7	+18.2	3	31.1	40.1	28.2	—	—	−1.9	+24.8
Colchester-Hants	+2.1	84.8	+5.5	3	42.7	53.5	3.2	—	—	+5.9	+6.4
Cumberland	+4.2	81.4	+9.2	2	45.2	54.1	—	—	—	+6.2	+6.1
Digby-Annapolis-Kings	+0.5	83.2	+0.0	2	41.7	57.6	—	—	—	+6.4	+6.2
Halifax[m]	+10.4	75.2	+11.7	6	47.0	50.4	2.2	—	—	−8.1	+9.8
Inverness-Richmond	+6.0	80.9	+9.2	2	52.5	46.9	—	—	—	−10.1	+10.2
Pictou	+6.5	87.7	+10.1	4	41.1	54.2	2.0	—	—	−9.3	+12.6
Queens-Lunenburg	+0.7	84.4	+5.3	2	49.1	50.2	—	2.1	—	−7.0	+6.9
Shelburne-Yarmouth-Clare	+3.4	81.1	+8.9	2	51.8	47.4	—	—	—	−8.8	+8.7
New Brunswick											
Charlotte	+5.9	86.4	+8.2	2	51.8	46.6	—	—	—	−0.1	+3.0
Gloucester	+2.5	80.3	+3.9	2	57.3	41.7	—	—	—	+0.2	+0.8
Kent	+3.7	86.1	+6.1	2	57.3	41.7	—	—	—	−8.1	+8.2
Northumberland-Miramichi	+2.7	81.4	+5.7	3	46.2	35.7	—	—	17.0[g]	−17.3	+5.3
Restigouche-Madawaska	+2.3	83.7	+5.2	2	44.6	54.0	—	—	—	−4.9	+25.2
Royal	−3.2	81.1	+0.5	2	40.5	58.4	—	—	—	+1.8	+4.0
Saint John-Albert	+1.1	77.6	+4.9	3	45.7	52.8	—	—	—	+9.4	+3.9
Victoria-Carleton	+3.5	78.0	+1.7	3	35.8	57.6	—	5.5	—	—	+8.8
Westmorland	+1.9	83.1	+3.1	4	50.1	41.5	3.5	3.6	—	+3.8	+2.0
York-Sudbury	+8.8	82.0	+1.4	3	47.7	48.9	2.3	—	—	+4.6	+6.5

TABLE D/6 (cont'd)

Constituency	Change[b] in electorate	Percentage voting 1957	Change in % voting 1953–1957	No. of candidates	Percentage of votes obtained by parties[c]					Change in vote 1953–57[d]	
					Lib.	P.C.	C.C.F.	So. Cred.	Other	Lib.	P.C.
Quebec											
Argenteuil-Deux-Montagnes	+ 6.5	82.1	+13.6	4	41.4	36.5	—	—	20.9[e]	−28.0	+ 7.2
Beauce	+ 3.3	85.4	+ 2.0	2	47.7	—	—	—	51.1[g]	+ 5.4	− 9.3
Beauharnois-Salaberry	+11.9	70.0	+ 1.2	3	64.7	14.3	—	—	19.6[c]	−10.3	− 9.3
Bellechasse	− 2.5	69.2	− 5.0	4	72.4	16.3	—	—	10.6[f]	+13.4	−24.0
Berthier-Maskinongé-Delanaudière	+ 2.0	79.0	+ 1.0	2	52.9	45.9	—	—	—	− 3.3	+43.6
Bonaventure	+ 3.9	82.3	+ 4.9	2	48.8	50.4	—	—	—	− 9.1	+ 9.7
Brome-Missisquoi	+ 1.4	80.5	+13.1	2	51.4	47.8	—	—	—	−11.3	+19.3
Chambly-Rouville	+16.6	76.9	+ 5.6	4	59.8	31.0	—	—	6.5[e]	− 5.6	+ 2.4
Champlain	+ 5.2	79.9	+ 0.5	2	57.3	41.6	—	—	—	− 5.5	+ 5.4
Chapleau	+ 0.5	74.7	+ 4.4	2	50.3	48.7	—	—	—	+ 1.0	+19.2
Charlevoix	+ 3.1	80.5	− 0.9	4	55.0	40.7	—	1.3	1.2[e]	− 4.0	+ 0.8
Chateauguay-Huntingdon-Laprairie	+12.2	71.1	+ 3.7	3	51.5	35.3	—	—	12.0[e]	− 9.2	− 3.0
Chicoutimi	+11.7	87.1	+ 4.7	2	51.1	—	—	—	47.2[g]	+17.8	—
Compton-Frontenac	− 2.8	86.1	+ 6.4	3	51.7	45.8	1.9	—	—	− 8.3	+ 8.0
Dorchester	+ 0.5	85.7	+ 1.4	2	50.7	48.0	—	—	—	− 1.9	+ 1.5
Drummond-Arthabaska	+ 1.5	78.8	+ 6.3	3	32.3	31.7	—	—	35.2[e]	+21.6	−13.6
Gaspé	+ 2.6	76.5	+ 0.6	3	48.2	48.5	—	—	2.2[g]	− 3.4	+ 2.1
Gatineau	+ 5.5	74.6	+ 4.2	3	58.2	29.8	—	—	10.9[e]	− 6.9	+ 0.0
Hull	+ 9.3	85.9	+ 7.5	4	44.1	13.9	—	6.7	33.9[e]	−29.8	− 7.3
Îles-de-la-Madeleine	+ 4.1	90.9	+ 3.2	3	52.9	—	—	—	46.6[g]	− 1.4	−45.0
Joliette-L'Assomption-Montcalm	+ 5.4	53.5	− 0.1	2	80.5	18.3	—	—	—	+ 1.4	− 1.5
Kamouraska	− 1.8	70.2	+ 4.9	2	47.4	—	—	—	51.3[g]	+ 1.1	− 1.9
Labelle	+ 3.6	82.1	− 1.7	2	45.6	53.4	—	—	—	+ 5.6	+ 7.3
Lac-Saint-Jean	+14.6	85.6	− 1.8	2	60.8	38.2	—	—	—	+ 4.9	+ 5.2
Lapointe	+ 3.3	82.0	+ 2.4	2	52.0	—	—	—	47.0[g]	+13.0	− 7.3
Lévis	+19.0	83.2	+ 2.4	4	71.0	27.9	—	—	—	+ 0.3	+ 0.6
Longueuil	+ 1.1	71.9	+ 7.5	2	57.9	32.8	5.3	—	—	+ 8.6	+13.2
Lotbinière	+ 1.0	88.7	+ 2.2	2	47.9	51.2	—	—	2.3[f]	+ 8.3	+ 8.4
Matapédia-Matane	+ 7.2	76.8	+ 3.3	2	51.0	47.7	—	—	—	+ 2.6	+ 2.2
Mégantic	+ 0.5	76.7	− 0.4	2	64.1	34.6	—	—	—	+ 2.3	+ 2.7
Montmagny-L'Islet	− 3.3	81.8	+ 6.7	2	58.9	—	—	—	40.0[g]	+ 8.0	−32.2
Nicolet-Yamaska	− 3.8	81.7	+ 2.1	2	48.2	50.9	—	—	—	+ 0.7	+38.5
Pontiac-Temiscamingue	+ 0.4	81.3	+ 8.1	2	51.9	47.3	—	—	—	+ 6.1	+ 6.4
Portneuf	+ 7.4	78.4	+ 5.0	2	57.7	41.3	—	—	—	−11.5	+11.4
Québec East	+ 2.2	75.7	+ 5.3	3	71.2	25.8	—	1.9	—	+ 6.7	+ 8.3
Québec South	+ 0.8	79.7	+ 8.5	4	61.2	33.4	—	—	4.4[h]	−12.9	+ 8.5
Québec West	+27.4	79.0	+ 4.5	4	46.9	43.5	—	2.1	6.0[e]	+27.1	+ 7.1
Québec-Montmorency		78.1	+ 1.1	2	63.1	35.7	—	—	—	+ 4.2	+ 4.4

TABLE D/6 (cont'd)

Constituency	Change[b] in electorate	Percentage voting 1957	Change in % voting 1953-1957	No. of candidates	Percentage of votes obtained by parties[c]					Change in vote 1953-57[d]	
					Lib.	P.C.	C.C.F.	So. Cred.	Other	Lib.	P.C.
Quebec (con'd)											
Richelieu-Verchères	+1.4	69.2	+1.5	3	80.4	3.8	—	—	14.2[f]	0.0	−13.3
Richmond-Wolfe	+3.6	76.6	+3.5	3	46.3	32.5	—	—	20.2[e]	−16.9	−2.8
Rimouski	+5.7	73.6	−2.5	2	59.5	39.6	—	—	—	+24.0	+5.6
Roberval	+6.2	81.6	−0.6	2	59.5	39.7	—	—	—	+9.8	+9.1
St. Hyacinthe-Bagot[a]	+2.2	80.2	—	2	45.5	53.6	—	—	—	—	—
St. Jean-Iberville-Napierville	+7.9	87.1	+20.6	2	51.5	1.4	—	—	45.5[f]	−35.4	−9.4
St. Maurice-Laflèche	+12.7	73.3	−2.5	4	58.6	24.1	13.7	—	2.4[g]	−5.3	−11.3
Saguenay	+29.2	64.4	+1.1	2	57.3	41.1	—	—	—	+7.5	+6.5
Shefford	+3.7	76.9	+0.8	2	62.1	36.5	—	—	—	−5.3	+4.9
Sherbrooke	+4.6	72.8	+2.9	2	61.9	37.1	—	—	—	−3.5	+3.7
Stanstead	0.0	77.6	+1.9	2	56.6	42.6	—	—	—	−2.9	+5.2
Temiscouata	−11.3	74.1	+5.3	2	57.9	40.6	—	—	—	+0.8	+2.3
Terrebonne[a]	+5.0	73.8	−3.7	2	59.4	39.5	—	—	—	—	—
Trois-Rivières	+8.3	83.5	+9.1	3	48.1	50.1	—	—	—	+1.5	+10.3
Vaudreuil-Soulanges	+1.1	73.7	+9.1	2	67.7	31.1	—	—	0.8	−10.4	+10.3
Villeneuve	+1.1	76.0	+9.3	4	37.8	23.0	7.4	—	31.0	−26.0	+7.1
Quebec: Island of Montreal											
Cartier	−2.3	65.3	+2.3	5	71.4	11.4	4.0	—	11.1[e]	+4.1	+4.9
Dollard	+28.0	66.9	+4.4	3	67.7	24.1	6.8	—	—	+4.3	+6.9
Hochelaga	+6.5	60.3	+0.1	4	74.5	14.7	3.5	—	6.1[p]	−0.4	+0.4
Jacques-Cartier-Lasalle	+31.5	74.3	+7.4	3	47.2	47.5	3.9	—	—	−11.4	+20.1
Lafontaine	−5.9	64.3	+5.8	3	72.4	21.4	5.1	—	—	−1.5	−1.5
Laurier	+7.8	65.7	+7.1	5	59.7	28.0	1.4	—	5.5[h]	−9.4	+2.6
Laval	+51.0	61.7	+3.2	4	59.7	12.6	2.7	—	23.5[q]	−10.1	−13.8
Maisonneuve-Rosemont	+20.5	60.6	+0.5	3	69.6	21.5	7.4	—	—	+28.2	+2.4
Mercier	+42.6	62.1	+0.1	3	73.6	24.8	—	—	—	+12.6	+7.9
Mount-Royal	+20.7	62.3	+8.0	3	59.7	35.4	3.6	—	—	−1.3	+1.8
Notre-Dame-de-Grace	+8.9	58.0	+11.4	3	40.4	56.4	2.4	—	—	+5.7	+7.0
Outremont-Saint-Jean	+0.3	63.4	+7.1	3	71.1	20.0	6.7	—	—	+3.3	−4.8
Papineau	+8.0	63.4	+4.3	3	77.3	13.2	8.1	—	—	+40.3	+5.0
Sainte-Anne	−13.6	69.9	+0.9	4	26.5	17.5	—	—	54.0[e]	−56.4	+5.8
St-Antoine-Westmount	+3.8	65.9	+4.8	2	54.4	44.3	—	—	—	−1.9	+8.1
Saint-Denis	+5.8	57.5	+5.2	4	67.4	18.1	4.0	—	9.2[e]	+3.1	+6.7
Saint-Henri	+5.8	64.4	+1.1	4	48.2	10.7	3.7	—	35.5[e]	−14.4	+8.7
St. Jacques	+14.1	48.0	+2.3	5	40.2	27.2	3.7	—	27.0[e]	−24.4	+5.1
St. Laurent-St. Georges	−13.4	54.3	+7.9	4	51.5	41.3	2.9	—	2.4[p]	−12.6	+10.0
St. Marie	−8.2	58.7	+1.0	3	59.7	33.5	3.6	—	—	−12.6	+11.2
Verdun	−2.1	64.7	+2.3	3	61.1	30.0	7.5	—	—	+6.4	+5.9

Table D/6 (cont'd)

Constituency	Change[b] in electorate	Percentage voting 1957	Change in % voting 1953–1957	No. of candidates	Percentage of votes obtained by parties[c]					Change in vote 1953–57[d]	
					Lib.	P.C.	C.C.F.	So. Cred.	Other	Lib.	P.C.
Ontario											
Algoma East	+50.3	65.5	− 2.5	3	51.5	34.6	12.9	—	—	−13.8	+ 0.8
Algoma West	+ 5.5	72.4	+ 5.9	3	42.8	35.1	21.1	—	—	− 7.8	+ 8.2
Brantford	− 1.0	78.8	+ 8.5	3	33.5	41.0	24.5	—	—	−10.6	+ 4.5
Brant-Haldimand	+ 3.6	82.0	+ 6.0	3	34.5	55.0	9.3	—	—	− 9.9	+ 6.9
Bruce	+ 3.4	84.6	+ 5.5	2	42.2	57.0	—	—	—	− 6.3	+ 6.2
Carleton	+14.3	82.4	+ 5.8	4	33.6	61.1	2.9	1.3	—	− 6.1	+ 6.7
Cochrane	+ 2.5	72.3	+ 1.0	4	44.0	22.1	17.0	—	15.6	− 2.0	−13.8
Dufferin-Simcoe	+ 6.6	75.2	+ 3.2	2	34.3	64.6	—	—	—	− 8.6	+ 8.6
Durham	+ 5.7	81.2	+ 5.8	4	41.0	44.0	11.5	2.4	—	− 4.8	+ 0.6
Elgin	+ 0.9	76.4	+ 4.3	4	29.1	59.2	4.9	5.6	—	−16.7	+ 5.9
Essex East	+ 8.5	75.4	+12.2	3	56.2	27.0	15.1	—	—	− 9.6	+ 8.8
Essex South	+ 5.7	75.6	+ 6.4	4	45.5	47.6	3.7	1.5	—	−12.8	+ 6.8
Essex West	+ 0.4	65.6	+11.5	4	42.4	31.4	21.6	2.3	—	− 9.3	+ 0.5
Fort William	+ 4.0	80.0	+ 6.7	3	37.7	34.9	—	1.0	26.1[e]	−14.3	+ 9.8
Glengarry-Prescott	0.0	85.7	+ 5.0	4	32.1	39.8	—	7.4	—	− 7.8	+ 9.7
Grenville-Dundas	+ 3.8	66.1	+ 0.9	3	30.2	61.5	—	—	—	−18.0	+ 2.3
Grey-Bruce	− 0.9	85.5	+15.2	3	41.2	58.0	—	—	—	−11.0	−17.8
Grey North	+ 2.7	83.9	+ 8.6	3	29.8	56.8	—	—	—	−12.4	+15.3
Halton	+38.8	76.6	+ 5.0	4	50.4	57.9	5.6	—	—	−14.0	+10.0
Hamilton East	+ 8.6	70.7	+10.2	4	28.0	37.6	26.3	3.3	—	−12.2	+ 8.2
Hamilton South	+19.0	72.9	+ 8.9	4	31.8	38.8	27.7	3.9	—	− 4.2	+ 8.6
Hamilton West	+ 5.3	72.9	+11.3	3	27.4	52.8	13.9	—	—	−13.1	+ 6.1
Hastings-Frontenac	+ 2.3	69.8	− 1.5	3	44.4	61.5	—	10.3	—	− 5.7	+ 2.7
Hastings South	+ 5.3	79.8	+ 2.3	2	41.4	52.0	—	2.3	—	− 5.9	+ 5.8
Huron	− 3.8	85.2	+ 3.6	3	47.2	57.6	—	—	—	− 9.1	+ 5.8
Kenora-Rainy River	+ 9.2	70.8	+ 1.8	3	47.2	31.3	20.7	—	—	− 7.3	+ 2.5
Kent	+ 1.6	71.5	+ 0.9	3	50.6	40.3	—	—	—	− 2.8	+ 0.5
Kingston	+ 7.9	78.6	− 1.4	3	44.0	44.6	3.5	6.6	—	−12.1	+ 1.6
Lambton-Kent	+ 1.7	75.0	+ 2.3	3	41.9	55.3	—	3.0	—	+ 0.1	+12.2
Lambton West	+ 9.6	75.4	+ 8.9	2	27.7	71.4	—	—	—	− 5.7	+ 5.0
Lanark	− 1.3	73.9	+ 2.4	4	46.4	47.4	6.3	—	—	−11.0	+ 8.4
Leeds	+ 2.0	86.1	+ 5.4	3	32.2	50.7	—	1.8	—	− 7.6	+ 0.3
Lincoln	+ 9.9	77.7	+12.5	4	32.6	51.8	9.9	4.6	—	−11.0	+12.4
London	− 3.9	73.6	+ 7.3	3	28.0	58.1	8.0	—	—	− 8.7	+10.4
Middlesex East	+18.7	77.4	+10.3	3	28.7	60.9	9.7	—	—	−10.4	+11.5
Middlesex West	+ 7.6	81.1	+ 5.7	3	52.6	52.6	3.7	—	—	−15.2	+14.0
Niagara Falls	+21.1	60.0	+ 1.6	2	53.4	45.6	—	—	—	− 5.6	+18.0
Nickel Belt	+10.6	75.7	+ 8.8	3	42.2	35.9	21.1	—	—	−15.7	+15.3
Nipissing	+ 5.1	73.3	+ 0.6	3	56.7	33.3	9.0	—	—	− 5.9	+ 6.4
Norfolk	+ 4.6	78.5	+10.0	3	39.5	55.7	—	3.5	—	−12.7	+14.1
Northumberland	+4.6	85.8	+ 3.5	2	47.0	51.9	—	—	—	− 6.9	+ 9.1

TABLE D/6 (cont'd)

Constituency	Change[b] in electorate	Percentage voting 1957	Change in % voting 1953–1957	No. of candidates	Percentage of votes obtained by parties[c]					Change in vote 1953–57[d]	
					Lib.	P.C.	C.C.F.	So. Cred.	Other	Lib.	P.C.
Ontario (Con'd)											
Ontario	+12.0	77.8	+17.9	3	25.0	42.3	31.6	—	—	−12.6	+ 0.7
Ottawa East	+ 7.3	78.1	+ 2.9	4	70.2	22.9	2.4	3.2	—	− 3.6	+ 2.4
Ottawa West	−10.0	77.8	+ 3.6	4	56.4	36.4	3.1	2.6	—	− 0.9	− 0.7
Oxford	+ 3.7	81.7	+ 9.7	3	27.5	67.9	—	3.1	—	−21.9	+18.3
Parry Sound–Muskoka	+ 2.8	79.3	+ 9.2	2	41.7	57.4	—	—	—	− 7.6	+13.8
Perth	+22.9	74.0	+ 8.2	4	29.7	56.2	9.7	2.6	—	− 6.6	+ 3.3
Peel	− 0.6	80.1	+ 6.4	2	35.3	64.0	—	—	—	−10.1	+10.2
Peterborough	+ 6.0	77.9	+ 2.1	4	30.1	60.1	6.8	2.0	—	−10.2	+ 8.0
Port Arthur	+ 9.6	73.8	+ 3.9	3	37.7	18.3	42.6	—	—	−11.9	+ 3.6
Prince Edward–Lennox	+ 5.8	77.5	+11.5	3	37.8	57.6	—	3.5	—	− 8.1	+ 3.6
Renfrew North	+12.4	83.0	+ 2.4	2	52.4	46.8	—	—	—	+ 3.1	+ 4.4
Renfrew South	− 0.5	87.5	+ 6.0	2	46.8	52.7	—	—	—	+ 8.6	+ 3.7
Russell	+41.6	76.9	+ 2.8	4	57.1	33.9	—	—	—	+ 7.9	+11.6
Simcoe East	+ 7.5	80.6	+ 7.3	4	35.5	54.2	3.9	3.2	3.1	− 9.7	+ 7.6
Simcoe North	+14.1	75.8	+ 4.1	3	37.1	61.8	6.0	—	—	−10.8	+ 9.8
Stormont	− 0.4	75.2	+ 0.9	2	52.8	43.2	—	—	—	−11.5	+10.7
Sudbury	+14.1	72.0	+ 4.5	3	45.5	39.9	—	2.7	—	− 5.1	+ 8.7
Timiskaming	+ 2.7	78.8	+ 5.2	3	35.5	28.7	13.6	—	—	− 3.8	+13.9
Timmins	− 1.1	76.9	+16.0	3	35.6	25.0	35.2	—	—	− 4.7	+ 4.3
Victoria	+10.3	78.3	+ 1.3	4	26.5	64.3	3.9	4.2	—	−14.9	+ 6.4
Waterloo North	+ 3.6	68.3	+ 3.9	4	42.0	35.4	19.5	2.4	—	− 7.6	+ 2.3
Waterloo South	+ 7.4	79.2	+ 7.2	4	29.8	46.8	16.0	6.1	—	−11.6	+13.4
Welland	− 1.6	72.8	+ 2.8	3	41.9	33.6	23.0	—	—	−12.6	+ 7.5
Wellington–Huron	+ 8.8	83.2	+ 6.2	2	37.5	61.6	—	—	—	−11.9	+11.7
Wellington South	+30.3	72.7	+ 3.0	3	28.3	54.1	16.6	—	—	−16.8	+11.7
Wentworth	+39.6	73.0	+ 9.3	3	26.8	57.2	14.7	—	—	− 7.7	+10.2
York Centre	+ 6.9	66.6	+ 7.2	4	33.8	46.6	16.3	1.6	—	− 9.7	+11.6
York East	+17.2	70.7	+12.3	4	26.0	50.6	19.7	1.8	—	− 6.5	+ 8.6
York-Humber	+27.2	71.9	+10.5	3	30.1	51.2	13.5	3.7	—	−10.2	+10.7
York North	+86.9	71.8	+ 4.2	3	35.1	58.1	—	5.4	—	−13.4	+16.8
York-Scarborough	+ 4.3	73.0	+11.4	4	29.3	55.5	11.7	2.1	—	−14.0	+14.1
York South	+38.9	65.9	+10.6	4	28.6	38.9	28.1	1.5	—	− 2.9	+ 9.5
York West		73.0	+11.6	4	27.7	54.8	13.4	2.8	—	− 6.7	+13.8
City of Toronto											
Broadview	−11.0	62.7	+ 8.3	3	21.4	58.7	18.7	—	—	− 8.2	+ 9.9
Danforth	+ 3.7	69.5	+ 9.3	3	22.7	50.0	26.1	—	—	−15.3	+ 9.6
Davenport	−14.2	69.3	+11.5	4	29.5	39.8	28.4	—	—	−11.0	+ 8.0
Eglinton	− 0.6	72.2	+11.4	3	22.7	67.9	7.5	—	0.7	−13.2	+12.2
Greenwood	+ 8.1	66.7	+ 8.4	3	20.4	52.7	25.6	—	—	− 8.2	+ 9.3
High Park	− 8.9	69.9	+ 9.0	4	36.0	45.3	15.0	2.0	—	− 7.1	+ 8.7
Parkdale	−10.6	67.6	+ 7.8	4	34.5	44.5	17.9	—	1.5f	−12.7	+13.7

TABLE D/6 (cont'd)

Constituency	Change[b] in electorate	Percentage voting 1957	Change in % voting 1953-1957	No. of candidates	Percentage of votes obtained by parties[c]					Change in vote 1953-57[d]	
					Lib.	P.C.	C.C.F.	So. Cred.	Other	Lib.	P.C.
City of Toronto (Con'd)											
Rosedale	− 6.9	68.9	+ 9.4	4	30.7	53.4	13.1	1.3	–	− 9.8	+14.4
St. Paul's	−12.0	63.2	+ 7.0	4	27.8	56.0	12.3	2.3	–	−10.8	+15.3
Spadina	−21.3	60.1	+ 6.5	5	38.4	41.9	12.3	1.9	2.7[p]	−16.9	+18.5
Trinity	− 7.5	61.4	+ 3.7	5	35.8	33.2	22.0	2.7	3.9[p]	− 4.3	+ 3.2
Manitoba											
Brandon-Souris	+ 4.0	77.9	+ 8.9	4	20.5	61.3	4.0	13.6	–	−14.5	+ 3.7
Churchill	+ 0.5	73.8	+16.3	4	31.0	38.4	11.6	18.5	–	− 9.0	+17.8
Dauphin	+ 7.9	76.4	+19.5	5	17.1	20.4	39.5	14.4	7.7[e]	−14.1	+ 7.2
Lisgar	− 3.1	75.8	+19.9	5	23.0	45.5	2.3	27.4	1.1	−22.0	+12.8
Marquette	− 7.0	83.5	+14.7	4	32.3	43.5	5.8	17.6	–	−22.0	+17.8
Portage-Neepawa	− 2.4	76.9	+18.4	4	29.6	42.7	7.5	19.6	–	−20.3	+11.5
Provencher	+ 6.4	67.9	+15.5	5	33.0	34.9	1.8	29.4	–	−32.3	+13.7
St. Boniface	− 4.0	75.9	+13.3	5	30.8	24.0	24.7	15.4	4.3[e]	−12.0	− 2.5
Selkirk	− 2.3	70.9	+16.7	4	32.6	12.4	43.8	10.6	–	−10.9	+ 2.5
Springfield	+12.6	74.1	+13.0	5	28.2	10.7	37.6	22.5	–	−21.6	+ 6.2
Winnipeg North	+ 2.4	73.2	+13.0	4	23.0	16.2	47.8	7.4	3.7[p]	− 6.3	+ 1.1
Winnipeg North Centre	+14.9	64.1	+16.1	4	17.3	20.5	53.7	6.0	–	−14.3	+ 3.7
Winnipeg South	+ 1.5	77.3	+16.1	4	27.3	51.1	15.3	5.0	–	−11.0	+13.2
Winnipeg South Centre	− 1.5	73.0	+17.3	4	25.0	49.6	17.7	6.7	–	− 7.9	+ 7.5
Saskatchewan											
Assiniboia	− 3.0	86.3	+ 9.0	4	39.9	8.7	46.8	4.1	–	+ 4.7	− 0.4
Humboldt-Melfort	− 7.2	79.9	+ 4.3	4	26.3	23.0	35.6	14.7	–	−12.1	+15.0
Kindersley	+ 0.8	86.1	+ 8.2	4	32.5	16.7	38.1	12.2	–	−12.9	+11.4
Mackenzie	−10.2	78.2	+ 5.7	4	29.7	18.4	40.5	10.9	–	−10.9	+13.8
Meadow Lake	− 1.1	73.9	+ 7.4	4	32.3	19.0	25.4	22.8	–	−11.0	+ 9.8
Melville	+ 4.6	85.4	+ 1.7	4	40.4	13.2	38.6	7.3	–	− 9.3	+ 7.5
Moose Jaw-Lake Centre	+ 5.8	80.0	+10.3	4	23.6	32.5	33.8	9.4	–	+ 1.6	+13.8
Moose Mountain	+ 7.9	81.3	+ 0.9	4	31.8	18.4	33.8	15.6	–	−14.6	+18.4
Prince Albert	+ 1.0	82.0	+ 2.5	3	21.9	52.8	24.8	–	–	− 1.7	+ 8.9
Qu'Appelle	+ 6.6	85.7	+ 5.4	4	30.2	34.0	23.4	11.8	–	− 8.1	+ 7.0
Regina City	+13.8	81.7	+ 9.1	6	30.3	25.6	35.4	7.2	0.8	−10.3	+14.0
Rosetown-Biggar	+ 2.2	83.8	+ 6.5	4	22.9	25.4	45.1	6.3	–	− 3.8	+ 8.6
Rosthern	+ 5.4	77.3	+ 3.7	3	36.1	—	30.8	32.7	–	+ 9.1	–
Saskatoon	+16.6	75.0	+10.1	4	20.0	38.0	35.4	5.9	–	+ 7.9	+19.5
Swift Current-Maple Creek	+ 1.0	82.1	+ 7.3	4	37.0	16.4	34.3	11.6	–	+ 6.0	+10.3
The Battlefords	− 3.6	80.3	+11.8	4	29.4	20.2	39.0	10.8	–	−15.5	+13.1
Yorkton	− 4.4	80.3	+ 8.0	4	37.3	10.4	43.1	8.7	–	+ 2.4	+10.4
Alberta											
Acadia	− 3.4	77.5	+10.9	4	29.7	9.4	7.7	52.7	–	−13.4	+ 9.4
Athabasca	− 4.1	71.0	+12.5	4	41.2	11.7	7.6	38.8	–	− 5.7	+11.7
Battle River-Camrose	− 2.0	75.2	+15.3	4	24.5	16.9	9.7	48.5	–	+ 0.2	+ 7.2

TABLE D/6 (cont'd)

Constituency	Change[b] in electorate	Percentage voting 1957	Change in % voting 1953–1957	No. of candidates	Percentage of votes obtained by parties[c]					Change in vote 1953–57[d]	
					Lib.	P.C.	C.C.F.	So. Cred.	Other	Lib.	P.C.
Alberta (Con'd)											
Bow River	+ 2.9	77.2	+12.6	3	23.6	37.0	–	38.8	–	– 6.7	+19.6
Calgary North	+20.0	70.8	+ 7.9	4	16.0	54.1	3.8	25.0	–	–11.4	+17.2
Calgary South	+12.9	72.6	+10.7	4	29.0	52.7	2.6	14.4	–	+ 0.2	+11.3
Edmonton East	0.0	70.5	+14.2	4	38.6	14.2	6.5	39.6	–	+ 4.3	+ 2.2
Edmonton-Strathcona	+28.8	73.4	+12.1	4	28.9	28.3	6.6	35.4	–	– 8.1	+11.6
Edmonton West	+30.3	69.9	+11.3	4	30.6	34.4	5.5	28.7	–	–12.0	+16.1
Jasper-Edson	+ 5.3	69.4	+ 6.4	4	28.6	20.0	10.6	40.0	–	– 8.0	+20.0
Lethbridge	+ 5.3	74.3	+ 8.8	3	31.9	14.7	–	52.6	–	+ 0.8	+ 4.4
Macleod	– 6.3	76.7	+ 9.7	5	24.6	26.2	5.2	43.4	–	+ 0.8	+ 6.2
Medicine Hat	+ 4.2	79.7	+11.0	5	35.6	10.2	5.4	46.5	1.6	–10.2	+ 4.2
Peace River	+ 6.0	71.1	+ 5.7	4	23.0	24.6	7.4	43.3	0.9	–13.4	+24.6
Red Deer	+ 4.5	72.2	+ 8.9	5	17.2	29.4	5.3	47.3	–	–12.9	+20.7
Vegreville	+ 6.0	77.6	+ 9.1	4	27.5	9.7	17.7	39.9	4.4[p]	–19.1	+ 9.7
Wetaskiwin	– 1.9	69.4	+11.5	4	21.2	19.7	13.1	45.4	–	– 3.8	+ 6.8
British Columbia											
Burnaby-Coquitlam	+25.6	76.2	+11.1	4	16.8	17.4	38.5	26.5	–	– 5.2	+ 6.4
Burnaby-Richmond	+34.0	72.8	+ 7.9	4	23.0	25.6	24.7	25.8	–	–11.0	+25.6
Cariboo	+10.8	68.5	+ 9.6	4	21.4	21.5	13.9	42.2	–	–12.5	+21.5
Coast Capilano	+23.3	77.8	+10.3	4	38.8	27.4	12.1	21.0	–	– 6.9	+17.6
Comox-Alberni	+16.5	69.8	+ 9.8	4	13.0	30.7	35.5	19.8	–	–12.8	+20.7
Esquimalt-Saanich	+16.2	79.8	+12.4	4	17.6	53.5	15.5	12.8	–	– 1.9	+ 7.7
Fraser Valley	+ 9.5	74.0	+ 8.7	4	18.2	23.9	18.7	38.4	–	–21.8	+23.9
Kamloops	+15.9	73.2	+ 7.9	4	15.8	46.9	9.2	27.4	–	– 0.8	+ 0.8
Kootenay East	+ 1.6	78.7	+ 7.3	4	31.2	13.9	26.9	27.3	–	+ 6.2	+13.9
Kootenay West	+ 1.5	75.3	+ 6.7	4	13.1	16.8	43.6	26.0	–	– 8.5	+11.2
Nanaimo	+10.9	76.5	+ 7.8	4	14.9	26.4	37.4	20.7	–	–10.8	+ 8.4
New Westminster	+20.2	76.8	+ 9.7	5	17.9	21.2	23.6	35.2	1.3	–12.8	+12.4
Okanagan-Boundary	+ 8.4	76.8	+ 6.2	4	13.5	25.9	29.8	30.3	–	–10.7	+25.9
Okanagan-Revelstoke	+ 2.4	79.9	+ 8.4	4	13.3	24.3	10.7	39.5	–	– 3.0	+ 6.4
Skeena	+ 6.7	63.9	+ 4.5	3	35.3	25.1	38.7	–	–	– 7.6	+25.1
Vancouver-Burrard	– 5.5	71.7	+12.0	5	15.5	46.1	13.7	22.6	0.9	–19.0	+29.2
Vancouver Centre	+ 4.0	65.4	+ 7.5	5	24.2	41.0	10.0	21.2	2.4[p]	–16.2	+32.4
Vancouver East	– 1.5	68.0	+ 8.6	4	10.7	17.9	47.0	23.2	–	– 5.4	+12.8
Vancouver Kingsway	+ 5.6	71.1	+ 8.6	4	16.0	25.4	34.0	23.5	–	– 1.8	+17.7
Vancouver Quadra	+ 1.8	77.4	+ 9.8	4	15.8	63.4	8.6	11.3	–	–10.8	+19.8
Vancouver South	+ 8.5	76.4	+10.5	5	20.9	44.5	13.4	18.0	2.3[p]	–15.5	+27.1
Victoria	+ 3.6	78.7	+10.3	4	27.2	44.5	9.2	18.7	–	–13.1	+26.5
Yukon Territory	+10.0	88.7	+12.8	2	49.5	48.2	–	–	–	– 7.5	+32.7
Northwest Territories											
Mackenzie River	+12.3	62.9	– 0.4	2	66.4	31.0	–	–	–	+18.5	– 6.4

[a] Mr. Benidickson in Kenora-Rainy River, Ontario is counted as a Liberal and Mr. Courtemanche in Labelle, Quebec, as a Conservative.

[b] The change is expressed as the difference in percentage points between the 1953 and 1957 electorates. 1953 is taken as the base year.

[c] Percentages do not add to 100.0 because of rounding and the omission of rejected ballots.

[d] The change is expressed in percentage points showing the difference in the percentage of votes obtained by each of the major parties in 1953 and in 1957.

[e] Independent Liberal.

[f] Independent Conservative.

[g] Independent.

[h] Includes an Independent Liberal.

[i] Adjusted for acclamation: percentage computed only for constituencies in which balloting took place.

[j] Adjusted to take account of each voter in Queens (P.E.I.) and Halifax (N.S.) having been eligible to vote for two candidates.

[k] For the constituencies included in each of the metropolitan areas see note q below. See also "The Fifteen Metropolitan Areas of Canada", inserted between pp. 154 and 155 in D.B.S., *Canada Year Book, 1956*.

[l] Acclamation in 1957.

[m] Elects two candidates.

[n] Acclamation in 1953.

[p] L.P.P.

[q] The regions are defined so as to resemble as closely as possible those established in D.B.S., *Statistics of the Economic Regions of Ontario and Quebec*, 1956. There follows a list of constituencies comprising the areas of Ontario and Quebec.

Area	Constituency
ONTARIO	
Eastern Ontario:	Renfrew N., Renfrew S., Lanark, Stormont, Grenville-Dundas, Leeds, Glengarry, Russell, Carleton, Ottawa E., Ottawa W.
Lake Ontario:	Kingston, Peterborough, Hastings-Frontenac, Hastings, S., Victoria, Northumberland, Durham, Prince Edward-Lennox.
Metropolitan Toronto:	All the Yorks, all the constituencies in the City of Toronto, Halton, Ontario, Peel.
Niagara:	Wentworth, Lincoln, Welland, Niagara Falls, Brant-Haldimand, all Hamilton constituencies.
Lake Erie:	Norfolk, Elgin, Oxford, Brantford, Middlesex W., Middlesex E., London.
Southwestern Ontario:	Lambton-Kent, Lambton W., Kent, all the Essex constituencies.
Upper Grand River:	Wellington-Huron, Wellington S., Huron, Perth, Waterloo N., Waterloo S.
Georgian Bay:	Bruce, Grey-Bruce, Grey N., Simcoe E., Simcoe N., Dufferin-Simcoe, Parry Sound-Muskoka.
Northeastern Ontario:	Nipissing, Sudbury, Nickel Belt, Algoma E., Algoma W., Timiskaming, Timmins, Cochrane.
Lakehead and North:	Port Arthur, Fort William, Kenora-Rainy River.
QUEBEC	
Northern Quebec:	Saguenay.
Gaspesia-South Shore:	Montmagny-L'Islet, Kamouraska, Témiscouata, Rimouski, Matapédia-Matane, Bonaventure, Gaspé, Iles-de-la-Madeleine.
Saguenay-Lake St. John:	Roberval, Lac St. Jean, Lapointe, Chicoutimi.
Quebec:	All Quebec constituencies, Bellechasse, Dorchester, Beauce, Lotbinière, Portneuf, Charlevoix, Lévis.
Three Rivers:	Berthier-Maskinongé-Delanaudière, Three Rivers, Champlain, St. Maurice-Laflèche, Nicolet-Yamaska.
Eastern Townships:	Brome-Missisquoi, Shefford, Drummond-Arthabaska, Compton-Frontenac, Stanstead, Sherbrooke, Richmond-Wolfe, Mégantic.
Montreal Region:	Joliette-L'Assomption-Montcalm, Labelle, Argenteuil-Deux Montagnes, Vaudreuil-Soulanges, Beauharnois-Salaberry, Chateauguay-Huntingdon-Laprairie, St. Jean-Iberville-Napierville, St. Hyacinthe-Bagot, Richelieu-Verchères, Terrebonne.
Metropolitan Montreal:	All constituencies on the Island of Montreal, Chambly-Rouville, Longueuil.
Northwestern Quebec:	Pontiac-Temiscamingue, Chapleau, Villeneuve, Hull, Gatineau.

Most of the metropolitan areas in Table D/5 are self-explanatory. To avoid confusion there follows a list of constituencies comprising those metropolitan areas where some ambiguity might arise.

METROPOLITAN AREA	Constituencies
Ottawa:	Carleton, Russell, Ottawa E., Ottawa W.
Quebec:	Quebec E., Quebec W., Quebec S.
Windsor:	Essex E., Essex W.
London:	London. Middlesex E.